Freedom To Learn for the 80's

Freedom To Learn for the 80's

Carl R. Rogers

With special contributions by

Julie Ann Allender
David Aspy
John Barkham
Kyle Blanchfield
Jerome Freiberg
Jeanne Ginsberg
Hugh Gunnison
Peter Ladd
Herbert Levitan

Barbara Shiel McElveny
"Winnie Moore"
Flora Nell Roebuck
William Romey
Ruth Sanford
Gay Leah Swenson
Anne-Marie Tausch
Reinhard Tausch
Alvin White

Merrill, an imprint of
Macmillan Publishing Company
New York

Collier Macmillan Canada, Inc.
Toronto

Maxwell Macmillan International Publishing Group
New York   Oxford   Singapore   Sydney

#8889965

This book was set in Bembo and Caledonia.
Production coordination: *Linda Hillis Bayma*
Text design: *Angela Foote*
Cover design coordination: *Tony Faiola*

Library of Congress Catalog Card Number: 82-061108

International Standard Book Number: 0-675-20012-1

Printed in the United States of America

10— 92 93 94

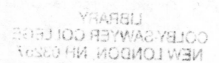

*I*t is in fact nothing short of a miracle that the modern methods of instruction have not yet entirely strangled the holy curiosity of inquiry; for this delicate little plant, aside from stimulation, stands mainly in need of freedom; without this it goes to wrack and ruin without fail.

—*Albert Einstein*

Contents

Introduction

꒰

Our educational system is, I believe, failing to meet the real needs of our society. I have said that our schools, generally, constitute the most traditional, conservative, rigid, bureaucratic institution of our time, and the institution most resistant to change. I stand by that statement, but it does not describe the whole situation. There are new developments—alternative schools, open classrooms, opportunities for independent study—all kinds of adventurous enterprises being carried on by dedicated teachers and parents. One of my purposes in bringing out this book is to encourage these new trends, these new hopes in the educational world, and to point the way to still further advances.

Another broader purpose in my writing is that I wish to aid in the development of our most precious natural resource—the minds and hearts of our children and young people. It is their curiosity, their eagerness to learn, their ability to make difficult and complex choices that will decide the future of our world. We need the help of all of our young—the despairing, alienated youth of the ghetto, the aimless, affluent youth, the serious, thoughtful children, the whole great mass of our young people—if we are to preserve this fragile planet and build a future world worthy of persons. The only way we can be assured of that help is to assist our youth to *learn*, deeply and broadly, and above all, to learn *how* to learn. No one book, no one person, can achieve such an aim, but we can all do our bit, and this volume is my contribution to that purpose.

It appears at a peculiar time in our history when many are saying that we must teach only the "basics," that we must *tell* children what is right and

1

wrong, that we must teach them to obey and follow. Large and powerful groups are insisting that students must not read certain books, that they must not be exposed to social issues, and that they must be presented with only one set of values (selected by these primarily conservative groups). They hold that students are in school to be *taught,* not to discuss problems or make choices.

In response to such pressures, many teachers are frightened and inhibited. A ninth grade teacher says, "I think twice about what I'm doing. Is there anything controversial in this lesson plan? If there is, I won't use it. I won't use things where a kid has to make a judgment."

I would like to dwell on that statement a moment. Ninth graders will soon be facing a world filled with controversy—political, social, international, as well as personal. They will be involved in making judgments, choices, decisions that will affect their own lives, their families, their society. Yet, to the extent that frightened attitudes prevail, such as expressed by this teacher, they will have no experience in school that will prepare them for life in this difficult world. They will not engage in discussion of controversial matters, will not face new and complex problems in need of solution, will not learn how to make responsible decisions and abide by the consequences.

This book takes a very different stance. It *believes* in young people. It gives evidence that in a genuinely human climate, which the teacher can initiate, a young person can find him or herself respected, can make responsible choices, can experience the excitement of learning, can lay the basis for living as an effective concerned citizen, well informed, competent in knowledge and skills, confident in facing the future.

A parent, who is also a teacher, sums it all up in expressing her worries about her son. "I want him to be able to evaluate opinions and be able to *think.* People who can't think are ripe for dictatorship!"

You will find in this book many examples of teachers who are real persons and who treat their students as real persons. You will discover the creative ways in which the minds of students are opened to the possibilities of "reading, writing, and arithmetic" and much, much more. You will see classrooms in which teachers have provided freedom with responsibility, a freedom in which the excitement of significant learning flourishes.

This volume is a revision of my earlier book with the same title. Some chapters have been retained with few changes because they still appear timely. More than half of the book is new material, from more recent experience.

In one respect the book is greatly changed. When *Freedom to Learn* was first written, the reports of students and teachers seemed to indicate that more and more significant learning took place in classrooms where there was a human climate, where attitudes and feelings could be expressed, where the student could choose from a wide range of options, where the teacher served as a facilitator of learning. *But,* there was almost no hard evidence available at that time.

Now, primarily because of years of devoted research by David Aspy and Flora Roebuck and their colleagues in this country, and by Reinhard and Anne-Marie Tausch and their students in West Germany, all that has changed.

In farflung studies involving hundreds upon hundreds of teachers and thousands of students from primary grades through technical schools, massive data have been accumulated. Very briefly, their work shows clearly that when a teacher is real, understanding, and caring, students learn more of the "basics," and in addition exhibit more creativity and problem-solving qualities. For the first time the humanistically oriented teacher has the *facts* to back up his or her classroom stance. As David Aspy puts it, "It *pays* to be human in the classroom." I regard the chapter reporting these researches and their findings as one of the most important in the book.

I would like to summarize the general aims of the book before giving a brief account of its organization and content. Here are some of the goals that are implicit throughout its pages.

● It aims toward a climate of trust in the classroom in which curiosity and the natural desire to learn can be nourished and enhanced.

● It aims toward a participatory mode of decision-making in all aspects of learning in which students, teachers, and administrators each have a part.

● It aims toward helping students to prize themselves, to build their confidence and self-esteem.

● It aims toward uncovering the excitement in intellectual and emotional discovery, which leads students to become life-long learners.

● It aims toward developing in teachers the attitudes that research has shown to be most effective in facilitating learning.

● It aims toward helping teachers to grow as persons, finding rich satisfaction in their interaction with learners.

● Even more deeply, it aims toward an awareness that, for all of us, the good life is within, not something which is dependent on outside sources.

Let me describe briefly the manner in which the book is organized.

In Section I, "Difficulties and Opportunities," I attempt to explore realistically some of the external forces and circumstances that make the teacher's profession a very difficult one today. Then I examine those elements within the teacher and the classroom that open up the possibility of discovering a richly interactive, growing life within the teaching profession.

Section II, "Responsible Freedom in the Classroom," permits a diverse assortment of teacher-facilitators to tell their own stories of excitement, frustration, and reward as they work to humanize their classrooms. From elementary school to graduate education, every level is represented, and a department chairman as well. My part in this is to try to clarify or illuminate some of the meanings in the accounts so vividly presented.

The third section, "For the Teacher," is intended to be of help to the teacher who wishes to take risks in innovation, who would like to move toward being a facilitator of responsible freedom. Some of the questions dealt with are: What is the nature of a facilitative relationship? How may it be implemented—in the teacher's own attitudes and in practical classroom management? What is involved in the education of humanistically oriented teachers? What about the issue of power—personal and institutional—the politics of education?

The fourth section "What Are the Facts?" is the work of four research workers. To my mind it provides the first adequate presentation of the hard-won data that confirms the value of person-centered attitudes in the learning process. I regard it as a cornerstone of the book.

Section V, "Some Disappointments in Innovation," deals briefly but frankly with an area in which the person-centered approach has shown little lasting success. It is the failure thus far to demonstrate that humanistically oriented educational institutions can continue that philosophy over an extended period of years. Some of the reasons are explored.

Section VI, "Philosophical and Value Ramifications," gives me the opportunity to present my philosophical stance: in regard to the ever present question of values; the issue of free choice in a world of determinism; the kind of person toward which we aim.

The final section "Do We Dare?" is brief. It gives a fresh summary of the advantages of a person-centered approach in the classroom. It also points to the resistance to change that is evident in our educational system and explores some of the reasons for this. It closes with a challenge to the reader.

The book is so constructed that while it follows a somewhat logical progression, almost every chapter may be read separately as complete in itself. Thus, the reader may move to the chapters of greatest personal interest and find that they make sense by themselves though there may be some loss of context.

I greatly regret that no one has as yet offered to authors a viable solution of the *he/she* problem. In many cases I refer to *him* or *her;* sometimes I designate the teacher as *she* and the student as *he;* sometimes I use *she* and *her* as the generic terms; occasionally I follow some compromise path. I am not completely consistent, but I am very much aware of the injustice done to women by the use of the generic *he,* and I have tried to remedy that situation as best I can.

It will be evident from the foregoing description that I have drawn heavily upon the experience of others. This will be even more clear as you read the book. I have wanted to show that a humanistic approach to education is not the product of one person, nor is it implemented in only one way. As you will see, teachers of different ages, different interests, different personalities, different subject matter fields, all find distinctive ways of creating in their own groups, classes, courses, or departments, an experience of responsible freedom in which creative learning can take place.

I would like to express my indebtedness to the persons who have contributed most significantly to this book. They are

Julie Ann Allender
David Aspy
John Barkham
Kyle Blanchfield
Jerome Freiberg
Jeanne Ginsberg
Hugh Gunnison
Peter Ladd
Herbert Levitan

Barbara Shiel McElveny
"Winnie Moore" (pseudonym)
Flora Nell Roebuck
William Romey
Ruth Sanford
Gay Leah Swenson
Anne-Marie Tausch
Reinhard Tausch
Alvin White

I feel a special indebtedness to my long-time assistant and loyal friend, Valerie Henderson. Her help in the production of the finished manuscript has been invaluable.

In addition to these who can be named, I am grateful to all the students who have, often in very enlightening and moving ways, contributed their reactions to the various classroom experiences. They have brought many experiences to life.

I hope that for you, the reader, the book will be a provocative signpost pointing toward what education might become in your own life and in that of the learners whom you influence.

Carl R. Rogers
La Jolla, California
1982

Difficulties
and
Opportunities

The Challenge of
Present-day Teaching

It was a sunny morning in early June, 1981. When I walked into the fifth grade classroom, the first impression was one of confusion. But as I watched, I saw that some children were quietly doing art work, and another group was working with a chemistry set. There was a somewhat noisy cluster of children around a new toy on the floor—of which more later. Three boys were taking photographs with a Polaroid, trying especially to catch objects or persons in motion. Off in one corner a number of children were rehearsing for the play that the class would put on in about ten days during the ceremonies ending the school year. One boy was closely observing a box of silkworms, which were starting to spin their cocoons. One girl was making up difficult arithmetic problems, writing them on the board. Mike, the teacher, moved from group to group, observing, and helping when asked, interested in what they were doing. His liking for the kids was obvious, and his openness with them.

Soon he spoke up in a strong, firm voice. "Please, everybody stop. I want your attention for a few minutes." To my amazement, everyone stopped immediately. It could only have been out of respect for and loyalty to him. "The group around the new toy is very noisy. I expect you can stand it, but I think it is probably disturbing others and, I'm afraid, disturbing classes in adjoining rooms. I wonder if we all want to work out a system for the quieter use of the toy? Let's take a vote." The show of hands indicated that though the class was divided, the majority did not want to take time to develop a system. "OK," Mike went on, "then will the group using the toy please find some way of reducing the noise." They began to discuss among themselves.

9

The toy puzzled me. He had purchased it and brought it in that morning. Only two people could use it at a time, and it involved pulling levers that put two tiny cars into a complicated race. Why had he brought it? As I watched, I realized that to use it without shouting for a turn, the boys and girls had to develop a cooperative system. Soon that was working. "I come after him." "Yeah, and I come after you." "Only three laps apiece." Now the noise was reduced, only the excited voices being raised when one or the other car was ahead.

I had, I learned, missed their reading period, half of which was spent on a standard workbook. Half the time they could read anything they wished from the school or public library.

As I continued to observe during the day, I was refreshed to realize again the incredible amount of curiosity possessed by a fifth grader. One boy with a flower he brought in used dictionaries, encyclopedias, and questions of me and another visitor until he had found how to spell *bougainvillea*, and learned the fact that the petals are actually leaves. A girl wrote for a long time in her journal, describing what she had been learning.

At the end of the day, I had ample opportunity to talk with Mike. The results of the standardized achievement tests had just come in, and the group had increased its percentile rating, showing that they had learned more in school subjects than would be expected during the year. Mike was not impressed, taking that pretty much for granted. The other personal learnings were more important to him. The increase in self-confidence, in creativity, in ability to make wise choices, the self-discipline of study—these were more significant to him. Then the personality changes. One boy, clearly headed for delinquency, a real "tough," was baffled when he realized that he could choose what he wanted to learn. Mike asked if he would like to have some things suggested to him. "I don't know," he said in a puzzled voice. "Give me one more day." Obviously, he was involved in an inner struggle. But the next day he had chosen something that *he* wanted to *learn*. Since then he has become a chess "expert" and had learned many other things as well. The "Mafia" in the sixth grade no longer seem so enticing.

One story amused me. Mike, in initiating the free program, had frequently stressed the fact that everyone is *always* learning *something*. One shy girl was very resistant to the whole idea. She kept turning in good work, but was unhappy. Sometimes she would say "Mr. R?" and when he replied, "Yes?" would say "Never mind." Then after several weeks, she came up to him and blurted out in an irritated voice, "Mr. R, what am I learning right *now*?" He laughed and said, "You're learning to have enough courage to confront an adult in order to try to get what you wish."

Before initiating his program, Mike had called a meeting of the parents and explained to them what he was about to do in giving the students more freedom to choose their own learning projects. Some were resistant, others very dubious. But as he talked to them about preparing children for life in the future and how important *choice* would be, he finally won their unanimous consent, though some felt sure it would not work. Now the parents have been much pleased with the results.

I was delighted to have made the acquaintance of a bright, sensitive young man who was so clearly being a person in the classroom, not a mask or a facade. And he was willing to learn from the children. He said that he had told the class that for him kindness was generally better than punishment, and that he didn't intend to punish them, but to try to help them. Then on a field trip to a museum, he felt tense and responsible for their behavior. After having clearly told the group that they were not to leave the museum room, one boy openly disobeyed. Mike went after him, grabbed him by the shoulders, and started to "blow off" at the boy. One of his group, a very timid girl, simply walked past the two and said, "Remember what you told us about kindness." Mike was so startled, it cooled his anger.

It all sounded better and better. Then came the shocker. Mike said, "I'm leaving at the end of this school year. I feel I'm not doing what they are paying me to do." Why? When parents are enthusiastic, children learning at an accelerated rate, growth in personal maturity evident, *why* would he be leaving? "The school is adopting policies I can't live with. There are to be, for example, stated punishments for every infraction of specified school rules, and all teachers are to use and enforce these punishments. Other policies are becoming more rigid, more bureaucratic. And besides," he added, "the other members of the teaching staff really don't like what I am doing. I feel I am being paid to be authoritarian, a disciplinarian, and I can't do that."

Mike's story is not the only one of its kind. The teacher who is human in the classroom is all too often a threat to other teachers, to administrators. And today there are other serious obstacles to becoming a teacher. So let us take a look at some of the discouraging aspects that a person needs to recognize if thinking of becoming one who promotes learning.

Obstacles

This is an extremely difficult time in which to become a teacher. It is also a challenging time, and much of this book will be devoted to ways of meeting that challenge. But I have no desire to overlook the very real negative elements that today are affecting educational institutions.

THE DECLINING SCHOOL

This is a period when education faces many disturbing circumstances originating outside itself. Budgets have been drastically cut throughout the country, affecting every type of education. Enrollments are dropping rapidly, because the children of the post–World War II "baby boom" have now completed their schooling, and we are feeling the full effect of the falling birth rate. So there are fewer opportunities for new teachers, and the average age of teachers is increasing.

THE IMPACT OF BUREAUCRACY

The schools are, to a degree never seen before, regulated from outside. State-designated curricula, federal and state laws, and bureaucratic regulations intrude on every classroom and every school activity. The teacher-student relationship is easily lost in a confusing web of rules, limits, and required "objectives."

One teacher gives her reactions to this situation. Here are excerpts from her journal. "Teaching frustrates me so much. There is always more to do, never enough time. There are stupid piles of paperwork or administrative duties which interfere with the real job in the classroom. . . .

"Teaching no longer offers the chance to be creative and stimulating. It's frustrating not to be able to try something different. How can you be a teacher without being creative? I feel angry when I feel stifled, not able to use everything that I've learned. . . .

"The students are not robots nor are the teachers, but with the demands of society for budget cuts and higher test scores, we are failing to realize that we are dealing with students who are feeling, total, human beings. . . .

"As a teacher, I feel I am expected to 'put in my time. Don't make waves, don't be creative or innovative.' This causes too many problems for the administrators because the students begin to think and ask questions that the administration can't or won't answer. . . .

"People are so afraid of creativity because that might cause change and undermine their sense of security. I really want to help my students find a sense of security within themselves so that the inevitable change will not scare them. One thing that we had better learn to cope with is *change!*"

Anyone close to education knows that the feelings of this teacher are representative of thousands of others.

DANGER FROM THE RIGHT

Currently, in this country, there is another force affecting and inhibiting the educational process. A number of conservative groups, with undoubtedly good intentions, are endeavoring to stamp out those elements in our schools that stress open discussion, free choice, or informal teacher-student relationships.

It is not difficult to understand the motives of these people. Our culture is changing at a tremendous rate, and rapid change is a frightening experience. So one very natural reaction is to try to go back to "the good old days" when everyone knew what was right, when life was much simpler, and education was narrowly defined. One can sympathize with this desire to turn the clock back and with the people who desire to do so.

But, unfortunately, these right-wing groups have a strength far beyond their numbers because they are backed by many millions of dollars, which come from TV ministers who reach large audiences and wealthy conservatives who believe that change must be stopped. As a consequence, they generate a very large amount of propaganda. Much of it endeavors to equate humanistic education with "secular humanism" (a philosophical religious movement), which is a gross misrepresentation. The effort is made to discredit everything humanistic in education. *Humanism* is regarded as being responsible for all the country's evils—low achievement, drug abuse, crime, and sexual promiscuity. It is very strange indeed in a nation that has always valued the individual to find education attacked for emphasizing the worth and dignity of each individual child. But in their hysteria, these groups have completely misunderstood the situation. An ad in the *New York Times* says, "Moral Majority, Inc. is . . . sick and tired of the way many amoral and secular humanists and other liberals are destroying the traditional family and moral values on which our nation was built (6, p.5).* I fear that *they* are the ones destroying our national values. Let me be specific.

An important aspect of this conservative movement is that its members believe that there is an absolute right and an absolute wrong. This is an entirely reasonable philosophical stance. It is when they carry it one step further and proclaim that *they* know the *truth* as to what is right and wrong that it becomes ominous. And when they go a great step further and insist that it is their view of absolute right and wrong that is to be taught in the schools, with no opportunity to differ from or even discuss the matter, then the movement becomes dangerous indeed. When they label those who disagree with epithets such as "anti-family" or "anti-God," they show themselves as opposed to the freedom of thought that is basic to our Constitution and to the American way of life.

The fact is that their view of what is right is often completely out of line with the thinking and wishes of the great majority of people. For example, most of the fundamentalist groups strongly oppose sex education in the schools. Yet a poll conducted by NBC and the Associated Press shows that of a representative sample of the American people, 75 percent approve of sex education in the schools. And of that group, of those who are parents of minor children, *80* percent approve (9)! This finding is confirmed by a recent Gallup Poll, commissioned by the White House Conference on Families, which reported that 79 percent of Americans think sex education should be taught with parental consent in the schools. Only 3 percent of parents refuse to permit their children to attend such courses (7). It is clear that the stand of the fundamentalist groups is *their* stand—to which they are entitled—but it does not represent the wishes of the American public.

I should like to be clear as to *why* the attitudes of this conservative movement are dangerous. Whenever one group in society (*a*) has proclaimed itself as having the moral truth, and (*b*) has insisted on imposing its view of the truth upon all, the result has been a tyranny over the human mind and often over the human body as well. Some of the darkest periods of history are characterized by this pattern. The most famous example is the Inquisition, where the Church proclaimed *the* truth and endeavored to impose it on all people, persecuting and punishing, even killing those "heretics" who disagreed. In modern times McCarthyism was similar, labeling as "Communist" anyone who disagreed with the narrow views of those who backed Senator McCarthy. Although ultimately unsuccessful, the degree of tyranny which was achieved and the many creative lives which were ruined by the persecution made it a social disaster of the first magnitude. Another example exists in Communist nations. The Communist party possesses *the* truth in these countries and any departure from the party line, any deviation of thought or deed,

---

*References are numbered in the text and listed alphabetically at the end of each chapter.

is punished. This seems to account not only for the drabness of intellectual and artistic life in Communist states, but for the steady flow of refugees escaping such rigidity. We cannot afford to let the same thing happen here.

The freedom for each person to think for him- or herself has been the hallmark of American greatness. Everyone is entitled to an opinion, and it is out of such diversity that creativity emerges. Truth gradually evolves out of the interaction of all.

The most shocking aspect of the conservative movement I am describing is that they wish to eliminate discussion in our schools because discussion implies that there might be some alternative to the "right" view which is to be taught and accepted. Student opinions are not to be sought or encouraged. The very title of this book would be unacceptable because it implies a freedom of thought, a freedom of choice in learning. In the view of the conservative movement, there is to be no freedom to learn. Students are to learn what is selected as best for them to learn. They are not to think for themselves, but to learn and accept the morally correct view that is to be taught. Teachers or students who disagree will be attacked. Educators and school administrators will need courage to stand up to these extremist pressures.

To the extent that this conservative movement is able to achieve its goals and to stifle freedom of thought and choice, the result will be tragically dangerous for our country. Never in our history have we been faced with so many serious and complex decisions. As citizens we will be called upon to play our part through neighborhood discussions, community gatherings, use of the news media, and through our votes in deciding these issues. What action should be taken in regard to the polluting of air and water in our community? What steps should be taken to deal with excessive drug use? How much of our personal and governmental income can we afford for health care? Who should provide sex education for the young? What are we to do about the crisis in our Social Security system that provides for the elderly? Shall a nuclear power plant be erected in our area? How far do we want to go in building up our military system and nuclear bombs and the neutron bomb? The questions go on and on. It is absolutely essential that young people learn early in life to consider complex problems, to recognize the pros and cons of each solution, and to choose the stand they will take on an issue. They must learn this process of intelligent choice, the weighing of the available data, and arriving at an informed decision. Learning to solve complex problems, social and scientific, is a primary objective for education. And it cannot be achieved in a situation where conformity to one dogmatic view is demanded. It cannot be achieved when free and open discussion is in any way inhibited. This is the very real danger posed by the aims of the conservative movement.

The views of this cluster of conservative groups have not gone unchallenged. The president of Yale University, Dr. Bartlett Giamatti, spoke for many when he addressed the freshman class. "A self-proclaimed 'Moral Majority' and its satellite or client groups, cunning in the use of a native blend of old intimidation and new technology, threaten the values of the nation.

"Angry at change, rigid in the application of chauvinistic slogans, absolutistic in morality, they threaten through political pressure or public denunciation whoever dares to disagree with their authoritarian positions; using television, direct mail and economic boycott, they would sweep before them anyone who holds a different opinion" (2).

The opposition to the conservative right is more than rhetorical. The National Coalition for Democracy in Education has been formed to stem this unhealthy, anit-democratic tide. It coordinates the efforts of many organizations and individuals and provides valuable services and protection to teachers and school systems who believe in educating the whole student.*

STUDENT DISSATISFACTION

Another negative element in education at the present time is the widespread dissatisfaction among students. Several dozen years ago this was documented by an educational journal when a request was sent out for student opinions for an issue on "Kids Talk about School." It was flooded with responses. The findings were summarized as follows: "3,157 students (U.S. and Canada, middle school, senior high, college and grad school, male and female, black and white, public and private, rich and poor) wrote and told us that *school is a BORE*" (5, pp. 5–6). The situation has not changed since that time. In fact, it has probably grown worse.

The student unhappiness is not confined to elementary, secondary, and college levels. A high-ranking physician was able to make informal contact with students in a "good" medical school. He met with nearly 200 of them to learn their opinions of their professional education. The meeting started hesitantly as he endeavord to draw them out, but "then the comments began—first slowly, then in a veritable avalanche—an outpouring of frustration, disappointment, and real rage came crashing down about me. (It) soon became an enormous interactive song of anger. . . . The message . . . was simple and monotonous. They felt they were being lectured to death. . . . Every day they sat passively while faculty, whom they did not know and who did not know them, spewed enormous boluses of facts at them. There were blistering testimonials about the poor quality of the lectures, of insufficient time for study, of the absence of personal contact with the faculty, of school unresponsiveness to their needs or their complaints. Try as I might I was unable to coax out countervailing opinions."

The students had developed an ingenious way of coping with this situation. They each contributed money to a fund. From this, selected students were paid to attend and record the lectures. These were transcribed, edited and reorganized, references added, and the material distributed to classmates. Although the class numbered 200, an attendance of 35 at a lecture was unusual, and sometimes as few as ten attended the lecture. "Even if there were only five students in the room, the lecturer would march to the podium and go through the whole incredible ritual of giving the lecture" (8, pp. 3–4).

So even in a medical school where students are intensely eager to learn in order to help their patients, the utter absurdity of the lecture system is clear. It is not, in most cases, a suitable mode of learning.

*The National Coalition for Democracy in Education, 108 Spring Street, Saratoga Springs, NY 12866, Howard Kirschenbaum, Executive Director.

Another reason for the boredom and unhappiness in our schools is the continual—and increasing—stress upon grades. One student writes to me, "I seem to always feel anxious and pressured at school. I'm beginning to realize how painful the process of strict external evaluation of my work is to me. . . . I love to explore the new ideas or concepts that I come across when I'm reading, but my current environment hinders this almost completely for me. . . . Must I achieve the same as everyone else and live unhappy and dissatisfied along the way? These are very real questions for me right now. I know I have expressed the feelings of so many frustrated college students and teens. I'm beginning to sense in myself that that frustration is turning into a type of hopelessness, and it is swallowing me up."

Still another reason for this feeling of "hopelessness" is the necessity of holding students against their will in schools that are little better than prisons. I remember vividly an experience that is as fresh in me today as it was when it occurred several years ago.

I was visiting an inner city school system that had worked wonders in many of its schools. Teachers and students were working together, learning together, and enjoying it. I was deeply impressed. I said to the administrator, "These schools are great, but there must be some schools you haven't been able to reach." He replied, "Yes, some of the junior high schools we haven't been able to touch." I said, "I'd like to see the worst." We visited it, a school in a severely impoverished ghetto area. The corridors were dark, with a few students furtively scurrying fearfully along. Every classroom door was locked, so that pupils could not get in or out. The doors originally had frosted glass windows, but most of these had been broken and replaced by plywood nailed over the opening. We selected a door at random and knocked. The teacher unlocked it from the inside and peered out suspiciously. When he recognized the school official, he opened it wide. It was a strange scene. His face was red, and he was breathing hard, holding a large paddle in his hand. It was impossible to tell which student he had just paddled because all the students, black and white, looked equally sullen and angry. Then began the farce. Laying down the paddle he said, "Now class, take your books and turn to page 73," and he started reading from his book. Very few students picked up their books. Their whole sullen stance was saying, "Just *try* to make me learn *anything*." We left, to spare him further embarrassment.

I have often thought of that class and that teacher. Imagine the poor student having each morning to get up and go to a classroom he hates. And even worse for the poor teacher, no matter how many faults he may have. Think of earning a living by going to a classroom each day where he knew he was hated. It would be intolerable. It was not surprising that in this school there had been assaults on teachers and pupils and a great deal of vandalism.

I was reminded of that school, and of others like it, when I read a portion of a commencement address by the president of Yale University in June, 1981. He said, "America cannot allow itself to transform the public schools into warehouses for the angry" (3). What a description that is of so many of our schools—"warehouses" for the bored, the unhappy, the angry!

Most tragic of all are the desperately hopeless youngsters. A teacher in one of our metropolitan cities has had the opportunity to work closely, over a period of time, with a small group of eight-year-olds from a deteriorating

ghetto area. As she has gained their confidence, their initial violence sub-
sides, and the underlying despair comes to light. One young girl, one of the
brightest, confides that she doesn't want to live. No one cares, and there is
no point to living. She has already made one suicide attempt, but was stopped
in time. A black youngster, an aggressive, active boy, says privately to this
teacher, "I'm going to be the first one of this group to be dead." When she
asks why, he says, "I don't want to live. I'm going to the top of a building and
jump off like Superman." The rest of the conversation gives evidence that he
means what he says. And these are eight-year-olds!

My granddaughter, Frances Fuchs, taught in a training program for adolescents who had been rejected by the regular schools. Early in the term
she asked them to write a brief statement as to what they envisioned for
themselves five years from now. Here is one of the statements. "In five years
I will either be dead or in the army or playing lead guitar in a band. I do
think the war will come before five years and most of us will be dead" (1).

More than half of this group believed they would be dead within five
years or living desperate lives in a polluted, overcrowded world.

Try to imagine what such young people must feel when they are told that
they must learn algebra or English grammar. How could such tasks have any
meaning when they are facing their own death in a nuclear war? All required
learning must seem trivial beyond belief.

We have no way of knowing how many of our young people see death as
being imminent, but I am sobered by one factual report. The National Urban
League reports that among young blacks between the ages of fifteen and
twenty-nine, suicide has become the number one cause of death. There are
undoubtedly many elements behind this finding. Nevertheless, to know that
in many classrooms today there are children and young people actively considering death, either by their own hand or in a nuclear holocaust, gives a
new and somber dimension to the educational experience, one that challenges us to our very roots.

I think I have said quite enough to indicate that our educational system
is suffering from many elements of a crippling sort: the decreased financial
resources, the dwindling enrollment, the tangled web of law and bureaucratic
regulations that so often dehumanizes the classroom, a dangerous right-wing
attack that aims to prevent freedom of thought and choice, and boredom,
frustration, rage and despair on the part of many students.

Yet the other side of the coin needs to be equally stressed. There are
school administrators with vision. There are teachers who inspire in their
students a lifelong love of learning. There are students for whom school is
the most exciting, most growing part of their lives. I want now to introduce
some of the fascinating challenges and opportunities that can make the teacher's task a most satisfying one.

What Does It Mean to Teach?

It would seem that to most people, teaching involves keeping order in
the class, pouring forth facts, usually through lectures or textbooks, giving

examinations, and setting grades. This stereotype is badly in need of overhauling.

I would like to quote a very sensitive, thought-provoking definition of teaching, written by the German philosopher, Martin Heidegger.

"Teaching is even more difficult than learning . . . and why is teaching more difficult than learning? Not because the teacher must have a larger store of information, and have it always ready. Teaching is more difficult than learning because what teaching calls for is this: to let learn. The real teacher, in fact, lets nothing else be learned than—learning. His conduct, therefore, often produces the impression that we properly learn nothing from him, if by 'learning' we now suddenly understand merely the procurement of useful information. The teacher is ahead of his students in this alone, that he still has far more to learn than they—he has to learn to let them learn. The teacher must be capable of being more teachable than the apprentices. The teacher is far less assured of his ground than those who learn are of theirs. If the relation between the teacher and the taught is genuine, therefore, there is never a place in it for the authority of the know-it-all or the authoritative sway of the official. It still is an exalted matter then, to become a teacher— which is something else entirely than becoming a famous professor" (4, p. 75).

I would like to underscore some of Heidegger's thoughts because they express some of the central themes of this book. The primary task of the teacher is to *permit* the student to learn, to feed his or her own curiosity. Merely to absorb facts is of only slight value in the present, and usually of even less value in the future. Learning *how* to learn is the element that is always of value, now and in the future. Thus, the teacher's task is delicate, demanding, and a truly exalted calling. In true teaching there is no place for the authoritarian, nor the person who is on an "ego trip."

It should be mentioned that Heidegger first gave the above statement as part of a lecture in 1951 or 1952. In other words, this kind of thinking about teaching is not new. It has very old roots. Yet in every era, it is a radical way because it departs so far from the ordinary picture of the teacher. What this book endeavors to do is to portray fresh ways of implementing this central idea in today's situation, in various sorts of school situations. It attempts to provide some practical answers to the question, "How can a teacher be creative in facilitating learning, and a love of learning, in the student?"

What Is Learning?

If the purpose of teaching is to promote learning, then we need to ask what we mean by that term. Here I become passionate. I want to talk about *learning*. But *not* the lifeless, sterile, futile, quickly forgotten stuff that is crammed into the mind of the poor helpless individual tied into his seat by ironclad bonds of conformity! I am talking about LEARNING—the insatiable curiosity that drives the adolescent boy to absorb everything he can see or hear or read about gasoline engines in order to improve the efficiency and speed of his "cruiser." I am talking about the student who says, "I am discovering, drawing in from the outside, and making that which is drawn in a real part of *me*." I am talking about any learning in which the experience of the learner progresses along this line: "No, no, that's not what I want"; "Wait! This is closer to what I'm interested in, what I need"; "Ah, here it is! Now I'm grasping and comprehending what I *need* and what I want to know!" This is the theme, the topic, of this book.

TWO KINDS OF LEARNING

Learning, I believe, can be divided into two general types, along a continuum of meaning. At one end of the scale is the kind of task psychologists sometimes set for their subjects—the learning of nonsense syllables. To memorize such items as *baz, ent, nep, arl, lud,* and the like, is a difficult task. Because there is no meaning involved, these syllables are not easy to learn and are likely to be forgotten quickly.

We frequently fail to recognize that much of the material presented to students in the classroom has, for the student, the same perplexing, meaningless quality that the list of nonsense syllables has for us. This is especially true for the underprivileged child whose background provides no context for the material with which he is confronted. But nearly every student finds that large portions of his curriculum are for him, meaningless. Thus, education becomes the futile attempt to learn material that has no personal meaning.

Such learning involves the mind only. It is learning that takes place "from the neck up." It does not involve feelings or personal meanings; it has no relevance for the whole person.

In contrast, there is such a thing as significant, meaningful, experiential learning. When the toddler touches the warm radiator, she learns for herself the meaning of a word *hot;* she has learned a future caution in regard to all similar radiators; and she has taken in these learnings in a significant, involved way that will *not* soon be forgotten. Likewise the child who has memorized "two plus two equal four" may one day in her play with blocks or marbles suddenly realize, "Two and two *do* make four!" She has discovered something significant for herself in a way that involves both her thoughts and feelings. Or the child who has laboriously acquired "reading skills" is caught up one day in a printed story, whether a comic book or an adventure tale, and realizes that words can have a magic power which lifts her out of herself into another world. She has now "really" learned to read.

Another example is given by Marshall McLuhan. He points out that if a five-year-old child is moved to a foreign country and allowed to play freely for hours with her new companions, with no language instruction at all, she will learn the new language in a few months and will acquire the proper accent too. She is learning in a way which has significance and meaning for her, and such learning proceeds at an exceedingly rapid rate. But let someone try to *instruct* her in the new language, basing the instruction on the elements that have meaning for the *teacher,* and learning is tremendously slowed, or even stopped.

This illustration, a common one, is worth pondering. Why is it that left to her own devices the child learns rapidly, in ways she will not soon forget, and in a manner which has highly practical meaning for her, when all of this can be spoiled if she is "taught" in a way that involves only her intellect? Perhaps a closer look will help.

A DEFINITION

Let me define a bit more precisely the elements that are involved in such significant or experiential learning. *It has a quality of personal involvement*—the whole person in both feeling and cognitive aspects being *in* the learning event. It is *self-initiated*. Even when the impetus or stimulus comes from the outside, the sense of discovery, of reaching out, of grasping and comprehending, comes from within. *It is pervasive*. It makes a difference in the behavior, the attitudes, perhaps even the personality of the learner. *It is evaluated by the learner*. She knows whether it is meeting her need, whether it leads toward what she *wants* to know, whether it illuminates the dark area of ignorance she is experiencing. The locus of evaluation, we might say, resides definitely in the learner. *Its essence is meaning*. When such learning takes place, the element of meaning to the learner is built into the whole experience.

WHOLE-PERSON LEARNING

Let me look at this from another angle. Education has traditionally thought of learning as an orderly type of cognitive, left-brain activity. The left hemisphere of the brain tends to function in ways that are logical and linear. It goes step by step, in a straight line, emphasizing the parts, the details that make up the whole. It accepts only what is sure and clear. It deals in ideas and concepts. It is associated with the masculine aspects of life. This is the only kind of functioning that has been fully acceptable to our schools and colleges.

But to involve the whole person in learning means to set free and utilize the right brain as well. The right hemisphere functions in quite a different way. It is intuitive. It grasps the essence before it understands the details. It takes in a whole gestalt, the total configuration. It operates in metaphors. It is aesthetic rather than logical. It makes creative leaps. It is the way of the artist, of the creative scientist. It is associated with the feminine qualities of life.

Ingmar Bergman sums up in a very pithy manner the way in which the two kinds of functioning come together in a learning which utilizes *all* our abilities. He says, "I throw a spear into the dark—that is intuition. Then I have to send an expedition into the jungle to find the way of the spear—that is logic."

Significant learning combines the logical *and* the intuitive, the intellect *and* the feelings, the concept *and* the experience, the idea *and* the meaning. When we learn in that way, we are *whole*, utilizing all our masculine and feminine capacities.

THE DILEMMA

I believe that all teachers and educators prefer to facilitate this experiential, meaningful whole-person type of learning, rather than the nonsense syllable type. Yet in the vast majority of our schools, at all educational levels, we are locked into a traditional and conventional approach that makes significant learning improbable if not impossible. When we put together in one scheme such elements as a *prescribed curriculum, similar assignments for all students, lecturing* as almost the only mode of instruction, *standard tests* by which all students are externally evaluated, and *instructor-chosen grades* as the measure of learning, then we can almost guarantee that meaningful learning will be at an absolute minimum.

DO ALTERNATIVES EXIST?

It is not because of any inner depravity that educators follow such a self-defeating system. They are inhibited by bureaucratic rules; they fear "making waves"; they frequently do not know the steps they might take to implement a practical alternative.

The fact that there are alternative ways to handle a classroom or a course—alternative assumptions and hypotheses upon which education can be built, alternative goals for which educators and students can strive—will, I believe, be amply illustrated in the chapters that follow.

THE BALANCE

We can look squarely at all of the elements that make teaching a difficult profession at this time in this country, and I have endeavored to suggest some of these roadblocks and dangers. But we can never escape the exhilarating fact that when a student's eyes light up with a new discovery, a new learning that pervades and illuminates his or her life, this makes all the hard work, the personal effort of teaching, completely worthwhile. How can that precious gleam occur more frequently? What can I, as an educator, do to kindle that spark? It is the purpose of this book to suggest some answers.

This is not a handbook of methods or techniques. It is primarily an approach to the teaching-learning situation, a philosophy if you will, but a philosophy come to life in the experience of many teachers, many students, who will be allowed to tell their own very diverse stories.

REFERENCES

1. Fuchs, Frances. "The Guru on the Labor Market." Unpublished manuscript, 1981.
2. Giamatti, A. Bartlett. Quoted in *New York Times,* 10 September 1981.
3. Giamatti, A. Bartlett. Quoted in *Time,* 11 June 1981.
4. Heidegger, Martin. *What Is Called Thinking?* (New York: Harper Torchbooks, 1968), p. 75. (Originally published in 1954 in Germany, *Was Heisst Denken?* Based on lectures given 1951–52.)
5. "Kids Talk about School." *Media & Methods* 5 (April 1969): 5–6.
6. Moral Majority, Inc. Quoted in *People for the American Way,* June 1981, p. 5.
7. *Planned Parenthood News,* Fall 1981, p. 2.
8. Rogers, D. E. "Some Musings on Medical Education. Is It Going Astray?" Unpublished paper, Robert Wood Johnson Foundation, 1981, pp. 3–4.
9. Today Show. *NBC,* New York, 8 October 1981.

As a Teacher,
Can I Be Myself?

Can We Be Human in the Classroom?

A teacher friend of mine, knowing I was going to write this chapter, posed this question to his class. One reply, typical of many, began, "Of course not!" and followed with some very eloquent reasons why both students and instructors believe that it is utterly impossible to be real whole human beings in a classroom situation.

THE USUAL CLASS

In the first place many an instructor, during all her* professional training and experience, has been conditioned to think of herself as the expert, the information giver, the keeper of order, the evaluator of products, the examination giver, the one who, at the end, formulates that goal of all "education," the *grade*. She firmly believes that she would be destroyed if she let herself emerge as the human being she really is. She knows that she is not as expert as she appears. She knows that as lecturer and information giver she has her good days and her bad ones, that sometimes she should receive a failing grade on her work. She knows, at some level, that if she let her mask slip, if she showed herself as she is, there would be questions to which she would have to answer, "I don't know." She realizes that if she fully interacted with

*Throughout this chapter, I will use feminine pronouns for the teacher or instructor, masculine for the student.

her students there would be some she would come to like very much, and others for whom she might feel real dislike. What then would happen to her "objectivity" in giving grades? Even worse, suppose some student she really liked did very poorly in his work. What a bind she would be in! Could she give a poor grade to someone she liked? Another risk is that if there were real interaction, some students would be bold enough to say that they found the class very uninteresting and having little relationship to the issues of real concern to them. In short, it would be *very risky* indeed to let students know her as a person. It would be risky within herself because she would be making herself vulnerable. It might well be risky in her profession because she would get the reputation of being a poor teacher and lecturer, of caring more about her students than about the content of the course, of having a noisy classroom where students talk a lot.

Hence, she—perhaps most instructors—prefers to play it safe. She will firmly fasten her mask, maintain her role of expert, retain her "objectivity" at all cost, and keep a proper distance between herself as the higher level role in the room, and the student in his lower role, and thus preserve her right to act as the judge, the evaluator, and sometimes the executioner.

But many a student has his facade, too, and often his mask is even more impenetrable than that of the instructor. If he wishes to be well thought of as a student, he attends class regularly, looks only at the instructor, or writes diligently in his notebook. Never mind that while looking so intently at the instructor, he is thinking of his weekend date, or while looking down, he is writing a letter in his notebook or wondering whether the family welfare check has arrived. He is sometimes truly desirous of learning what the instructor is offering, but even so his attention is contaminated by the two questions, "What are this teacher's leanings and biases in this subject, so that I can take the same view in my papers?" and "What is she saying that it is likely she will ask on the exam?" If the student asks questions, his questions will have the two-fold purpose of showing his own informed knowledge and will also tap a known reservoir of interest and information in the instructor. He does not ask questions that might embarrass or expose ignorance. It makes no difference what he thinks of the course, his instructor, his fellow students. He shuts such attitudes carefully within himself because he wants to pass the course, to acquire a good reputation with the faculty, and thus move one step further toward the coveted degree, the union card which will open so many doors for him once he has it. Then he can forget all this and enter real life.

So, for thousands upon thousands of students it is far too much of a risk to be a whole human being in the classroom. For the student it would mean letting his feelings show—feelings of indifference, resentment at the discrimination he feels is aimed toward him, occasional feelings of real excitement, feelings of envy toward classmates, feelings of upsetness about the unpleasant family situation he just left, or the terrible disappointment or real joy he is experiencing with his girlfriend, his desire to learn important things, his sharp curiosity about sex or psychic phenomena or government policies— you name it. For him, as for the instructor, it is much safer to button his lip,

preserve his cool, serve his term, cause no ripples, and get his paper credentials. He is not willing to take the *risk* of being human in class.

Perhaps I am too harsh, but I am sure you realize that this charade is
played out every school term by thousands of instructors and hundreds of
thousands of students.

In this so-called "educational" atmosphere, students become passive,
apathetic, bored. Teachers, trying day after day to prevent their real selves from
showing, become case-hardened stereotypes, and eventually burn out. Here
is some evidence from the student side—a panel of eight students in the
Boston area, from eighth grade through college, from various economic levels:

> School is just a place to meet your friends. Classes are something you have
> to live through.

> Lectures are so *boring!*

> I like some teachers as friends. But when they get into their *teacher* roles,
> they're boring, too.

> Students don't have the guts to *confront* the teachers and administrators
> and tell 'em what they *feel*.

> Before I went to school, I just dug books and encyclopedias. By the end of
> the first year, I wouldn't look at a book.

> I'd like to see a complete wipeout. Burn all the schools to the ground and
> start over.

Now the question I want to raise is, "Is this angry dissatisfaction *necessary?*" Could a classroom be a place of exciting meaningful *learning*, having
to do with live issues? Could it be a place where *mutual* learning takes place,
where you learn from the others, and they from you; where the "instructor"
learns from the class, and the class from the instructor? I not only think it is
possible, I have seen it happen! If I didn't believe very deeply that this could
come true in thousands of classrooms, I would not be writing this book.

But how? Let's get down to the nitty-gritty.

MY OWN LEARNINGS

I found my way into being human in class by somewhat of a back-door
entrance. As a psychological counselor, dealing with students and others in
personal distress, I had found that talking to them, giving advice, explaining
the facts, telling them what their behavior meant, did *not* help. But little by
little, I learned that if I trusted them more as essentially competent human
beings, if I was truly myself with them, if I tried to understand them as they
felt and perceived themselves from the *inside*, then a constructive process
was initiated. They began to develop clearer and deeper self-insights, they
began to see what they might do to resolve their distress, and they began to
take the actions that made them more independent and that solved some of
their problems.

But this learning, important to me, made me question my role as a teacher. How could I trust my clients in counseling to move in constructive directions, when I was not nearly so trusting of my students? Thus, I began a groping, uncertain change in my approach to my classes.

To my surprise, I found that my classrooms became more exciting places of learning as I ceased to be a *teacher.* It wasn't easy. It happened rather gradually, but as I began to trust students, I found they did incredible things in their communication with each other, in their learning of content material in the course, in blossoming out as growing human beings. Most of all they gave me courage to be myself more freely, and this led to profound interaction. They told me their feelings, they raised questions I had never thought about. I began to sparkle with emerging ideas that were new and exciting to me, but also, I found, to them.

I believe I passed some sort of crucial divide when I was able to begin a course with a statement something like this: "This course has the title 'Personality Theory' (or whatever). But what we do with this course is up to *us.* We can build it around the goals *we* want to achieve, within that very general area. We can conduct it the way *we* want to. We can decide mutually how we wish to handle these bugaboos of exams and grades. I have many resources that I have on tap to be available, and I can help you find others. I believe I am one of the resources, and I am available to you to the extent that you wish. But this is *our* class. So what do we want to make of it?" This kind of statement said in effect, "We are *free* to learn *what* we wish, *as we wish.*" It made the whole climate of the classroom completely different. Though at the time I had never thought of phrasing it this way, I changed at that point from being a *teacher* and *evaluator,* to being a *facilitator of learning*—a very different occupation.

The reaction was not all positive by any means. While some students very quickly felt released and began to take initiative, others felt primarily suspicious. "This sounds good, but frankly we've taken so much guff from teachers, we don't believe you. How are you going to grade us?" Others were indignant. "I paid good money to come here and have you *teach* me, and now you're saying we'll have to learn the stuff ourselves! I feel cheated." But since I could understand very well how students could have these negative reactions and tried to make my understanding clear, several things happened. They had discovered already that one could challenge the instructor and even criticize him and not be put down, rebuked, or humiliated. This in itself made the class totally different from any other class they were in. Little by little the concept of *responsible freedom* was *experienced*—not intellectualized, not talked about, but just experienced in the feelings and emotions and intellects of the students. And then, in different ways and at different rates, they began to *use* it.

A man named Samuel Tenenbaum, who was in a summer school graduate course with me, wrote what it was like to be in that class—the surprise and the indignation of the students, the growing excitement, the closeness among class members, the incredible amount of learning, the self-insights that were a product of that class. He is writing of a time when I had become quite fully what I wanted to be in relation to a class—namely, a resourceful, fallible, human facilitator. I used his account in one of my books (2, pp. 297–313), and you might find it of interest.

With more experience, I came to feel that the resentment and hostility I aroused at the outset was not really necessary. Consequently, whether out of cowardice or wisdom, I have come to provide enough limits and require-ments, which can be *perceived* as structure, so that students can comfortably start to work. It is only as the course progresses that they realize that each "requirement" separately, and all of them together, is simply a different way of saying, "Do exactly what you wish to do in this course and say and write exactly what *you* think and feel." But freedom seems less frustrating and anxiety-laden when it is presented in somewhat conventional sounding terms as a series of "requirements."

To make clear what I mean I will give an example taken from one course.

Requirements

There are several aspects of the course which will be required. These are as follows: I wish to have a list of the readings you have done for the course turned in before the end of the course with an indication of the way you have read the book. For example, you might list a book and state, "Chapters 3 and 6 were read thoroughly." You might list another book and state, "Skimmed the book and found it was over my head." You might list another book and say, "I got so much out of this book that I read it twice and made careful notes on chapters 5 through 12." You might state, "I was repelled by the whole point of view and only read enough to become convinced that I was disgusted with the author." In other words, what is wanted is an honest account of what you have read and the depth to which you have read the material you covered. The books do not necessarily have to be on this reading list.

The second requirement is that you write a paper, which may be as brief or as lengthy as you wish, about your own most significant personal values and the ways they have changed or not changed as a result of this course.

A third requirement is that you turn in to me a statement of your own evaluation of your work and the grade that you think is appropriate. This statement should include (*a*) the criteria by which you are judging your work; (*b*) a description of the ways in which you have met or failed to meet those criteria; and (*c*) the grade that you think appropriate to the way you have met or failed to meet your own criteria. If I find that my own estimate of your work is quite at variance with yours, I will have a personal talk with you, and we will see if we can arrive at some mutually satisfactory grade that I can in good conscience sign and turn in.

The final requirement is to be your personal reaction to the course as a whole. I would like this turned in to me in a sealed envelope with your name on the outside. You are at liberty, however, to mark on it, "Please do not open until the final grades have been turned in." If you mark the envelope in this fashion, I assure you I will honor your request.

In this reaction I would like you to state very honestly what the course has meant to you, both positively and negatively. I would like any criticisms you have to make of the course and suggestions of ways in which it might be improved. This in short is your opportunity to evaluate the course, the instructor, and the manner in which the course has been carried out. It will in no case have any influence on your final grade, but if you are fearful that it might have such an influence, please mark your envelope as suggested, and I will not open it until all grades have been turned in.

A final grade in the course will not be turned in until all of these requirements have been fulfilled.

Perhaps this example indicates how much freedom can be given in a framework that appears conventional. I believe it also suggests that instructions to students can be stated in a human way.

I had to learn the hard way that I should never *say* I was granting some degree of freedom, or some degree of trust, that I was not willing to back up with my whole being. When I granted some freedom and then felt I had to take it away, the resentment was incredible. It is better not to give it at all, I learned, than to extend it and then attempt to bring the authority back into my own hands. Where the freedom or trust was limited in certain ways, I had found that those limits had better be *explicit*. "I want this course to be as free as possible, but the department requires that we cover these two texts, and an examination written and graded by the department will be given on those texts." Or, "I would just like to say, 'Give yourselves the grade you think is fair,' but I realize that I must sign the grade sheet, giving it my approval, so I believe the grade must be mutually acceptable. If I find a discrepancy between my subjective evaluation of your work and your subjective evaluation, we will discuss it together and try to agree on a reasonable grade." (I found that I more frequently insisted on a higher grade than argued that a high grade was doubtfully deserved.)

All this had a great effect on the students and a great effect on me. I found myself so much freer to permit variety in student work—poems and art work and experience in community work sometimes became student projects. More important to me was the fact that I felt far freer to express vague, ill-formed ideas (creative ideas are initially almost always half-baked) and to receive enormous stimulation from the discussion of them. Also, I felt more free—since I was no longer the power—to let a student know how I felt. "I don't know how others feel, but I resent the amount of class time you take with your talking," or "When you speak, it is always so much to the point, so incisive, I wish you would speak up more often."

The effects of such human learning in a classroom persist. Just yesterday I received a letter from a young woman (no, no longer so young) with whom I have had no contact for more than fifteen years. In one paragraph, she says, "I have always meant to tell you that the two course sequence with you twenty years ago (!!!) was the only genuine educational experience I found in about nine years of college and grad school at four different universities. I have never read so much psychology or with such pleasure as I did that year. The contrast between that and the rest was very painful." I can scarcely remember her, but she for twenty years has remembered a class where she was free to learn and to be.

A NEW TYPE OF CLASSROOM

Why am I telling you all this personal experience? Because I think that, from what I have been saying, you and your students might invent a way to develop a climate of free and creative learning in your class. You are not me, nor are your students the ones I have had, so the laying down of rules, or telling you this is the way a class should be, is no answer. I am simply suggesting that if students and instructor discuss the issue openly, ways might be found in which all could be whole human beings in the classroom. Occasionally, I have known "miracles" to follow from such discussions, but much more often, it is painful, growthful struggles that ensue—in the instructor, in each student, in the interactions of the whole group. It is only at the end of the course, or even afterward, that individuals may disclose how valuable it has been to attempt to be a whole human being in a classroom interaction.

Here are a few statements written, after the course was over, by students in a high school psychology course where discussion was free. Not even the most sensitive issues such as sex and drugs were barred, and movies, books, tape recordings, drawing materials, and many other resources were made available. The course was facilitated—certainly not taught—by Dr. Alice Elliott.

I think that there should be more classes where students would be able to speak out!!!

In this class, people seemed to be more truthful than they are in other classes, and they seem to be aware of other people's feelings.

The class helped me to become more aware, a more interested person. I feel more independent and more like an explorer. I want to search, to know more.

This class has helped me realize more than before that I am an individual. I do not want to be measured with other people, but as myself.

This class or subject is about the greatest thing that ever happened to me in school, 'cause this subject makes you realize the object in your life. What are you doing in this world and what do you want to do in this world?

This class has made me realize that I am not the only person in the world, and everyone has just as many problems as I have. It also helped me to understand more fully why some people do the things that they do.

Ever since I started school and began to understand what I was doing I dreamed that one day it would be different. I never liked books and things that were written. I have learned more by being aware of what others liked and disliked.

For the last two years I have been a put-on. I've realized what I was, so I have changed. I try to be myself, do and say what I feel, not afraid of what people will think.

These statements come from a classroom where the teacher is a real person, who cares for adolescent young people and lets them know that she can understand their thoughts and feelings.

AN ILLUSTRATION OF CLASSROOM
CHANGES

While working on this chapter, I received a surprising letter from a high school student describing a dramatic change in his math teacher. I was sufficiently interested that I wrote to the teacher, asking to know more of her experience. It was indeed a dramatic story, almost melodramatic, and I thought that it could not be used since readers would be put off, feeling that it was "too good to be true." On further thought, it seemed to me that the very sudden change in this teacher, occurring in a few weeks, was much like the more gradual change I have observed in many teachers over a period of months or even years. So I have decided to present the material from both the students and the teacher in this high school geometry class. Only the names have been changed.

Here are some statements from the letter I received from Pete, telling of the "miracle."

> It's been exactly two months and eleven days since a miracle took place at our public high school. A certain teacher came to school that Monday, March 9, as a completely different person. Yes, Mrs. Winnie Moore (an Algebra I and Plane Geometry teacher at our school) had changed. . . .
>
> We sit in a circle, kids teach kids. But in these classes we don't just learn math. We learn about life. . . .
>
> As I said earlier, Winnie changed my outlook on life. I now have a goal to work for—to become a teacher and to get this marvelous new way to work. I now can communicate with other people; I get along better with my parents; I care deeply about many things, and I notice things that I never noticed before. All this change in me came about because of this new method. . . .

He also included statements from a number of other students who had been through the same experience. I will quote a few of them later. I must admit that my first reaction was, "What the hell do you suppose happened to that teacher?" Since Pete had given me her name, I wrote to her some weeks later to find out, asking, among other things, if she had been in an encounter group experience since it can sometimes produce a sharp change of this sort. She replied that she had not, but wanted to tell me about "certain events that led up to my change in the classroom."

She had been taking an evening course in counseling during the winter in which she had come across some of my writings and the qualities that I have found to be productive of both learning and personal growth—genuineness (or realness), deep empathic understanding, and a warm, loving acceptance of the person as he/she is. She continues:

> . . . These concepts intrigued me and, to my astonishment, I was able to use them in the next week. A student of mine who was deeply troubled came to visit me at my home. Paul is fifteen and well experienced with drugs. I sensed his desperate need to communicate to and with someone, and I felt God had designated me to be that someone. (I am sure the phenomenon could be thoroughly explained in psychological terms.) I tried

to hear him at every level possible until I had internalized his difficulties almost to an intolerable extent. Suddenly, I realized how painful life seemed to him. More shocking still, I realized what he felt like as a student in *my class*. I was adding to his pain. I watched his agony at taking one of my quizzes. It became my pain, too.

On Wednesday of that week I did some role playing in the evening counseling class. I had been chosen the week before to play the part of a client with a personal problem. I played a deeply troubled person who was thinking of suicide. In that role I believe that I played both Paul and me intertwined. The woman who played the counselor was astonished and told me, "If you can do this, you can do anything." She was, it seemed, almost on the verge of tears.

I then went through an extraordinary experience on the following Friday—March 6—in which my husband, John, helped me to communicate with Paul. The three of us sat on the floor, and John started things off by saying that we all had to be very honest with each other even though that was difficult. I could not speak for a long time. Paul began to get tears in his eyes, so I moved toward him and whispered to him. I do not remember all that I said, but the words came very easily. I told him that I was sure that he had been trying to kill himself. (Later, he told me of four or five attempted suicides.) I also told him that I would see that he would not feel that lonely or despondent again. He told me that nobody had ever cared for him before. A bit later I was so released by this communication that I felt filled with power and strength. I really had reached somebody! The strength that I felt seemed to pour into Paul. I ran across this description in a personality text of Maslow's "oceanic feeling":

> limitless horizons opening up to the vision, the feeling of being simultaneously more powerful and also more helpless than one ever was before, the feeling of great ecstasy and wonder and awe, the loss of placing in time and space with, finally, the conviction that something extremely important and valuable had happened, so that the subject is to some extent transformed and strengthened even in his daily life by such experiences.

This was my experience! I had a fantastic feeling for four days. I could no longer tolerate the walled-in teacher that I had been. I had to change my teaching because I had to be true to myself. Teaching in the traditional way hurt me. I also had to show Paul that I could change, and then he could change. On the following Monday I changed all my classes as my students related to you. Paul was very dependent on me for several months, but our relationship now has eased into a friendship. He seems independent and more confident with his peers. . . .

So that was what happened to her! Clearly, she had been through a conversion experience with profound effects. (I am always suspicious of conversions that take place because of external circumstances—an inspiring speaker or group pressure—but conversions that are brought on by internal experiences are quite different and tend to be lasting.) The work that she and her husband did with Paul may be questioned by many readers. Was she qualified to undertake the counseling of such a seriously disturbed boy? The alternative—to turn away a boy who had taken the great risk of coming to her for help—is, in my judgment, a definitely hurtful thing, and I am glad she took the risk. There must have been a real psychic connectedness for her to "know" intuitively that he wished to commit suicide. I regard her initial whispered statement to him as very risky indeed, only justified by the fact that her intuition proved correct. I would have been more comfortable with a much more tentative communication on her part.

But however we view her counseling sessions with Paul, the effect on her was profound. She had let herself move inside the world of one of her students, and not only experienced the pain he was in, but the further pain she was causing him in her class. (Imagine the tremendous difference it would make if every teacher felt, even for a few moments, the way his or her class was being experienced by each and every student!) In Mrs. Moore, this profoundly empathic involvement with Paul caused her to change her whole way of being in her class. That this change was very observable is evidenced by the statements of other students in addition to Pete, two of which are given here.

> A fellow: . . . The things it's done for my geometry class cannot be put down in words on paper. But it all came about because Mrs. Moore was honest with us and with herself and took this small step. The things this small step did for me and the class and my education and my outlook on life just cannot be said adequately. I've gotten to learn so much about so many people in that class and I've gotten the will to work on geometry.

> A girl writing to Mrs. Moore: . . . I finally got myself believing that teachers were robots programmed to hurt people. I finally realized I had to shut them out and not listen to them for they scared me out of my mind. . . . My 3rd grade math teacher would call me stupid, lazy, and ungrateful when I messed up on a quiz or didn't understand my homework. She scared me so that when it was time to take a test, I was so scared of flunking that I flunked every one. My parents thought it was because I wasn't studying enough, so all my privileges were taken away and I was made to go to bed at 7:30 so that I would be rested for my next terrifying day at school. . . . It was like a dream—here a teacher was finally realizing that her students need her and want her to be their friend and to help them understand so many puzzling things! When I left your class, I felt like crying out to everyone that someone *does* care.

I believe it is very rare and most unusual for a teacher and a classroom to change so suddenly. But whether slowly and gradually, or in a short period as here, the response of students is overwhelming. To find a teacher who is human, to be treated as a human being in a class is not only a very precious experience, but one that stimulates the learning of facts, as well as self-understanding and improved communication with one's fellows.

How Can I Become Real?

Thus far, there have been frequent references to "being real," "being one's real self." What do these phrases mean fundamentally? I would like to approach these issues from several angles.

In the first place, such queries are common ones. As I have known young men and women intimately in counseling relationships and encounter groups, and less intimately in courses and seminars and personal discussions, I have found one profound question underlying much of the surface talk. It appears that for almost all of them the question they are seeking to answer is, "Who am I, really? Can I ever discover or get in touch with my real self? Will I ever feel any assurance or stability in myself?" And these questions are not only those of the young, but of countless older men and women too.

THE SEARCH FOR IDENTITY—A MODERN PROBLEM

We are, perhaps all of us, engaged in a struggle to discover our identity, the person we are and choose to be. This is a very pervasive search—it involves our clothes, our hair, our appearance. At a more significant level, it involves our choice of values, our stance in relation to parents and others, the relationship we choose to have to society, our whole philosophy of life. It is, in these days, a most perplexing search. As one college woman says:

> I'm confused. Just when I think I'm getting my head together, I talk with some fellow who's sure he knows what life is all about. And because I'm uncertain, I'm really impressed. And then when I get away I realize that's *his* answer. It can't be the answer for me. I've got to find my own. But it's hard when everything is so loose and unsure.

I see this search for one's real self, for identity, as much more of a problem today than in the historical past. During most of history, it made little difference whether the individual discovered himself. Perhaps he lived a more comfortable life if he did not because the identity he lived was defined for him. It is interesting to think ourselves back into feudal times. The serf was expected to *be* a serf throughout his life and his children after him. In return he was permitted to eke out a meager living, most of his work going to support the lord of the manor, who in turn protected him. The nobleman was, in a more luxurious way, also constricted. He was the lord, responsible for his followers, and his children would continue the role of the nobleman. In our own country, during one dark period of our history, the slave was always the slave, and the master always the master. The difficulties of abandoning these role identities are still painfully with us.

While this rigidity of the defined role seems incredibly restrictive to us now, this should not blind us to the fact that it made life simpler in many ways. The cobbler knew that he and his sons would always be cobblers; his wife knew that she and her daughters would always be primarily servants of their husbands. There were almost no options, and peculiarly enough this gave a type of security that we have left behind. Perhaps one of the few analogies that is comprehensible to us is the peacetime army. Many men and women have come to accept this life with more satisfaction than they had supposed possible. There are almost no decisions. They are told what to wear, how to behave, where to live, what to do. They can gripe as freely as they wish, without any responsibility for their lives. They are *given* an identity, *told* who they are, and the agonizing personal search that most of us must go through is at least temporarily abrogated.

It is for reasons of this sort that I say the search for one's real self is a peculiarly modern problem. The individual's life is no longer defined (though it may be influenced) by one's family, social class, color, church, or nation. We carry the burden ourselves of discovering our identity.

I believe the only person today who does not suffer this painful search for self is the person who voluntarily surrenders his or her individual identity to some organization or institution that defines the purposes, the values, the philosophy to be followed. Examples would be: persons who completely commit themselves to some strict religious sect that is sure of all the answers; persons who commit themselves to a rigorous ideology (whether revolutionary or reactionary) that defines their philosophy, their lifestyle, and their actions for them; persons who give themselves completely to science or industry or traditional education (though there are large cracks in the certainties of all these institutions); or, as mentioned, give over their lives to the military. I can thoroughly understand the satisfactions and securities that would cause individuals to make such commitments partly in order to gain a certain comfort. Yet I suspect that the majority of young people prefer the more painful burden of choosing to be the uniqueness that is involved in discovering the real self. I know personally that is my choice.

One of the most common fears of persons who are trying to discover who they really are inside is that this undiscovered "me" will turn out to be a worthless, bizarre, evil, or horrible creature. Something of this is expressed by a searching student: "I feel my mind is open, kind of like a funnel, and on top there are sparks and exciting things, but down deeper in the funnel it's dark, and I'm afraid to go down in there because I'm scared of what I might find. I'm not going to do it just now." This attitude is a very frequent one indeed.

PATHWAYS TO SELF

There are a number of ways in which individuals pursue this goal of becoming themselves. Some lives have been badly distorted or warped by early childhood. For them the search for solidity in themselves, for their own real self, may be a long or painful one. Others who have been more fortunate are already in the process of discovery and have an easier time. Some are sufficiently frightened by the risks involved in the search that they endeavor to freeze themselves as they are, fearful of any road that would lead into unknown territory. I will briefly describe several of the ways in which people venture, as they search for the "real self."

ONE PATHWAY—PSYCHOTHERAPY

More and more people these days are seeking to find themselves through psychotherapy. The success of this venture depends heavily on the person and the attitudes of the therapist. My colleagues and I have singled out three attitudes—three ways of being—that are especially important in a therapeutic relationship, and exhaustive research has confirmed this belief. The first is a realness or genuineness in the therapist. He is what he seems to be. His internal being is matched by his external expression. The second is a nonpossessive, nonjudgmental caring—a type of love that creates a safe atmosphere for the person seeking help. The third is the therapist's ability to listen in a very special empathic way, leading to an acceptant understanding of the inner world of the client. This feeling of being fully understood without being judged is a very precious experience and one that enables the client to move forward.

But this description is from the side of the counselor or therapist. Some years ago I tried to draw from my experience with many individuals seeking help a subjective picture of the way therapy feels to the client, and I am going to quote it here. I should point out that what I describe in a few paragraphs is a process that may take weeks, months, or even years to complete. When a person seeks help from a therapist best described as person-centered, here is the process as it feels to the client. First is the fearful, risky start.

> I'm afraid of him. I want help, but I don't know whether to trust him. He might see things that I don't know in myself—frightening and bad elements. He seems not to be judging me, but I'm sure he is. I can't tell him what really concerns me, but I can tell him about some past experiences which are related to my concern. He seems to understand those, so I can reveal a bit more of myself.

> But now that I've shared with him some of this bad side of me, he despises me. I'm sure of it, but it's strange I can find little evidence of it. Do you suppose that what I've just told him isn't so bad? Is it possible that I need not be ashamed of it as a part of me? I no longer feel that he despises me. It makes me feel that I want to go further, exploring *me,* perhaps expressing more of myself. I find him a sort of companion as I do this—he seems really to understand.

> But now I'm getting frightened again, and this time deeply frightened. I didn't realize that exploring the unknown recesses of myself would make me feel feelings I've never experienced before. It's very strange because in one way these aren't new feelings. I sense that they've always been there. But they seem so bad and disturbing I've never dared to let them flow in me. And now as I live these feelings in the hours with him, I feel terribly shaky, as though my world is falling apart. It used to be sure and firm. Now it is loose, permeable and vulnerable. It isn't pleasant to feel things I've always been frightened of before. It's his fault. Yet curiously I'm eager to see him and I feel more safe when I'm with him.

> I don't know who I am any more, but sometimes when I *feel* things I seem solid and real for a moment. I'm troubled by the contradictions I find in myself—I act one way and feel another—I think one thing and feel another. It is very disconcerting. It's also sometimes adventurous and exhilarating to be trying to discover who I am. Sometimes I catch myself feeling that perhaps the person I am is worth being, whatever that means.

> I'm beginning to find it very satisfying, though often painful, to share just what it is I'm feeling at this moment. You know, it is really helpful to try to listen to myself, to hear what is going on in me. I'm not so frightened any

more of what *is* going on in me. It seems pretty trustworthy. I use some of my hours with him to dig deep into myself to know what I *am* feeling. It's scary work, but I want to *know.* And I do trust him most of the time, and that helps. I feel pretty vulnerable and raw, but I know he doesn't want to hurt me, and I even believe he cares. It occurs to me as I try to let myself down and down, deep into myself, that maybe if I could sense what is going on in me and could realize its meaning, I would know who I am, and I would also know what to do. At least I feel this knowing sometimes with him.

I can even tell him just how I'm feeling toward him at any given moment and instead of this killing the relationship, as I used to fear, it seems to deepen it. Do you suppose I could be my feelings with other people also? Perhaps that wouldn't be too dangerous either.

You know, I feel as if I'm floating along on the current of life, very adventurously, being me. I get defeated sometimes, I get hurt sometimes, but I'm learning that those experiences are not fatal. I don't *know* exactly *who* I am, but I can feel my reactions at any given moment, and they seem to work out pretty well as a basis for my behavior from moment to moment. Maybe this is what it *means* to be *me.* But of course I can only do this because I feel safe in the relationship with my therapist. Or could I be myself this way outside of this relationship? I wonder. I wonder. Perhaps I could. (2, pp. 67–69)

I hope that gives a clearer understanding of how one's real self emerges in psychotherapy. In case you are speculating as to whether clients would agree with this description, here is a portion of a letter from Melanie. She is twenty-four years old, with experience as a teacher. She read one of my books and wrote me about her therapy.

. . . The therapist's decision to commit himself emotionally to me really enabled me to feel safe in the relationship. The humanness of feeling that followed was beautiful. The therapist's confidence . . . led me to move away from fear and mistrust of people into love, away from hostility and regressive acts into understanding and maturity. Because I felt and accepted love from this one human being (a situation I never had in all my life), I was able to accept myself as a loved person. I felt worthwhile and beautiful. It was only then that I could undergo the pain of seeing myself as a very separate human being and of accepting all responsibility for my own life. I felt safe enough to open my eyes and really see for the first time. I saw love and hate, joy and sorrow, beauty and ugliness. But through it all, I was fortunate to have the strengths given me to support me through turbulent times. In three and one-half years I moved from being a frightened, distrustful, withdrawn, and tense human being to a warm, loving, aware, calm, and creative woman. I reached across a stormy sea to the shores of maturity. . . .

I've found a new life, an aliveness and a sense of adventure. I found within me the strengths to give to others the love and understanding to help them grow in confidence and independence. I have returned to teaching where I have found joy in watching children who, in the right atmosphere, break through their defenses and reach out, who take the risk to bridge the gap from their separateness to mine. . . .

I think this illustrates very well the importance of finding in some other person trust, acceptance, and love if one is to become one's self, to become a separate person in one's own right. Clearly Melanie is now offering that kind of relationship in the atmosphere she creates for her pupils at school.

THE INTENSIVE GROUP—ANOTHER PATHWAY

It is increasingly common for people to have some sort of experience in an intensive group. They exist under many different labels—encounter group, T-group, human relations group, sensitivity group, among others. The ones most pertinent to our present interest are those that are held in connection with university courses, often with a variety of purposes, including the opportunity for the student to grow in the understanding and acceptance of self.

A number of medical schools have organized such groups for students just entering medical school. The groups include the students, the faculty members who will be teaching them, and members of the administrative staff. Students who are married are encouraged to invite their spouses. The sessions are held away from campus in some informal, camp-like setting. When facilitated by an experienced person, holding the sort of attitudes described above for a psychotherapist, the outcomes are very meaningful for most participants. They build solid, personal, "first name" relationships with faculty, develop friendships with other students, and make progress in discovering who they are underneath the usual facade.

I, and many other instructors, have included such intensive group experiences as a part of a course. My own preference is for two weekend groups, one early in the course and one toward the end. I would like to give some examples from a course of thirty students in which three former students assisted as facilitators. I have chosen reactions that bear on the issue of discovering one's true self.

> I had always wanted to be loved, accepted, and esteemed and felt that this could only be brought about by certain values which came from others, that *I* could not rock the boat, and how *I* really felt didn't matter. In our first encounter group I felt mixed up but good when I related some of my deep personal problems, when the feedback was pleasant, when I tried to truly see myself. But I found that maybe wasn't really me after all. Maybe there was another me who had something to say, but did he have the "right to speak up?" [He tells how he began to express his feelings and] . . . here I was truly relating to others how I was *really* feeling, actually being aware of what I was experiencing. As I write this I am becoming emotional and have very wet eyes at this moment.

> I feel that I am definitely moving away from "oughts" and meeting expectations, that I don't always have to please others, that I can become myself and actually become aware of what I am experiencing, and that this isn't any crime and I do have some rights. Truly a significant change in some of

my personal values. I find that I am moving more toward trusting myself though this is going to take time.

*   *   *

Since the last workshop encounter I have been turned on and have been experiencing myself, my wife and children, and my work, in a clearer, more involved, more meaningful way. Ideas, thoughts, emotional insights keep bubbling up and influencing me toward freer, more open behavior in these areas. I attribute these changes to my workshop experiences.

*   *   *

As I reflect on the experiences afforded me in the small groups I realize that I had developed a kind of channeled perception; that is, I was filtering out those things that didn't fit my idea of the way the thing "ought to be."

Small group members helped me to see my irrational behavior, not only by pointing it out to me, but by being open and interacting with each other. . . . As the group sessions drew to a close I began to experience a good feeling. I had developed a desire to face my problem in a positive way and in so doing I have since learned that what I had feared for five years really wasn't so important.

Since the basic encounter group experiences I believe that I can learn to accept myself. I am well aware that this will take time but I feel certain that as I learn to be less critical of myself I will be happier. I am sure that this course has helped me in this regard.

*   *   *

I became tellingly aware of the fact that I have been trying to *prove* myself. I don't have to prove myself. All I really have to do, that is, my only responsibility, is to *be* myself. I value myself more as a person—my dependency needs, my anxieties, my proving needs, my inadequacies, and limitations, as well as my warm feelings for others, my knowledge, my competencies, my worthiness, my potential.

Not everyone profits from such group experience. In this class there was one negative reaction.

My negative reaction to the course is that for me personally it is a depressing experience to see how many truly deeply troubled people we have in our group, some with personal troubles so deep and complicated that I fear they will never overcome them. Of course, on the other hand, I can be thankful that I am not in their shoes but somehow this feeling doesn't seem to overcome the concern that these weekends generated in me, for the many troubled people we have drifting around as associates in this life. . . . I myself personally received no help from these group encounters . . . but I accept the fact that they are of immense value to my troubled associates.

Perhaps these student statements (with the exception of the last) are evidence of the progress individuals make toward finding and being a deeper, more authentic self.

THE LIFETIME TASK OF SELF-DISCOVERY

This process of self-discovery and self-acceptance and self-expression is not something that goes on only in therapy or in groups. Many people have neither of these experiences. For those who do, the therapy or the group exists for only a limited time. But for all of us, the search to become the person we most uniquely are, is a lifetime process.

I believe this is one reason why biography holds a fascination for so many readers. We like to follow the struggle of an individual to become what he or she is capable of becoming. For me, this is illustrated by the book I have just finished, telling the life story of Georgia O'Keeffe, the artist. There are many steps in her development. At fourteen, the inwardly independent but outwardly conforming girl won a gold medal for her ladylike "deportment" at a strict Catholic school. But by the age of sixteen, she was beginning to dress in a "tailored, midwestern corsetless style" (in 1903!) which was to be a characteristic throughout her many years. And at age twenty-nine she locked herself in her studio and analyzed all her work up to that point with "ruthless detachment." She could tell which paintings had been done to please one professor and which to please another. She could tell which had been influenced by well-known artists of the day. "Then an idea dawned on her. There were abstract shapes in her mind integral to her imagination, unlike anything she had been taught. 'This thing that is your own is so close to you, often you never realize it's there,' she later explained . . . 'I could think of a whole string of things I'd like to put down but I'd never thought of doing it because I'd never seen anything like it.' . . . She had made up her mind. This was what she would paint" (1, p. 81).

As you can imagine, this decision was the initial step toward becoming the great artist of her mature years. Though she is in her nineties now, she has relentlessly pursued that goal of painting her own unique perceptions— of the desert, of bleached bones, of huge and gorgeous flowers—to the point that one has only to look at one of her paintings to realize "That's an O'Keeffe."

Like Georgia O'Keeffe, each of us is the artist or the architect of his or her own life. We can copy others, we can live to please others, or we can discover that which is unique and precious to us, and paint that, become that. It is a task which takes a lifetime.

BECOMING REAL

Let me try to summarize what it means to me to find one's real self. In the first place it is a process, a direction, not some static achievement. In my estimation no one is ever completely successful in finding all her real (and ever-changing) self. But there are certain characteristics of this process. Persons move away from hiding behind facades and pretenses, whether these have been held consciously or unconsciously. They move toward a greater closeness to, and awareness of, what they are inwardly experiencing. They find that this experiencing is exceedingly complex and varied, ranging from wild and "crazy" feelings to solid, socially approved ones. They move toward accepting all of these experiencings as something they can own—that they are persons with this enormous variety of reactions. The more they own, accept, and are unafraid of their inner reactions, the more they can sense the meanings they have for them. The more all this inner richness belongs to them, the more they can appropriately *be* their experiences. An individual may become aware of a childish need to depend on someone, to be cared for and protected. In appropriate situations she can let herself *be* that child-ish, dependent self. She may discover that certain situations anger her. She can more easily express that anger as it arises, in the situation which arouses it, rather than suppressing it until it pours out explosively on some innocent victim. A man can discover soft, tender, loving feelings (especially difficult for men to own) and can express these with satisfaction, not shame. So these persons are moving toward being a wider range of their feelings, their atti-tudes, their potential. They have built a good relationship with what is going on within themselves. They begin to appreciate and like, rather than hate and mistrust, all their experiencings. Thus, they are coming closer to finding and being all of themselves in the moment. To me this is the way the person moves toward answering the question, "Who am I?"

THE EXCITEMENT OF SELF-DISCOVERY

I should like to close this chapter with one more illustration from the course that included two weekend encounter groups. This is not written by a young man, but by a man who has been a teacher, a high school principal, has carried heavy administrative responsibility. Yet it is clear that he is just taking the first steps in finding and being himself. It seems tragic that he could have lived for more than thirty years without discovering himself. Yet his pride in taking these steps, and the excitement of getting acquainted with himself, shine through his remarks:

> As I sit at my desk to begin this paper, I have a real feeling of inner excitement. This is an experience that I have never had. For as I write I have no format to follow and I will put my thoughts down as they occur. It's almost a feeling of floating for to me it doesn't seem to really matter how you, or anyone for that matter, will react to my thoughts. Nevertheless, at the same time, I feel that you will accept them as mine regardless of the lack of style, format, or academic expression. . . . My real concern is to try to communicate with myself so that I might better understand myself.

> I guess what I am really saying is that I am writing not for you, nor for a grade, nor for a class, but for *me*. And I feel especially good about that, for this is something that I wouldn't have *dared* to do or even *consider* in the past.

> You know I guess it bothers me if others don't think well of me . . . But I now realize that I really want people to like me *now* for what I *am*, for what I *really* am, not just for what I pretend to be.

THE CHALLENGE

I hope that this chapter has opened a door and given you a glimpse of what is beyond. It is a door to being fully alive in the classroom. Also, it is a door to being more fully yourself. Some of you will want to close that door because what is on the other side seems too risky, too emotional, too frighteningly self-responsible, and the paths it leads to seem too uncertain and unknown. Others may wish to peer cautiously inside, and to take a few tentative steps. Others will feel, "This is for me," and realize from the examples given that it can come about.

REFERENCES

1. Lisle, Laurie. *Portrait of an Artist: A Biography of Georgia O'Keeffe.* New York: Washington Square Press, 1980.
2. Rogers, Carl R. *On Becoming a Person.* Boston: Houghton Mifflin, 1961.

Responsible Freedom
in the Classroom

A Sixth Grade
Teacher Experiments

I feel that the diary constituting the first section of this chapter (1) speaks directly to the classroom teacher who is harassed by pupil apathy, by discipline problems, by complaining parents, by a set curriculum, by the daily difficulties involved in being continuously in contact with a large and varied group of students. The diary is a deeply human document. I hope that it will have the meaning for teachers of all levels that it has had for me—a feeling that there is a basis for hope, even in "impossible" classroom groups. I trust that it will release other teachers to be adventuresome and honest—with themselves and their students—and risk themselves by taking steps the consequences of which cannot be guaranteed but which depend upon trust in human beings.

A Teacher's Diary: Barbara J. Shiel

This past year was my thirteenth year of teaching elementary school. I have taught all six elementary grades. The class mentioned in the document (originally intended only as a kind of personal diary) was one of the most difficult I had ever worked with in terms of discipline, lack of interest, and parental problems. There were thirty-six in the group, with an I.Q. range of 82 to 135. There were many who were "socially maladjusted," "underachievers," or "emotionally disturbed."

I had exhausted my resources in an attempt to cope with the situation, but had made very little progress. The many discipline problems were notorious: they were constantly in the office or "on the bench" for varied offen-

45

ses; their attitude and behavior kept them in constant trouble. Several were suspended for short periods. In addition, the parents were uncooperative and/or defensive. Most of them had a history of blaming the teachers or the school for the child's problems.

MARCH 5, WE BEGIN:

A week ago, I decided to initiate a new program in my sixth grade classroom, based on student-centered teaching—an unstructured or nondirective approach.

I began by telling the class that we were going to try an "experiment." I explained that for one day I would let them do anything they wanted to do—they did not have to do anything if they did not want to.

Many started with art projects. Some drew or painted most of the day. Others read or did work in math and other subjects. There was an air of excitement all day. Many were so interested in what they were doing that they did not want to go out at recess or noon!

At the end of the day, I asked the class to evaluate the experiment. The comments were most interesting. Some were "confused," distressed without the teacher telling them what to do, without specific assignments to complete.

The majority of the class thought the day was "great," but some expressed concern over the noise level and the fact that a few "goofed off" all day. Most felt that they had accomplished as much work as we usually do, and they enjoyed being able to work at a task until it was completed without the pressure of a time limit. They liked doing things without being "forced" to do them and liked deciding what to do. They begged to continue the "experiment," so it was decided to do so, for two more days. We would then reevaluate the plan.

The next morning I implemented the idea of a "work contract." Each child was to write his contract for the day—choosing the areas in which he would work and planning specifically what he would do. Upon completion of any exercise, each student was to check and correct his own work, using the teacher's manual. The work was to be kept in a folder with the contract. Resource materials were provided, suggestions made, and drill materials made available to use when needed.

I met with each child to discuss plans. Some completed theirs in a very short time. We discussed as a group what this might mean, and what to do about it. It was suggested that the plan might not be challenging enough, that an adjustment should be made—perhaps going on or adding another area to the day's plan.

I found I had much more time, so I worked, talked, and spent the time with individuals and groups. At the end of the third day, I evaluated the work folder with each child. To solve the problem of grades, I had each child tell me what grade had been earned.

Also at this time, the group wrote a second evaluation of the experiment, adding comments their parents had made. All but four were excited and enthusiastic about the plan and thought school was much more fun. The four still felt insecure and wanted specific assignments. I talked with them about giving the experiment time—sometimes it took time to adjust to new situations. They agreed to try. The rest of the class was thrilled at the prospect of continuing the rest of the year.

The greatest problem I've encountered is discipline. I have many problem individuals in my class, and there was a regression in terms of control when the teacher's external controls were lifted. Part of the difficulty stems from the fact that I let the children sit where and with whom they liked. The "problems" congregated together, spent much of their day fighting (verbally and physically), "bugging" each other, and generally accomplishing very little, which brings to mind another problem for me—internally. I am having a difficult time watching them do nothing and am concerned at times about their progress, achievement, etc. I have to remind myself constantly that these pupils were "failing" under the old program and never turned in completed assignments under the old regime either. They only *looked* like they were doing something.

I've considered the possibility of moving some of the seats in the problem area, but I realize that I would be defeating an important aspect of the program if I reestablish my control. If we can survive this period, perhaps in time they will develop greater *self*-control.

It is interesting to me that it is upsetting to them, too. They all sit close to my desk and say it is too difficult this new way. The "temptation" is too great. This would indicate that they are not as recalcitrant as they seemed.

The class has been delighted in general. They even carry their projects and work outside and have the whole school interested and talking about the idea. And I've heard the story that they think I've really changed (since I've stopped trying to make them conform to my standards and rules, trying to make them achieve *my* goals!!).

The atmosphere is a stimulating, relaxed, happy one (discounting the problem-area upheaval).

An interesting project has developed. I noticed that some of the boys were drawing and designing automobiles. I put up a big piece of paper for them to use as they wished. They discussed their plans and proceeded to do a mural on the history of cars, incorporating their designs of cars of the future. I was delighted. They used the encyclopedia as a reference, as well as books on cars they brought in. They worked together, and some began models and scrapbooks, boys who had produced very little, if anything, so far this year.

Other ideas began to appear in other areas. The seed of initiative and creativity had germinated and began to grow.

Many children are doing some interesting research in related (and unrelated) areas of interest. Some have completed the year's "required" work in a few areas, such as spelling.

Most important, to me, is the evidence of initiative and self-responsibility manifested.

MARCH 12, PROGRESS REPORT:

Our "experiment" has, in fact, become our program—with some adjustments.

Some children continued to be frustrated and felt insecure without teacher direction. Discipline also continued to be a problem with some, and I began to realize that although the children involved may need the program more than the others, I was expecting too much from them, too soon—they were not ready to assume self-direction *yet*. Perhaps a gradual weaning from the spoon-fed procedures was necessary.

I regrouped the class—creating two groups. The largest group is the non-directed group. The smallest is teacher directed, made up of children who wanted to return to the former teacher-directed method, and those who, for varied reasons, were unable to function in the self-directed situation.

I would like to have waited longer to see what would have happened, but the situation for some disintegrated a little more each day—penalizing the whole class. The disrupting factor kept everyone upset and limited those who wanted to study and work. So it seemed to me best for the group as a whole as well as the program to modify the plan.

Those who continued the "experiment" have forged ahead. I showed them how to program their work, using their texts as a basic guide. They have learned that they can teach themselves (and each other) and that I am available when a step is not clear or advice is needed.

At the end of the week, they evaluate themselves in each area—in terms of work accomplished, accuracy, etc. We have learned that the number of errors is not a criterion of failure or success. Errors can and should be a part of the learning process. We learn through out mistakes. We also discussed the fact that consistently perfect scores may mean that the work is not challenging enough and perhaps means we should move on.

After self-evaluation, each child brings the evaluation sheet and work folder to discuss them with me.

Some of the members of the group working with me are most anxious to become "independent" students. Each week we will evaluate their progress toward that goal.

I have only experienced one parental objection so far. A parent thought her child was not able to function without direction.

Some students (there were two or three) who originally wanted to return to the teacher-directed program are now anticipating going back into the self-directed program. (I sense that it has been as difficult for them to readjust to the old program as it would be for me to do so.)

MARCH 19, PROGRESS REPORT:

Today, from my point of view as a teacher, has been the most satisfying since we began our new program.

It began with an individual evaluation with each child in the teacher-directed program. (I had had conferences with the nondirected group the preceding day.) Several of the children in the former group felt that they were ready to go back into the nondirected group. They had decided they liked the freedom after all and thought they understood the responsibilities involved. It was decided that they would try it for one week to see if they really were ready. I would help them at any time they needed help with their work plan or actual work.

At this point, I have only six in the teacher group. One wants to be in the other group, but since her mother was the one parent who complained, I told her she must discuss it at home first.

We had an oral evaluation; one of the topics discussed was parental reaction. One boy said his mother said it sounded as if I had given up teaching! Another boy said his father told him that he had tried self-responsibility with him before, and he thought I was nuts to try it with so many at once!

We discussed what we could do to help our parents understand the program. It was suggested (by the children) that we could take our weekly work folders home to show what we were actually accomplishing and that since the intangible work was on the work contract, it could be discussed as well.

The rest of the day was spent with as little interference as possible by me. Groups and individuals proceeded with their plans. It was a productive, rewarding day.

The days have fluctuated between optimism and concern, hope and fear. My emotional temperature rises and falls with each rung climbed on the ladder of our adventure.

Some days I feel confident, buoyant, sure that we are on the right track—on other days I am assailed by doubts. All the teacher training, authoritarian tradition, curriculum, and report cards threaten and intimidate me.

I must exercise great control when I see a child doing nothing (productive) for most of a day. Providing the opportunity to develop self-discipline is an even greater trial at times.

I've come to realize that one must be secure in one's own self-concept to undertake such a program. In order to relinquish the accepted role of the teacher in a teacher-directed program, one must understand and accept one's self first. It is important as well to have a clear understanding of the goals one is endeavoring to work toward.

In another statement written later, Shiel describes the elements of a school day during the "experiment." I insert it here in order to give more of a picture of how the students, as well as Shiel, operated:

A Sample Day in the Class

Each day began informally; the first task of each individual was to design his or her work plan, or "contract." Sometimes children planned with one or two others. There was constant self-grouping and regrouping, withdrawal from a group for independent work.

As soon as the contract was made, the child began to study or work on his plan. He could work as long as he needed or wanted to. Because I was not free to discard the state-devised curriculum time schedule, I explained the weekly time-subject blocks to the children. This was to be a consideration in their planning. We also discussed sequential learning, especially in math, mastering a skill before proceeding to the next level of learning. They discovered that the text provided an introduction to a skill, demonstrated the skill, and provided exercises to master it and tests to check achievement. When they felt they were ready to go on, they were free to do so. They set their own pace, began at their own level, and went as far as they were able or self-motivated to go.

I have been constantly challenged, "But how did you teach the facts and new concepts?" The individuals inquiring apparently assume that unless the teacher is dictating, directing, or explaining, there can be no learning. My answer is that I did not "teach." The children taught themselves and each other.

When individuals or groups wished to share their projects, learnings, or research with the class, or when there were audiovisual materials of general interest to the class, it was announced on the board and incorporated into the individual planning. For example, if we had a film on South America, the entire class viewed it; but what they did with the film was up to the individual. They could outline it, summarize it, draw pictures of it—or ignore it if they chose.

Whenever the children felt the need to discuss individual, group, or class "problems," we arranged our desks in a seminar circle and had a "general semantics" session. We also functioned as one group in music (singing) and in physical education.

Since evaluation was self-initiated and respected by the teacher, there was no need for cheating to achieve success. We discovered that "failure" is only a word, that there is a difference between failure and making a mistake, and that mistakes are a part of the learning process.

In art, the children were free to explore with materials: paper, paints, crayons, chalk, clay, etc., as well as with books and ideas. They discovered for themselves, through manipulation and experimentation, new techniques and new uses of media. No two "products" were alike—although there was considerable dependency on the discoveries of others in the beginning. In time, individuals developed confidence and openness to experimentation. The results were far more exciting than those achieved in teacher-directed lessons in spite of the fact that I consider art my greatest strength, or talent!

The children developed a working discipline that respected the individual need for isolation or quiet study, yet allowed pupil interaction. There was no need for passing of notes or "subversive" interaction. There was respect for meditation and contemplation as well as for overt productivity. There were opportunities to get to *know* one another. The children learned to communicate *by communicating*.

Final Entry

APRIL 9, PROGRESS REPORT:

I prefer the term *self-directed* to *nondirectional* in describing our program. I believe it better describes the goals, as well as the actual implementation, of the program.

It is directed, in the sense that we must work within the structure of the curriculum, the specific units of study. It is self-directed in that each child is responsible for his own planning within this basic structure.

At this point, I have only four pupils who are not in the program. I try to provide a period each day for them when they are able to assume some responsibility, make some decisions. They are children who need much additional help and are insecure and frustrated without my guidance.

As I went through the process of putting grades on report cards, I began to realize that the most valuable aspects of the children's growth could not be evaluated in terms of letter grades. For some, there is no observable change, or it is intangible—yet one senses growth, a metamorphosis taking place.

Day to day one can sense the growth in communication, in social development. One cannot measure the difference in attitude, the increased interest, the growing pride in self-improvement; but one is aware that they exist. And how does a teacher evaluate self-discipline? What is easy for me may not be easy for someone else.

The report cards are only an indication, but I know the children will be pleased as I am at the improvement in their grades and the great decrease in citizenship checks.

In evaluating their work, I find them to be fairly perceptive, aware of their capacity and how it relates to their accomplishment. I rarely need to change grades. When I do, sometimes I must upgrade!

I mentioned earlier how many "problems" there have been in this class—both disciplinary and emotional. This program in fact developed out of an attempt to meet the challenge that the "problems" presented. At times, I felt whipped, defeated, and frustrated. I felt I was making no headway and resented my policing role.

Since our program has been in full swing, I've found that I've undergone change, too. Early in the year I could but bide my time until I could send the "gang" onward and upward—at least see them off to the seventh grade.

I find now that I see these children with different eyes, and as I've watched them, I've begun to realize that there *is* hope. I have asked to take this class on, in a self-contained situation, to seventh grade. Scheduling may prevent this becoming an actuality, but I feel these children would continue to progress toward self-actualization within the framework and freedom of the self-directed program.

I feel that now that the mechanics of the program are worked out, now that there is greater understanding and rapport between the children and myself (since I have discarded the authoritarian role), there is greater opportunity for self-growth, not only creativity, initiative, imagination, but self-discipline, self-acceptance, and understanding.

At times when I see children who are not doing what I think they ought to be doing, I must remind myself again of the ultimate goals and the fact that they did not produce "required" work when it was assigned previously. They may be drawing something that is not esthetically pleasing to me, but they *are* drawing, and it *is* imaginative! They may not be "busy," but they may be *thinking.* They may be talking, but they are cooperating and learning to communicate. They may fight and respond with signal reactions—abuse one another verbally—but it may be the only way they know. They may not do as much math, but they understand and remember what they do do.

Best of all, they are more interested in school, in their progress. I would venture that this program might result in fewer dropouts and "failures" in school.

It is not the panacea, but it is a step forward. Each day is a new adventure; there are moments of stress, concern, pleasure—they are all stepping stones toward our goal of self-actualization.

I continued the program until the end of the term, two months past the last report. In that time, there was a continuing change in these children. They still argued and fought among themselves but seemed to develop some regard for our social structure: school, adults, teachers, property, etc. And as they began to better understand themselves, their own reactions, the outbursts and quarrels diminished.

. . . They developed values, attitudes, standards of behavior *on their own* and lived up to those standards. They did not become "angels" by any means, but there was a definite change. Other teachers and playground supervisors seldom had to discipline them and commented on the change in behavior and attitude. They were rarely in the office for infractions, and there was not one parental complaint the balance of the year! There was a tremendous change in parental attitude as the children evidenced success and growth, both academic and social.

I have neglected to mention the students who were not problems and those who are above average academically. I firmly believe that the gifted children were the ones who benefited most from this program. They developed a keen sense of competition among themselves, interest in mutual projects, and they sailed ahead, not being restricted by the slow learners. Their achievement was amazing to me.

I found that the children who had the most difficulty learning also made great progress. Some who had been unable to retain the multiplication tables (which should have been learned in fourth grade) were able to multiply and divide fractions (!) with a minimum number of errors by June.

I cannot explain exactly what happened, but it seems to me that when their self-concept changed, when they discovered they could, they did! These slow learners became fast learners. Success built upon success.

. . . I am well aware of the fact that in many schools or districts I would have not been allowed the freedom I was permitted to have.

Both my principal and superintendent were interested in, and gave support to, my effort. The schedule was structured to enable me to continue on to a self-contained seventh grade. Then it was learned that the people who had been hired for the intermediate positions did not have elementary credentials and therefore could not take my place. I had to be put back into a sixth-grade position. The children, the parents, and I were very disappointed.

Partly as a result of this disappointment, Shiel accepted another position. She did not, however, lose all contact with her class. The following autumn a report came to her.

> I received a letter from my principal this week in which he states: "I must relate to you . . . that your former students are dedicating themselves to building rather than destroying . . . really, you can take honest breaths about your contribution . . . as I have not had any negative dealings with any of your former pupils, even those who unfortunately find themselves in poor environments. . . . Your "impress" method or whatever, seems to have done the job, and their commitment (to you really) is something to behold. . . ."

Shiel concludes:

> If three months of "self-direction" produced such tangible results at this age level, imagine the potential inherent in a program of greater length! It is an exciting thing to contemplate. . . .

Comments on the "Experiment"

Although Shiel's account speaks for itself, I should like to point out some salient features of the way in which she dealt with this "experiment" and some of the learnings that I see as transferable to other educational situations.

Commitment

Shiel was clearly and deeply committed to a philosophy of reliance upon self-direction and freedom as leading to the most significant learning. This commitment was not a rigid one; indeed her personal doubts and waverings are one of the most significant features in her account because they indicate that such an approach can be carried through by imperfect, uncertain individuals, who are by no means clothed in self-assurance. But my point is that this was not simply a technique or "gimmick." Although she calls it an *experiment*, it was an experiment in which she believed and about which she had convictions.

The importance of this commitment is shown in a brief paragraph in one of her letters to me. She says, ". . . Several other teachers tried my idea and failed. Primarily, I think, because they did not really believe in it, but were moved to action by the enthusiasm and progress of the children and by my own enthusiastic reports."

To give self-direction and freedom to children can clearly be a complete failure if it is simply a new "method." Commitment and conviction are essential.

Internal Locus of Evaluation

Though the ideas Shiel implemented in her approach had undoubtedly been absorbed from various sources, it is very clear from her document that this is *her* experiment. She trusted her own judgment of what to try and when to retreat. She was not trying out a scheme devised by someone else.

This maintenance of what I term an *internal locus of judgment* is highly important. *She* decided when her new program was not working as she wished. *She* decided that two classes, the self-directed and the teacher-directed, were necessary, even though this had not been a part of her initial plan. By being open to the evidence in the situation, including her own feelings and intuitions, and basing her judgments on that evidence, she kept herself flexible in the situation. She was not trying to please someone else or to follow some "correct" model. She was living and acting and deciding in a fluid situation. She was even aware of the elements most threatening to her and faced those frightening aspects of the experience openly in herself.

Aware of the Realities

The way in which she adjusted to the demands of a required curriculum and the necessity of report cards excites my admiration. The way her pupils accepted those outside demands is, I think, not surprising. Children as well as adults can accept reasonable requirements placed on them by society or by the institution. The point is that giving freedom and self-direction to a group makes it easier for the members to accept the constraints and obligations surrounding the psychological area in which they are free. So her students "covered" the required work and went on to undertake more interesting activities. They even worked out a mutually satisfying solution to the vexing problem of report cards.

Group Problem Solving

One of the evidences of Shiel's commitment to the group and its potentiality is the way in which she handled unexpected problems. I doubt if she had clearly foreseen the parental skepticism that arose in regard to her plan. But here, as in other areas, she put her trust in the capacity of the group to deal with the problem. Free discussion of the situation brings out very constructive ways of helping to resolve the issue.

Experience

If this had been Shiel's first year of teaching, could she have carried off her experiment? I do not know. Certainly her years of experience in teaching gave her assurance in dealing with everyday classroom situations and perhaps gave her the security to launch out in a very new direction.

On the other side of this coin is the fact that the kind of relationship she had built up with pupils over the years was the very element that changed most markedly. The students were the first to notice this change, and in the diary Shiel mentioned their comments with some amusement, as though the change existed only in their own perceptions. Later she recognized how profoundly her relationship with the members of the class had changed. Thus, one might argue that a new teacher would have less to unlearn. I leave it as an open question.

Support

Shiel was, of course, fortunate to have the interest and support of her principal and superintendent. Backing and security make risk taking easier. Yet it is quite possible to underestimate the probability of such support. I have known of instances in which teachers simply assumed that no support would be forthcoming from a superior, only to find that when they *asked* if they might try something different, wholehearted backing was forthcoming. Administrators are people, too, and often welcome change and experiment. At least they deserve the chance to make a decision as to whether or not they will support a new venture on the part of a teacher.

Communicability to Others

After one more year of experimentation with a self-directed curriculum, Shiel was invited to become coordinator of a new program (in another district) to be designed for "educationally disadvantaged" children and their teachers and administrators. The aim of the program developed in such a way that it not only endeavored to provide an experiential, self-directed curriculum for the children, but also the same kind of opportunity for the teachers. Teachers, too, need support and understanding as they face the struggle and pain of trying to change perceptions and behaviors. Shiel reports her experience.

> The participating teachers spent the morning working with the children, then met in the afternoon with a psychologist in an encounter group, to explore together the morning experiences and their feelings and attitudes. The purpose of the workshop was not to show "one way," but to illustrate that possibly "other ways" exist. We wanted the teachers to experience self-direction in the same milieu that was provided for the children. Almost every teacher experienced great anxiety and apprehension in working with these problem children in an atmosphere of freedom. For all concerned, it was an emotionally trying time, painful—as growth can sometimes be. However, various forms of evaluation indicated the workshop was successful in helping teachers change their perceptions and attitudes.

One teacher was unable to cope with the situation and eventually resigned. The general reaction from teachers, students, and parents ranged from favorable to enthusiastic, and more than thirty additional teachers signed up for a new workshop.

We will present more about this workshop approach in later chapters. Suffice it to say here that it is in part an opportunity for exploration of self and one's relationship with others. Shiel concluded her report with the following words.

> Writing in retrospect, one can never capture the actual tears, pain and guts that go into such exploration. Many of us went deep into our inner selves and discovered that our anxieties, hostilities, and needs profoundly affect us as teachers. The structure of the system can be a refuge of sorts, and to deliberately "rock the boat" can be terribly threatening.

> For me, the experience of finding myself an "instant administrator" (lacking preparation or courses), was a new challenge—at first frightening. "Could I do it? What if I 'failed?' Had I gotten in over my head?" I found it difficult to wear so many hats, and I learned that my patience with the "child" in big people is more limited than it is with little people. I learned that to *be truly* facilitating is quite different from articulating about facilitating.

Certainly this whole program is evidence that the approach Shiel used with her own sixth-grade class can, in its essential attitudes, be conveyed to others. But it is clear that this new learning on the part of teachers can only be effective when they *experience* greater self-direction, greater freedom to communicate. It is *not* conveyed on an intellectual level.

Summary

I am deeply indebted to Barbara J. Shiel, the author, for her willingness to have this material used. It is of special practical help because it portrays her own uncertainties and confusions, as well as those of her students, as she launched into this new approach. Clearly it takes courage to attempt the new, and many teachers at every level would lack this courage.

Shiel's experience is most certainly not a model for another teacher to follow. Indeed, one of the most meaningful elements in this account is that she risked giving freedom to her pupils only so far as she dared, only so far as she felt reasonably comfortable. Thus, it is an account of a changing, risky approach to a classroom situation by a changing, risk-taking human being, who felt at times defeated and at times very moved and stimulated by the consequences of what she was attempting.

REFERENCES

1. Shiel, Barbara J. "Evaluation: A Self-directed Curriculum, 1965." Unpublished manuscript, n.p., 1966.

A French Teacher
Grows with Her
Students

❧

What about high school students? Is it possible to trust them to want to learn? Can they make appropriate choices of what to learn?

Talking with Gay Swenson (now Dr. Swenson, a psychologist), I learned of her experiences in teaching French a number of years ago. Since she had ample notes and material on which to base an account, I encouraged her to write of her experience. At first she was reluctant, but the scales were tipped when she was visited by a fourteen-year-old high school freshman and his father. The boy had his French textbook with him since he knew she had taught French and spoke it fluently. The cover of the text looked familiar to her. She says, "It was the same text I had used as a high school student more than twenty years ago!" This helped her to decide that her experiences were still relevant today and might well be helpful to teachers of, and those preparing to teach, any subject content. So she shares her very personal zigs and zags of growth as a French teacher and the exciting growth of her students in the pages that follow (1, pp. 115–27).

Grammar and Growth

I BEGIN

When I began substitute teaching in 1966–67, many factors were in my favor. I was young, enthusiastic, and very committed to French and Social Studies, my two major fields, so my experiences were quite rewarding. At the end of that year I was accepted for a teaching position at a high school well known and respected for its innovative atmosphere. I spent the summer preparing materials, audio-visual aids, and sample lessons for French.

57

That fall semester I applied the best principles gleaned from my recent graduate education courses and entertained the students with humor and "personality." I sometimes felt as though I were tricking them into learning something through cleverness and catchy techniques. Apparently they were enjoying it for the most part, so in the name of good pedagogy, to "keep them motivated" I continued. At the end of the year I felt rather satisfied that we had enjoyed ourselves together; they liked the new teacher, and they had learned a considerable amount of French as well. My department head, principal, and fellow teachers gave me encouraging feedback about my potential as an exceptional teacher, and I was given an intern to supervise the following year, a rare assignment for an untenured teacher.

Yet I felt something was missing. My "great" lesson plans sometimes mysteriously fell through unpredictably, and my modest ones would succeed as well as if I had spent hours preparing them. I would reason that the success or failure was probably related to the time of day, the heat of the season, their or my personal lives, or any other possible chance variable. At the worst, I would take out my frustration of crisis-filled days by angrily saying they could just "go home and turn on their darn TVs if what they expected was entertainment from me all the time". . . they were here to learn, and it wasn't all fun, etc., etc.

Among these highs and lows, a pattern clearly emerged that later developed into an incipient principle. I noticed that whenever learning involved either: 1) *creativity* from the individual, 2) *personal choice* by the student in determining a project or 3) *controversy* around an issue applicable to their personal world, learning invariably occurred, lasted, and something intangible flourished for us all. Following is an example that illustrates these observations.

Two students chose to teach the entire class for a week in French 1. The students were to select the concepts they wanted to teach, design appropriate approaches and audio-visual aids, teach the unit, develop and administer tests for it and then grade the students. They were then to evaluate their own and the class response to their efforts. The entire class was electric with various reactions during and after the unit—amusement, enthusiasm, anger, frustration, but always aliveness. They readily criticized clarity or lack of it in the lessons, the tests, grading, etc. The results for both the learners and teachers, including myself, were significant: 1) generally high grades overall, 2) clear evidence of skill acquisition, 3) a voiced insight into the difficulties inherent in developing a coherent lesson comprehensible to everyone and therefore, 4) empathy for teachers. The key principles which appeared most clearly here were that involvement and excitement occurred when learning was self-directed and initiated by personal choice of the student. This early experience of freeing students to learn was to be the foundation for further changes in me as a teacher the following years.

The importance of controversy as a catalyst for learning in class appeared frequently as we began to discuss current issues relating to their private lives and the larger world. Although we may not have all felt similarly, we discussed delicate issues openly in French whenever we could at whatever level of competency, from beginning French on. I shared my personal values and views with them as they did with me. It seemed to be unique for them, and us, to do this, and they would strain to speak in French to get their ideas across. Finally, significantly, they seemed to find it very supportive that I respected them and valued their worth as persons enough to engage in controversial dialogues. They often expressed this to me in the anonymous class evaluations which I requested regularly.

With this and similar experiences behind me I was beginning to develop some clearer sense of direction. During the summer I did intensive reading on innovative education and attended conferences given by people concerned with educational and social change.

SCHOOL IN TRANSITION

Our school itself had long been planning and preparing for a major structural and social change, which occurred during my second year of teaching. Later this innovation was to involve the community at large in several ways. The change was marked most overtly by our school beginning "modular or flexible scheduling," an event exciting and challenging to us all. Modular scheduling is a pattern of class attendance similar to that at universities. Classes meet at stated times throughout the day and week rather than following a lock-step order hour after hour. Classes vary in length from 20 minutes to 2 hours, depending on the course; they vary in size from 8 students to nearly 200, and in numbers of teachers involved, from one to teams of five. Students are scheduled into classes from 60% to 90% of the day, and therefore have varying amounts of "open" or "free" time. The problems and advantages of flexible scheduling are numerous, and vary depending on the individual perspective. I personally found it a long overdue approach to dealing with several aspects of compulsory education.

One significant change built into the new schedule and a precursor to the total change I attempted later, was the small group seminar. As applied in the Foreign Language Department, this was designed to provide more time for listening and speaking. The third-year language students met in seminar once a week for 45 minutes in groups of not more than 12. The material and content used for these conversation seminars was based on vocabulary lists topically organized around the house, body, clothes, idioms, and specific situational dialogues such as movies and restaurants. If done with some imagination by the teacher, the students took to it and used the time well. But again, it was when the content involved an issue which concerned *them* that they really tried to get their ideas across to one another. The effectiveness of such an approach remained vividly with me as we continued. So I began to make lists of issues which the students had suggested, and appropriate vocabulary upon which to build oral skills. Some of the topics which students suggested and we discussed were: sex, drugs, ecology, communes, school curriculum, grading, drinking, dating, driving, prejudice, politics, parents, peace, and . . . teachers. The changes in student participation were amazing. Their fluency developed, their interest and involvement increased, and ideas buzzed through the small room as opinions differed, emotions flared and they struggled to communicate all this "en francais." Student evaluations indicated that it was generally fun to be learning.

EARLY CONTRACTING

Despite innovations in schedule and curriculum, emphasis on small group discussions and student-led lessons, I felt that there was still no fundamental change in the class structure and hierarchy system. It was still the teacher who held the power and control in matters of attendance, curriculum and grading. There were still students who were unchallenged, bored or felt held back. I wanted to find alternatives for these people. I tried several alternatives, each very different. They gave me incentive to later apply such principles to an entire class.

One such alternative approach was that selected by two very capable young women in third-year French. We worked out an inter-departmental approach for English and French. One young woman studied children's literature in her English classes and created her own book—a fairy tale written in French and illustrated by her as well. Additionally, in cooperation with her friend, the two of them analyzed and compared American and French romantic poetry. Each wrote serious papers on poetry styles and translated a series of very difficult poems by Victor Hugo, attempting to retain the flavor, sound and imagery of the originals. This they did well. To this day, both young women retain an active interest in French, corresponding or visiting with me once or twice a year.

EMERGING VALUES

With such small successes after two years of teaching, several values were solidified for me. Yet I still had many concerns about the learning process. There were pitfalls and potentials in freeing students to learn; therefore how to best maximize the potentials became the issue.

I asked myself, "How does one meet all the different needs of all these different students so that they are using both their scheduled in-class time and free time creatively and uniquely?" Related to this concern was how to keep the students in class and involved while they were there, for with the new flexible schedule there was an initial heavy pattern of cutting, or selective class-cutting and nonproductive use of open time. I did not personally have heavy cutting. I assumed it had something to do with the kinds of students I was lucky enough to have and perhaps more importantly with something different we were doing together in class.

Operating primarily on this latter assumption, I began my third teaching year with the belief that all the best features of the partially individualized approach which I had experimented with so far could be and should be made a permanent part of the structure of the class. Having that summer just finished reading *Freedom to Learn*, the book by Carl Rogers, I felt even more strongly about making a commitment to individualized learning.

SELECTING A CLASS

But where to begin? I certainly couldn't radically individualize all my classes at once since this year I was to teach all five levels of French. What would be my criteria for selecting a class? After taking some time to come to know the various groups, I selected one which had the widest cross-section of potential.

THE FREE LEARNERS

The "free learners" then in 1969–70 were to be my third-year French class. In make-up, it was a class of 28 students, mostly sophomores, a few juniors and a couple of seniors. They ranged from very motivated, sophisticated and good-willed people, to not so, in any of the above, who in the past had been more than willing to let me know when they were bored or uninvolved. The class met three times a week for about an hour, then in addition once a week in a conversation seminar and again once a week in a large group with the other two French teachers' third-year classes for a film or lecture.

I did not begin the "project approach" as we came to call it, in the fall. Still afraid of the risk, hesitant, procrastinating, I stopped myself by my own fear that they would not "get in" the necessary grammar if given too much freedom of choice. Instead I reached into my bag of tricks and tried to make palatable the usual short stories, grammar, dictations, essays and listening comprehension.

At the same time I was coordinating the development of a tutorial program whereby some 300 French students would be tutored by volunteer fellow students in addition to their regular assigned class time. This monumental logistical effort took much energy, many hours, and some guts and nerve, which I consequently did not put into the project approach. While a rational "stopper" it also gave me incentive, for this experience did teach me much about self-motivated teaching/learning which later became applicable in our project.

HESITANT STEPS

My first hesitant attempt to de-structure the class involved *MY* planning a unit, rather highly structured at that, based on the words and music of Jacques Brel; a unit which *I* developed in advance *FOR* the students. Today I see my hesitancy apparent in the very pronouns used above. Even at the end of the unit I felt that were I to do it again I would leave the course principally in the hands of the students to develop and coordinate. Although the unit was highly enjoyable according to the students, I believe that it would have been much more imaginative and importantly, more meaningful, had they initiated it themselves.

After Christmas vacation we began to use another textbook. The students did *not* want to return to the traditional approach, so they suggested forming groups again to work on different chapters, present them to the class, build their own vocabulary lists and tests as they had in the Brel unit. But this time it was old hat. They were quickly bored with the pattern as well as with the light nature of the book itself; the semester was nearly over and we were going nowhere. They were annoyed and I began my old line of "you just want to be entertained." We had several frank and painful sessions on what was wrong with the class. They were just not interested anymore. Some even wanted to drop French. We were all discouraged and I became even more resistant to freeing them to learn their own way. Yet this very crisis acted as the final push that helped me to plunge in with them into a turbulent and buoyant sea of change.

RESEARCHING AND SELF-SEARCHING

First, if they weren't interested anymore, what would renew their interest? I asked and they told me in a series of preference sheets—poetry, music, art, history, fashion, drama, cartooning, cooking, literature of every sort, philosophy, and even grammar. For weeks, the students and I dug out every bit of written or audio-visual material we had on hand in the language department, researched additional school library resources and added from our own personal home libraries and record stocks. The pile of literature alone included works from *Peanuts, Winnie the Pooh* and *The Red Balloon* to Brel, Piaf, Baudelaire, Verlaine, La Fontaine, Molière, Sartre, Camus, Villon, Prévert and others. It took the form of short stories, poetry, music, magazines, anthologies, college texts and references on every aspect of literary analysis, history or grammar.

From these materials I made up what came to be known familiarly as "the cart"—a moveable book cart and overhead projector overflowing with records, tapes and books from which groups or individuals were to select their initial project when the spring semester began.

THE PROJECT

As we began this totally individualized approach, there were organizational and personal issues to be dealt with carefully and constantly. How we dealt with them varied from day to day as we moved along, but the general themes occurred fairly consistently as follows:

To deal with the personal aspects of the change we had informal groups or class meetings. Some of the issues dealt with at length were, 1) the problems and opportunities involved in this approach, 2) the responsibilities to oneself and others, 3) confronting the frustrations as they appeared and not allowing feelings to build up, 4) handling feelings of great expectations with an individualized program and the possible disappointments and sense of failure when goals changed or did not materialize. In time we were to express precisely this wide emotional spectrum and more—anxiety, acting out, anger, false starts and frustrations, sadness in facing one's lack of self-directive abilities, need to blame, problems with working in groups or alone—all had their day in each of us. Every feeling and issue demanded attention, caring, understanding and encouragement. We gave it to each other as individuals or as a class. Later I will give examples from specific incidents which will vividly demonstrate this aspect of the change.

A second factor requiring creative solutions was the ongoing logistics problems, such as 1) the mechanics of developing a personal contract, 2) choice in selecting a project, 3) use of time, 4) keeping accurate records of one's work progress and a record of newly learned materials, 5) being responsible to turn in materials when completed and deciding when one was ready to take tests on work done, perhaps developing these tests from one's unit for oneself or other group members, 6) selecting new goals as one project was completed, 7) altering goals and/or demanding more work from the "cart" or elsewhere. The underlying theme in all the above was personal and shared responsibility for constant movement and change.

A third and crucial learning or more accurately—unlearning—process occurred as the students became more involved in their projects and completed them: that of evaluation. Here the adjustment involved learning to look inward for signs of progress and growth and not through peer comparison or teacher evaluation alone. At first we experienced a high level of resistance to self-evaluation. This was not surprising, for the evaluating responsibility is a difficult one for teachers to abdicate and for students to assume after years of conditioning. **During this** project I found it a vital shift to make, if the students were to learn to become self-evaluators rather than persons waiting for the traditional authority to say yes-that-is-good, you-are-right, go-on. As with the logistics issue, students learned to assume this responsibility, or rather to share it with me, with varying degrees of efficiency and comfort. This again required guidance and encouragement which hopefully led to personal satisfaction at the growth experienced.

As the projects got further underway the realities of the physical situation itself were both frustrating and humorous. It was not unusual to see me and several students lugging tape recorders, record players, and slide projectors across campus to class, then later, running off to the next class with materials scattering windward en route. Sudden room changes, assembly day schedules, or switches in the time a student was to present a project to the class added to the flurry of activity and the need for constant flexibility. Having taken a deep breath and settled down in one location for the day, the creative chaos began. Since each student had selected an individual or group activity, an unprepared visitor might walk into a room where he would find one group acting out a scene from a play, another reading a story aloud or translating, a single student silently spread out on the floor over an art project or engrossed in a poem, nearby a friend leaning over the record player, struggling to hear it over a neighboring tape recorder in the corner; others would be trying to grasp the emotionality of the use of the subjunctive, calling for help from me while the usual conversation "nuts" would be talking away in French about men, sex, life, or the current ecological crisis, and of course, someone would be goofing off altogether in English until I came close by, while others coolly handled it all. Over the din and to the astonishment of our visitor some anxious soul might yell, "I don't know what the hell I'm doing and this chaos is driving me crazy."

Admittedly, there was all that seeming chaos. The physical, philosophical, logistical and emotional factors were ever present. It was not an easy change for the students or for me. It was an exciting one, for there was a vitality and aliveness present through it all. We never knew if that vitality would take the form of guilt, anger and blame, or jubilance and joy at the discovery or accomplishment of the moment. It was an electric time.

DOUBTS IN THE COMMUNITY

In the language of the graduate education school, what has been discussed up to this point has remained primarily in the "affective domain" . . . what actually happened to the "cognitive progress" of the student? In other words, "what did they really learn that we can measure?"

Correlated closely to the question of "measurable results" are two events which had an impact on the effectiveness of the project approach. One event affected us particularly as a class and the second involved the entire school.

First, during the spring our school came under heavy criticism from a vocal minority in the community as to the merit of this new flexible schedule in which students were given so much freedom to determine how they used or abused their time. In this regard the group was strongly supported by a local newspaper. As the conflict intensified there were days and nights of meetings. Student, parent and faculty committees were formed pro and con and conciliatory. There were long weeks of anxiety and pressure on everyone with hope for resolution of the impasse.

Many of my students and I were deeply involved in the issues during the entire spring semester both in and out of class. Our minds were often not involved with the "cart." Putting the cart before the horse in this case would have been not only a cliché and bad pun but a catastrophe as well. However, in class our small group discussion seminars were like local town meetings where the conflict was played out in miniature—in French.

During this dialoging an esprit de corps developed and intensified among us in support of the school and its innovations while students also offered fine suggestions for modifying the system to improve it. School ended with the issues still smoldering to burn again the following year.

A second event which affected us personally as a class was my health. During this period I became quite ill. Only five weeks after having begun the project approach, I was in the hospital for 10 days and home for a month following. The adjustments to this event were hardest on the teachers replacing me. For her or him, the project was at the least a surprise, and at the most, a shock. Often appalled at what was going on—or not going on— in class, one substitute would rapidly retreat to be replaced by another and another. For students it was easier in some respects since they were in charge as they had been all along. Since it was their individual responsibility to help the substitute, my files and desk were opened to them and they knew where "the cart" was and the materials and equipment to be checked out. They would tell a substitute not to worry; they knew what they were doing, then phone me at the hospital to ask where something was or tell me which student was teaching with the sub for that week. Often they would visit the hospital or my home during their open time, bringing with them delightful presents, jokes, good wishes, and significantly, serious questions and concerns about their work in French. During this period I believe they felt a responsibility and freedom rarely experienced in the normal classroom situation—a choice to goof-off and/or grow, as they felt inclined, and to reap the appropriate harvest.

FRUITS OFF THE CART

Four weeks later when I returned with barely a month left of school and not much spark or gumption, fears bubbled up in my stomach. I feared that the fruits of their individual efforts would be stunted or blemished due to the halting, hit and miss nourishment. I wondered if my faith and values built up over the last years would have some foundation in fact. Answers to these inner questions would be the crucial telling point as to the merit of the project we had ventured into together.

When it came time to present the results or "harvest," the creative individual and group efforts which had emerged out of the not so well nurtured soil of confusion and first attempts were astonishing. The fruits were so much more abundant than I had ever expected that I could hardly believe it. Following are the collected examples of such growth—work and play and learning.

1. One girl wrote some 15 papers and personal essays in French on poetry, music and literature.

2. One student read 12 short stories and condensed them into an imaginative single French composite, developing tests, vocabulary and grammar units on each of the readings.
3. Several students translated and drew popular or original cartoons in French.
4. One student made a pictorial adaptation of a poem from newspaper clippings and explained the story line in French orally.
5. Many students adapted stories and poems which they had first translated, into art forms—collages, pictures and photos.
6. Several students read, listened to tapes, analyzed and wrote essays based on the Fables of La Fontaine and the underlying themes.
7. Students studied grammar and applied the points learned in various story form or essay or personal journals.
8. Several students read and learned vocabulary from dozens of poems by various French poets and discussed in French the significance to them personally.
9. Singers Piaf and Brel continued to be popular sources for looking at personal values and life meanings.
10. Tales such as *The Red Balloon* and *Babar the Elephant* were approached from direct translation to acting out, writing about or developing increasing grammar competency and vocabulary.
11. Many students wrote their own poetry or journals expressing intimate feelings from their inner lives.
12. Grammar study was continued in differing formats. Those students continuing a traditional intensive approach covered much more material than I would normally have assigned during the same time period.

COMPARATIVE FACTS

During such a similar period of seven weeks' time, we would normally have read some short stories or *The Little Prince* together as a class and done grammar, dictations and listening comprehension as we had in the past. Indeed, 80% of the students did at least three different projects each, and everyone did at least one project which included translation, a paper, testing and vocabulary and grammatical growth. Only one person turned in no work at all. She read poetry in class when she was there. When she was not we took time together to discuss the effect of her choice for the following school year and in her personal life at home and elsewhere.

EVALUATIONS

Obviously there were drawbacks and advantages to the approach as seen by the students and myself. As abstracted from their written evaluations at the end of the school year, the following points were mentioned either repeatedly or with decided emphasis in individual cases.
1. My absence was mentioned most frequently. Many felt it had led to less productivity, particularly for those students who were experiencing a need for more direction. This need was not expressed by just one type of student or learner but came from an A-plus student, a timid student fearing self-direction, another student needing to be "pushed," she said, in order not to flunk, and one who "would have done better if you had told me what to do more."
2. Mistranslations occurred. When work was done alone or in a group, since they could not or would not always check with me or a dictionary

for every idiom or grammatical subtlety, some inaccurate learning took place.

3. Several students expressed a desire for a more rigid system of deadlines o be set by me. This was to include expectations for each week, a demand to turn in or achieve so much during a specific time slot. Old conditioning feels safe and operates well.

4. Some students admittedly did not do work commensurate with their ability. They did not set or achieve goals well or clearly, and one did not even come to class very often. These same students did learn something valuable about themselves in the process according to their reports.

5. Many wished more oral work in French such as that provided for in the small conversation seminars held once a week.

6. Some students feared they may not have learned traditionally enough to prepare them for demanding college work.

On the more positive side the gains were clearly stated. In terms of the subject matter students frequently expressed a sense of excitement, involvement, renewed interest or intensified interest in French. Many said they read more in French and enjoyed it more for themselves, often voluntarily not even submitting it for a project but just doing it from getting "turned on." In personal terms they expressed good feelings about group cooperativeness in becoming noncompetitive learners, helpers to learn together, thus minimizing competition; they valued highly the removal of fear about tests; they praised the warm, relaxed feelings in class. The fairly neutral students expressed increased interest because the goals did not seem so unattainable since they could choose a project more appropriate to their level of competency or commitment. All types of learners appreciated the freedom to create, the feeling of self-direction and responsibility, the elimination of pressure to cheat, the facing of their own potentials and limitations and ability to direct and pace their learning process. Lastly, and frequently mentioned, was the feeling that they will remember what they did much longer and with greater joy. Only one student in the project approach suggested returning to the traditional classroom method.

My personal point of view as a participant in this project naturally reflects my own bias and valuing process. Additionally, my views express as well my sensibility to young people and a respect for my own intuitive and intellectual strengths, therefore I would like to share some conclusions with you.

1. A new and significant element to me was that student learning was not spatially one-dimensional, i.e., occurring only in class. Outside of class, in the offices, under the trees, in the halls, students would be found discussing "their" poet or writer with someone else with a real notable concern and excitement. Nor was learning limited to "the assignment." They would sit together with friends and become interested in some other person's project. Often they exchanged books, bought or "borrowed" copies of their own, or kept books long after projects were over. It was common practice to stop in the office for additional references or help from me or just to talk in French and/or English. We went places together and spoke French in the car and at the park or museum or restaurant until it was "too much, let's stop." Perhaps some changes were merely because they now had time outside of class to do this. Perhaps not merely that.

2. Very significant to me was the fact that we became learners together. Since I obviously was not an expert in every one of the areas in which they often became immersed, I was discovering and researching along with them. I did not know all the grammar nor the entire French literary vocabulary, and we all accepted this perfectly comfortably. I was never afraid to say "I don't know" and they became more and more comfortable and pleased with this reality.

3. The changes in personal growth and in interpersonal relationships among students and between student and teacher were highly visible and moving to me. We were very open about our moods, and let each other know clearly where we were when we sensed some changed feelings. Anger, joy, grief, belly-laughs and tears were freely shown by me and them. It was not unusual to hear from them or from me "you may notice I talk too much so stop me when you've had enough," "I am really depressed today, can you handle this for me for a while until I get out of it?" "I just had this huge fight and my head's in a mess," "The most fabulous thing happened to me this weekend!" "I'm sorry, I really wasn't listening to you at all," "you've given me so much," "I really love you," "I'm really getting angry," "you don't give a damn about me!" We discussed our problems around sex, drugs, abortion, etc., at length, very openly both in the small seminar hour or outside of class as a group. When I was in the hospital a miniature rose tree was sent with a note from *The Little Prince* saying "tu es unique au monde," among dozens of individual presents, visits, etc. I know that every teacher has experienced such caring and concern which in no way relates to the approach or the curriculum; however I do feel that the context in which we operated during the year made such ways of relating easier. The growing trust that each of us was of very special value and worth to the other in some way, and most importantly of increasing value to ourselves as we emerged intellectually and emotionally, facilitated the possibility of the following occurrences.

When I had been particularly upset about a possible personal change in my life, my emotions were rather transparent. So there would be flowers on my desk, notes, and special caring contacts with many sensitive students. One day a student came to me in my office and sat down and from a real sense of her own worth as a supportive human being, regardless of our differences in age, "roles," etc., said, "Mrs. Swenson, you don't seem to be your usual self these days. A lot of us are really concerned. I know we're only students, but you are so often there when we're upset, we want you to know that if you want to talk about it, we'd like to listen." I am still deeply touched recalling this incident, both for the caring for my well being and for the self-respect that this young woman's statement exemplified. Movement toward maturity is more than mastery of subject matter alone, and together that past year we had been enabling such mutual growth.

OLD FEARS

However, as the year came to an end the old feelings held fast, the old fears reappeared in students and in me. In gestalt terms, what had been "ground" for some time was emerging as "figure" in the form of doubts. Have they learned as much as they would have with a traditional method? Will they do well on those ever present, and important, achievement tests? Questions such as, "Will they learn values and ideals needed for their own worth? Will they become free learners? Will they concern themselves with humanity's needs?" fell back in timid retreat.

We were all faced with those fears, students and I both, this first time around, so before final exam week I told them we had better review fast in grammar areas we might not have "covered" well enough individually. I suggested they go through the grammar workbook we had used the earlier part of the year and intermittently since and we would take an 80-point multiple-choice test, all verbs and grammar, with one change. During the three hour final they would bring up each page as they finished it, I would mark the incorrect answers with a dot and they would be given a second chance to determine the right answer. Only this time they had to justify and explain their answer indicating in writing or orally that they understood the rule behind its selection; in that way the factor of guessing or chance selection was to be eliminated. We did this. The test was very difficult and results excellent, frequently without the added second chance for many students. Some, of course, had still "never understood" grammar and several of these had been the most creative students in the class. When I asked the class how it was that they had done so well, the answer was a comment, both humorous and sad, on our usual approach to learning. "What difference does it make? You always study for the final the week before—then forget everything the next day. So we did the same thing this time. The only difference was we did a lot more interesting things all year long too."

All but three of the 28 students who were not graduating continued on into fourth year French the following year, expressing hope that the class would be organized—or rather not organized—as it had been this year.

SOME CONCLUSIONS

Having outlined the major drawbacks and personal and academic potentials of our project, I would like to summarize the major beliefs which I hold some years after initiating the program. These values and premises had been long incubating in me as "inner promptings." When I listened to them and acted upon them, these beliefs became tangible evidence that learning can be self-directed, as postulated in *Freedom to Learn*. In fact, many of the values listed below closely resemble those stated by Rogers.

I strongly feel that:
1. The curriculum can be self-selected by the student, based on his or her own current interests and abilities;
2. There can be self-testing, self-evaluation, self-set goals, which are valid;
3. Frequent evaluation of the effectiveness of a program can occur by a combination of input from the individual learner, the teacher, the entire class;
4. Such an approach requires miniature "encounter groups" or "keeping-current sessions" which might be highly charged with complaints, positive feelings, mixed feelings and creative problem-solving;
5. When interests alter, change need not be considered failure or something about which to feel guilty but rather a self-selected, re-routing of direction and growth;
6. Cooperation rather than competition can accrue and be encouraged;

7. Grades can be based on individual expectations and will differ greatly; this will mean that one student's "A" will be very different from another student's "A";
8. Varying amounts of time will be put in by different students, at different time periods, some coming in for additional work because they are shy in class, less confident in one area or because they want more in-depth intense work in addition to that in class, and others may invest very little time or effort;
9. Students can be involved at every level possible in designing curriculum or selecting materials and approaches to achieve their goals;
10. Language learning is fundamentally a cultural and oral communicative tool which can increase insights and understanding among diverse people and can aid in decreasing disharmony and stereotypic reactions to differences, therefore,
11. The most appropriate and satisfying content for conversation seminars are student-selected controversial topics which they might discuss with a young French person of their own age; and lastly,
12. Values and beliefs regarding the human condition can be integral to the study of literature and grammar.

DOING IT YOUR WAY

Implementing such a belief system can be risky, frightening, and open to challenge. It will take considerable preparation on the part of the teacher both psychologically and in the way of research. However, as the project continues, even more potential will emerge or be suggested by fellow students and teachers. It can be an electrifying and varied experience when team-taught by excited cooperative colleagues; it can be made more convenient by a language center where materials and equipment and "ambiance" are available in one location; students can help develop a core cultural approach (such as that used by our Spanish team in our school); mini-courses can evolve based on student interests such as crafts, drama, politics, or social action, and can be led by the students themselves.

None of the above is necessary to begin. All that is needed is one's courage, one's students, and one's commitment to trust the human ability to discover one's self. It is then we begin to become more of what we really are—free excited learners and growers.

POSTSCRIPT

Years later, letters and visits continue to come from students who shared the experience described above. The contents reassure me that the problems encountered and the opportunities offered during that time helped these young people to become more competent decision-makers and very importantly, open, risking adults, affirming their person-hood.

In closing I think of a student from whom I heard only this week. The woman writes, "I think a lot about my experiences there, especially the cooperative group of friends (teachers and students) and the stimulating environment and intellectual excitement which I have rarely experienced anywhere else, even at the University, which I thought would be better. . . . The environment there was so rich for me and I could explore so many directions. . . . I remember being awakened to something new every day. . . . The places I've lived and studied have not been nearly so supportive or rather have not encouraged the kind of growth I experienced in our class."

So I am touched and encouraged to know that our ways of coming together academically and personally have lasted through the years beyond the classroom time and space; that it did indeed offer as an alternative more humanistic classes where people were persons together as well as learners.

Comments

I would just like to underscore some of the elements I see as especially important in Dr. Swenson's account, most of them already stated by her.

It is a splendid example of the way a teacher starts by taking small risks, small enough that he or she can afford to fail. As each risky step provides new learnings and new confidence, the teacher can go on to greater and more pervasive innovation in permitting students to take responsibility. To put it another way, providing responsible freedom in the classroom is not an all or none thing. It is a gradual growth process, involving both the teacher and the students.

It is clear that the underlying philosophy is the all-important thing. This fundamental philosophy of belief in the potentiality of each student can then be flexibly implemented. Techniques, or special teaching methods, are secondary.

It is clear that from the outset Mrs. Swenson was committed to students and her subject. She was eager to learn from each experience. It is on a personal foundation such as this that her philosophy of education developed, became enriched, and increased her capacity for permitting students to grow.

It is fascinating to watch her growth from an occasionally accusative and evaluative teacher to one who listened to and learned from students. "You just want to be entertained," "Don't think school is all fun," changed to "What would renew your interest?"—and they told her! It is clear that this kind of learning process *demands* a teacher who is continually growing.

Her increasing openness in expressing her feelings—whether joy, anger, or conviction—as being her *own* feelings, with room for others to have different feelings, is striking.

Her caring for her students comes through in many ways and is fully reciprocated when she was ill, and most movingly, by the young woman who offered her help in a psychological crisis.

Involving parents and community was a most valuable step in a crisis situation. Dr. Swenson says, "It was a reminder of how important it is that we listen to each other and to the multiplicity of voices and views before, during, and after an innovation."

As to the students, it fascinated me to see them become cooperative learners, competent decision makers, responsible leaders (especially while she was ill).

It is not at all surprising that, in the climate Mrs. Swenson initiated and which they all helped to create, they learned far more French than would have occurred in a traditional class. And in addition they learned to live responsibly and creatively with themselves and with others.

One last amusing point. The students are quite right that learning in order to pass an exam need take only a relatively small amount of time, and that when this fact is faced, there is ample time for creative personal and group learning.

It is exciting to see how both teacher and students, though focused on learning a particular subject matter—French—can also learn and grow in personal responsibility, in openness of communication, in an increased sense of self worth, in creativity, and in warm interpersonal relationships. That these learnings lasted for years afterwards adds to the significance of the whole experience. I feel indebted to Gay Swenson and to her students for permitting us to see this extremely pervasive, ever-changing learning process.

REFERENCES

1. Swenson, Gay. "Grammar and Growth: A French Connection." *Education* 95 (1974):115–27. Used by permission. Revised for this chapter.

An Unusual Science
Course in a University

*S*uppose you are a cautious, conscientious instructor in a conventional university. The subject in which you specialize is a complex and growing science, involving an intricate knowledge of a multitude of facts and techniques. You have been committed to a lecture approach, and your lectures have been well prepared. Is it possible for you, without damage to your students, your subject, or yourself—and without offending your university—to introduce more of freedom to learn into your course? Dr. Herbert Levitan is such a professor, his subject is neurophysiology, and he attempts such a change. I would like him to tell his own story, as it appeared in publication (2, pp. 19–27). I have shortened his account somewhat, with his permission, and I also insert my own comments from time to time, to give my understanding of what went on.

An Experiment in Facilitating the
Learning of Neurophysiology

INTRODUCTION

When I began teaching six years ago, I adopted a format familiar to most professors and students. My purpose was to provide advanced undergraduate and graduate students with a reasonable breadth and depth of understanding of what neurobiology could be about, so that they would be prepared for further training in the field. As the instructor, and presumably the most experienced and knowledgeable, I assumed complete responsibility for planning the course. I developed a syllabus, composed lectures, wrote examinations, constructed laboratory exercises, and specified requirements.

The course acquired a reputation among students and faculty of being good, but requiring a lot of hard work. Some students flourished under the challenge I presented, but many floundered. As a result, enrollment dropped dramatically in subsequent years from 120 to 60 and then to 40 students. The class size decreased further as each semester proceeded because students who could not keep up with the work dropped out. The drop-out rate ran 30–40% most years.

I learned a tremendous amount by preparing for the lectures and designing new laboratory exercises. My teaching assistants shared my enthusiasm, supported the standards I set, and also learned a considerable amount from their association with the course.

What a true picture this gives! The lecturer, if he is thorough and professional, learns a great deal by preparing his lectures. It is a fine learning experience for him.

But for the students? Clearly they are "voting with their feet." Whether it is the lectures or the required work that is most repelling, they do not like to take the course, so enrollment shrinks drastically. But once in the course, the judgment is in a way, still more severe. At least a third of them drop out *during* the course. Here are two types of nonverbal feedback, and the student message is clear—"For a variety of unverbalized reasons, we do not like this course! It is not giving us the learning we want."

With each year my view of teaching changed subtly. I gradually attempted to cover less material in lecture, and to give the students more time to do fewer laboratory exercises. I took more time to answer student questions, to ask questions of the students, and to request their participation in raising questions in lecture. I began to believe that the most important skill the students should obtain from the course was the ability to formulate good questions, questions which would provoke them to examine the subject in more depth. I found that I did not enjoy the job of requiring students to do a variety of tasks which I had selected, even though I truly thought them important and worthwhile. I derived little satisfaction from the antagonism that this engendered in students, and did not look forward to the anxiety such a test of power and wisdom produced in me.

I speculated that perhaps an atmosphere in which the students could 1) call upon their own diverse, previous experience and curiosity, 2) explore new topics in a manner best suited to them individually, 3) avoid direct competition for a grade, and 4) actively participate in deciding what they wanted to do as a class and individually, would be more conducive to significant learning. It might also expand the options available for exploration and study, and place the responsibility for learning on the students themselves. I saw myself as a coordinator/facilitator, helping all the students to achieve their individual goals, and as one of several sources of feedback for the student's activities.

Dr. Levitan got the message. He is re-evaluating not only his methods, which he modifies, but his whole philosophy of education. He is internally making a revolutionary change—from being a lecturer, an authority, to being a facilitator of student learning and student purpose. He is embarking on a whole new direction. He is not trying a new "technique." He is searching out a way of being with which he can be comfortable.

But fortunately this is not something that he tries to achieve overnight. Over several years he makes gradual changes in his mode of class interaction, until he is inwardly ready to take a major risk. This is certainly the most appropriate and successful way of change—a gradual, step by step process.

> Reflecting on my own approach to learning new things, and the generally positive response of the students to my attempts to have them raise questions, I began to feel more strongly that opportunities for student participation in their own learning should be maximized. I began to feel confident that the students could and would accept the responsibility implied. I was further encouraged to attempt something new by the writings of Carl Rogers on "student-centered" learning (3; 4, pp. 69–89; 5, pp. 279–96; 6, pp. 384–428) and by several graduate students with whom I shared the evolution of my thoughts.

> In the spring of 1979 I offered a course in neurophysiology which was conducted in a manner quite different from the way I had previously offered it, and probably quite different from most science courses offered at the University. The following reflections document what happened during the semester, and may offer insight and encouragement to others interested in the education of scientists.

ORGANIZATION AND CONDUCT OF COURSE

A. *Beginning*

I came to the class the first day prepared to follow one of two options. In one case the course would follow a syllabus, schedule, and tasks which I had outlined. The other option called for the students themselves to determine the syllabus and how the class would be conducted. As the students entered they picked up a memo which read as follows:

Memo to: Students Enrolled in Neurophysiology
From: Herbert Levitan

> My principal goal in this course is to create the conditions whereby you have the freedom to pursue a study of neurophysiology in a manner which best suits you.

> I do not consider you to be empty receptacles into which I must attempt to pour a collection of facts which I find interesting. Rather I ask you to actively participate in deciding what you wish to learn and how you want to learn it, based upon your previous experience and interests.

> I hope that in this process you will become capable of asking fundamental questions about the subject, and develop the confidence and independence to answer them using your own resources and initiative. I also hope, and fully expect, that I, too, will learn about areas of neurophysiology which previously I had no motivation to explore.

If some of you are uneasy about participating in a course structured in this way please share your feelings with us. I myself am apprehensive about how the course will evolve and turn out but I feel the risk is worth taking.

The discussion which followed was recorded on magnetic tape, as were almost all subsequent class discussions. I can thus ascribe comments to students and myself with a fair degree of accuracy. Copies of these recordings were also made available to the students. At my invitation many students expressed their interests and what it was they wanted to study or learn about in greater detail. At one point a student commented, "I really like the way you put this memo. I am used to a teacher giving a syllabus or something very structured the first day of class. This was more open and I like the idea." I appreciated her directness and told her so.

Acknowledging the diversity of interests which had been expressed I noted that in my experience the instructor tends to ignore the diversity of interests and background of the students in the class and tries to fit everybody into his or her mold. On reflection it did not seem right to me that I should impose upon the students my background and inclinations. I thought that the course might be more dynamic and interesting (for me) if I gave greater consideration to where the students were coming from and where they wanted to go. Such an approach involved a significant risk from my perspective because I did not know if it would work.

After additional students expressed their interests and aspirations, I offered to outline what I thought was a spectrum of the possible ways to proceed. We could then vote on the style that best suited our collective purposes. At one end of the spectrum, an instructor would provide an outline, a reading list, establish tasks (e.g. exams and papers), set due dates and conduct evaluations, without any explanation or justification to the students. In the next category an instructor would do these same things but justify them, by explaining the logic of the organization and the reason for the tasks. While the students could not alter the course plan, they would have some appreciation for the "method behind the madness." A third alternative provides an opportunity for student input. Such a course might begin by reflecting the interests of the instructor. Subsequently, but presumably early in the course, the emphasis would change so as to reflect more the curiosity of the students and the questions raised by them as a result of what was initiated by the instructor. The students could also provide more input as to the tasks to be performed. They might for example help to write the exams, and decide what should be done in the laboratory. At the other end of the spectrum the students would participate from the start in deciding what should be covered in the course. They would help make up a course outline, which would be modifiable with time to reflect the increased sophistication and changing needs of the students. The students would decide with the instructor what tasks should be carried out, whether there should be exams and/or whether other tasks would be encouraged (such as research a paper). These possibilities for conducting a course thus run the gamut from authoritarian to egalitarian. The class then shared their feelings about these possibilities, expressing varying degrees of support, reservations and modifications, responding to each other's ideas as much as to mine.

In the initial memo to the class and in his conduct of the discussion, we get a clear picture of Levitan's way. He is tentative and open. He is not trying to force freedom on those who might be frightened by it. He is prepared to offer a range of options. He is feeling his way openly and honestly—an approach that would inevitably calm student anxieties, and build their faith in him.

> About midway through this first class I asked whether anyone felt disturbed by this lack of organization and if so to share their feelings with us. Some structure was thought to be important by several students because they had many other commitments, classes, and labs to schedule. In response a student offered the opinion that the usual environment in which students are obliged to block out specific times for doing certain tasks did not provide a good learning environment. One should not be pressured into meeting deadlines set by others, he felt, but be free to go to the library to pursue topics of interest as they arose.
>
> During this discussion I mentioned that I felt that listening to lectures was a very inefficient way to learn. One student responded that she did not learn during lectures, but they provided her with material to think about a later time. Another student said he wanted me to present material in lecture or seminar format with discussion possible because he felt that I knew more about neurophysiology than he did.
>
> When asked by another in the class why he felt that way, the student responded that I had been at it for awhile. The individual who challenged initially was not satisfied with that reply, but as he hesitated a moment to retort, the student said to me, "OK, let me give a lecture." I said that it would be more appropriate to ask the students. The response of the class surprised me by its good sense. One said: "I don't know; how prepared are you?" "Biophysics," he said, "I could come up with something." "Make it interesting and you'd be more than welcome," was a response. At the conclusion of this exchange, I suggested that students were welcome to prepare a lecture for the class. The student's "credentials" really wouldn't matter. A willingness to listen, expressed by the class, would give the potential lecturer the confidence to do a fine job, and both the lecturer and the class might gain a lot. It is significant I think, and appreciated only in retrospect, that the exchange occurred only partly in jest, which allowed this student to propose at a later date that he be permitted to give a lecture.

Some ideas and feelings are so serious that it seems safer to express them as a joke. The idea of one of the students giving a lecture is so "far out" that it is made—and received by the instructor—as being a humorous fantasy. At this point neither the student nor the instructor could have accepted the feeling implied in the challenge. The feeling, quite clearly, was "In some ways I am fully equal to you—even in intellectual knowledge." The class responds acceptantly and creatively.

> Towards the end of the first class meeting I asked: "Does anyone feel that this discussion is a waste of time?" "It's not for me at all," a student responded. "I was very intimidated . . . because I had very little experience about the subject matter . . . I just walked in really fearful (because of what she had heard about the course previously) and I feel a lot better about the whole thing . . . It appears that there is going to be a substantial amount of

student involvement and it won't be all you telling us what you expect."
Another student said: "The more time you do spend like this the more open
minds will become in class . . . so they can let it all hang out and learn." At
this time no one expressed any reservations about the time we had been
spending on organization. I reminded them of the other important decisions
which we had yet to make and which would take some more of our time,
but I thought that this was preferable to having me make all the decisions
and imposing the procedure on them. . . .

I was very encouraged by the number of students who participated at the
first class meeting, and the frankness of their contributions. A majority of
the students present seemed to have expressed their views, interests, and
reservations in the discussion, and I sensed from what had been said that
the students were at this point cautiously optimistic about what might
happen.

At the beginning of the second meeting, I provided the students with an
accounting of who their classmates were, and asked for their response. This
information came from cards I had asked the students to fill out at our first
meeting. There were 7 juniors, 21 seniors, and 15 graduate students, rep-
resenting areas such as Zoology/Biology (21), Entomology (1), Psychology
(4), Physical Therapy/Education (3), Mathematics (2), Engineering (5), Physics
(1), Biochemistry/Chemistry (5), and Independent Studies (1). The question
of class composition was raised by an undergraduate after our first meeting.
He apparently felt intimidated by the nature of the comments and contributions made by his fellow students and was concerned that he might be at
a disadvantage if he had to compete with mostly graduate students. In
discussing the diversity represented by the list, it became apparent that no
one group or individual had a clear advantage over the others. Someone
said, "so many grads and postgrads in the class . . . would be able to add
that much more to the class." Another said she, as an undergraduate, felt
the competition with graduate students would encourage her to work harder
to make up for the maturity they might have.

When a group is permitted some freedom, the diversity that emerges is
astonishing, and the unique importance of each individual becomes more
evident. The instructor helped in this process by at least giving out the
educational and professional categories into which they fell. If a brief written
statement of interests and life situation had been requested from each student and distributed to the class, the personal diversity would have been
even more marked.
It is interesting, in the light of the information given here, to picture
again the conventional lecture system. Imagine how totally inappropriate it
is to give a series of lectures on neurophysiology (or any other subject) to
such a group, with their vast differences in interests, needs, and attitudes. It
is a miracle if much real learning takes place in such a lecture system.

I hoped that by airing the students' feelings they would realize that they
each had something to offer. Our organization of the tasks to be done could
lead to cooperative instead of competitive feelings and this might remove
some of their anxiety. I said that the only imposition we had on what we do
in class was the obligation to submit a grade at the end of the semester, but

I believed we had a lot of flexibility in deciding how to arrive at that grade. Decisions about what tasks the students could perform and what criteria should be used for evaluating these tasks could be made as we went along. I expressed my inclination that in the end each of them would decide themselves what their own grade for the course would be.

At this second meeting I also handed out a list of the topics which the students had contributed at our previous meeting. The list represented their interests and obviously reflected the diversity in the type and extent of their previous experience. I asked them to examine the topics with the objective of organizing our interests into a coherent, logical syllabus. To aid in this process I suggested they consider the following questions: 1) what it is we wish to know about each topic (in as much detail as our current experience allows), and 2) what background material we need to have in order to appreciate fully the information we gather on the topic.

The list of topics that were of interest to the students covered a wide range. There were broad topics such as "Developmental neurobiology—development of neuronal form and function," and also quite specific topics such as "Computer simulation of neuronal function." There were nineteen items in all—enough for several courses.

There was lively interaction about the way the content of the course might be organized and a first step was decided on.

As a consequence of the discussion which followed it was decided that I should present some background or "core" material on the workings of nerve cells and their interactions, since many expressed the desire to have an overview, and this seemed to most of the class to be basic to all their other interests. Then we would review where we had been and discuss what to do next.

B. *Students' Comments on Beginning of Course*

The students' written comments concerning the beginning of the course confirmed the attitude of cautious optimism and uncertainty which I sensed during early class discussions. They wrote in diaries: "It sounds great that we will be deciding our own syllabus," and they looked forward to a class in which it might be possible to begin with questions based on phenomena they were already aware of. But they were also "kind of scared as to what will happen in the end . . . because . . . we're faced with a wide variety of topics to choose from and the responsibility of prudent decision."

Having the students decide the format of the course was "an interesting approach for mature students (but) how will immature students fare?," another wrote, adding that "it really (is) uncomfortable to have to decide what we want to get out of the course . . . (and) the issues of grading." Many felt uneasy at the beginning because they were "used to the professor dictating the grounds of the course. That way I knew what I would be up against." The key to resolving these fears seemed to be expressed by a student after he talked at length with the teaching assistant. He wrote, "I've decided that for me this course will be successful because of the mutual trust between (the instructors) and the students."

I believe this student statement catches a most important aspect of Levitan's approach that has not been specifically verbalized. He has been scrupulously honest and open with the group—presenting the possibilities of the new freedom, his own uneasiness in experimenting, the choice of other options. He has listened very carefully to student opinions and feelings, willing to understand attitudes quite different from his own. He has shown real concern for the students, eager to hear those who were disturbed by or opposed to the directions they were taking, and responsive to requests, such as the student who had asked to know the composition of the class. There can be little doubt that he came across as a real person, without facade; that he understood the range of their feelings and accepted them; that he respected and prized the student and his or her attitudes. In brief he had exemplified the three attitudinal conditions that have been shown to facilitate growth in both therapy and education. Consequently, though students might feel uneasy and frightened by the *situation*, the instructor's attitudes were such as to build *trust* in him as a *person*. Through all the specific steps and the verbal interactions in class, it is these all-important attitudinal components which show through, which constitute the basic dynamics of the interaction between the facilitative instructor and the diverse learners. They have already learned one of the most important elements—that this is a person they can trust.

C. *The Lecture Process*

Before lecturing on the "core" material I wanted the students to realize that they would be getting primarily my view of and my approach to the subject. I also wanted to have their input and utilize their questions to motivate the class. I begin by trying to think about how they might approach the nervous system, what questions they might have on first viewing the system. Given these observations I asked what questions occurred to them and listed their responses on the board. These questions were then organized into a mini-syllabus, and I provided a list of relevant references consisting of textbooks, review articles and original papers.

Based upon our readings or other previous experiences, the students or I would then make suggestions about how we might design experiments to get answers to these questions. The limitations of various experimental designs were discussed in the process. The results of an experiment using these suggested experimental techniques would then be provided. Based on these observations other questions would be raised and the procedure repeated.

In sum, the lecture periods consisted of (1) raising questions based upon the current state of knowledge of the students, (2) considering what information they would have to have in order to answer the questions raised, (3) suggesting experimental procedures which might provide the required information, and (4) considering new questions which would arise as a result of the information gathered. Each such question session served as a branch point at which a choice had to be made concerning which direction to take. In this sense the course syllabus was not predetermined but flexible.

I cannot help but point out that in this series of steps in what were called "lecture periods," the students were not only learning *about* a science, they were *experiencing* the very process of a true science.

The following description of the content of the interaction may not be of specific interest to the reader, but it illustrates well the enormous range of topics covered when one is responsive to student questions and needs. The instructor has been willing to use himself as a resource, but the students draw him far beyond a usual lecture coverage.

> Reviewing the topics which were discussed by the class it appears that most of the items which the students expressed initial interest in were considered in some way. Approximately the first two-thirds of the "lecture" time was devoted to discussing the properties of nerve cells and their interconnections (excitability and voltage dependent membrane conductances, nerve conduction, synthesis, storage and release of neurotransmitters, and the initiation of changes in postsynaptic cells). This naturally involved discussion of aspects of cellular and comparative neurophysiology, neuropharmacology, nervous control of muscle activity, the cellular basis of behavior and experimental techniques. Photoreception and the mammalian visual system, and current theories of the nature of memory were also discussed. The students considered aspects of human and comparative neuroanatomy, and carried out a computer simulation of excitability independent of the formally scheduled lecture and laboratory time. Individual students explored a variety of additional subjects as indicated by the annotated bibliographies and papers they included in their portfolios at the end of the semester.

> The course was thus much more interesting and challenging for me than would have been the case had I alone determined its direction. As one student observed, "This class required alertness, thinking and application of already known phenomena, something which are not required in most other classes. The students seemed actively engaged in the lecture, developing the points together; or dispersing the point with opposing views, but at least there was interaction between minds."

Levitan shows an easy attitude toward the "structure vs. nonstructure" issue. He exhibits readiness to share his expertise in an informal lecture fashion, but readily departs from that to follow student interests. There is, however, enough of a skeleton structure that the class does not go through a period of chaos, as often happens if they are suddenly faced with the full responsibility for deciding the content of the course.

Clearly the class has reached the desirable state described by Paolo Friere. "Through dialogue, the teacher-of-the-students and the students-of-the-teacher cease to exist and a new term emerges: teacher-student with student-teachers. The teacher is no longer merely the-one-who-teaches, but one who is himself taught in dialogue with the students, who in turn while being taught also teach. They become jointly responsible for a process in which all grow" (1, p. 67).

Dr. Levitan tells at length of the class discussion of the scheduled three hours per week of laboratory time. The class told of their past experience with "labs," positive and negative, and considered what purposes these hours could serve. They also discussed the circumstances involved in writing reports, which could range from a creative experience to a dull task. When students were concerned that they might not collect significant data, the instructor pointed out how much one can learn from mistakes and negative findings. The document continues:

D. *Organization of Laboratory*

As a result of extended discussion it appeared that the general consensus of the class was that the purpose of a laboratory should be:

1. Provide another activity (besides listening, reading, or watching) whereby the student can acquire a firmer understanding and appreciation of basic principles and current paradigms.
2. Provide an opportunity for students to appreciate the experimental observations upon which the currently accepted principles, paradigms and dogma are based, i.e., the experimental basis for the current dogma.
3. Gain an appreciation for the limitations which apply to the generally accepted paradigms.
4. Gain technical experience.
5. Gain an appreciation for the kinds of questions one can reasonably ask and how one might proceed to answer them experimentally.
6. Have an opportunity to test or evaluate their understanding of the material.

To accomplish these objectives, most of the students felt that demonstrations by the instructor should be minimized and as many students as possible should have hands-on experience with the various tasks required to carry out the experiments. By repeating some aspects of "key" experiments, an appreciation for the experimental basis of the current dogma could be obtained. When asked whether they preferred experiments which illustrated "key" non-trivial points or trivial, easily accepted points, they were inclined towards the former. An appreciation of the limitations of the dogma could be gained by becoming aware of the assumptions made and the experimental conditions. Analyzing data, interpreting results, and comparing their conclusions with others might aid this process.

A varied technical experience could be gained by performing such tasks as dissection, checkout and manipulation of instruments, and recording data. I asked the students whether they thought the experiments should utilize current, state of the art technology and instrumentation or be of historical interest with appropriate instrumentation, and whether the experiments should provide a conceptual and technical challenge to execute or be trivial to execute. More specifically they were asked whether they preferred to attempt experiments which:

1. were fail safe, guaranteed successful,
2. had a high probability of success, i.e., more than 75% rewarded on first attempt,
3. had a moderate probability of success, i.e., 25% would be successful the first time, 50% the second and 75% the third time,
4. had a low probability of success, i.e., 10% the first time, 25% the second, and 30% the third,

5. were "impossible," wherein no success was probable the first, second or third times, even for the very experienced, but after a dozen experiments the success rate would approach 50–60%?

Most students appeared to prefer category (3) although they felt that category (5) probably approached more closely the conditions of original research.

It is of interest that when students are given the opportunity to choose their own laboratory tasks, they choose a more difficult pathway than the "cookbook" type of experiments, which are usually assigned.

They have also worked out for themselves a set of purposes that will provide them with a real experience of scientific work. Lab periods often fail miserably in developing this appreciation.

In order to gain an appreciation for the capabilities of the experimental system, the students chose to make use of laboratory instruction sheets I had previously prepared. They apparently felt more comfortable beginning with instructions in a cookbook manner. It was understood, however, that they were always free to explore other questions, and design other experiments. What was recorded and how it was recorded by the participants was left to the students to decide. I recommended that the decision as to what and what not to record be an active one rather than one made by default. I also suggested that the students organize their groups such that one individual accepted responsibility for recording what was happening. This record could subsequently be distributed over his or her signature to other participants. Other group members could indicate their role in the experiment as well (e.g., dissector, instrumentation technician, etc.) to make the record complete.

To evaluate their efforts in the laboratory and test their understanding of the material interested students had the option of writing a report of their activities and seeking feedback from the instructor and their peers. A handout on the preparation of laboratory reports which I had previously prepared was made available for those who wished guidance in deciding what should be included. Those who submitted reports were expected to critique the reports of at least two others and I suggested they address particularly, such questions as:
1. Does the introduction correctly and clearly state the principal objectives of the experiment?
2. Is the description of methods complete enough to allow an understanding of what was done and how?
3. Are the observations clearly described? Are the analyses of results clear?
4. Is the interpretation of data logical? Is a comparison made with relevant literature? Are differences considered and limitations of dogma recognized?
5. Are the references to published material complete and correct?

No grades were to be assigned. It was left to the authors of the reports to use the critiques as they wished to enhance their understanding of the material and improve their ability to communicate that understanding to others.

E. *Laboratory: Student Comments*

The students also expressed their satisfaction and dissatisfaction with the organization and conduct of the laboratory by writing notes in their diaries or in their course evaluations. Their comments ranged from feeling "that the lab could have used more structure as well as a more rigid requirement" to finding "the atmosphere in lab very conducive to learning . . . (permitting) good interaction to occur between our lab partners." Some students made suggestions for improving the laboratory experience. "Demonstrations–followed by 'hands-on' labs–would have been (enormously) helpful," wrote one. Another found it difficult to find adequate time to satisfy his curiosity about how the equipment worked and suggested that students be allowed to help set up the apparatus. In this time students could "ask basic, fundamental, elementary questions about the apparatus in the absence of pressure to perform an experiment," and they might also help to reduce the instructor's work load. He added that setting up might also give the students "practice for doing it in the future in some other setting, like grad school or on a job." Another student came "home from labs saying that this is really what science is all about, . . . what it is (like) to be a scientific researcher." The "loose structure" allowed the students the freedom to linger over and discuss phenomena they found interesting and to "try new ways of investigating those phenomena." This would not have been possible, he thought, if one had specific deadlines to meet. The possibility of writing laboratory reports evoked a variety of responses. One student "realized" the lab reports should be long and should cover material in great depth. She decided that she would not gain much from such a time consuming task and so did not submit any reports. Another student regretted not handing in for evaluation any information gathered during the lab. He found the experience beneficial, however, because "it helped to point out the areas that I need to concentrate upon if I am to continue any type of research." For one student who had never before been required to write "formal lab reports," with an introduction, methods and results, the task was very difficult. He found that writing all the reports proved "to be a very useful experience, and one that will obviously be useful for me in the future since I plan on going to graduate school. Looking over my reports I was surprised to see how much my lab reports improved. My first lab report had no comparisons with the current literature. My last two are well supported by the current literature."

An indication of the depth of interest stirred in the students was the development, largely through student initiative, of two projects somewhat outside of the course: a "mini-course in neuroanatomy;" and a computer simulation of aspects of the nervous system.

In both of these Dr. Levitan helped a great deal through making resources available; he permitted students to use his personal books on the topic, made human brains available for dissection, found a room and a volunteer instructor for the first project; then for the second he put them in touch with the Computer Center and advised them on how to begin their work.

The number of students involved in these projects varied, as students dropped out when the limit of their interest was reached. There were frustrations and dissatisfactions, but for the students who chose to persevere, these projects brought much satisfaction and the impetus to explore further in these new directions.

F. *Examinations*

Many of the students assumed we would have exams but were uncertain of how it would come about given the way the course was evolving. In preparation for discussing the matter of exams I asked the students to draw upon their vast experience and consider two questions: (1) whether they would derive any benefit from preparing for an exam, and (2) whether they would derive any benefit from taking an exam.

Studying for an exam, several students suggested, provided an opportunity for organizing a broad body of material, more so than if one were reviewing material to write a paper, for example. It also allows one to get feedback of one's understanding of that material. Being obliged to organize a body of material gives one the opportunity to observe relationships between subjects that might have been missed when they were previously covered sequentially. On the other hand it was the experience of another student that preparing for exams most often had the aspect of trying to figure out what the instructor wanted and guessing what might be asked. Were it not for this game it could be a valuable experience. "Having to second guess the instructor usually means that you don't get a chance to study what you are really interested in."

One of the values of taking exams is the opportunity it offers for feedback on whether your organization of the material and understanding of it is logical and accurate, suggested a student. Another recalled the value of questions written in such a way as to correlate previously isolated or unrelated material. The student then has an opportunity to learn something new while taking an exam. This can happen when the questions allow a new synthesis or a discovery that principles applicable to one situation are in fact applicable to others not previously considered.

A student who appreciated the value of this said she "would rather not find this out during an exam, but rather on a less formal basis." The pressure to perform in the confines of an hour also made the experience of taking exams unpleasant for some. But one student felt that the anxiety produced by knowing one has an hour to perform was not necessarily bad, and that she often felt relieved to know that the exam would be completed within a finite time and very relieved when it was all over. One way to alleviate the tension often accompanying exams, a student suggested, was to allow take-home exams. Another thought that the method of grading exams was also crucial to how one felt about the exam process.

We then considered how the exams should be created (i.e. by whom); how they should be taken (in class, at home, by everyone or not at all); how they should be evaluated (what criteria should be used, how should the various aspects be weighted) and by whom.

Someone suggested that the students themselves could write questions on the body of material covered based on things they thought they would like to know and should know. To avoid missing points that others find important, the comments and criticisms of other students could be invited. "Making up clear and unambiguous questions is a fine art which comes with long years of experience," thought a member of the class. Questions made up by students therefore are typically very unclear and ambiguous, in this student's experience, and he would prefer to have the instructors rewrite questions submitted by the class. This procedure avoided an aspect of learning and taking exams which I thought should perhaps also be evaluated. By writing an exam the students would be inviting feedback on their ability to communicate clearly.

The students were concerned about their ability to make up questions which would challenge the rest of the class and which they could answer correctly. Being able to support clear, logical statements was more desirable, I thought, than "correct" answers. They were concerned about being too narrow in their selection of questions and missing many aspects of the material. I thought it was important to develop the skill to identify the key points in a body of knowledge, rather than having to depend on others. They were concerned about the time it would take to accomplish all of this. Some students preferred to be given questions to answer which had all these desirable characteristics, and others wanted to limit in some way the time invested in the exam process.

One student, responding to another's desire to have a numerical grade of his effort on an exam, said that the options being proposed offered "a golden opportunity to break out of that old mold. I am so familiar with those traditional tests that given the choice I am not willing to submit myself to it. You don't get the opportunity very often to get out of that. We are so ingrained (in the old mold) that it is like we are sitting here wanting to submit to anything they'll do to us."

Those students interested in attempting to answer questions posed by others could choose from the pool available. Upon completing their answers they could refer to those provided. If desired, the authors and respondents could confer with each other and/or with additional source material in order to enhance their understanding and resolve any differences.

It was left to the individual students to decide whether or not to participate in any of this activity.

Any material generated as a result of participating in the examination process should be included in the Portfolio presented by the students at the conclusion of the course, and used to support their final course grade.

G. *Examinations: Students' Comments*

Through entries in their diaries and in their course evaluations the students expressed their thoughts on the examination process they helped design. The following statements are extracted from these documents.

One student related that he had previously taken a graduate level course in neurophysiology at another university and "knew he had a good knowledge" of the material. But he "learned a lot more making up exams." He found it difficult and very time consuming to make up questions in the multiple choice format which he had chosen, and finally did not turn in for evaluation the first exam he made up "because he didn't think his questions were 'good enough.'"

Another student didn't hand in an exam because he felt that writing questions for himself would not be an effective use of his time. He decided after reading over the material covered so far in the course that he understood it well and that he would test himself by trying to answer exam questions which other students submitted or those which I had made up in previous years.

Another found that ". . . creating exams was very beneficial because I learned that posing unambiguous questions is very often difficult." He found himself "interested in asking questions I wanted to answer because they were valuable to me."

Most agreed that making up an exam was more difficult than taking one. "The exams were extremely challenging," said one student, "and I am proud of how mine turned out. They provided an excellent way for me to synthesize and condense the course material. The most rewarding experiences when writing the exams were when I wrote a question that I could not answer, and had to keep digging into the material until I found the answer. I never dropped a question because it was too difficult!"

To turn the bugaboo of "exams" into a profound learning experience is something Levitan achieved to a remarkable degree. To discover how difficult it is to pose good questions, and for some to come to enjoy the process of asking and answering tough questions, is a learning those involved will never forget.

This whole section is fascinating to me. The initial discussion of the pros and cons of exams, the enormous freedom experienced by the students in handling this issue, the diverse personal learnings of those who developed and answered questions is remarkable.

One unverbalized element of this section is the subtle climate of the class. To discuss such an emotion-laden topic as exams with no feelings of panic, points to only one conclusion: the students felt sure that whatever the outcome it would not be unfair or personally threatening. This speaks volumes about the instructor's way of being in the class.

H. *Student Lecture*

About halfway through the semester one of the students asked if he could give a lecture to the class. (I had completely forgotten that on the first day of class this same student had a somewhat tongue-in-cheek exchange with the class about students giving lectures.) He wanted to present in greater detail the thermodynamic basis of some material we had previously covered in class. Admitting skepticism, to myself at least, I suggested he write a proposal, outlining what he wanted to do and how, which he should submit to the class for their response. With his outline he included a questionnaire which addressed the conditions under which the class might want to hear what he had to say. The class was overwhelmingly receptive to this student's proposal! An uncertainty arose only because half the class wanted to hear the lecture during class time and a half wanted to schedule it another time. The only feasible way to resolve this conflict was to hold both the regular class and the "guest" lecture at the same time in different rooms, allowing students to choose between the two.

The "guest" lecturer handed out the details of what he had to say several days before the meeting so that everyone would have access to his efforts. About 10 students attended the lecture/discussion he conducted, and their responses to his "debriefing" questionnaire indicated a very favorable reaction to his efforts and to the idea of "allowing," or encouraging students to develop and deliver lectures. The student was obviously pleased with his effort but said, interestingly enough, that once he had prepared the handout detailing what he had to offer, it did not matter to him very much whether a convenient meeting time could be arranged. He had already gotten out of the experience most of what he wanted.

I would like to comment very briefly here. It is clear that the *process* of learning—in this case the preparation of the lecture—is the valuable element. The specific outcome—the delivery of the lecture—is definitely less important.

EVALUATION OF COURSE

A. *Students' Self-evaluation*

The question of evaluation kept arising as we spoke of the various tasks and activities the students could carry out in the process of learning what it was they wanted to learn. The students repeatedly asked how I was going to evaluate them, a question which reflected their past experience in courses in which their ultimate objective was to please the instructor. While granting that an instructor's critique and evaluation of students' work are of great importance, I was strongly inclined to have the students themselves play a major role in evaluating themselves and each other. I wanted them to have the experience of attempting a self-evaluation on the basis of feedback received on documents they had written and submitted. I wanted them to gain confidence in their ability to realistically and fairly evaluate themselves and thereby arrive at a letter grade which could be submitted to the University. The character of the evaluation process evolved as the course went on.

All the students wishing to have a grade submitted to the University in recognition of their participation in a neurophysiology course were required to submit a portfolio containing all written material which reflected the work they had done during the semester. In addition the students were asked to submit a diary or journal containing their insights, perception of progress and their reflections on the conduct of the course, as well as a justification of the grade they wanted submitted. I reminded them that I reserved the right, and indeed felt the obligation, to give them feedback on the grade they assigned themselves. I made clear, however, that I would respect their final decision on the grade they wished to have submitted.

The process of self-evaluation was new for most of the students, and difficult for many of them. A majority reflected very seriously on their self-evaluations, and submitted honest, sometimes agonized, commentaries on the conduct of the course and their response to the responsibilities and burdens it placed on them. Particularly revealing were statements made in their diaries, statements which reflected their daily activities, problems, successes, anxieties, insecurities and triumphs. I quote from some of these below.

"I suppose I could compare my progress to the others in the class but I got the idea that we were to feel a mood of cooperation not competition, so that is not a valid way to gauge my progress. So I guess that just leaves me to fend for myself, as it were (I'm beginning to think that this was the idea all along . . .). Sitting through three days of a symposium (at the National Institutes of Health) whose list of speakers read like the Who's Who of neurobiology and really being able to understand the ideas presented, surprised me. To be honest, I did not realize I understood the subject matter that well. . . . Realizing where I started with the course work and where I am now, I deserve an A."

"Based on the amount of time I spent in (class) compared to the amount of time I could have spent and the number of concepts I could have learned I give myself the grade of C for the course. I did not think a higher grade was justified simply because I did not make a formal attempt at synthesis of a topic of interest (term paper, exam, etc.). Also a lower grade would not reflect the amount of time I placed in the course and my satisfaction with what I have learned."

"Evaluating myself is difficult but I will try and be objective. I feel I've come a long way since the start of the course. Instead of just learning facts I learned how to ask questions and approach a problem. . . But more importantly (I learned) how to discover more on my own. I believe my effort in this course is worth a B."

And finally, "I need to show the medical schools that I am capable of doing hard science, and am not afraid of doing so. I am hoping that the fact that I have taken this course will look good on my record. Perhaps I am being too honest with this admission.

"I fear that I spent too much time synthesizing material for my understanding in the early part of the course and not enough time trying to come up with a written product. This question of quantity of written work produced on a personal scale (and not as compared to other students) is the main reason why I have given myself a B."

The distribution of grades submitted for the course was: 33% A, 45% B, 20% C, 2% D.

I wish more of the students had kept more complete diaries for their own, as well as my benefit. One individual wrote a paragraph summarizing what was done each time the class met either in lecture or lab and what impact it had on him. Most wrote less frequently, but from my reading of the comments they are honest statements, and reveal a great deal about the positive and negative aspects of the course, and the learning process. Perhaps the most significant aspect of the students' comments was their focus on the students themselves, what they did or did not do, how they grew, what they learned, etc. I detected relatively little commentary about the personality, style, or knowledge of the instructor. That is, the students appeared to place the responsibility for the learning process clearly on themselves. Some of their comments follow:

I first wish to express my admiration for the very thorough, broadly based, carefully planned process of evaluation. Levitan's goals include having the students play a major part in evaluation, and everything he does works toward the fulfillment of that goal, which is openly discussed with the group throughout the course. The procedures adopted were admirably suited to achieving that goal.

The students responded by setting up their own criteria for judging their work and progress, and these criteria are as diverse as the students themselves. The growth in student maturity as they wrestle with the problem of a grade is evident in their statements.

Levitan's observation at the end of this section is typical. When students are responsible for their own learning, the facilitator must find his satisfactions in seeing their growth and progress and in his own learnings with the class. He will not be rewarded with much praise as the brilliant lecturer might be. The rewards are there, but they are subtle and personal.

The students' evaluation of the course (rather than their own work) is sampled in the comments that follow.

B. *Students' Evaluation of Course*

"What was done this semester in (class) was a remarkable attempt to undermine some standard education procedure. During the first few weeks, the class as a whole was inundated with questions which are normally decided by the professor. The class seemed (as a whole) quite impatient. (One could almost hear the words 'we came to learn [Neurophysiology], so why can't we get started).' Some students voiced an opinion that a freedom to choose was great and that it was a much better idea than a structured situation. Of course other students said exactly the opposite. Those who felt a liberal atmosphere would be conducive to greater depths of understanding were surprised to find how little they could work when nothing was actually 'due.' (This is not all that surprising when considering that for more than 15 years students are conditioned to study for in-class exams and turn in mandatory assignments.) Those opting for more structure, realized, I think, that with a little self discipline one could learn a great deal."

"It was planned in the beginning of the semester that Dr. Levitan (as the prime holder of wisdom in the classroom) would lecture on a set of 'core topics' without which other interesting areas of neurophysiology could not effectively be attacked. After this introduction, students were to branch off into whatever they chose to do. Clearly the course unfolded a little differently. Part of this change of plans was occasioned by the nature of the discussion in class. Even though topics to be discussed were outlined ahead of time, each was approached with a sense of discovery. Data were presented at times and conclusions asked for, and at other times hypotheses (from the class and/or Dr. Levitan), listed and experiments asked for to differentiate between them. The class as a whole, it seemed to me, enjoyed this encounter session with science. Enthusiasm in the subject matter was at times quite high (e.g. on several occasions there was argument among students on the interpretation of some data—clearly something quite different from what one usually finds in a science course . . .). Overall I think a class such as the one we experienced this semester is suitable to a group of students who are willing to interact in the classroom, do a reasonable amount of background reading for the discussion, and who are interested in the subject matter being discussed. Regardless of how one classifies oneself with respect to this group of students, an experience like this semester will help formulate one's opinion about other educational methods, taken usually without question."

"The method of democratically deciding on what areas we would investigate in class was laborious at times, though the results seemed to please everyone . . . I much prefer only having to worry about my own standards for judging my achievement and understanding of the material. Too often exams force a student to learn the material in the teacher's way, and this detracts from the excitement one experiences in learning new material."

"This course has indeed been a unique experience. It makes one think much more than other courses at this university. But for someone to come into this course, who has not done much independent work, it is quite a shock. It is hard to organize and be productive without someone constantly telling one what to do if one's not used to it . . . I think this could be a problem for some people . . ."

"I think the new flexible format of the course is conceptually an excellent idea. However, I am the product of a system built around assignments, deadlines, and conventional examinations. Therefore, with this course graded by the flexible method and four other courses graded by the more conventional methods I tend to give less attention to this course than it merits due to lack of well-defined requirements."

"While I can appreciate the reasoning behind the course structure I am in disagreement with the method. I personally feel that democracy has no place in the classroom for an introductory course. A benevolent dictator (can more efficiently) teach a course covering a lot of new material. My reasoning is this: I primarily want an instructor to dump as much material on my head as possible per classroom hour. This allows me to go home and sift through this information, organize it and recognize what I don't understand. Also (and probably the main reason), it saves me a lot of time. The days you strictly lectured and answered questions were excellent and very enjoyable. The days we discussed how and what to do were, in one word, a drag."

"This whole course has been a stretching experience for me. Never before have I been responsible for so much material in one course, and never before have I not been spoon-fed the material by the professor. I can honestly say that neurophysiology was only a portion of what I learned. I also learned how to be responsible for keeping up with assignments, how to write exams, and the necessity for being well read in journals . . . I would like to extend my thanks and appreciation to Dr. Levitan, (the T.A.), and the entire class for making this course very rewarding for me."

The proportion of students completing the course was greater this semester than at any time in the previous six years. Only one student dropped the course, and he went out of his way to explain that his decision was based on extraneous circumstances.

These are unusually thoughtful analyses of a unique and stimulating experience. They reflect the objective, cautious approach of the scientifically inclined—and perhaps have caught some of this attitude from their instructor!

By far the most significant comment is the unspoken one. *Not one student* intentionally dropped the course, compared to the 30–40 percent dropout rate in the earlier lecture courses by the same instructor! When there is freedom to choose, to learn at one's own pace, to select the most relevant areas for oneself, there is a magnetism to the experience that *holds* the learner. This constitutes not only a satisfaction for the student, but a very rewarding nonverbal evaluation of the facilitator.

C. *Summary Evaluation*

I struggled for some time with the feeling that "structuring" the course in the way I have described made me very vulnerable. The students might take advantage of *me*. They might do less than *I* thought they should and less than students in the past had been required to do. They might not take the initiative, accept responsibility, and show *me* that they could learn on their own. They might fall prey to the explicit pressures and requirements of other courses and not realize the great pleasure from learning something oneself. But I found that taking sole responsibility for the course content and requirements was an unrewarding burden. In the power struggle related to such an autocratic procedure, no one wins very much of consequence, and little learning of lasting importance takes place.

With practice one gets better at learning, at educating oneself. Some students who had been "trained" to educate themselves by parents or special education programs, recognized their advantage with respect to others in the class, and expressed it to me. They were grateful for the opportunity to exercise that option again at the University. They also reflected upon their stuttering start, their floundering and initial frustration until they learned how to learn.

Those in the class who had not previously had the opportunity to experience these symptoms exhibited and reported the tell-tale signs. The process takes time, proceeds faster in some than in others and should not really have an end point. But the beginning, the initial experience is often clearly delineated. Perhaps in the future some of the students will let me know that this course served as the beginning for them.

Heading the list of things I would do differently next time is improving my role as facilitator of the learning process. One way to accomplish this would be to organize and summarize more extensively and explicitly the contributions which the students have made during previous class discussions. This would serve to show the students that in fact much had been accomplished in what appeared to be rambling, apparently unfocused, question-raising discussions. Such periodic summaries would also help the class to focus on new questions and problems.

In sum, I feel the course was a step closer to the way I think it should be than it was previously. It was a step I very much enjoyed taking.

SOME CONCLUDING COMMENTS

I have only a few observations to add to Dr. Levitan's summary.

One element that shows through again and again is that the instructor felt himself very much a part of the group. He does not impose his ideas or feelings, but neither does he hold back their expression. He is very much a participant and appears to feel easy about making his contributions, whether as a teacher-learner, or as a learner-teacher. Thus, I am sure he came across in a natural way as a real person. The extent to which this contributes to the development of trust in the group cannot be overestimated.

Another fact that deserves comment is that a humanistic approach, facilitative attitudes, and self-determined learnings are just as appropriate in a "hard" science course as in the so-called "soft" subjects. This approach works well in everything from advanced mathematics to the study of literature. It is as applicable in a college science course as in an elementary grade reading class. This account helps to document that fact.

Everything in this course evolves gradually. Nothing comes to a dramatic (or traumatic) confrontation. Thus, the instructor agrees to some lectures, but these rapidly evolve into largely student-directed learning. The problems of examinations and of the final grade are discussed and handled piecemeal until a satisfactory pattern emerges. Probably this gradualness is due to the personal style of the instructor. He does not hold rigidly to his views or values, but deals with each situation flexibly within himself and with the class. This quality reduces the shock and resentment that are sometimes found when students are faced with the necessity of making responsible choices.

To me Dr. Levitan's account of his "experiment" is an inspiring addition to the documentation of a person-centered approach in education. I believe it warrants careful study by every teacher and teacher-to-be.

REFERENCES

1. Friere, Pado. *Pedagogy of the Oppressed.* New York: Seabury Press, 1970.
2. Levitan, Herbert. "Science Education: An Experiment in Facilitating the Learning of Neurophysiology." *The Physiologist* 24 (February 1981): 19–27.
3. Rogers, Carl R. *Freedom to Learn.* Columbus, OH: Charles E. Merrill Publishing Co., 1969.
4. Rogers, Carl R. "Power or Persons: Two Trends in Education." *On Personal Power: Inner Strength and Its Revolutionary Impact.* New York: Delacorte Press, 1977.
5. Rogers, Carl R. "Significant Learning: In Therapy and Education." *On Becoming a Person.* Boston: Houghton Mifflin, 1961.
6. Rogers, Carl R. "Student-Centered Teaching." *Client-Centered Therapy: Its Current Practices, Implications, and Theory.* New York: Houghton Mifflin Co., 1951.

Other Facilitators of
Freedom

One of the most prevalent misunderstandings of a person-centered approach in education is that it is applicable only in certain kinds of subjects or in certain special situations. We have, in previous chapters, observed it in action in an elementary grade, in the learning of a foreign language, and in a technical science course. In this chapter I wish to show how differently it can be implemented in the widest variety of situations.

I believe also that by presenting the experience of very diverse individuals it will become clear that we are not talking about a method or a technique. A person-centered way of being in an educational situation is something that one grows into. It is a set of values, not easy to achieve, placing emphasis on the dignity of the individual, the importance of personal choice, the significance of responsibility, the joy of creativity. It is a philosophy, built on a foundation of the democratic way, empowering each individual.

So in this chapter you will find:

● A science teacher whose bold effort at creating freedom in his classroom is marred by one mistake.

● A department chairman who believes in the democratic process and goes the limit in empowering both students and faculty.

● A mathematician who learns what constitutes a nurturing environment for creative thinking.

● A teacher of teachers who uses childhood memories as a way of changing teacher attitudes.

● A counselor in a conventional school who cultivates a limited garden plot of freedom, the fruits of which are highly nutritious and long-lasting.

Courage, Integrity and One Mistake

I am quite aware that up to this point I have presented examples in which both the process and the outcome of the learning were positive for the instructor as well as for the student. I should like now to present an innovative course in which, in my judgment, a real error was made with some unfortunate consequences.

Dr. John Barkham teaches environmental science in an English university. He sent me a long, very thoughtful analysis of a course that he taught in a most innovative manner (2). The course was a valuable learning experience for the instructor as well as the students. I cannot in a short space do credit to the dedicated way in which Barkham prepared for the course and evaluated it, using ingenious research methods. I wish to focus only on some of its salient features, quoting from his report. Though it is unfair to the course as a whole, I wish to emphasize some of the things he did and did not do, which in my judgment constituted serious mistakes, keeping the experience from becoming all that it might have been.

Barkham had been moving toward an innovative style for some time.

> Over a number of years I have been developing and changing my approach to teaching Ecosystem Management. . . . In 1978 I began to realize the potential power of participatory learning in groups. (He tells of developing discussion groups during 1979–80). At this point I read two books for the first time which have influenced me enormously. Adam Curle's *Education for Liberation* (3) got to my guts and gave me a little revolutionary zeal, Carl Rogers' *Freedom to Learn* (5) confirmed those feelings but actually helped me find the tools I was at that precise moment looking for to facilitate my students more effectively. If you want to be stuck where you are in your thinking about teaching, don't read either of these books.

He is very honest about his internal struggle, stating it in a way that will ring true with many teachers.

> I realized for the first time that many students' difficulties in "EcoMan" in 1979–80 actually mirrored my own confusion of role. They could hear me saying, "I want to give you freedom to explore . . ." but what they *felt* was that I was simply controlling and, at worst, manipulating them in another way. And indeed I was. Giving freedom and responsibility to students for their own learning is a very scary business. I was scared of the possible consequences, of losing control. After all, if I know so much more than the students surely I have a *duty* to put it all there before them? And anyway they wouldn't respect me if I allowed them to think that their ideas are as important and as valid as my own. . . . I know what is important; what is important is the syllabus and all students must accept that I know best, etc., etc. These were some of the fears in me which in general I failed to articulate to myself. So, I realized that if the students were to feel genuinely free, I would genuinely have to leave go of the reins. Having read Rogers' book, I immediately wrote the handout for the course 1980–81 in the space of a day.

This handout, which was given several months before the course began to the thirty-seven students who had signed up, is exceedingly thorough and detailed, an eleven-page single-spaced document. A brief segment will give its tone and purpose.

> Can you and I together run a really worthwhile third-year course with so many people involved. . . . My own personal goal for this course is to give you all possible freedom to pursue the study of ecosystem management and nature conservation. You are not the empty vessels into which I will pour some of the contents of my own vessel. I must remember all the time that this is *your* course, not mine. You have expressed an interest by signing up, and my role must be as facilitator: to enable you as far as my own skills allow to pursue your interest. I want to set up an environment in which freely self-directed and creative learning can take place.

An initial trace of an inner conflict which definitely affected the course is already evident. Note the discrepancy between "you and I together" and "this is *your* course, not mine." Which statement will he stand by?

The handout goes on to various topics. He suggests the questions by which the student can define his or her own goals. He outlines the resources, which are many—books, field trips, outside experts. He suggests the kind of projects on which students might embark. He deals at length with the problem of assessment of student work, stating as his aim "to work out together a solution to this problem which satisfies the University while at the same time not destroying our freedom to learn, the ethos of the course. I think this will be the main item on the agenda for our first meeting." He also lets them know that he will ask for a report at the end of the course, signed or anonymous, evaluating the instructor and the experience of the course, negatively or positively.

In describing the resources available, he states that one of the resources is "me."

> My perception is that, at least initially and for some of you, how to use me most effectively will be a tricky problem. You're used to a lecturer making all or most of the running. Now you've got to run yourselves. I'm sure you can overcome this problem.

> What do I think I have to offer which may facilitate your learning? What *I* think I have may be different from what *you* think I have! Here are some things I think I can offer and which you may wish to use at some point. (He then lists his experience and his interests.)

> There may be other ways in which you expect me to help. To facilitate your use of me I must be available to you in a predictable way. Here are the times I will nearly always be so, at least during the Autumn Term. (He gives a list of his office hours.) Almost certainly you will need to book my time in advance. Please do it wisely, out of perceived need, because almost certainly there will be many calls upon my time. *You must make it clear precisely what you want of me and how you are going to use me so that I can prepare accordingly.* If I don't understand or cannot meet your de-

mands or take exception to them I will say so. Otherwise I will do my best to oblige.

In this offering of himself, there appears to be a certain formality and distance which is out of line with the rest of the handout.

He concludes the statement by giving the date, hour and place of the first meeting, and concludes with this rather abrupt statement.

I will start the meeting at 3:30 and, within five minutes, hand it over to you to manage as you think fit. I suggest at least the following items for the agenda.

(He lists questions about how groups might form, the use of outside experts, the problems of examinations and assessment, etc.) It appears clear from this final statement, that he is distancing himself still more from the course. The first meeting had some of the chaos which any such learning experience involved, but he was not a significant part of it.

The initial class meeting was tense and anxious. I introduced it and then relinquished control and direction. Obviously most students found it very difficult to handle themselves in such a large group. There were many bids and counter-bids for leadership and many silent members. Much of the time was spent thrashing the issue of assessment, and worries about such a course with an exam at the end of it were freely expressed.

That he had indeed left himself out of the course is told in two uneasy— but revealingly honest—excerpts.

By and large the early weeks were very anxious ones for me. After the first meeting, a few of the students I never saw again for the entire course. I found this difficult to handle. I could only make one response: I had given them freedom and if they wished to use it to work entirely on their own then it was their decision for which they were responsible. The fear in me that in some cases no work was being done at all could neither be substantiated nor denied.

My activities. Apart from sitting worrying, I eventually freed myself to take my own independent action. I had intended, apart from responding to student requests, to use any available time for my own new learning in nature conservation, thereby making myself a more effective resource person for the students.

The gap in leadership of the group was not left empty.

One student by this time had taken a leadership role in organizing events. He was determined to get things moving and took all manner of initiatives, carrying others along with him—arranging seminars, etc., etc.

Professor Barkham did take two initiatives. He invited a number of professional nature conservationists to meet informally with the class, and these meetings were well attended and appreciated. Significantly, he did not lead one of these sessions.

He also gave a few lectures. The first was at the request of the students, in which he stated his personal values in the area of nature conservation. The students enjoyed this particularly.

The outcomes of the course, as shown by student productivity and their reactions and evaluations, were generally satisfactory or better. It was, for most of the class, a period of independent study. One rather typical reaction follows.

> "I think that the structure of the course is good in enabling you to develop your own lines of thought. From the outset it is made clear that you are on your own. This encouraged me to look at the course as more of a voyage of self-discovery than just another course. Also because there are no 'set' things to do, I found myself able to develop more freely than if lectures were set. It is impossible to become indoctrinated doing this course . . . I think that the course actually teaches you how to be interested."

The students wished he had taken a more active role.

> "Your contribution was inadequate to my mind. I would have preferred more talks . . . or even real seminars . . . where you actually have to prepare something."

> "I personally feel you should play a larger part—not in the sense of lecturing, but in guiding the discussions. . . ."

Comments

I should like to comment on Barkham's experience. He was clearly ambivalent as to whether it was to be "our" course or "your" course, but his actions made it definitely the latter. He effectively left himself out of the group experience, and once out he had no way back except to intrude. This he did apologetically. He says in his report that when he decided to give some lectures, it was "not simply a response to their anxieties . . . or mine about my lack of usefulness." When he arranged for the informal sessions with visitors, he speaks of "my justification for taking this initiative." Clearly he felt he had no real right to take action in the course.

Although I believe Professor Barkham made a real error in shutting himself out of his own course, I feel very sympathetic. I recall vividly a weekend session with an important high-level faculty group that had the purpose of helping them rethink their educational goals. Like Barkham, I made it clear that it was *their* group, and they could use the time as they wished. To my dismay, they chose to spend it mostly in small talk, and I had no effective way of changing the situation. If it had been *our* group, my anger at the waste of precious time could have been voiced as a participant member and would have been heard. As it was, I chalked up the weekend as a real disaster.

In my case, and I suspect in Barkham's, the error was made out of an excess of zeal in trusting others. What I failed to do was to trust *myself* to be a useful member of the group. Thus, I cheated them of what I might have contributed. I feel the same thing can be said of Barkham. He lost the opportunity to be a co-participant, and even more important, missed out on the chance to be a *co-learner.*

The second consequence of shutting himself out of the course is that the stimulation and creativity that comes from full and open interaction of the members with each other was lost. Because he kept himself and his feelings to himself—sitting uneasily in his office—the group tended to react in the same way. They held some discussion groups, but for the most part they went each their own way in independent study. This is one excellent way of learning, but it would have been greatly enriched if there had been regular sessions facilitated by the instructor. In the climate of freedom thus created, one mind strikes sparks in another, one person's fresh insight stirs many creative reactions in others, and the dynamics of the group process enhances the process of learning in all.

As I see it, the instructor's isolation from the group robbed both him and the members of important co-learnings. Then the failure to develop a facilitative *group* experience, robbed them all of many creative insights that would almost certainly have occurred.

This was a bold experiment carried out with great attention to detail, and its outcomes were largely good. But it could have been a great deal more valuable for instructor and students had it not been for one error in implementation, the instructor's failure to regard himself as a significant learning member of the group.

Geology Goes Radically Democratic

Bill Romey had a dream of how learning might take place in geology and the earth sciences. He finally found a home for his ideas at St. Lawrence University. I will let him tell of his plan in his own words (6, pp. 680–96). *

> In discussions at St. Lawrence the dream of an academic department focusing on its people rather than any narrow construct called a discipline was set forth. The university bought the dream, and initial conversations suggested an open willingness to support implementation. The plan involved the following elements:
> 1. Independent project work at all levels, for all students and faculty, would replace all standard courses.
> 2. Students would evaluate their own work.
> 3. Students would keep portfolios of their own work as an alternative means of showing what they had accomplished. There would be no more examinations of conventional types.
> 4. Students and faculty would participate fully and equally in the governance of the department.
> 5. Students would define for themselves what they wanted to study in the

department, when, for how long, and with whom. "Geology" and "geography" would be given the widest possible interpretations.

6. The faculty would accept responsibility, in cooperation with the students, to create and maintain a rich and stimulating learning environment for the benefit of all.

7. The department was to run as an open organism with free access for everyone in the university, whether or not they were formally enrolled for credit.

8. Everything was to be negotiable and faculty members and students would agree not to try to use power on, to manipulate, or to try to control anyone else.

9. The community would strive to create and maintain open communication leading to respect for each other and for the physical facilities. Friendship, mutual support, and closest possible interpersonal relationships would be sought.

10. Each person would function both as a teacher and as a learner.

11. A horizontal administrative structure would give all participants equal power, authority, and access. The chairmanship was to be a coordinating position for at least minimal integration of a horizontally organized group like ours into a larger university context organized in a strictly vertical hierarchy. The chairmanship would rotate.

12. The department would evolve from its primarily preprofessional orientation toward a more liberal department where general learning about the earth would be at least as important as the preparation of narrowly defined geological and geographic specialists. Thus, businessmen, politicians, musicians, historians, linguists, and people going out into almost any career would have a chance to become more aware and knowledgeable about the earth.

Comments

As one might imagine, problems quickly arose. One big issue was around grading. Romey and his group finally gained acceptance for a system in which there were only two evaluations recorded with the registrar: either *credit*, or *continuing* (in progress). In other words there were no grades at all, in the usual sense of comparative evaluations.

The other major issue revolved around the faculty of the five areas involved in this experiment. Some of the instructors became very uncomfortable with the lack of scheduled courses. So gradually such courses were reintroduced. After five and one-half years, the program had become a dual system, with over sixty percent of the students in project oriented groups, the remainder in labeled courses of a more traditional sort.

It is difficult to evaluate such a far reaching experiment. One outside observer notes, "By a narrow measure, the experiment could be said to have failed, since some faculty have returned to older ways of teaching. But to talk of this return as a simple reversion would be a mistake. The atmosphere has been wholly transformed and this has affected even the conservative teachers more profoundly than they themselves may realize. Moreover, if the objective was to set up an environment offering the maximum range of choices for the learner, the experiment has been a great success. . . . The diversity of teaching styles and assumptions is obvious to everyone in the department, so that there is a heightened consciousness about education among the students" (8, pp. 16–17).

What Romey and a few colleagues have done is to establish what is, in essence, an alternative college within a fairly conventional liberal arts university. Furthermore, this alternative college is daringly democratic. Why is it that we so much prefer to teach democracy than to practice it? Here the students and faculty participate in all important decisions. It is even democratic enough to permit divergence from innovation. Neither faculty nor students are *forced* to be free. They can choose the mode of learning and teaching with which they are most comfortable. The extent to which they have departed from a hierarchical system is astonishing. This is a small revolution growing in a healthy fashion inside of a larger conventional university envelope. It could be a model for others.

It is significant that during the five years the experiment has been underway, the number of students majoring in this field has nearly tripled. The number of seniors completing honors theses, mostly of publishable quality, has increased. The number of students going on to graduate school has shown a slow but steady increase. Clearly students are learning, and enjoying learning, in this program.

Creative Knowledge—Born of Love and Trust

Alvin White of Harvey Mudd College in Claremont, California, is an unusual teacher of mathematics. Years ago he described his experiment in making a course in "Calculus of Variations" (I don't know what that means, either!) a human, person-centered learning experience (10, pp. 128–133). It was such a growing learning process for all concerned that he has continued in ever bolder ventures—educating faculty members, trying out even more unique ideas in the classroom. In a recent report he tells of a remarkably varied seminar whose primary purpose was to learn how we gain knowledge and how we create. His account has some fascinating aspects (11).

An experience sometimes has such a profound effect that it leads one to infer general principles of which the particular is an instance. If the insights are true, then the general illuminates the particular which evoked it.

I shared such a fortunate experience with students at M.I.T. several years ago. The quiet glow of remembrance still inspires me. The Division for Study and Research in Education offered me a visiting professorship and an invitation to lead a seminar of my choice for the 1976 spring term. The invitation was an opportunity to consider questions which are common to all disciplines, and therefore are studied by very few, if at all. I proposed a series of questions:

"How do people obtain knowledge? What are the limits of certainty? What is the relation between general and scientific knowledge? What is the role of beauty, simplicity, or intuition in creative discovery? Our present knowledge in the arts, humanities, and sciences is the legacy of creative imagination. How can this legacy influence education at all levels?"

Appropriate readings were suggested. The scope was at once frightening and exhilarating to me. Being a visitor encourages audaciousness.

There were twelve students. Artificial intelligence, biology, computer science, electrical engineering, environmental studies, linguistics, mathematics, physics and visual arts were represented. The group was interdisciplinary or multidisciplinary. Our experience was transdisciplinary or transcendent! We reported on, considered and discussed the writings of various authors in search of answers. The answer, however, as to how we were obtaining knowledge was, for us, embedded in the process and its context.

We were scheduled to meet twice a week from 9:00 to 10:30 A.M. We quickly found ourselves continuing the discussions until noon. Everyone cancelled other morning appointments. Students invited their professors to participate. Visitors would ask permission to observe quietly, although their reticence was usually soon overcome. One student remarked that the popularity of our seminar among visitors was probably because openness, honest listening, and caring for each other were evident. Every contribution was accepted in a nonjudgmental way. No one was forced to speak, and everyone had a chance to speak. We examined writings by Dewey, Kant, Polanyi, Popper, Russell, and others.

The last week of the term was a time to discuss and evaluate the seminar. Why was it so successful? What had happened to us? How had we been transformed from strangers to a group of friends and colleagues? It was as if we had chanced upon a semester-long celebration, and like Alain-Fournier's Wanderer, we had been caught up in the spirit of the place. A student observed that this was the first course where her presence in the room had "made a difference."

Why had the seminar been so remarkably satisfying? What had we learned and what should we do if we wanted to find that spirit of celebration again? An unexpected answer emerged; one that answered some of the questions of the seminar as well as the questions about the seminar. The answer which came from one of the students in a moment of insight was "Love and Trust."

What did that phrase mean? The concept came from the process of our exploration, not from any of the disciplines represented. Love and trust contributed to the spirit of celebration and were essential ingredients in the process of obtaining knowledge. Some instances were remembered where those ingredients were absent, and then only minimal learning had occurred. Should love and trust have been such a surprising answer? Was my surprise a legacy of my formal education? In the past was I too unseeing to have noticed those qualities, or is my memory influenced by the cruelties and meanness often found in the academic scene? The students and I recognized our experience as real and exceptional. The rarity of such an experience for us made us treasure it. And yet, would such an answer be considered sentimental or worse?

Love and trust seem far removed from mathematical logic or electrical engineering as they are encountered in the classroom. Yet if we are engaged in learning and teaching, then all of the disciplines share the process involved in intellectual imagination and creation. Love and trust were natural parts of our learning in the group setting. We came together, attracted by the description of the seminar. Some progress toward understanding was made. Our understanding, however, went beyond the seminar.

Perhaps my surprise came from the absence of love and trust as explicit items in the syllabus or objectives of any course or table of contents of a text. The syllabus is focused on the discipline. How we obtain knowledge is considered outside of the discipline and is therefore usually not discussed. Traveling on the road, however, is as important as finding the road of knowledge. Obtaining knowledge is presumably an objective of a course. Why not assume that our seminar was the natural mode and that teaching and learning without love and trust are unnatural? Reflection on that seminar has been an impetus to seek confirmation that the student's insight about our success was an instance of a general principle; that those who adopt this mode are not sentimental, but are natural.

Mathematics is considered by some of the uninitiated to be devoid of any emotional content. By extension, perhaps, the teaching and learning of mathematics may be thought to be independent of emotional content. Recently, however, the concept of Mathematical Anxiety has been recognized (9). In describing programs to overcome Math Anxiety at Wesleyan, Stanford and Mills College, the consensus was that notwithstanding any superficial differences in the various approaches, there was a common element that was probably essential to their successes. That element was that the anxious student knew that there was someone who could help him or her, and who had faith in the student's ability to succeed. Whatever the cause of anxiety, the cure was love and trust between two people.

In addition to reading what others had said about knowledge, the seminar itself was an example of how one obtains knowledge. The supportive, anxiety-free environment of our seminar is a simple idea, although it may be difficult to achieve. And the idea is not unanimously endorsed by teachers or students. We, however, found it liberating. The students studied with joy and a sense of ownership and personal meaning. Our discussions were not only an aid to memory and an occasion for sharing ideas and insights; they were for the *creation* of ideas and insights. Knowledge was created by the process of our discussions.

Comments

For a mathematician to be striving toward the establishment of love and trust as the basic elements in his classroom is so "far out" as to be almost unbelievable. Yet a human climate fosters learning in mathematics, in philosophical issues such as concerned his seminar, in "hard" sciences, as well as in psychology and the humanities.

White's work has been of especial interest to me since it is often assumed that a humanistic approach to learning applies only to the "soft" subjects. He has demonstrated that it not only applies to the learning of such subjects as calculus, but that it induces creative new learnings in mathematics, or as in this seminar in epistemology—the investigation of human knowing.

In the manuscript of which the foregoing is a part, Alvin White shows that various philosophies and a national committee have come to much the same conclusions as his seminar, though couching their views in slightly more academic language. He says, "Now my surprise is not about a student's insightful answer; it is that whereas I thought a new frontier had been discovered, I now see that it is a well marked path!" It is indeed a well-marked path, trodden over many years by many people. Yet it has always remained the path of the minority. Society as a whole, education as a whole, has not dared to trust, and certainly not dared to love. Yet the teacher who is bold enough to include these ingredients is opening a gate to creative learning for both student and instructor.

Fantasy in Teacher-Training

Dr. Julie Ann Allender uses a special method to help teachers to become aware of experiences that inhibit or promote real learning (1). Her way would, I believe, be especially appropriate to the in-service training of teachers.

> For the past eight years I have been training teachers—part-time at Temple University—the methods of teaching affectively and effectively, i.e. differences between traditional and open education. Basically, the major variables are the instructor, the style of teaching, group dynamic techniques, a grading system based on a contract system, and open education techniques based on people such as Rogers, Maslow, Dewey.

> At the beginning of each course I begin on a negative note looking at the problems of education. I call it "mis-education." We look at how learning has been prevented. We look at how teachers create an unpleasant atmosphere for themselves and for their students. We look at how students' motivation and curiosity are stifled. We look at students' and teachers' fears and resentments. We begin by looking at what doesn't work and then for the next two-thirds of the course we look at what does work. What does enhance learning? What promotes curiosity? What creates a pleasant positive atmosphere conducive to learning? What does motivate students and increases curiosity? We look at students' and teachers' appreciations AND their resentments. We learn how to give constructive feedback.

> One of the first things I do in order to orient the class into thinking about what the problems are or what doesn't work is to form a circle on the floor and pass out a multitude of stories that I label as "mis-education stories," and I have the students read them aloud to the group. Many of the stories are well known, others are less well known, ones that I have collected over the years.

> This activity always stimulates feelings of shock and horror at the realization that many of these stories are true and as the students begin talking about them among themselves they begin to tell each other their own horror stories about their schooling experiences, and the reality of these "mis-education" stories begins to set the stage for many of the following experiences and learnings that we will share together during the semester.

It is at this point that I introduce the 4th Grade Fantasy Activity. I tell everyone to find a comfortable spot, to close their eyes and I then turn off the lights. (This always produces a lot of stirrings and giggling. Remember that most of these students are used to a traditional lecture series.) I then proceed to have them quietly breathe deeply for 2–3 minutes, listening to the air flowing in and out of their bodies, and then 2–3 minutes tensing and untensing each part of their bodies beginning from the feet up to the head. When I feel they are relaxed I begin the activity.

I take them (in fantasy) out of the room and back to their elementary school building. I have them slowly walk up and look all around them as they approach the building, trying to take in all that they can. I then inform them that they are 4th graders and that it is time for their classes to begin so they should hurry along to their classrooms. (I also offer 5th grade for those who have trouble remembering 4th grade.) I have them spend about 10 minutes in their 4th grade fantasy classrooms with me guiding them. We look at the students' desk arrangements, where the teachers' desks are, what was on the walls, the atmosphere of the classroom, their feelings of being there, etc. I give them plenty of time to really concentrate on what it was like for them in that classroom and then . . . it is the end of the school day. Everybody gets ready to leave. I then instruct my students that when they are ready to return to our classroom here they should slowly open their eyes. When all eyes are open I then turn on the lights.

The next step is for them to quietly draw a diagram or picture, not too elaborate, of their classroom and when that is finished I have them find 3 other people, getting into groups of four, and sharing with that group of four what each person's 4th grade classroom was like. As one final piece, when this process is finished I have the whole class come together and share with each other the things that the small groups had discussed.

I have used this fantasy activity in recent years with a total of about 195 students, mostly educated in Philadelphia. Of these students I *never* had *more than one* student per class who had had anything but a traditional row by row structured classroom. Some of the teachers' desks were in differing spots of the room (to the side, back or front) but otherwise the classrooms were all the same. The desks were all in single or double rows and the furniture never moved. Some of the more rigid school rooms even had the desks nailed to the floor. It was NOT unusual to have at least two students in each classroom who came from Catholic parochial schools in which they had had 50 to 90 pupils *per* classroom *per* teacher. To my class this information was shocking. To me it is becoming common knowledge. After three or four years, I was no longer surprised. Saddened, yes, at how the size and rigid class structure affected their learning, but not surprised.

How does this affect learning? Well, the next step in my process was to have the students brainstorm or throw out words that came to mind. Words that could be placed on the board under one category; words that describe learning. The left half of the board being positive and right side of the board being negative. Each time the board filled up very quickly . . . well, at least half of the board did . . . words that described learning to them through *their* eyes. . . .

The right side would always be overflowing. Students could not wait to put up their words concerning what was negative. However, with the left side, the positive side, I would have to prod and pull to get even half as many positive words up there. The negative words were mainly concerned with discipline, behavior, punishment, hidden agenda items, grades, tests, etc. Nothing to do with learning. Words such as *embarrassment, fearful, failure, sit up straight, don't talk, no noise*, etc. The positive side had to do with *escaping* school; recess, lunch, vacation, meeting friends, and again . . . nothing to do with learning. Once in a while a teacher's name would get in under the positive side as a friend, caring and considerate, but that was rare.

I guess what I did not realize was how much information I as an instructor have and might be sitting on. This is just one example, but it is true. It is very powerful. These 195 students represent a great many schools and if their education is thought to be so negative by them, then something is wrong with education and we need to get more of these true stories published. We need to encourage more schools to use affective/effective means of educating. This is not to say positive learnings and positive recollection do not exist concerning education. The 3 or 4 students that I have had (out of the total 195) that have experienced *open education* did not feel very different. Their descriptions of the classrooms all varied. I could never put them in a box and describe their learning situations as easily as I did the other 190! These students tended to begin my class on a more positive note. Their words of recalling their 4th grade classrooms were positive. In fact, most of the positive words on the board would come from these few students. It did not take me the 14 weeks to get them to trust education. They began excited and remained so throughout the course. It is the other 97– 98% who have only experienced the traditional and have had limited other experience that have very few positive memories of their educational process. Encouragingly enough by the end of the course I can get most of these students to really become active and interested learners. However then the inevitable happens. The ultimate question is asked . . . "What now? Do we have to go back to the other teachers and their traditional style of teaching which we do not like?" And sadly I must reply, "Yes. However there IS a light at the end of that tunnel." I tell them, "Now at least you know the difference and you DO have the power to change things."

Comments

When we contemplate the full meaning of this experience, the shock is great. Here are classes of teachers or teachers-in-training. Presumably they would not have chosen that profession if they had not found some value in their education. Yet when they think back on their schooling, the feelings are almost all negative, and even the positive feelings have to do with escaping from school. Their experience has been composed of fear, failure, humiliation, resentment, constriction. These are the important learnings—the personal ones. The *content* of their courses—what they were *supposed* to have learned—doesn't even come to mind! What an incredible fact! We have paid our taxpayers' money in order to have our children scarred, damaged, hurt, and stultified—changed from eager learners into active rebels against education.

The stupidity and tragedy of it all is that this outcome is completely unnecessary. That this is so is shown by the reaction of the very few students who have experienced an open, varied, individualized education. They have not been scarred. Why do we, as a community, continue to insist on a school experience that damages, when a proven alternative exists? The question is a most troubling one.

Freedom Part-Time and Its Consequences

The basic ideas and philosophy of this book are not new. They have many roots in the past. I should like to illustrate that with an account of an innovative project in one school that started with the dissatisfaction felt by one person in the early sixties. Then the story is completed by a participant telling of the project's impact, then and now—fifteen years later.

The project is a most unusual one. It involved both students and teachers for part-time only. The pupils ranged from slow learners in seventh grade to gifted eleventh graders. Out of thirty to thirty-five periods in a week, the students spent from six to ten in *EXP*, as the program was called, and the teachers and the coordinating counselor approximately the same. The enormous flexibility of scheduling required was possible only because the project had the full support of the principal.

Here is the account of an eight-year program, as told by the person most responsible, Ruth Sanford (7).

> This experiment in learning began with an almost desperate need to save myself. As a counselor with administrative responsibilities in a public school district, I had felt for some time that I was dying a little every day. I had begun to feel like a shock absorber, taking in the pressures, the anxieties and frustrations of students, parents, administrators, teachers, the board of education and the community, trying to be at the same time an advocate for student growth and learning. It seemed to me that everyone was losing, especially me. There had to be a better way! Unless I could find one, my energies and enthusiasms would ebb away and I would become another drop-out from the educational system.
>
> One of my strong points is, I believe, that once I have gained an insight, I do something about it.
>
> My first step was to apply for a sabbatical leave, which I used for research into "Creativity, Intelligence and Achievement in a Public Secondary School: Implications for the Classroom." It grew the following year into an experiment in education in which I, a counselor, worked first with a group of teachers, and later with those teachers in their classrooms. Our purpose was to create a climate in which the creative urge to growth and the excitement of learning would be nurtured. Much to our surprise we found that in the nurturing climate which we were striving to create, we ourselves were nourished, and found within ourselves a renewal of excitement in learning.

The next eight years were the most vital and adventurous of my professional life—up to that time.

The program kept the title chosen by the students, "EXP," although its form and the students involved varied from year to year depending upon the grade level and the school schedule for that grade. Perhaps like many living creatures, plant and animal, characteristics most essential to its survival were its adaptability and its will to live. It provided a place and a time for students to learn what they wanted to learn—in their own way—an opportunity to supplement and synthesize their regular schedule of required subjects.

The principal of the building, having shared in the enthusiasm of the preliminary workshop groups, was cooperative in setting up his master schedule. Some groups met two double periods each week plus time usually allotted to art, music and reading; others met one or two periods daily with adjacent free periods used, with student consent, to make larger blocks of time available for films, discussions and art work. The "prep" and free periods of teachers were also so placed in the schedule that they could meet once each week for workshop and processing sessions with the counselor or counselors.

We centered the subject content around a loose-leaf "Living Textbook"* divided for convenience into what we called "The Four Worlds": the natural world, the esthetic world, the technological world and the human or social world. The Introduction was a personal message to the learner, assuring her/him that "worlds" could be combined or separated into others or ignored, saying to the learner, "This is the beginning of your book. The moment you make a change, add, delete or rewrite, illustrate an article, make something and include a photograph of it, or do a page of your own, it becomes uniquely yours, living as you are living and changing. Even if today you only write a note in the margin it becomes yours."

We also used as a focus the "Being and Becoming" film series, developed by Dr. Drews under a federal grant. These films presented self-actualizing men and women, at work, at play, with their families and in their communities—as whole persons. The films, by selection, challenged the men/women career stereotypes presenting, for example, a woman judge, a man artist, a woman doctor. The "Living Textbook" together with the films, stimulated heated discussions on ideas and values, prejudices and ambitions. They encouraged original work, wide reading; some students were stimulated to become authorities on topics of special interest to them, often newly found interests. We discovered later that some of this adventuring spilled over to after school hours and family dinner tables—even to social gatherings of their parents.

Some students worked almost exclusively in their "Living Textbooks" and "hated" the films; some "loved" the films and did very little in their "LTBs"; some were highly verbal in class and others rarely spoke; some withdrew and worked on sculpture or mobiles while others wrote poetry or stories—

---

*Patterned after the "Living Textbook" developed by Dr. Elizabeth Drews, then at Michigan State University.

or gazed at the sky. A few who had never written an acceptable "composition" talked with a student friend or with one of the adults in the group, into a recorder, then edited a transcription and were amazed at the result— "Did I write that?"

For purposes of measurement and "feedback" most of the sessions were taped, in whole or in part, ready to be played back on request. Playback of tapes, along with the group process of establishing confidentiality and trust became important parts of the learning process. After years of feeling manipulated by adults, trust came slowly, but by the second semester it became, for many, permission to be a whole, real person in the classroom.

Students, teachers and counselors involved directly in the program, teachers who knew students only in "outside" classes, and parents, all had a part in the evaluation process, and a brief composite of the evaluations was placed in the student's folder along with the transcript of academic record. There were no grades.

Students, adult members of the groups and parents also evaluated the *program*. One boy wrote, "This is the first time in nine years of school that I felt I had a PLACE". Another said, "This course did nothing for me", then added, "Except to give me a few new ideas on education". A tenth grade girl asked, "Why is it that in this class with no teacher I have learned more than in my other classes with regular teachers?". An eleventh grade student wrote, "This EXP has brought me nothing but trouble. When I have an idea now or disagree with someone, I speak up. Usually the teacher doesn't like it, especially if I disagree with the teacher."

We learned that we could not measure a student's participation or learning by what was apparent in class. One young woman, whom the teachers and counselor had felt "probably gained the least" from the program, came back four years after she graduated from high school to tell us with great excitement about what her EXP experience was meaning to her in her practice teaching. She was full of questions about the planning—"Or", she asked, "did it just happen that way?"

Teachers learned that students, on the whole, accomplished more without the goad of grades, and that discipline problems diminished, much to their surprise.

In general, students in these groups showed an improvement in their English and social studies grades following their experience; most were more selective in the subjects in which they did well, most were observed by other-subject teachers to be more self-directed in their work and more able to weigh values in class discussions rather than "to see issues in terms of black or white"; most took a more active part in diversified activities associated with special interests after a year or more in the program.

Now, eight years after EXP ended as a formal program, there is a lasting effect on the teachers who were closely involved. I am in personal touch with four of the five who constituted a core of the experiment. Two of them use almost the same words: "After those years in EXP, I could never be the same again." One is in administration, one teaching music, another English, the fourth works with disadvantaged children and adults in an impoverished farming community. In every case they continue to see learning as a partnership, to trust others to choose, to participate, to learn. EXP is still having its effect.

We are also seeing the impact on education of some of the participating students, who are now themselves teachers or counselors. The long-lasting impact of the EXP experience is best exemplified by the story that follows. It is written by one of the young women who was for two years a participant and another year a student assistant. Her account has special meaning for me because my notes at the time describe her as "a mousey, shy girl who didn't open her mouth in the group until almost the end of the first semester, and then with tentative uncertainty." This memory is supported by her own comments at the end of her first year in EXP.

Jeanne Ginsberg writes of what it was like for a student (4).

Looking Back
SHOCK AND CONFUSION

EXP—my first impression was that I had stepped into a carnival funhouse; nothing was as it should have been. There were no grades; teachers offered minimal direction, students were addressed with the same respect given adults.

There seemed to me to be little point in working or in participating since there were no external standards to meet. Even in our discussions there seemed to be no right or wrong answer. Most students seemed to feel the way I did and our beginning discussions were somewhat dull, guarded comments punctuated by long silences.

Even then, teachers did not interfere. I began to feel that something was not right and that no one was doing anything about it. I began to feel anxious as the realization hit me that since there was no external approval or punishment—no adult with a special knowledge and power telling me what was "right," I was going to have to figure out for myself what was "right," what *I* wanted to get from this experience. If someone was going to make this interesting or meaningful or fun, it would have to be me.

It was this realization which helped me to open and fill with light and air and movement, a door which until that moment had been tightly closed. The first component of the program which caught my attention was the film series. I come from a home in which the roles and options for men and women are clearly defined. There are correct and incorrect ways to behave in each situation and there was a tremendous amount of fear associated with any move away from the standard ways of acting.

The film series "Being and Becoming" (I remember an interesting discussion about what these words mean and how they fit together) represented unconventional professions and did not always present the "proper" (that word again) gender for that role. Suddenly the options, which had previously been so constricted, widened for me. I began to gain a sense of independence and enthusiasm and self-respect.

LEARNING AND SELF-DISCOVERY

Soon after this, I read one line in an article from the "Living Textbook" which suggested the possibility that dolphins had a language of their own and that a man named John Lilly was studying this language. The idea that people could actually learn to decipher dolphin language, in a sense to realize what it felt like to be a mammal living in the sea and to share their history, caught hold of me and I began to explore this tidbit of information for no end other than my own interest. I wrote to John Lilly, found articles and books in the library, talked to people about my findings, and felt enthused about something *I* had discovered at school for the first time. Eventually I turned my exploration into a paper for a biology class and received an A+. The difference, however, was that I did this paper for myself. The grade was incidental.

I gradually stopped doing things for a teacher's approval and started doing things because I wanted to do them. How did this happen? I think one of the main factors was that the teachers seemed to accept everything I said. They didn't approve or disapprove; there didn't seem to be any judgment attached. They simply seemed interested. So, there was no point doing something for someone else's reaction.

As I stopped doing things for someone else I began to realize what *I* was interested in; what *I* wanted to learn; what was important to *me*; essentially, who I was. I began emerging from the shell of my parents' and teachers' expectations and into my own self.

FREEDOM VS. RIGIDITY

Perhaps the image which is most vivid to me now, years later, is that of the difficult trip down one hallway, through a crosswalk, and down another hallway to the left from EXP to Latin class. The entire trip took no more than two minutes but within that time I had to adjust myself from what seemed to me at fourteen years old the difference between life and death.

Life: I think of change, action, conflict, colors, feelings, risk-taking, growth, choices. Death: I think of stagnation, sluggishness, no conflict, grays, controlled emotion, certainty, and no choice—the belief that there is only one way to do or think or feel. I remember reading a statement of Maya Angelou's: "Children's talent to endure stems from their ignorance of alternatives." In EXP I was asked to think about things, to delve more deeply, to explore, to feel, to develop and to be myself. Our textbook was the *Living* Textbook. The class provided a place to "jump off" into material, into discussions, into interaction, and into the world outside of the classroom. It was an introduction into a way of relating to the world and to other people.

In Latin class, I was told to sit in a row in alphabetical order by my last name; the notes to be copied from the board made up our notebooks. Our text was a translation of *Julius Caesar.* The teacher moved up and down the rows to see that we were copying the notes neatly and exactly. A test was given daily on the material we were instructed to memorize the evening before. Home*work:* work in the most dead sense of the word. I remember practically nothing of my two years of Latin study. No wonder I was often late for this class, had nightmares about it, and dreaded eighth period.

THE PRESENT IMPACT

Now I am a teacher of emotionally disturbed and neurologically damaged children. In developing my own style of teaching I thought back to the walk between Experimental and Latin class and the feeling of darkness I experienced on that walk. These particular children need a tremendous amount of order and structure in their routine and work since their inner worlds and perceptions are often fraught with disorder and confusion. Yet, I have learned that while modes of learning can be classified into certain groups (visual learner, auditory learner, kinesthetic learner) there are as many learning styles as there are children. One child needs to learn math through understanding and experimenting with the concept. Another needs to learn the rote operation, practice it fifty times, and only then begin to understand the concept. A child who throws his reading book on the floor every day may be doing so because he perceives the symbols on the page to be jumping up and down. Another child who is presently enamoured with dinosaurs (I remember my dolphins) has become an expert on the subject and learned division only when I superimposed the problems on the back of a dinosaur. Each child is unique to me and I find one of the most exciting aspects of teaching is discovering and working with these differences.

It is most important to me to make the learning experience meaningful and personal by encouraging the children to *use* their minds rather than simply *accept* information. I want to challenge the one dimensional viewpoint and offer alternate ways of experiencing the world. In this way, I hope each child can feel in part responsible for his or her own learning experience.

This sometimes gives the class the appearance of being slightly more noisy or disorganized or less disciplined than a traditionally run classroom. Actually, tremendous planning and a very carefully organized program must be developed in order to enable disturbed (or for that matter, any child) to make discoveries and come up with ideas and conclusions based upon their own experience.

I think one of the most difficult insights for the children in my class to gain is that there may be more answers or viewpoints than their own. As one child screamed when I was helping to process a fight between him and another child: "Case is closed! He did it on purpose. Why won't you believe me? *I'm* right and *he's* wrong!!" Actually, the other child had hit this child with a ball accidentally because he has severe problems with eye-hand coordination. The first child only *perceived* the hurt as purposeful.

When I heard this, I felt frightened. It brought back old memories of Nazi Germany where Jews, gay women and men, really anyone who expressed a differing viewpoint to the government was deemed not deserving to be free or even to survive. It brought up new fears of a "Moral Majority" who *know* they are right; of a proposed Family Protection Bill which forbids the federal government from interfering with issues of child or wife abuse, forbids Legal Services Corp. from using money for cases involving abortion, divorce, homosexual rights or busing to achieve racial desegregation, and over thirty more subsections which would destroy the work and progress American people have made over the years. It brought up fears of the rising power of the Ku Klux Klan and the killer of Black children in Atlanta. If I react to this child's statement or run my classroom with the same closed and stuck finality of his thought pattern, I believe I am helping to feed this child's pathology and helping to create an individual who is incapable of empathy or reason or the possibility of change.

Very simplistically, in order to form valid opinions, I feel a child must learn how to listen, to consider what he's heard, to form an opinion based on his new information as well as his past experience, culture, and individual personality, and to express this opinion. I usually devote a large part of my curriculum to developing these skills with lessons as structured as copying letters or words exactly from a model, to sharing a personal experience in three full sentences, to writing creative stories on a specific topic, to discussing feelings and thoughts, and value systems.

I can trace a great deal of my excitement with the learning and growth process to the Experimental class. "Experimental"—even the name suggests that anything can happen if only you open your eyes and mind and ears and feelings. I hope that I carry this excitement with me into my classroom in a way that the children can feel its energy and power.

Comments

To insert a radically free learning environment into a conventional school, on a part-time basis, is a really wild pattern. Why did it work? It had the backing of the principal. It involved many of the regular teachers and the regular counselor, thus defusing much of the criticism that would have arisen if the program had been brought in by outsiders. It did not force anyone— teacher or student—to do anything. It simply provided an opportunity. Students used this opportunity in such constructive ways that the program sold itself to parents and to those who at the outset were skeptical.

As I read the two accounts, I am struck by the many valuable learnings that occurred. There was clearly an increase in: ability to take initiative, excitement about learning, independence of thought, ability to make choices, ability to organize a project and persist in it, creativity, openness and honesty, the appreciation of self.

All this came about in a climate of nonjudgmental caring, stimulating resources, and a trust in the student.

There are three elements in Jeanne Ginsberg's statement that stand out vividly. One is the contrast between the living joy of self-directed learning and the deadening nightmare of a highly traditional class. Another is the evidence that the impact of EXP was lasting. Clearly it has affected her teaching. She does not try to duplicate EXP in her class because her students have special problems and structure is required. But her attitudes are those fostered by EXP.

Finally, the program played a part in helping her to become a thoughtfully independent citizen, willing to make and voice her own considered judgments on personal, moral, and political issues. And she is helping even her disadvantaged students to become similarly thoughtful citizens, also.

I can only conclude that an experience of freedom to learn, even if it is only for a few hours a week, can have a positive influence which lasts for many years.

CONCLUDING REMARK

I am indebted to the six people who have permitted us to enter their diverse worlds through writing of their experiences. I am also indebted to the students who come so expressively into the stories.

I trust that the point has been made that any facet of education is drastically altered when the person responsible for it holds a humanistic, person-centered view. Revolutions—major or minor—occur.

REFERENCES

1. Allender, Julie Ann. "Fourth Grade Fantasy." *Journal of Humanistic Education* 6 (1982):37–38.
2. Barkham, John P. "Environmental Sciences 365: Ecosystem Management." Evaluation of the course, 1980–81.
3. Curle, Adam. *Education for Liberation*. London: Tavistock Publications, 1979.
4. Ginsberg, Jeanne. Looking Back. Personal document, 1981.
5. Rogers, Carl R. *Freedom to Learn*. Columbus, OH: Charles E. Merrill Publishing Co., 1969.
6. Romey, William. "Radical Innovation in a Conventional Framework." *Journal of Higher Education* 48 (1977).
7. Sanford, Ruth. Eight Years of an Experimental Program. Personal document, 1981.
8. Sugnet, C. J. "Metamorphosis of a Geology Department." *Change*, July 1977.
9. Tobias, S. *Overcoming Math Anxiety*. New York: W. W. Norton, 1978.
10. White, Alvin M. "Humanistic Mathematics: An Experiment." *Education*, Winter 1974.
11. White, A. "Process and Environment in Teaching and Learning." In White, A. (Ed.), *New Directions for Teaching and Learning: Interdisciplinary Teaching, No. 8*, San Francisco: Jossey-Bass, 1981.

For the Teacher

The Interpersonal
Relationship in the
Facilitation of Learning

This chapter is passionate and personal, as it endeavors to probe my relationship to the learning process and the attitudinal climate that promotes this process. It has been presented in different forms at different times, the first at Harvard University (10, pp. 1–18). It has, however, been changed and revised for this volume. I believe that it expresses some of my deepest convictions in regard to the process we call *education*.

* * *

I wish to begin this chapter with a statement that may seem surprising to some and perhaps offensive to others. It is simply this: Teaching, in my estimation, is a vastly over-rated function.

Having made such a statement, I scurry to the dictionary to see if I really mean what I say. *Teaching* means "to instruct." Personally, I am not much interested in instructing another in what she should know or think, though others seem to love to do this. "To impart knowledge or skill." My reaction is, why not be more efficient, using a book or programmed learning? "To make to know." Here my hackles rise. I have no wish to *make* anyone know something. "To show, guide, direct." As I see it, too many people have been shown, guided, directed. So I come to the conclusion that I *do* mean what I said. Teaching is, for me, a relatively unimportant and vastly overvalued activity.

But there is more in my attitude than this. I have a negative reaction to teaching. Why? I think it is because it raises all the wrong questions. As soon as we focus on teaching, the question arises, what shall we teach? What, from our superior vantage point, does the other person need to know? I wonder

*This chapter is a revised version of a presentation first published in *Humanizing Education*, ed. R. Leeper, ASCD, NEA, 1967. Copyright © by the Association for Supervision and Curriculum Development, NEA.

if, in this modern world, we are justified in the presumption that we are wise about the future and the young are foolish. Are we *really* sure as to what they should know? Then there is the ridiculous question of coverage. What shall the course cover? This notion of coverage is based on the assumption that what is taught is what is learned; what is presented is what is assimilated. I know of no assumption so obviously untrue. One does not need research to provide evidence that this is false. One needs only to talk with a few students.

But I ask myself, "Am I so prejudiced against teaching that I find no situation in which it is worthwhile?" I immediately think of my experiences in Australia long ago. I became much interested in the Australian aborigine. Here is a group that for more than 20,000 years has managed to live and exist in a desolate environment in which modern man would perish within a few days. The secret of the aborigine's survival has been teaching. He has passed on to the young every shred of knowledge about how to find water, about how to track game, about how to kill the kangaroo, about how to find his way through the trackless desert. Such knowledge is conveyed to the young as being *the* way to behave, and any innovation is frowned upon. It is clear that teaching has provided him the way to survive in a hostile and relatively unchanging environment.

Now I am closer to the nub of the question that excites me. Teaching and the imparting of knowledge make sense in an unchanging environment. This is why it has been an unquestioned function for centuries. But if there is one truth about modern man, it is that he lives in an environment that is *continually changing*. The one thing I can be sure of is that the physics that is taught to the present day student will be outdated in a decade. The teaching in psychology will certainly be out of date in twenty years. The so-called "facts of history" depend very largely upon the current mood and temper of the culture. Chemistry, biology, genetics, and sociology are in such flux that a firm statement made today will almost certainly be modified by the time the student gets around to using the knowledge.

We are, in my view, faced with an entirely new situation in education where the goal of education, if we are to survive, is the *facilitation of change and learning*. The only man who is educated is the man who has learned how to learn; the man who has learned how to adapt and change; the man who has realized that no knowledge is secure, that only the process of *seeking* knowledge gives a basis for security. Changingness, a reliance on *process* rather than upon static knowledge, is the only thing that makes any sense as a goal for education in the modern world.

So now with some relief I turn to an activity, a purpose, which really warms me—the facilitation of learning. When I have been able to transform a group—and here I mean all the members of a group, myself included—into a community of *learners*, then the excitement has been almost beyond belief. To free curiosity; to permit individuals to go charging off in new directions dictated by their own interests; to unleash the sense of inquiry; to open everything to questioning and exploration; to recognize that everything is in process of change—here is an experience I can never forget. I cannot always achieve it in groups with which I am associated, but when it is partially or largely achieved, then it becomes a never-to-be forgotten group experience. Out of such a context arise true students, real learners, creative scientists and scholars, and practitioners, the kind of individuals who can live in a delicate but ever-changing balance between what is presently known and the flowing, moving, altering problems and facts of the future.

Here then is a goal to which I can give myself wholeheartedly. I see *the facilitation of learning* and the *aim* of education, the way in which we might develop the learner, the way in which we can learn to live as individuals in process. I see the facilitation of learning as the function that may hold constructive, tentative, changing *process* answers to some of the deepest perplexities that beset humankind today.

But do we know how to achieve this new goal in education or is it a will-o'-the-wisp that sometimes occurs, sometimes fails to occur, and thus offers little real hope? My answer is that we possess a very considerable knowledge of the conditions that encourage self-initiated, significant, experiential, "gut-level" learning by the whole person. We do not frequently see these conditions put into effect because they mean a real revolution in our approach to education and revolutions are not for the timid. But we do, as we have seen in the preceding chapters, find examples of this revolution in action.

We know—and I will briefly mention some of the evidence—that the initiation of such learning rests not upon the teaching skills of the leader, not upon scholarly knowledge of the field, not upon curricular planning, not upon use of audiovisual aids, not upon the programmed learning used, not upon lectures and presentations, not upon an abundance of books, though each of these might at one time or another be utilized as an important resource. No, the facilitation of significant learning rests upon certain attitudinal qualities that exist in the personal *relationship* between the facilitator and the learner.

We came upon such findings first in the field of psychotherapy, but now there is evidence that shows these findings apply in the classroom as well. We find it easier to think that the intensive relationship between therapist and client might possess these qualities, but we are also finding that they *may* exist in the countless interpersonal interactions between the teacher and pupils.

Qualities that Facilitate Learning

What are these qualities, these attitudes, that facilitate learning? Let me describe them very briefly, drawing illustrations from the teaching field.

REALNESS IN THE FACILITATOR OF LEARNING

Perhaps the most basic of these essential attitudes is realness or genuineness. When the facilitator is a real person, being what she is, entering into a relationship with the learner without presenting a front or a façade, she is much more likely to be effective. This means that the feelings that she is experiencing are available to her, available to her awareness, that she is able to live these feelings, be them, and able to communicate them if appropriate. It means that she comes into a direct personal encounter with the learner, meeting her on a person-to-person basis. It means that she is *being* herself, not denying herself.

Seen from this point of view it is suggested that the teacher can be a real person in her relationship with her students. She can be enthusiastic, can be bored, can be interested in students, can be angry, can be sensitive and sympathetic. Because she accepts these feelings as her own, she has no need to impose them on her students. She can like or dislike a student product without implying that it is objectively good or bad or that the student is good or bad. She is simply expressing a feeling for the product, a feeling that exists within herself. Thus, she is a person to her students, not a faceless embodiment of a curricular requirement nor a sterile tube through which knowledge is passed from one generation to the next.

It is obvious that this attitudinal set, found to be effective in psychotherapy, is sharply in contrast with the tendency of most teachers to show themselves to their pupils simply as roles. It is quite customary for teachers rather consciously to put on the mask, the role, the façade of being a teacher and to wear this façade all day removing it only when they have left the school at night.

But not all teachers are like this. Take Sylvia Ashton-Warner, who took resistant, supposedly slow-learning primary school Maori children in New Zealand, and let them develop their own reading vocabulary. Each child could request one word—whatever word he wished—each day, and she would print it on a card and give it to him. *Kiss, ghost, bomb, tiger, fight, love, daddy*—these are samples. Soon they were building sentences, which they could also keep. "He'll get a licking." "Pussy's frightened." The children simply never forgot these self-initiated learnings. But it is not my purpose to tell you of her methods. I want instead to give you a glimpse of her attitude, of the passionate realness that must have been as evident to her tiny pupils as to her readers. An editor asked her some questions, and she responded: "A few cool facts you asked me for . . I don't know that there's a cool fact in me, or anything else cool for that matter, on this particular subject. I've got only hot long facts on the matter of Creative Teaching, scorching both the page and me" (3, p. 26).

Here is no sterile façade. Here is a vital *person*, with convictions, with feelings. It is her transparent realness that was, I am sure, one of the elements that made her an exciting facilitator of learning. She doesn't fit into some neat educational formula. She *is*, and students grow by being in contact with someone who really and openly *is*.

Take another very different person, Barbara Shiel, whose exciting work in facilitating learning in sixth graders has been described earlier. She gave her pupils a great deal of responsible freedom, and I will mention some of the reactions of her students later. But here is an example of the way she shared herself with her pupils—not just sharing feelings of sweetness and light, but anger and frustration. She had made art materials freely available, and students often used these in creative ways, but the room frequently looked like a picture of chaos. Here is her report of her feelings and what she did with them.

I find it maddening to live with the mess—with a capital M! No one seems to care except me. Finally, one day I told the children . . . that I am a neat, orderly person by nature and that the mess was driving me to distraction. Did they have a solution? It was suggested there were some volunteers who could clean up . . . I said it didn't seem fair to me to have the same people clean up all the time for others—but it would solve it for me. "Well, some people like to clean," they replied. So that's the way it is. (13)

I hope this example puts some lively meaning into the phrases I used earlier, that the facilitator "is able to live these feelings, be them, and able to communicate them if appropriate." I have chosen an example of negative feelings because I think it is more difficult for most of us to visualize what this would mean. In this instance, Miss Shiel is taking the risk of being transparent in her angry frustrations about the mess. And what happens? The same thing that, in my experience, nearly always happens. These young people accept and respect her feelings, take them into account, and work out a novel solution that none of us, I believe, would have suggested. Miss Shiel wisely comments, "I used to get upset and feel guilty when I became angry. I finally realized the children could accept *my* feelings too. And it is important for them to know when they've 'pushed me.' I have my limits, too" (13).

Just to show that positive feelings, when they are real, are equally effective, let me quote briefly a college student's reaction, in a different course:

. . . Your sense of humor in the class was cheering; we all felt relaxed because you showed us your human self, not a mechanical teacher image. I feel as if I have more understanding and faith in my teachers now. I feel closer to the students too. . . .

Another says:

. . . You conducted the class on a personal level and therefore in my mind I was able to formulate a picture of you as a person and not as merely a walking textbook.

Another student in the same course:

. . . It wasn't as if there was a teacher in the class, but rather someone whom we could trust and identify as a 'sharer.' You were so perceptive and sensitive to our thoughts, and this made it all the more 'authentic' for me. It was an 'authentic' *experience*, not just a class. (7)

I trust I am making it clear that to be real is not always easy, nor is it achieved all at once, but it is basic to the person who wants to become that revolutionary individual, a facilitator of learning.

PRIZING, ACCEPTANCE, TRUST

There is another attitude that stands out in those who are successful in facilitating learning. I have observed this attitude. I have experienced it. Yet, it is hard to know what term to put to it so I shall use several. I think of it as prizing the learner, prizing her feelings, her opinions, her person. It is a caring for the learner, but a nonpossessive caring. It is an acceptance of this other individual as a separate person, having worth in her own right. It is a basic trust—a belief that this other person is somehow fundamentally trustworthy. Whether we call it prizing, acceptance, trust, or by some other term, it shows up in a variety of observable ways. The facilitator who has a considerable degree of this attitude can be fully acceptant of the fear and hesitation of the student as she approaches a new problem as well as acceptant of the pupil's satisfaction in achievement. Such a teacher can accept the student's occasional apathy, her erratic desires to explore byroads of knowledge, as well as her disciplined efforts to achieve major goals. She can accept personal feelings that both disturb and promote learning—rivalry with a sibling, hatred of authority, concern about personal adequacy. What we are describing is a prizing of the learner as an imperfect human being with many feelings, many potentialities. The facilitator's prizing or acceptance of the learner is an operational expression of her essential confidence and trust in the capacity of the human organism.

I would like to give some examples of this attitude from the classroom situation. Here any teacher statements would be properly suspect since many of us would like to feel we hold such attitudes and might have a biased perception of our qualities. But let me indicate how this attitude of prizing, of accepting, of trusting appears to the student who is fortunate enough to experience it.

Here is a statement from a college student in a class with Dr. Morey Appell:

> Your way of being with us is a revelation to me. In your class I feel important, mature, and capable of doing things on my own. I want to think for myself and this need cannot be accomplished through textbooks and lectures alone, but through living. I think you see me as a person with real feelings and needs, an individual. What I say and do are significant expressions from me, and you recognize this. (1)

College students in a class with Dr. Patricia Bull describe not only these prizing, trusting attitudes, but the effect these have had on their other interactions.

> . . . I still feel close to you, as though there were some tacit understanding between us, almost a conspiracy. This adds to the in-class participation on my part because I feel that at least one person in the group will react, even when I am not sure of the others. It does not matter really whether your reaction is positive or negative, it just *IS*. Thank you.

*   *   *

> . . . I appreciate the respect and concern you have for others, including myself. . . . As a result of my experience in class, plus the influence of my readings, I sincerely believe that the student-centered teaching method does provide an ideal framework for learning; not just for the accumulation

of facts, but more important, for learning about ourselves in relation to others. . . . When I think back to my shallow awareness in September compared to the depth of my insights now, I know that this course has offered me a learning experience of great value which I couldn't have acquired in any other way.

*   *   *

. . . Very few teachers would attempt this method because they would feel that they would lose the students' respect. On the contrary. You gained our respect, through your ability to speak to us on our level, instead of ten miles above us. With the complete lack of communication we see in this school, it was a wonderful experience to see people listening to each other and really communicating on an adult, intelligent level. More classes should afford us this experience. (7)

I am sure these examples show that the facilitator who cares, who prizes, who trusts the learner creates a climate for learning so different from the ordinary classroom that any resemblance is purely coincidental.

EMPATHIC UNDERSTANDING

A further element that establishes a climate for self-initiated, experiential learning is empathic understanding. When the teacher has the ability to understand the student's reactions from the inside, has a sensitive awareness of the way the process of education and learning seems *to the student*, then again the likelihood of significant learning is increased.

This kind of understanding is sharply different from the usual evaluative understanding, which follows the pattern of "I understand what is wrong with you." When there is a sensitive empathy, however, the reaction in the learner follows something of this pattern, "At last someone understands how it feels and seems to be *me* without wanting to analyze me or judge me. Now I can blossom and grow and learn."

This attitude of standing in the other's shoes, of viewing the world through the student's eyes, is almost unheard of in the classroom. One could listen to thousands of ordinary classroom interactions without coming across one instance of clearly communicated, sensitively accurate, empathic understanding. But it has a tremendously releasing effect when it occurs.

Let me take an illustration from Virginia Axline, dealing with a second grade boy. Jay, age seven, has been aggressive, a trouble maker, slow of speech and learning. Because of his "cussing," he was taken to the principal, who paddled him, unknown to Miss Axline. During a free work period, Jay fashioned very carefully a man of clay down to a hat and a handkerchief in his pocket. "Who is that?" asked Miss Axline. "Dunno," replied Jay. "Maybe it is the principal. He has a handkerchief in his pocket like that." Jay glared at the clay figure. "Yes," he said. Then he began to tear the head off and looked up and smiled. Miss Axline said, "You sometimes feel like twisting his head off, don't you? You get so made at him." Jay tore off one arm, another, then beat the figure to a pulp with his fists. Another boy, with the perception of the young, explained, "Jay is mad at Mr. X because he licked him this noon."

"Then you must feel lots better now," Miss Axline commented. Jay grinned and began to rebuild Mr. X (5, pp. 521–33).

The other examples I have cited also indicate how deeply appreciative students feel when they are simply *understood*—not evaluated, not judged, simply understood from their *own* point of view, not the teacher's. If any teacher set herself the task of endeavoring to make one nonevaluative, acceptant, empathic response per day to a student's demonstrated or verbalized feeling, I believe she would discover the potency of this currently almost nonexistent kind of understanding.

What Are the Bases of Facilitative Attitudes?

A "PUZZLEMENT"

It is natural that we do not always have the attitudes I have been describing. Some teachers raise the question, "But what if I am *not* feeling empathic, do *not*, at this moment, prize or accept or like my students. What then?" My response is that realness is the most important of the attitudes mentioned, and it is not accidental that this attitude was described first. So if one has little understanding of the student's inner world and a dislike for the students or their behavior, it is almost certainly more constructive to be *real* than to be pseudoempathic or to put on a façade of caring.

But this is not nearly as simple as it sounds. To be genuine, or honest, or congruent, or real means to be this way about *oneself*. I cannot be real about another because I do not *know* what is real for him. I can only tell, if I wish to be truly honest, what is going on in me.

Let me take an example. Early in this chapter I reported Miss Shiel's feelings about the "mess" created by the art work. Essentially she said, "I find it maddening to live with the mess! I'm neat and orderly and it is driving me to distraction." But suppose her feelings had come out somewhat differently in the disguised way that is much more common in classrooms at all levels. She might have said, "You are the messiest children I've ever seen! You don't take care about tidiness or cleanliness. You are just terrible!" This is most definitely *not* an example of genuineness or realness, in the sense in which I am using these terms. There is a profound distinction between the two statements, which I should like to spell out.

In the second statement she is telling nothing of herself, sharing none of her feelings. Doubtless the children will *sense* that she is angry, but because children are perceptively shrewd, they may be uncertain as to whether she is angry at them or has just come from an argument with the principal. It has none of the honesty of the first statement in which she tells of her *own* upsetness, of her *own* feeling of being driven to distraction.

Another aspect of the second statement is that it is all made up of judgments or evaluations, and like most judgments, they are all arguable. Are these children messy, or are they simply excited and involved in what they are doing? Are they *all* messy, or are some as disturbed by the chaos as she?

Do they care nothing about tidiness, or is it simply that they don't care about it every day? If a group of visitors were coming, would their attitude be different? Are they terrible, or simply children? I trust it is evident that when we make judgments, they are almost never fully accurate and hence cause resentment and anger as well as guilt and apprehension. Had she used the second statement, the response of the class would have been entirely different.

I am going to some lengths to clarify this point because I have found from experience that to stress the value of being real, of *being* one's feelings, is taken by some as a license to pass judgments on others, to project on others all the feelings that one should be "owning." Nothing could be further from my meaning.

Actually the achievement of realness is most difficult, and even when one wishes to be truly genuine, it occurs but rarely. Certainly it is not simply a matter of the *words* used, and if one is feeling judgmental, the use of a verbal formula that sounds like the sharing of feelings will not help. It is just another instance of a façade, of a lack of genuineness. Only slowly can we learn to be truly real. For first of all, one must be close to one's feelings, capable of being aware of them. Then one must be willing to take the risk of sharing them as they are, inside, not disguising them as judgments, or attributing them to other people. This is why I so admire Miss Shiel's sharing of her anger and frustration, without in any way disguising it.

A TRUST IN THE HUMAN ORGANISM

It would be most unlikely that one could hold the three attitudes I have described, or could commit herself to being a facilitator of learning unless she has come to have a profound trust in the human organism and its potentialities. If I distrust the human being, then I *must* cram her with information of my own choosing lest she go her own mistaken way. But if I trust the capacity of the human individual for developing her own potentiality, then I can provide her with many opportunities and permit her to choose her own way and her own direction in her learning.

It is clear, I believe, that the teachers whose works are described in the preceding chapters rely basically upon the tendency toward fulfillment, toward actualization, in their students. They are basing their work on the hypothesis that students who are in real contact with problems that are relevant to them wish to learn, want to grow, seek to discover, endeavor to master, desire to create, move toward self-discipline. The teacher is attempting to develop a quality of climate in the classroom and a quality of personal relationship with students that will permit these natural tendencies to come to their fruition.

LIVING THE UNCERTAINTY OF DISCOVERY

I believe it should be said that this basically confident view of the human being and the attitudes toward students that I have described do not appear suddenly, in some miraculous manner, in the facilitator of learning. Instead, they come about through taking risks, through *acting* on tentative hypotheses. This is most obvious in the chapter describing Miss Shiel's work, where, acting on hypotheses of which she is unsure, risking herself uncertainly in new ways of relating to her students, she finds these new views confirmed by what happens in her class. The same is definitely true of Mrs. Swenson. I am sure the others went through the same type of uncertainty. As for me, I can only state that I started my career with the firm view that individuals must be manipulated for their own good; I only came to the attitudes I have described and the trust in the individual that is implicit in them because I found that these attitudes were so much more potent in producing learning and constructive change. Hence, I believe that it is only by risking herself in these new ways that the teacher can *discover*, for herself, whether or not they are effective, whether or not they are for her.

I will then draw a conclusion, based on the experiences of the several facilitators and their students that have been included up to this point. When a facilitator creates, even to a modest degree, a classroom climate character- ized by all that she can achieve of realness, prizing, and empathy; when she trusts the constructive tendency of the individual and the group; then she discovers that she has inaugurated an educational revolution. Learning of a different quality, proceeding at a different pace, with a greater degree of pervasiveness, occurs. Feelings—positive, negative, confused—become a part of the classroom experience. Learning becomes life and a very vital life at that. The student is on the way, sometimes excitedly, sometimes reluctantly, to becoming a learning, changing being.

THE EVIDENCE

The research evidence for the statements in the last paragraph is now very convincing indeed. It has been most interesting to watch that evidence accumulate to a point where it seems irrefutable.

First, in the 1960s, several studies in psychotherapy and in education led to some tentative conclusions. Let me summarize them briefly, without presenting the methods used. (These can be learned from consulting the references given.)

When clients in therapy perceived their therapists as rating high in genuineness, prizing and emphatic understanding, self-learning and thera- peutic change were facilitated. The significance of these therapist attitudes was supported in a classic research by Barrett-Lennard (6).

Another study focused on teachers. Some teachers see their urgent prob- lems as "Helping children think for themselves and be independent"; "Get- ting students to participate"; etc. These teachers were regarded as the "positively oriented" group. Other teachers saw their urgent problems as "Getting students to listen"; "Trying to teach children who don't even have the ability to learn"; etc. These were termed the negatively oriented group. It was found that their students perceived the first group as exhibiting far more of empathy, prizing, and realness than the second group. The first group showed a high degree of facilitative attitudes, the second did not (8).

An interesting study by Schmuck (12) showed that when teachers are empathically understanding, their students tend to like each other better. In an understanding classroom climate, every student tends to feel liked by all the others, has a more positive attitude toward self, and a positive attitude toward school. This ripple aspect of the teacher's attitude is provocative and significant. To extend an empathic understanding to students has effects that go on and on.

The foregoing are samples of the many small studies that began to pile up. But it could still be asked, does the student actually *learn* more when these attitudes are present? Back in 1965 David Aspy (4) did a careful study of six classes of third-graders. He found that in the three classes where the teacher's facilitative attitudes were highest, the pupils showed a significantly greater gain in their reading achievement than in those classes with a lesser degree of these qualities.

Aspy and a colleague, Flora Roebuck, later enlarged this research into a program that extended for more than a decade. The overwhelming evidence that they accumulated is presented in a later section, "What Are the Facts?" Their study makes it very clear that the attitudinal climate of the classroom, as created by the teacher, is a major factor in promoting or inhibiting learning.

EVIDENCE FROM STUDENTS

Certainly before the research evidence was in, students were making it clear by their reactions to student-centered or person-centered classrooms that an educational revolution was underway. This kind of evidence persists to the present day.

The most striking learnings of students exposed to such a climate are by no means restricted to greater achievement in the three R's. The significant learnings are the more personal ones—independence, self-initiated and responsible learning, release of creativity, a tendency to become more of a person. I can only illustrate this by picking, almost at random, statements from students whose teachers have endeavored to create a climate of trust, of prizing, of realness, of understanding, and above all, of freedom.

Again I must quote from Sylvia Ashton-Warner one of the central effects of such a climate. ". . . The drive is no longer the teacher's, but the childrens' own . . . the teacher is at last with the stream and not against it, the stream of childrens' inexorable creativeness" (3, p. 93).

If you need verification of this, here is one of a number of statements made by students in a course on poetry led (not taught) by Dr. Samuel Moon.

> In retrospect, I find that I have actually enjoyed this course, both as a class and as an experiment, although it had me quite unsettled at times. This, in itself, made the course worthwhile since the majority of my courses this semester merely had me bored with them and the whole process of "higher education." Quite aside from anything else, due mostly to this course, I found myself devoting more time to writing poetry than to writing short stories, which temporarily interfered with my writing class.
>
> . . . I should like to point out one very definite thing which I have gained from the course; this is an increased readiness on my part to listen to and to seriously consider the opinions of my fellow students. In view of my past attitude, this alone makes the course valuable. I suppose the real result of any course can be expressed in answer to the question, "Would you take it over again?" My answer would be an unqualified "Yes." (9, p. 227)

I should like to add to this several comments from Dr. Bull's sophomore students in a class in adolescent psychology. The first two are midsemester comments.

> This course is proving to be a vital and profound experience for me. . . . This unique learning situation is giving me a whole new conception of just what learning is. . . . I am experiencing a real growth in this atmosphere of constructive freedom . . . the whole experience is challenging.

*   *   *

> I feel that the course had been of great value to me. . . . I'm glad to have had this experience because it has made me think. . . . I've never been so personally involved with a course before, especially *outside* the classroom. It has been frustrating, rewarding, enjoyable, and tiring!

The other comments are from the end of the course:

> . . . This course is not ending with the close of the semester for me, but continuing. . . . I don't know of any greater benefit which can be gained from a course than this desire for further knowledge.

*   *   *

> . . . I feel as though this type of class situation has stimulated me more in making me realize where my responsibilities lie, especially as far as doing required work on my own. I no longer feel as though a test date is the criterion for reading a book. I feel as though my future work will be done for what *I* will get out of it, not just for a test mark.

*   *   *

> I think that now I am acutely aware of the breakdown in communications that does exist in our society from seeing what happened in our class. . . . I've grown immensely. I know that I am a different person than I was when I came into that class. . . . It has done a great deal in helping me understand myself better . . . thank you for contributing to my growth.

*   *   *

> My idea of education has been to gain information from the teacher by attending lectures. The emphasis and focus were on the teacher. . . . One of the biggest changes that I experienced in this class was my outlook on education. Learning is something more than a grade on a report card. No one can measure what you have learned because it's a personal thing. I was very confused between learning and memorization. I could memorize very well, but I doubt if I ever learned as much as I could have. I believe my attitude toward learning has changed from a grade-centered outlook to a more personal one.

If you wish to know what this type of course seems like to a sixth grader, let me give you a sampling of the reactions of Miss Shiel's youngsters, misspellings and all.

> I feel that I am learning self ablity [*sic*]. I am learning not only school work but I am learning that you can learn on your own as well as someone can teach you.

*   *   *

I like this plan because there is a lot of freedom. I also learn more this way than the other way you don't have to wate [*sic*] for others you can go at your own speed rate it also takes a lot of responsibility. (13)

Or let me take two more, from Dr. Appell's graduate class:

. . . I have been thinking about what happened through this experience. The only conclusion I come to is that if I try to measure what is going on, or what I was at the beginning, I have got to know what I was when I started—and I don't . . . so many things I did and feel are just lost . . . scrambled up inside. . . . They don't seem to come out in a nice little pattern or organization I can say or write. . . . There are so many things left unsaid. I know I have only scratched the surface, I guess. I can feel so many things almost ready to come out . . . maybe that's enough. *It seems all kinds of things have so much more meaning now than ever before.* . . . This experience has had meaning, has done things to me and I am not sure how much or how far just yet. I think I am going to be a better me in the fall. *That's one thing I think I am sure of.* (2, pp. 143–48)

*   *   *

. . . You follow no plan, yet I'm learning. Since the term began I seem to feel more alive, more real to myself. I enjoy being alone as well as with other people. My relationships with children and other adults are becoming more emotional and involved. Eating an orange last week, I peeled the skin off each separate orange section and liked it better with the transparent shell off. It was juicier and fresher tasting that way. I began to think, that's how I feel sometimes, without a transparent wall around me, really communicating my feelings. I feel that I'm growing, how much, I don't know. I'm thinking, considering, pondering and learning. (1)

I can't read these student statements—sixth grade, college, graduate level—without being deeply moved. Here are teachers, risking themselves, *being* themselves, *trusting* their students, adventuring into the existential unknown, taking the subjective leap. And what happens? Exciting, incredible *human* events. You can sense persons being created, learnings being initiated, future citizens rising to meet the challenge of unknown worlds. If only one teacher out of one hundred dared to risk, dared to be, dared to trust, dared to understand, we would have an infusion of a living spirit into education that would, in my estimation, be priceless.

The Effect Upon the Instructor

Let me turn to another dimension that excites me. I have spoken of the effect upon the *student* of a climate that encourages significant, self-reliant, personal learning. But I have said nothing about the reciprocal effect upon the instructor. When she has been the agent for the release of such self-initiated learning, the faculty member finds herself changed as well as her students. One such says:

To say that I am overwhelmed by what happened only faintly reflects my feelings. I have taught for many years but I have never experienced any-thing remotely resembling what occurred. I, for my part, never found in a classroom so much of the whole person coming forth, so deeply involved, so deeply stirred. Further, I question if in the traditional setup, with its emphasis on subject matter, examinations, grades, there is, or there can be a place for the "becoming" person with his deep and manifold needs as he struggles to fulfill himself. But this is going far afield. I can only report to you what happened and to say that I am grateful and that I am also humbled by the experience. I would like you to know this for it has enriched my life and being. (11, p. 313)

Another faculty member reports as follows:

Rogers has said that relationships conducted on these assumptions mean "turning present day education upside down." I have found this to be true as I have tried to implement this way of living with students. The experi-ences I have had have plunged me into relationships which have been significant and challenging and beyond compare for me. They have inspired me and stimulated me and left me at times shaken and awed with their consequences for both me and the students. They have led me to the fact of what I can only call . . . the tragedy of education in our time—student after student who reports this to be his first experience with total trust, with freedom to be and to move in ways most consistent for the enhance-ment and maintenance of the core of dignity which somehow has survived humiliation, distortion, and corrosive cynicism. (1)

Too Idealistic?

Some readers may feel that the whole approach of this chapter—the belief that teachers can relate as persons to their students—is hopelessly unrealistic and idealistic. They may see that in essence it is encouraging both teachers and students to be creative in their relationship to each other and in their relationship to subject matter, and feel that such a goal is quite impos-sible. They are not alone in this. I have heard scientists at leading schools of science and scholars in leading universities, arguing that it is absurd to try to encourage all students to be creative—we need hosts of mediocre technicians and workers, and if a few creative scientists and artists and leaders emerge, that will be enough. That may be enough for them. It may be enough to suit you. I want to go on record as saying it is *not* enough to suit me. When I realize the incredible potential in the ordinary student, I want to try to release it. We are working hard to release the incredible energy in the atom and the nucleus of the atom. If we do not devote equal energy—yes, and equal money—to the release of the potential of the individual person then the enormous discrepancy between our level of physical energy resources and human energy resources will doom us to a deserved and universal destruction.

I'm sorry I can't be coolly scientific about this. The issue is too urgent. I can only be passionate in my statement that people count, that interpersonal relationships *are* important, that we know something about releasing human potential, that we could learn much more, and that unless we give strong positive attention to the human interpersonal side of our educational dilemma, our civilization is on its way down the drain. Better courses, better curricula, better coverage, better teaching machines will never resolve our dilemma in a basic way. Only persons acting like persons in their relationships with their students can even begin to make a dent on this most urgent problem of modern education.

Summary

Let me try to state, somewhat more calmly and soberly, what I have said with such feeling and passion.

I have said that it is most unfortunate that educators and the public think about, and focus on, *teaching*. It leads them into a host of questions that are either irrelevant or absurd so far as real education is concerned.

I have said that if we focused on the facilitation of *learning*—how, why, and when the student learns, and how learning seems and feels from the inside—we might be on a much more profitable track.

I have said that we have some knowledge, and could gain more, about the conditions that facilitate learning, and that one of the most important of these conditions is the attitudinal quality of the interpersonal relationship between facilitator and learner.

Those attitudes that appear effective in promoting learning can be described. First of all is a transparent realness in the facilitator, a willingness to be a person, to be and live the feelings and thoughts of the moment. When this realness includes a prizing, a caring, a trust and respect for the learner, the climate for learning is enhanced. When it includes a sensitive and accurate empathic listening, then indeed a freeing climate, stimulative of self-initiated learning and growth, exists. The student is *trusted* to develop.

I have tried to make plain that individuals who hold such attitudes, and are bold enough to act on them, do not simply modify classroom methods—they revolutionize them. They perform almost none of the functions of teachers. It is no longer accurate to call them *teachers*. They are catalyzers, facilitators, giving freedom and life and the opportunity to learn, to students.

I have brought in the cumulating research evidence that suggests that individuals who hold such attitudes are regarded as effective in the classroom; that the problems that concern them have to do with the release of potential, not the deficiencies of their students; that they seem to create classroom situations in which there are not admired children and disliked children, but in which affection and liking are a part of the life of every child; that in classrooms approaching such a psychological climate, children learn more of the conventional subjects.

But I have intentionally gone beyond the empirical findings to try to take you into the inner life of the student—elementary, college, and graduate—who is fortunate enough to live and learn in such an interpersonal relationship with a facilitator, in order to let you see what learning feels like when it is free, self-initiated and spontaneous. I have tried to indicate how it even changes the student-student relationship—making it more aware, more caring, more sensitive, as well as increasing the self-related learning of significant material. I have spoken of the change it brings about in the faculty member.

Throughout, I have tried to indicate that if we are to have citizens who can live constructively in this kaleidoscopically changing world, we can *only* have them if we are willing for them to become self-starting, self-initiating learners. Finally, it has been my purpose to show that this kind of learner develops best, so far as we now know, in a growth-promoting, facilitative relationship with a *person*.

REFERENCES

1. Appell, Morey L. "Selected Student Reactions to Student-centered Courses." Unpublished manuscript, Indiana State University, 1959.
2. Appell, Morey L. "Self-understanding for the Guidance Counselor." *Personnel & Guidance Journal*, October 1963, pp. 143–48.
3. Ashton-Warner, Sylvia. *Teacher.* New York: Simon and Schuster, 1963.
4. Aspy, David N. "A Study of Three Facilitative Conditions and Their Relationship to the Achievement of Third Grade Students." Unpublished Ph.D. dissertation, University of Kentucky, 1965.
5. Axline, Virginia M. "Morale on the School Front." *Journal of Educational Research*, 1944, 521–33.
6. Barrett-Lennard, G. T. "Dimensions of Therapist Response as Causal Factors in Therapeutic Change." *Psychological Monographs*, 76 (Whole No. 562), 1962.
7. Bull, Patricia. "Student Reactions, Fall, 1965." Unpublished manuscript, New York State University College, 1966.
8. Emmerling, F. C. "A Study of the Relationships Between Personality Characteristics of Classroom Teachers and Pupil Perceptions." Unpublished Ph.D. dissertation, Auburn University, Auburn, Alabama, 1961.
9. Moon, Samuel F. "Teaching the Self." *Improving College and University Teaching, 14* (Autumn 1966):213–29.
10. Rogers, Carl R. "The Interpersonal Relationship in the Facilitation of Learning." In *Humanizing Education,* edited by R. Leeper, pp. 1–18. Washington, D.C.: NEA, 1967. Copyright by Association for Supervision and Curriculum Development.
11. Rogers, Carl R. *On Becoming a Person.* Boston: Houghton Mifflin, 1961, p. 313.
12. Schmuck, R. "Some Aspects of Classroom Social Climate." *Psychology in the Schools 3* (1966): 59–65; and "Some Relationships of Peer Liking Patterns in the Classroom to Pupil Attitudes and Achievements." *The School Review 71* (1963): 337–59.
13. Shiel, Barbara J. "Evaluation: A Self-directed Curriculum, 1965." Unpublished manuscript, n.p. 1966.

Becoming a Facilitator

✣

A Magic Wand

*N*ot long ago, a teacher asked me, "What changes would you like to see in education?" I answered the question as best I could at the time, but it stayed with me. Suppose I had a magic wand that could produce only one change in our educational systems. What would that change be?

I finally decided that my imaginary wand, with one sweep, would cause every teacher at every level to forget that he or she is a teacher. You would all develop a complete amnesia for the teaching skills you have painstakingly acquired over the years. You would find that you were absolutely unable to teach.

Instead, you would find yourself holding the attitudes and possessed of the skills of a *facilitator of learning*—genuineness, prizing, and empathy. Why would I be so cruel as to rob teachers of their precious skills? It is because I feel that our educational institutions are in a desperate state; and that unless our schools can become exciting, fun-filled centers of learning, they are quite possibly doomed.

You may be thinking that "facilitator of learning" is just a fancy name for a teacher and that nothing at all would be changed. If so, you are mistaken. There is *no* resemblance between the traditional function of teaching and the function of the facilitator of learning.

The traditional teacher—the *good* traditional teacher—asks her or himself questions of this sort: "What do I think would be good for a student to learn at this particular age and level of competence? How can I plan a proper

135

curriculum for this student? How can I inculcate motivation to learn this curriculum? How can I instruct in such a way that he or she will gain the knowledge that should be gained? How can I best set an examination to see whether this knowledge has actually been taken in?"

On the other hand, the facilitator of learning asks questions such as these, not of self, but of the *students:* "What do you want to learn? What things puzzle you? What are you curious about? What issues concern you? What problems do you wish you could solve?" When he or she has the answers to these questions, further questions follow. "Now how can I help him or her find the resources—the people, the experiences, the learning facilities, the books, the knowledge in myself—which will help them learn in ways that will provide answers to the things that concern them, the things they are eager to learn?" And, then later, "How can I help them evaluate their own progress and set future learning goals based on this self-evaluation?"

The attitudes of the teacher and the facilitator are also at opposite poles. Traditional teaching, no matter how disguised, is based essentially on the mug-and-jug theory. The teacher asks himself, "How can I make the mug hold still while I fill it from the jug with these facts which the curriculum planners and I regard as valuable?" The attitude of the facilitator has almost entirely to do with climate, "How can I create a psychological climate in which the child will feel free to be curious, will feel free to make mistakes, will feel free to learn from the environment, from fellow students, from me, from experience? How can I help him recapture the excitement of learning that was natural in infancy?"

Once this process of facilitation of wanted learning was underway, a school would become for the child, "My school." He or she would feel a living, vital part of a very satisfying process. Astonished adults would begin to hear children say, "I can't wait to get to school today." "For the first time in my life I'm finding out about the things *I* want to know." "Hey, drop that brick! Don't you break a window in *my* school!"

Beautifully, the same phrases would be used by the retarded child, the gifted child, the urban child, the underprivileged child. This is because every student would be working on problems of real concern and interest, at the level at which he or she could grasp the problem and find a useful solution. Each would have a continuing experience of success.

Some educators believe that such individualized learning is completely impractical because it would involve an enormous increase in the number of teachers. Nothing could be further from the truth. For one thing, when children are eager to learn, they follow up their own leads and engage in a great deal of independent study on their own. There is also a great saving of the teacher's time because problems of discipline or control drop tremendously. Finally, the freedom of interaction that grows out of the climate I have so briefly described makes it possible to use a great untapped resource—the ability of one child to help another in his learning. For John to hear, "John, Ralph is having trouble carrying out the long division that he needs to solve his problem. I wonder if you could help him?" is a marvelous experience for both John and Ralph. It is even more marvelous for the two boys to work together, helping each other learn, *without* being asked! John *really* learns long division when he helps another learner understand. Ralph can accept the help and learn because he is not shown up as being stupid, either in public or on a report card.

It is a risky thing for a person to become a facilitator of learning rather than a teacher. It means uncertainties, difficulties, setbacks—and also exciting human adventure, as students begin to blossom. One teacher who took this risk told me that one of her greatest surprises was that she had more time to spend with each child, not less, when she set each child free to learn.

I cannot stress too strongly how much I wish that someone could wave that magic wand and change teaching to facilitation. I deeply believe that traditional teaching is an almost completely futile, wasteful, overrated function in today's changing world. It is successful mostly in giving children who can't grasp the material, a sense of failure. It also succeeds in persuading students to drop out when they realize that the material taught is almost completely irrelevant to their lives. No one should ever be trying to learn something for which one sees no relevance. No child should ever experience the sense of failure imposed by our grading system, by criticism and ridicule from teachers and others, by rejection when he or she is slow to comprehend. The sense of failure experienced when one tries something one wants to achieve that is actually too difficult is a healthy one that drives him or her to further learning. It is a very different thing from a person-imposed failure, which must devalue him or her as a person.

What Is the Way?

If a teacher is desirous of giving students a freedom to learn or becoming a facilitator, how then can this be achieved?

I cannot answer for anyone else as there are many ways by which one may change. So I am simply going to speak personally and raise the questions that I would ask myself if I were given responsibility for the learnings of a group of children. I have tried to think about what I would ask myself, the things I would try to learn, the things I might try to do. How would I meet the challenge posed by such a group?

What Is It Like?

I think the first question I would raise is: What is it like to be a child who is learning something significant? I believe the most meaningful answer I can give is to speak from my own experience.

I was a very good boy in elementary and high school. I got good grades. Frequently I annoyed my teachers by being clever enough to get around the rules they had set up, but I was not openly defiant. I was a very solitary boy with few friends, isolated from others by a very strictly religious home. My family moved from a suburban setting to a large farm with acres of woodland when I was thirteen. At that time the Gene Stratton-Porter books were popular, which involved a wilderness setting and made much of the great night-flying moths.

Shortly after we moved to the farm, I found a pair of luna moths—great pale green wings with purple trimmings—on the trunk of an oak tree. I can still see the six-inch spread of shimmering green with its iridescent lavender spots, bright against the shaggy black bark. I was enthralled. I captured them, kept them, and the female laid hundreds of eggs. I got a book on moths. I fed the baby caterpillars. Though I had many failures with this first brood, I captured other moths and gradually learned to keep and sustain the caterpillars through their whole series of life changes: the frequent molting of their skins, the final spinning of their cocoons, the long wait until the next spring when the moths emerged. To see come out of its cocoon a moth with wings no bigger than a thumbnail and within an hour or two to develop a five to seven-inch wingspread was fantastic. But most of the time it was hard work; finding fresh leaves every day selected from the right varieties of trees, emptying the boxes, sprinkling the cocoons during the winter to keep them from drying out. It was, in short, a large project. But by age fifteen or sixteen, I was an authority on such moths. I knew probably twenty or more different varieties, their habits, their food, and those moths that ate no food during their lifespan, only during their period as caterpillars. I could identify the larvae by species. I could spot the big three- to four-inch caterpillars easily. I never took a long walk without finding at least one caterpillar or cocoon.

But it interests me as I look back on it that to the best of my recollection I never told any teacher and only a very few fellow students of this interest of mine. This consuming project wasn't in any way a part of my *education.* Education was what went on in school. A teacher wouldn't be interested. Besides, I would have so much to explain to her or him when after all they were supposed to teach me. I had one or two good teachers whom I liked during this period, but this was a personal project, not the thing you share with a teacher. So here was an enterprise at least two years in length, scholarly, well researched, requiring painstaking work and much self-discipline, wide knowledge and practical skills. But to my mind it was, of course, *not* a part of my education. So that is what real learning was like for one boy.

I am sure that significant learning is often very different—for girls, for the urban child, for the physically handicapped child. But keeping this aspect of my own childhood learning in mind, I would try very hard to find out what it is like to be a child who is learning. I would try to get inside the child's world to see what had significance for him. I would try to make school at least a friendly home for such meaningful learning wherever it might be occurring in the child's life.

Can I Risk Myself in Relationship?

A second cluster of questions I would ask myself would run along these lines: Do I dare to let myself deal with this boy or girl as a person, as someone I respect? Do I dare reveal myself to him and let him reveal himself to me?

Do I dare to recognize that he may know more than I do in certain areas—or may in general be more gifted than I?

Answering these questions involves two aspects. One is the question of risk. Do I dare to take the risk of giving affirmative answers to the queries I have raised? The second aspect is the question of how this kind of relationship can come about between the student and myself.

I believe that the answers may lie in some kind of intensive group experience, a so-called communications group, human relations group, encounter group, or whatever. In this kind of personal group it is easier to take the risk because the group provides the sort of psychological climate in which relationships build.

I am reminded of a very moving film: *Because That's My Way* (4), in which a teacher, a narcotics agent, and a convicted drug addict were participants. At the conclusion of this filmed group, the high school drug addict said with wonderment in his voice, "I've found that a teacher, a cop, and a drug addict are all human beings. I wouldn't have believed it!" He had never found such relationships with teachers in school.

We have found much the same thing in our conferences on humanizing medical education. Here one of the outstanding learnings in the intensive groups is that of the physicians-in-training discovering that their department chairmen, medical school deans, and faculty members are human beings, persons like themselves. They regard this as incredible. We had the same experience in dealing with the Immaculate Heart school system at both the high school and college levels: students and teachers were able to relate as persons, not as roles. It was a totally new experience on both sides.

Although I have seen the highly positive results of an open and personal relationship between learner and facilitator, this does not mean that it would be easy for me to achieve it in every class or with every student. I know from experience that to show myself as I am—imperfect and at times admittedly defensive—seems to be a personal risk. And yet I know that if the relationship between myself and my students were truly a relationship among persons, much would be gained. If I were willing to admit that some students surpass me in knowledge, some in insight, some in perceptiveness in human relationships, then I could step off the "teacher pedestal" and become a facilitative learner among learners.

What Are the Students' Interests?

Another question I would ask myself would be, "What are the interests, goals, aims, purposes, passions of these students?" I would want to ask the question not only collectively, but individually. What are the things that excite them, and how can I find out?

I may be overconfident, but I think the answer to this question is an easy one. If I genuinely wish to discover a student's interest, I can do so. It might be by creating a climate in which it is natural for interests to emerge. Although young people have been greatly deadened by their school experience they do come to life in a healthy psychological atmosphere and are more than willing to share their desires.

It impresses me as I think back that I can recall no teacher who ever asked me what my interests were. That seems an amazing statement, but I believe it is a true one. Had a teacher *asked*, I would have told her about wild flowers and woodland animals and the night-flying moths. I might even have mentioned the poetry I was trying to write or my interest in religion, but no one asked.

Although more than sixty years have gone by, I remember one question a teacher penciled in the margin of a freshman theme. I had written, I believe, about something I had done with my dog. Alongside the description of some action I had taken, the teacher wrote, "Why, Carl?" I have always remembered this marginal note, but it is only in recent years that I realize the reason for the memory. It stands out because here was a teacher who seemed to have a real personal interest in knowing why I, Carl, had done something. I have forgotten all the other wise comments written on my themes, but this one I remember. To me it shows how rarely it comes across to a student that a teacher really wants to know some of the motives and interests that make the student tick. So if I were a teacher, I would like very much to make it possible for students to tell me just these things.

How Can I Unleash the Inquiring Mind?

A fourth question I would ask myself is, "How can I preserve and unleash curiosity?" There is evidence to show that as children go through our public school system they become less inquiring, less curious. It is one of the worst indictments I know. The provost of the California Institute of Technology has told me that if he could have only one criterion for selecting students it would be the degree to which they show curiosity. Yet it seems that we do everything possible to kill, in our students, this inquisitiveness, this wide-ranging, searching wonder about the world and its inhabitants.

A professor whom I know in a California university is finding his way of preserving the zest of inquiry. He wrote a letter to me in which he said, "I want to tell you about some of the outcomes your *Freedom to Learn* has had for me and my students . . ." (5). He told me how he decided to adapt each of his psychology courses to make them freer:

> I was careful to explain to the students the assumptions underlying the approach we were going to try. I further asked them to consider seriously whether or not they wanted to take part in such an "experiment." (My courses are elective. . . .) No one decided to drop out. We—the class and I—created the course as we went along. (There were sixty in the class.) It was the most *exciting* classroom experience I have ever had, Carl! And, as it turned out, the students were equally excited. They turned in some of the best work . . . that I have ever seen from undergraduates. Their excitement was contagious. I found out later, from several different sources, that

students in this course were constantly being asked by roommates, by peers in the cafeteria, etc., "What did you do in class today?" "How is the course going?" I had a constant stream of students requesting to visit the class.

Perhaps the most meaningful evaluations for me came from those students who said that they had not learned as much as they could have, *but that this was their own fault:* they took the responsibility for it. There is so much more to tell, Carl, but I don't want to belabor the point. What I did want is that you know how enthusiastically these students responded to the opportunity to learn—in ways that were important for *them.* And how freeing it was for me as a fellow-learner.

Resources

Another question I would be asking myself is, "How can I imaginatively provide resources for learning—resources that are both physically and psychologically available?"

I believe that a good facilitator of learning should spend the majority of preparation time in making resources available to the young people with whom he or she works. To a large extent with all children, but outstandingly with bright children, it is not *necessary* to *teach* them, but they do need resources to feed their interests. It takes a great deal of imagination, thought, and work to provide such opportunities.

My son is a physician. Why? Because in a forward-looking school in the junior year of high school, each student was given a number of weeks and considerable help in trying to arrange a two-week apprenticeship. My son was able to obtain the consent of a physician who found himself challenged by the naive but often fundamental questions of a high school boy. He took Dave on hospital rounds and home visits, into the delivery room and the operating room. Dave was immersed in the practice of medicine. It enlarged his very tentative interest into a consuming one. Someone had been creative in thinking about resources for his learning. I wish I could be that ingenious.

Creativity

If I were a teacher, I hope that I would be asking myself questions like this: "Do I have the courage and the humility to nurture creative ideas in my students? Do I have the tolerance and humanity to accept the annoying, occasionally defiant, occasionally oddball questions of some of those who have creative ideas? Can I make a place for the creative person?"

I believe that in every teacher-education program there should be a course on "The Care and Feeding of Infant Ideas." Creative thoughts and actions are just like infants—unprepossessing, weak, easily knocked down. A new idea is always very inadequate compared to an established idea. Children are full of such wild, unusual thoughts and perceptions, but a great many of them are trampled in the routine of school life.

Then, too, as the work of Getzels and Jackson (3) showed, there is a difference between those students who are bright and those who are both bright and creative. The latter tended to be more angular in their personalities, less predictable, more troublesome. Can I permit such students to be—to live and find nourishment in my classroom? Certainly education—whether elementary, college, or professional training—does not have a good record in this respect. So Thomas Edison was regarded as dull and stupid. Aviation only came about because two bicycle mechanics were so ignorant of expert knowledge that they tried out the wild and foolish idea of making a heavier-than-air machine fly. The educated professionals would not have wasted their time on such nonsense.

I would hope that perhaps in my classroom I could create an atmosphere of a kind often greatly feared by educators, of mutual respect and mutual freedom of expression. That, I think, might permit the creative individual to write poetry, paint pictures, produce inventions, try out new ventures, without fear of being squashed. I would like to be able to do that.

Is There Room for the Soma?

Perhaps a final question would be, "Can I help the student develop a feeling life as well as a cognitive life? Can I help him or her to become what Thomas Hanna calls a *soma*—body *and* mind, feelings *and* intellect?" I think we are well aware of the fact that one of the tragedies of modern education is that only cognitive learning is regarded as important.

I see David Halberstam's book, *The Best and the Brightest,* as the epitome of that tragedy. Those men who surrounded Kennedy and Johnson were all gifted, talented people. As Halberstam says, "If those years had any central theme, if there was anything that bound these people, it was the belief that sheer intelligence and rationality could answer and solve anything." Certainly they learned that viewpoint in school. So this complete reliance on the cognitive and the intellectual caused this brilliant group to lead us little by little into the incredible quagmire of the Vietnam war. The computers omitted from their calculations the feelings, the emotional commitment, of little people in black pajamas who had little equipment and no air force, but who were fighting for something they believed in. This omission proved fatal. The human factor was not put into the computers because "the best and the brightest" had no place in their computations for the feeling life, the emotional life of individuals. I would hope very much that the learning that took place in my classroom might be a learning by the whole person—something difficult to achieve, but highly rewarding in its end product.

An Example

You may well ask if there are schools in which the teachers could give generally positive answers to the questions I have raised. There are many such schools, but one is carefully described by Jerome Freiberg (2). It is a high school in Houston, Texas. We may visit it through Freiberg's words. He acknowledges his indebtedness to superintendent of schools, Billy Reagan, and the principal, Norma Lowder, for sharing the successes of this innovative school.

High School for the Performing and Visual Arts

Upon approaching its address on Austin Street near downtown Houston, one first sees a proud but weathered edifice with "Temple Beth Israel" carved into the stones above the front entrance. Since 1971 this renovated synagogue has served as the home for the High School for the Performing and Visual Arts of the Houston Independent School District. In the intervening years, eight temporary buildings have been wheeled onto the grounds to accommodate the expanding enrollment and space is often borrowed from buildings across the street. The campus of renovated and temporary buildings houses 500 students drawn from every part of the city and from the surrounding suburban areas which lack such a facility, from every ethnic group, from every lifestyle and from every socio-economic level. Here they spend three hours per day in their art areas (dance, drama, instrumental music, vocal music, media arts or the visual arts) and the remaining four hours in academics or electives.

The opening of HSPVA represented the first attempt by any public school in the nation to correlate concentrated training in the arts with the conventional academic high school curriculum. It was the first of Houston's alternative schools and has served as the model for the magnet schools which followed. It has a full-time staff of 34, several additional part-time certified teachers, but the principal, Norma Lowder, points out that each year, as many as 40 or 50 professionals who may not have certification as teachers but who have a wealth of expertise to share, are invited to the campus to teach special classes, to conduct workshops, to present lectures and demonstrations.

Upon entering the campus the visitor is drawn into its climate of informal camaraderie. There is neither the repressed silence of a custodial atmosphere nor the noise of the disengaged and idle. Instead, there is the busy hum of activity—earnest discussion, purposeful movement.

"I look for teachers who are not rigid; who are flexible enough to recognize that geometry class may be a total loss today because the orchestra is playing in Jones Hall tonight; then, because geometry suffered through this, a teacher who will say 'You may have the kids for some of my time today to work on geometry,'" explains Mrs. Lowder. Close friendships among faculty members develop from this sense of community and mutual help, and the spin-offs from this include a high level of job satisfaction and a low rate of turnover for HSPVA teachers, a condition which, along with the frequent occasions for individualized instruction and tutorial help offered to students by the faculty members, enhances the quality of teacher-student relationships as well.

Interestingly, and consistent with findings reported later in this book, young people consistently perform among the highest in the district academically, producing a high proportion of merit scholars.

In 1979, of the thirty nationally selected presidential scholars, three came from HSPVA. Numerous awards line the walls of the school's offices. Because the student body is drawn from a wide area, parents are seldom physically present at the school. For students whose ethnic ties bind their families closely to their neighborhoods, coming to HSPVA represents perhaps their first venturing beyond their cultural boundaries. Parental support is strong, however, and the community takes pride in the school and often requests performances from the student groups.

We asked a group of June, 1980, graduates how they felt about their experiences at the HSPVA. The following are representative responses from three graduates:

SUSAN: HSPVA let me be myself and let me grow pretty much on my own. I was never forced into a mold, but was allowed to be an individual, allowed to do my artwork the way I felt it should be done.

JOHN: In order to be very real you have to know all the facets of yourself and that's a process that takes a long time. Once I allowed that to sink in it just made me feel that much easier about learning. I can learn now. I can take things, and I can actually see my development. It is a very confident feeling.

SANDRA: Attending school at HSPVA can be described in one word: it is an EXPERIENCE. Although this experience may be different for each individual student, the basic foundation of creativity, growth and learning is there for everyone.

                  From the very first day a student walks on campus, he is exposed to creativity. Creativity at HSPVA is one thing that is never lacking—there seems to be a constant flow of it, not only *within* each art area, but also *between* them. One art area is always serving as inspiration for another. Students at HSPVA are not *afraid* of their creativity; instead, they are proud of it, and are free to express it in many ways, both in their individual art areas and in their academic subjects as well.

                  As a result of this creative freedom, the HSPVA student has the opportunity to grow to his highest potential in anything he does. He is exposed to many different philosophies and ideas, and thus is provided a broad base from which to grow and form his own beliefs.

                  Much of this growth results from the student being given the opportunity to be around people involved in *all* the arts, and thus learning many different ways of looking at things. Because of this exposure, he becomes open to many different kinds of expression, and

not only does he learn about different areas of the a
but he also learns a great deal about life and about
himself as well.

HSPVA is definitely a very exciting, special place to
be.

It is a compelling experience to watch these students. Here is a setting in
which their sense of promise and self-worth can flower. It is clearly a school
in which the teachers have become facilitators of learning.

Comments

I am fascinated by the fact that these students make no particular mention of their teachers, but simply of the psychological climate in which they
were enveloped. The rewards of an excellent facilitator are different from the
rewards of a brilliant teacher. One study showed that in later years people
could quite vividly remember the brilliant teachers they had had, but were
quite unable to remember what they had learned in those classes. They
could, however, remember in detail every learning experience they had
themselves initiated. The students just quoted will never forget the zest for
creative learning they developed at this high school.

I often think the best facilitator was described by the Chinese philosopher Lao-Tse, 2500 years ago. I will close this chapter with that description.

A leader is best
When people barely know he exists,
Not so good when people obey and acclaim him,
Worst when they despise him.
But of a good leader, who talks little,
When his work is done, his aim fulfilled,
They will all say "We did this ourselves." (1)

REFERENCES

1. Bynner, W. *From the Way of Life According to Lao-Tse.* New York: Capricorn
   Books, 1962. (Translation.)
2. Freiberg, Jerome. "High School for the Performing and Visual Arts." Unpublished
   manuscript, University of Houston, 1980.
3. Getzels, J., and Jackson, P. *Creativity and Intelligence.* New York: Wiley & Sons,
   1962.
4. McGaw, W. H., Rogers, C. R., and Rose, A. *Because That's My Way* (film).
   Lincoln, Nebraska: Great Plains TV Library, 1971.
5. Rock, L. Personal correspondence, 1972.

Methods of Building
Freedom

❧

"Could I do this in my classroom?" This question, it seems to me, would be raised by the teacher who has been favorably impressed by the preceding chapters. In this chapter, I have pointed to some of the specific ways in which teachers have been able to provide opportunities for more self-reliant learning. I hope these ideas will give both reassurance and stimulation to the teacher who wishes to step into the chilly waters of classroom innovation.

*I*f you want to give your students a freedom to learn, how can you do it? We've reviewed those personal and subjective attitudes basic to the creation of such a climate. And there is no doubt that the teacher who is in the process of achieving these attitudes will develop modes of building freedom suited to his or her own style, one that grows out of free and direct interaction with students. Yes, you will undoubtedly develop a growing methodology of your own—always the best procedure.

Yet it is quite natural for those who are taking the risk of being creative to want to know what others have tried and what ways they have found to implement these personal attitudes in the classroom in such a way that students can perceive and use the freedom offered to them. It is the purpose of this chapter to set forth briefly a few of the approaches, methods, techniques that have been successfully used by teachers who are endeavoring to give a freedom to learn.

147

Building Upon Problems Perceived
as Real

It seems reasonably clear that for learning of the sort we are discussing, students must be confronted by issues that have meaning and relevance for them. In our culture, we try to insulate our students from any and all of the real problems of life, and this insulation constitutes a difficulty. It appears that if we desire to have students learn to be free and responsible individuals, then we must be willing for them to confront, to face problems.

It would seem wise for any teacher to try to draw out from students those problems or issues that are real for them and also relevant to the course at hand. Since, in general, students are so insulated from problems, it may be necessary to confront them with situations that will later become real problems to them. It is possible to set up circumstances that can involve students and confront each one with a problem that becomes very real.

Young human beings are intrinsically motivated to a high degree. Many elements of the environment constitute challenges for them. They are curious, eager to discover, eager to know, eager to solve problems. A sad part of most education is that by the time our children have spent a number of years in school, this intrinsic motivation is pretty well dampened. Yet the motivation is there, and it is our task as facilitators of learning to tap that motivation, to discover what challenges are real for young people, and to improve the opportunity for them to meet those challenges.

Providing Resources

Teachers concerned with the facilitation of learning rather than with the function of teaching organize their time and efforts very differently than do conventional teachers. Instead of spending great blocks of time organizing lesson plans and lectures, facilitative teachers concentrate on providing all kinds of resources that can give students experiential learning relevant to the students' needs. These teachers also concentrate on making such resources clearly available by thinking through and simplifying the practical and psychological steps the student must go through in order to use the resources. For example, it is one thing to say that a given book is available in the library. This means that the student may look it up in the catalog only to find that it is already on loan. Not every student will have the patience or interest to wait for the book to return. I have found that if I can make a shelf of books and reprints available for loan in the classroom, the amount of reading done and the resulting stimulation to use the library in pursuing individual needs grow by leaps and bounds.

In speaking of resources, I am thinking not only of the usual academic resources—books, articles, work space, laboratory room and equipment, tools, maps, films, recordings, and the like. I am also thinking of human resources—people who might contribute and interest students. Frequently, there are people in the community who might be brought in to illuminate certain problems with which the students are concerned. But clearly, the teacher is the most important resource. By making himself or herself as a person, his or her knowledge and experience clearly available to the students, help can be given without imposing. The facilitator can outline the particular competences he or she possesses, and the students can call for help in those areas.

We have examined some of the ways in which a teacher may thus make himself or herself available. Shiel made herself available for individual consultation, for students who were having difficulty with the tasks on which they were working. Swenson made herself available in ways too numerous to list. Levitan helped the students set up the "mini-courses" they desired, responded to their request that he give some lectures, made his own books available. Romey arranged it so that students could sit in on any course in the department. Sanford took the students on field trips. Without exception, all of the teachers who have presented their stories made themselves personally available in the class sessions.

Richard Dean, of the California Institute of Technology, has taught a course in higher mathematics in a very free fashion. He provided "feedback" sheets in which he tried to summarize the major problems discussed or resolved in each session (as well as the problems opened up and not resolved) for the use of the class. A student coming into any class meeting was supplied with a feedback sheet from the previous session; the information helped students refresh their minds on what the class had done. Later Dean stated that any student could volunteer to provide a feedback sheet also; in this way, both he and some of the students shared in summarizing the discussions. In addition, Dean or students frequently would add their own analysis of what had gone on or their own solution to issues and problems that had been raised.

If instead of the time now spent on planning for prescribed curricula, lectures, and examinations, we spent it instead on the imaginative provision of a multitude of resources for learning, we would come up with all kinds of new ways of surrounding students with a learning environment from which they could choose those elements that best met their needs.

Use of Contracts

One open-ended device that helps to give both security and responsibility within an atmosphere of freedom is the use of student contracts. There is no doubt that this also helps to assuage the uncertainties and insecurities the facilitator may be experiencing. We have seen how Shiel quite quickly made use of daily contracts with her students. Contracts allow students to set goals and to plan what they wish to do. Contracts provide a sort of transitional experience between complete freedom to learn whatever is of interest and learning that is relatively free, but that is within the limits of some institutional demand or course requirement.

Arthur Combs has used a type of contract for college and graduate students that has some interesting features. He explains at the beginning of the course that each student may obtain any grade he chooses. Students who desire to take a passing grade in the course and receive credits for it may certify that they have read a certain amount of assigned textbook material and then pass examinations covering the material. No stigma is attached to this decision. Students who want higher grades must plan for themselves, individually, work that would justify a B or an A grade. Once the work is completed, the student will receive the contracted grade. This removes any fear and apprehension from class sessions and makes genuinely free discussion possible. Students can differ with the professor without feeling that they may be endangering their grade. They can express what they really feel and think.

Contracts are also helpful in resolving doubts that may exist in the mind of the instructor or the student. If the teacher is dubious that students will be responsible learners and if some students have difficulty believing they can learn without being pushed, then time spent developing contracts will be very helpful to both. Indeed, a number of initial hours in the course may be given over to this process.

Using student contracts is one way to evaluate students based on a shared view of both quantity and quality. Traditionally, teachers have decided upon criteria for an A grade without including any input from the students. With the use of student contracts, the student has an opportunity to share in decisions about evaluation. Contracts can be used for providing activities, motivation, and reinforcement to help students achieve cognitive objectives. Contracts can be used in any subject matter or at any grade level. Like many classroom techniques, contracts should be recognized as an *aid* to learning and not the only method of teaching.

A SPECIFIC EXAMPLE

Since contracts are such a helpful bridge between conventional approaches and a classroom of greater freedom, a very specific description of how a contract may be used is presented here. This experience is contributed by Dr. Jerome Freiberg (1).

> An independent study contract was developed with a sixth grade student in a social studies class (see p. 152). Our particular course of study was African history, and this contract is related to the study of Africa. One day in class Cynthia asked, "How can people survive if Africa is hot and there's not enough food?" We sat down and discussed the assumptions made in her question—a) that Africa is hot; and b) that there was no food. (The assumptions developed by the student were very similar to hypotheses. There should only be a few assumptions as too many may signal the need for a more specific question.)
>
> The first step in using the contract was to explain its function and how it operates in general terms. As we went through the process of explaining the use of contracts, the student was allowed to decide her level of participation. (Developing a contract with one student was a good way to ease into the use of student contracts. It allowed the teacher to see the problems associated with individualizing instruction, difficulties of evaluation, and the use of resources.)

Once the contract is written, both parties must try to abide by it. In this particular case (this was Cynthia's third contract), the length of the project was two or three weeks. (It may be desirable to begin with contracts of a much shorter duration and gradually increase their scope.)

It is important to interact with the student to find out how things are going—if the contract is too difficult, or if it is too easy and not challenging the student.

We scheduled a student-teacher conference every Tuesday and as needed during the time of the contract. We also felt it desirable to schedule regular independent working time for Cynthia. This time was scheduled so that she could use resources in the library, but if this was not necessary on a particular day, she could work independently in the classroom. The decision to work in the library or classroom was Cynthia's.

The question that is posed at the top of the contract is really being answered by the activities developed by both the student and the teacher. A rainfall map allowed the student to see that it does snow in parts of Africa and that there is a great deal of rain and vegetation. The interview with two people who are from different parts of Africa allowed her to get some more input about Africa. A log of films and slides was used to describe the kinds of things the student had seen in the film. She agreed to present the findings of her questions to the class, at which point both the class and the teacher were able to question Cynthia. During this period of time, the class had also been discussing Africa, and Cynthia had been in class, except for Tuesdays when she went to the library. Cynthia completed much of the regular classwork, and also worked on her independent study project (the two overlapped).

Contracts can be written for any length of time. First contracts are of short duration; later they can be expanded according to the student's own abilities. It is important that one vary the activities, combining reading, writing, artwork, interviews, oral presentation, and reports in the activity section of the contract. If films are not available, use books. Allow the student to progress to the point of going to the library, rather than using library work as an initial activity.

It's important, initially, for you and the student to sit down and go over the possible resources. It is also important that the contract be signed and dated. Now that you have completed reviewing the contract, it might help to list the elements involved.

ELEMENTS OF A CONTRACT

1. Decide if the contract will be short term or long term.
2. Develop a general format for a contract.
3. Gather resource material and information.
4. You should have a few feedback sessions with the students on their progress.
5. State in the contract how the student will be evaluated.
6. Begin with one student and if the operation is successful begin the process with another student.

Independent Study Contract

Cynthia S.
Mr. Freiberg

Question: How can people survive if Africa is hot and there is not enough food?

Assumptions:
1) Africa is hot
2) There is no food

Independent Study Time: Every Tuesday if needed Cynthia will go to the library.

Length of Project: Two-Three Weeks

Scheduled Meetings with Mr. Freiberg and Cynthia S.: Every Tuesday plus meetings as needed.

Activities: Cynthia will find out the answers to the above questions by presenting her findings in the following form:

1) Weather-Rainfall Maps
2) Interview of Mr. Awad and Mr. Schikongo with a list of ten questions.
3) Diary of Films and Slides on Africa.
4) Cynthia will present the findings of her questions to the class.
5) Cynthia will answer questions about the topic from Mr. Freiberg and the class.

Evaluation: Cynthia will receive an "A" if all the above (1-5) are answered

Possible Resources: Almanac
Atlas
Films and Slides in Library
Mr. Schikongo and Mr. Awad Interview
Books in the Library

Signed: _____
Cynthia S.

_____
Mr. Freiberg

QUESTIONS YOU SHOULD ASK
YOURSELF

1. What is to be done in the contract?
2. Who will do it? (Students may work in groups after their first attempt at contracts has been successful.)
3. What will the student have at the end of the contract?
4. What is the expected outcome for the student? (What will he take away with him?)
5. How will you evaluate numbers three and four?
6. What resources will be needed?
7. Where will the student find resources on his own?

Something that may help you write contracts more effectively could be sitting down, perhaps during one of your inservice programs, and simply writing a contract with another teacher. For example, you could role play a student and the other person could role play the teacher. You could negotiate a contract, switch the roles, and then negotiate another contract. You could see how close your contract comes to some of the criteria in this particular activity.

USING THE COMMUNITY

Another avenue of approach is to use the learning resources of the community. Suppose a student chose to interview ten (or twenty) black members of the community (or Chicanos) and an equal number of whites, as to their attitudes on racial issues. To do the background study that would enable him to do this, to learn how to approach people and how to *listen,* to analyze his notes to discover the salient points of racial conflict in this community, would be *far* more valuable learning than any classroom course I could imagine. And if the interviewing was done by a mixed team of black and white (or Chicano and white), it would be so valuable it should be presented to the community in some way.

There are many other types of community projects. A group of students at Caltech in Pasadena decided to study the smog problem in Los Angeles and finally developed such an impressive plan that they were financed by a federal grant.

One other type of possibility might be mentioned. If a student is particularly interested in working with people, he might, with the instructor's help, apprentice himself to a working psychologist, psychiatrist, or social worker in the community. He might enroll in an encounter group or a peer group for individuals similar to himself. He might, in other words, wish to learn psychology *experientially.*

All these very tentative suggestions add up to one major view that I hold—that students, if given real freedom, frequently come up with very exciting learning experiences that they have developed on their own and from which they profit deeply. They can become *searchers* after knowledge, not passive and temporary recipients of it. They can enter into the *process* of learning and discover what an adventure it is.

PEER TEACHING

The tutor-tutee relationship is one mode of promoting learning that has many advantages both for the student being helped and for the older or more advanced student doing the teaching.

A noteworthy project of this sort was carried out by two faculty members of the University of Cincinnati (3). They carefully selected seventy-six sixth grade children to be tutors for an equal number of second and third graders. The children were in inner city, suburban, and rural schools. The subject was mathematics.

They selected sixth grade students on the basis of personality, achievement, sense of responsibility, and enthusiasm. They found that these students already had a very good idea of what it took to facilitate learning. There were three training sessions of thirty minutes each. Letters were sent to parents of both tutors and tutees, explaining the project and enlisting their support.

On the basis of observation and teacher suggestions tutors were matched with tutees. There were six thirty-minute tutoring sessions during a two-week period.

An evaluation of this very brief experiment showed that many of the tutees increased their mathematical skills, only 12 percent showing little or no progress. Perhaps a more important observation indicated that they "showed greater confidence, more motivation to work, and an improved attitude toward mathematics." The main complaint of the tutors was that there were not enough tutoring sessions. "Tutors gained in their own self-assurance and their willingness to assume responsibility." Several of them worked hard to extend and improve their own knowledge of mathematics (3, p. 431).

Especially in a time of reduced budgets and large classes, tutoring is a resource that might be much more heavily used with gains for all concerned.

Division of Group

It does not seem reasonable to impose freedom on anyone who does not desire it. When students are offered the freedom to learn on their own responsibility, there should also be provision for those who do not want this freedom and prefer to be instructed and guided. Shiel recognized this problem and divided her sixth graders into two groups—one self-directed and one conventional. The fact that the children had freedom to move back and forth between these two approaches made this a very happy solution. Dean, in teaching higher mathematics, made it possible for students who did not like the freedom to transfer into conventional sections of the same course.

Such easy solutions may not always be possible, but the facilitator of learning will always wish to consider the problem. If students are free, they should be free to learn passively as well as to initiate their own learning. Perhaps further development of programmed learning will offer another alternative. Those students who prefer to be guided on a carefully predetermined path of learning may choose to take the programmed learning. Those who prefer to follow their own directions and initiate their own learning can meet as a group or follow any of the various patterns that have thus far been described.

Organization of Facilitator-Learning
Groups

Is it possible to provide any freedom of learning within large classes? This question is often and deservedly raised. Weldon Shofstall, teaching prospective high school teachers, has come up with an interesting way of handling this problem (6). He sets the climate for the class with some general comments:

> I am a facilitator of learning, and you are the learner. There is no teacher in the traditional sense. Whether you learn or not is entirely your own personal responsibility. My sole job is to allow you to take this responsibility by using your own initiative . . . I am always available for personal conferences. You are urged and advised to start these personal conferences during the first week. . . .
>
> In addition, personal conferences are very helpful to me as your facilitator because I wish also to be a learner. I can learn only if you raise questions, objections, and make suggestions to me personally.

He then provides for the formation of relatively autonomous "facilitator-learning" groups.

> You will be assigned to an FL group of from seven to ten students. Within this group you can either waste your time and the time of others, or you can find this one of the most stimulating and worthwhile learning experiences you have ever had. For most of you there will be no middle ground. . . . I will attend your FL group upon the invitation of the group only. Please let me know the day before if you want me to attend your group meeting.
>
> The FL group should select a chairman. It is suggested that the chairman serve for not more than one week at a time. The chairman is the group moderator and must report to me before every FL group meeting. In addition to selecting a chairman, one member of the group should be designated as the group reporter. This person will report to me after each group meeting. It is suggested that the group plan the FL group work and make assignments for not more than two meetings in advance. . . . Failure on the part of individual members to *prepare* for the group meetings is a serious handicap to the effective functioning of the group.

At the end of these courses, Shofstall asks that the students write letters to new students who will be taking the course the following year. Here is an excerpt from one of those letters:

> To begin with, friend, if you have gone through all of your college career sitting in lectures, taking notes on what the teacher wanted you to get, reading what the teacher wanted you to read, writing or reporting what the teacher wanted you to write or report on, and taking tests over what the teacher wanted you to know at the end of his course—and you *like* this method of education—then drop this course. . . . But if you are willing to try honestly and sincerely to become involved with assuming responsibility for your own learning, then welcome!

There are many other ways of dividing up large classes into small, functional, self-motivated groups. Members can be clustered in terms of special interests or in terms of particular topics and in other ways. The description of Shofstall's method is simply intended to indicate that if we are willing to give as much attention to planning for the facilitation of learning as we ordinarily do for the preparation of lectures, many of the seemingly insuperable problems can be resolved.

The Conduct of Inquiry

A specialized type of participative and experiential learning, which has been receiving increasing emphasis in recent years, has been developing in the field of the sciences. Various individuals and national groups have been working toward a goal of helping students to become inquirers, working in a fluid way toward discovery in the scientific realm.

The impetus for this movement grows out of an urgent need to have science experienced as a changing field, as it is in the modern world, rather than as a closed book of already discovered facts. The possession of a body of knowledge *about* science is not an adequate achievement for the student today. Today's aim is to get the student away from the misleading image of science as absolute, complete, and permanent.

In order to achieve this aim, the teacher sets the stage for a mind-set of inquiry by posing the problems, creating a responsive environment, and giving assistance to the students in the investigative operations. This environment makes it possible for pupils to achieve autonomous discoveries and to engage in self-directed learning. They become scientists *themselves*, on a simple level, seeking answers to real questions, discovering for themselves the pitfalls and the joys of the scientist's search. They may not learn as many scientific "facts," but they develop a real appreciation of science as a never-ending search, a recognition that there is no closure in any real science.

It is obvious that if prospective teachers are to engage in this kind of stimulation of inquiry among their pupils, they must have experienced it themselves. It follows that courses in teacher training must be taught in the same fashion as just described if teachers themselves are to experience the satisfaction of self-initiated discovery in the scientific realm.

This new development in the area of science constitutes a deep challenge to present concepts of teaching. Current educational practice tends to make children less autonomous and less empirical in their search for knowledge and understanding as they move through the elementary grades. This trend is strictly at variance with the aim of those who focus on inquiry. When children are permitted to think their way through to new understandings, the concepts they derive in the process have greater depth, understanding, and durability. They have become more autonomous and more solidly based in an empirical approach.

There is a need to offer teachers a variety of learning experiences. Today, more than ever, the educational system and teachers, in particular, are faced with a continuing barrage of seemingly insoluble problems. However, we continue to give teachers fifteenth century tools to deal with twenty-first century education. The gap between the verbalization of problems and the solutions of those same problems becomes wider. As educators we need to offer those tools that are closest to being practical. We do not expect a carpenter to build a house with a hammer. Why do we expect teachers to build the educational foundations of children with only one approach?

Like any of the methods described in this chapter, the procedures involved in developing an inquiring state of mind can themselves become simply more ways of imposing a teacher-directed curriculum on the students. I have known this to happen. None of the *methods* mentioned in this chapter will be effective unless the teacher's genuine desire is to create a climate in which there is freedom to learn.

Programmed Instruction As Experiential Learning

As educators well know, there has been a vast and explosive development in the field of programmed instruction. This is not the place to review these developments or the theory of operant conditioning upon which programmed instruction is based. It is appropriate, however, to point out that programmed instruction may be used in a variety of ways. It can be seen as potentially providing for all learning, or it may be seen as one new and very useful tool in the facilitation of learning. As Skinner has pointed out, "To acquire behavior the student must engage in behavior" (8).

In the development of programmed instruction, there has been a tendency toward shorter programs, rather than toward the development of whole courses covering a total field of knowledge. To me, the development of these shorter programs suggests the most fruitful way in which the student may be involved in the use of teaching machines. When learning is being facilitated, the student will frequently come across knowledge gaps. Here the flexibility of programmed instruction is invaluable. A pupil who needs to know how to use a microscope can find a program covering this knowledge. The student who is planning to spend three months in France can use programmed instruction in conversational French. The pupil who needs algebra, whether for the solution of interesting problems or simply to get into college, can work on a program of instruction in algebra.

Used in these ways, there is no doubt that a competently developed program can provide students with the opportunity for immediate experiences of satisfaction, competency in a body of knowledge, the feeling that any content is learnable, and an understanding of the learning process. Emphasis on immediate reinforcement and reward, rather than on punitive or evaluative measures, is another factor in favor of programmed learning. Used flexibly, programmed learning can constitute a large forward step in meeting the massive needs for functional learning of subject matter.

But programmed learning has great potential risks if it is unwisely used. If it becomes a substitute for thinking in larger patterns, if it becomes a way of stressing factual knowledge above creativity, then real damage may be done. But if it is perceived as an instrument that may be used to achieve flexibility in education, then it is a powerful tool that psychology has contributed to education.

The Encounter Group

A very important example of a development that fosters a climate for significant learning is the encounter group. This approach is of help in educating not only students, but teachers and administrators, for the newer goals in education. The encounter group has been used in educational institutions, but relatively few teachers or administrators have had experience with it. There has, however, been a burgeoning use of the intensive group experience in the various helping professions and in the development of business executives and government administrators. Under a variety of labels—T-group, the laboratory group, the sensitivity training course, the intensive workshop in human relations, the encounter group—this approach has become an important part of the development of leaders in both their personal and professional functioning (5).

It is difficult to describe briefly the nature of such a group experience because it varies greatly from group to group and from leader to leader. However, the group usually begins with little imposed structure; the situation and the purposes are up to the group members to decide. The leader's function is to facilitate expression and to clarify or point up the dynamic pattern of the group's struggle. In such a group, after an initial "milling around," personal expressiveness tends to increase. An increasingly free, direct, and spontaneous communication occurs between members of the group. Facades become less necessary. Defenses are lowered, and basic "encounters" occur as individuals reveal hitherto hidden feelings and aspects of themselves and receive spontaneous feedback—both negative and positive— from group members. Some or many individuals become much more facilitative in relationship to others, making possible greater freedom of expression.

In general, when the experience is a fruitful one, it is a deeply personal experience resulting in more direct person-to-person communication, sharply increased self-understanding, more realness and independence in the individual, and an increased understanding and acceptance of others. Although much still remains to be learned about the intensive group experience in all its forms, it is already clear that encounters help to create in most members of the group, attitudes highly conducive to experiential learning.

Self-Evaluation

The evaluation of one's own learning is one of the major means by which self-initiated learning becomes also responsible learning. It is when the individual has to take the responsibility for deciding what criteria are important to him, what goals must be achieved, and the extent to which he has achieved those goals, that he truly learns to take responsibility for himself and his directions. For this reason, it seems important that some degree of self-evaluation be built into any attempt to promote an experiential type of learning.

We have already seen a number of ways of implementing self-evaluation. Shiel settled the problem of grades by mutual discussion with her pupils.

Swenson worked cooperatively with her students to establish highly individualized grades, as did Levitan. In a class of mine, the students were primarily responsible both for the criteria and for the grade assigned. In classes like Combs', fulfillment of the contract is itself a completion of the self-evaluation. Shofstall provides for his students summaries of learnings and self-evaluations made by previous students so that they have some notion of the task. During the whole course, students analyze their personal strengths and weaknesses and confer with other members of the group to have feedback. Class grades were decided upon by representatives selected by each group, who met with the instructor to make their recommendations.

It is obvious that there are many patterns to follow in making an appraisal of personal efforts and learning. The particular pattern is far less important than the feeling of responsibility for intelligent pursuit of specific learning goals. One student may choose a very rigid goal such as simply amassing a certain amount of testable information in the field of study. Another may use a course to become more spontaneous in learning, more open to a wide range of stimuli, or free to be himself in reacting to the available resources. Obviously the criteria will be very different for these two individuals. Yet each has functioned as a responsible, professional person functions in society.

Other Sources

I have purposely limited this chapter to a few general areas and methods that the teacher may wish to consider. There is a wealth of other ideas and ingenious procedures, described by those who are directly involved in classroom teaching. Three volumes (of several) that would prove helpful to the teacher eager to humanize the classroom are:

The Psychology of Open Teaching and Learning: An Inquiry Approach, edited by M. L. Silberman, J. S. Allender, J. M. Yannoff. Boston: Little, Brown & Co., 1972. This contains well-selected and stimulating articles.

Learning Guide for Those Who Can Teach, by H. J. Freiberg, J. M. Cooper, and K. Ryan. Boston: Houghton Mifflin, third edition, 1980. Written by authors with much classroom experience.

Learner-Centered Teaching: A Humanistic View, by Gerald J. Pine and Angelo V. Boy. Denver, Colorado: Love Publishing Co., 1977. Written out of a rich experience by two teachers. Contains helpful lists of books, films, and organizations that are devoted to a humanistic approach in education.

How Effective Is Open Teaching?

All of our examples thus far and the methods described could be classed under the heading of open teaching and learning. This has been well defined as: "An open approach to the teaching-learning process which recognizes the valid wish of every student to be involved in some way in the direction of his own learning. It respects children's natural impulse to learn and understands the ways they gain and create knowledge. Of special concern, it changes the function of a teacher from 'telling information' to one of providing choice and facilitating inquiry activity" (7, p. 3).

Open education has been evaluated in many research investigations. Horwitz (4) and Walberg et al., in two separate reviews of 102 such studies, came to similar conclusions. "Open education, authentically implemented, consistently reaches its goals in creativity, self-concept, school attitudes, curiosity and independence" (9, p. 102). Horwitz tabulates the studies in a way that illustrates this conclusion even more dramatically, as Table 1 shows.

TABLE 1 Overview of Results

Variable and Number of Studies	Results (Percent of Studies)			
	Open Better	Traditional Better	Mixed Results	No Significant Differences
Academic Achievements (102)	14%	12%	28%	46%
Self-Concept (61)	25%	3%	25%	47%
Attitude toward School (57)	40%	4%	25%	32%
Creativity (33)	36%	0%	30%	33%
Independence & Conformity (23)	78%	4%	9%	9%
Curiosity (14)	43%	0%	36%	21%
Anxiety & Adjustment (39)	26%	13%	31%	31%
Locus of Control (24)	25%	4%	17%	54%
Cooperation (9)	67%	0%	11%	22%
(Overall average)	(39%)	(4%)	(24%)	(33%)

SOURCE: R. A. Horwitz, "Psychological Effects of the 'Open Classroom.' " *Review of Educational Research*, 49 (1979): 71–85. Reprinted by permission of the publisher.

Note that there is not one area in which traditional education is superior to the open approach. However, in academic achievement there is no significant difference. In fact, a study by Good (2) concludes that in mastery of basic skills, direct instruction is superior to open teaching. In a later chapter, however, we shall find that when teacher *attitudes* are considered, even basic skills are more readily learned in humane classrooms.

Concluding Remarks

I trust that this chapter has made it clear that if you wish to create the conditions for responsible self-directed learning, there are a number of methods already at hand that are congenial to this approach. A few of these have been discussed, and reference made to other sources. These will, I hope, serve as a stimulus to the facilitator, but in the long run your own personality and style will determine the methods you use.

It is reassuring to know, as you work toward creating a classroom climate of responsible freedom, that the relevant research studies show that your students will profit, in ways highly important for their future living in a changing world.

REFERENCES

1. Freiberg, H. Jerome. Recipe of Classroom Ideas. In W. R. Houston and S. White, eds., *Professional Development Modules.* Houston, Texas: Professional Development Center, College of Education, University of Houston, 1973.
2. Good, T. "Teacher Effectiveness in the Elementary School: What We Know About It Now." *Journal of Teacher Education,* 30 (1979): 52–64.
3. Hill, J. C., and Tanveer, S. A. "Kids Teaching Kids: It Works." *Educational Forum,* 45 (1981): 425–532.
4. Horwitz, R. A. "Psychological Effects of the 'Open Classroom.'" *Review of Educational Research,* 49 (1979): 71–85. Copyright 1979, American Educational Research Association, Washington, D.C.
5. Rogers, C. R. *Carl Rogers on Encounter Groups.* New York: Harper & Row, 1970.
6. Shofstall, W. P. "Training High School Facilitators of Learning." Unpublished manuscript, Arizona State University, 1966.
7. Silberman, M. L.; Allender, J. S.; and Vannoff, J. M., eds. *The Psychology of Open Teaching and Learning: An Inquiry Approach.* Boston: Little, Brown & Co., 1972.
8. Skinner, B. F. "Why We Need Teaching Machines." *Harvard Educational Review,* 37 (1961): 377–98.
9. Walberg, H. J.; Schiller, D., and Haertel, G. D. "The Quiet Revolution in Educational Research." *Kappan,* 61 (1979): 179–83.

Developing Person-centered Teachers

❧

Somehow in the United States, we have managed to transform one of the most rewarding of all human activities into a painful, boring, dull, fragmenting, mind-shrinking, soul-shriveling experience. (12, p. 207)

*T*his statement of Hall's describes all too accurately the present state of education. While our society as a whole is basically responsible for this situation, the institutions for the training of teachers have played an important part in creating this dismal picture. The schools of education, throughout the country, where young people receive their pre-service and in-service training, are, by and large, in a sorry state. They tend to be rigid bastions of conventional thinking and practice, and highly resistant to change. On many university campuses, education courses are looked upon as a boring waste of time.

Fortunately, there are exceptions, institutions where a human climate for learning is created, where prospective teachers experience the excitement of discovery—both in regard to themselves and the subject matter they will teach. They find it rewarding to be a part of a dual process—the process of becoming more of themselves, and the process of promoting and facilitating learning in their students.

I have been privileged to know of a few of these innovative programs. They are by no means confined to this country. I have before me a description of a program at the University of Ottawa, Canada, carried on by a team of faculty members. One of them states very concisely the principles he has found valuable in helping student teachers develop new ways. I would like to quote these.

1. That change in approach must be gradual for most teachers.
2. That change should hinge on some simple specific behavior that the teacher can use as both goal and criteria.
3. That it is essential to gradually change the locus of decision making if any significant change in the dynamics of the process is to occur.
4. That students must assume the responsibility to evaluate, before other changes can genuinely occur.
5. The allowing of students to accept the right to make true subject matter decisions is highly traumatic for teachers. (3)

His stress on the necessity of a gradual *process* of change is most certainly a healthy one, growing out of his experience. His last point is dramatically stated but very true. When students choose what they wish to learn, the teacher is often shocked to realize the extent of the revolution that is taking place.

The universality of the challenge of innovative education, and the similarity of student reactions the world over, is shown by letters and a paper from the opposite side of the earth—from the University of Malaya, Kuala Lumpur, Malaysia. There Mary Catherine Symons was impelled to try something new in teacher training. She had found her students were often bored. Besides, "I have come to the conclusion that few students ever refer to their lecture notes when they go out for practical teaching." But primarily she wished to develop self-reliant, independent teachers. So she started a project which would give the teachers-in-training the *experience* of self-directed learning. Both she and the students went through the ups and downs with which we have become familiar in earlier chapters. She felt excited and apprehensive in beginning the experiment, discouraged and unsure at times, and ended the course with a critical evaluation of what she had done, and revised plans for the next year.

Three excerpts from her diary give the flavor of her experience.

Today was the first day I met my students as a group and I explained the framework of the course to them. I began by stating that the freedom that I would be giving to them to pursue their interest(s) might seem strange and new and even perhaps threatening. However, I told them that it was the student himself who could decide what was of interest to him and what was needed to satisfy his/her needs. To get a clearer picture of what I was attempting to do, students were recommended to read any or a few of the first six books or articles listed in the Learning Resources. (A list of twenty books that she handed out.)

(Two days later) three of my students came to see me to discuss their work contract. Perhaps one of the main difficulties that they were facing was the lack of direction, as throughout their education they had been told what to do and what not to do. I, too, have been plagued with doubts and fears. Did I trust my students enough to learn on their own? Then I reminded myself that I had already started on it and that there would be no turning back.

(One week into the course) an outcome of this approach was my reading books on the Teaching of the English Language. Previously I had confined myself to a few areas that were of interest to me but I was now reading more widely so that I could be of greater help to my students. I felt that I had to help them more. Undoubtedly I would learn more about myself during these weeks.

The student reactions have a familiar ring. Here are three.

This is indeed the most challenging and brain-taxing course that I have had so far in my school life. . . . It is a change from the usual type of teaching, and being implemented at University level it provides the starting point for the training of more flexible teachers who would, hopefully, allow more intellectual freedom to their future students.

I do not think the course was successful. . . . Personally I feel that most Malaysian students (other than the very hardworking ones) find it very difficult to work without receiving any push. All this time, this has been provided by the teachers/lecturers. They are guided, prodded and made to work. When left on their own they neglect their work.

While on one hand, I welcome the liberty bestowed, yet on the other hand, the years of traditional training and following what is set, cast shadows of uncertainty and even a feeling of helplessness. In spite of initial misgivings and doubts, I have come to value this "Freedom to Learn". . . students are encouraged to develop initiative, and a sense of responsibility is also instilled.

Ms. Symons concluded that she would continue her experiment the following year. "However, I think that students should be given the opportunity to decide which approach they would like to follow as not all students are in favor of independent learning. But in the Malaysian context some degree of 'guided freedom' would be more appropriate. Also, I have to learn how to be a more effective teacher-learner" (17).

It is heartening to know that the effort to educate potential teachers in ways that help them become more self-directed, responsible, human facilitators of learning, is not limited to this country. In working along these lines, one is part of a worldwide network of educators who believe in young people, who are able to trust them as capable human beings with a great potential for learning.

The St. Lawrence Story

The teacher-education program on which I wish to focus most of my attention is one with which I have been in contact for a number of years, and which I was able to visit and observe. It is a program at St. Lawrence University, Canton, New York, a modestly sized private university. It has been described by two of its leaders, Hugh Gunnison and Peter Ladd, both in a report by Hugh (10) and in a paper written by both (11). I am drawing on all of this material to give a brief but coherent account of the development and present status of the program.

Its Roots

Almost fifteen years ago, the St. Lawrence experiment in a person-centered approach to teacher education began. The impetus, the ideas and the thrust for the undergraduate teacher education experiment are a direct result of the graduate counselor education program (14, pp. 91–97). For nearly twenty years this small program has been deeply committed to a person-centered approach in the training of counselors. It was in response to the idea of training teachers as counselors that the St. Lawrence experiment began.

The Setting

St. Lawrence is a small, coed, nondenominational, private liberal arts college in northern New York State. The school is typical of the private colleges of the Northeast and allows a flexibility that only a small privately endowed school can entertain. It is free, to a large extent, from the constant wranglings for bureaucratic power found in the larger universities. Fortunately St. Lawrence prides itself as a college where teaching is stressed as much as research and grant-seeking. The Department of Education argued that if the school were to compete with the less expensive state teachers colleges an experimental and different alternative had to be offered. St. Lawrence had to provide a program different in degree and in kind than could be found on other campuses.

The Program

In this setting we have developed a comprehensive undergraduate program where student teachers are helped to become human beings in the teaching situation.

The first essential component in the development of a program that centers around the student-as-person, is to present to student teachers and participating supervising teachers a solid research base which undergirds the general thrust of the St. Lawrence program. Through findings of such researchers as Carl Rogers, David Aspy, Flora Roebuck and Arthur Combs, the Teacher Education Program establishes a solid research base both in implementation and evaluation of the student teacher (9, pp. 162–70). This basic approach is also closely aligned to the graduate Counselor Education Program at St. Lawrence (14, pp. 91–97) which exemplifies a highly experiential and phenomenologically based approach to counseling. In the same manner, the Teacher Education Program has been developed from a phenomenological perspective where there is a continual refocusing on the student teacher as a person.

A phenomenologically based teacher education program at a liberal arts college provides a very different set of preconditions and values than are found in the more conventional teacher education programs. St. Lawrence's program is built on a strong liberal arts tradition which is the foundation for the student teaching experience. This is followed by an introductory course in the Education Department which focuses on the prospective student teacher's perception and understanding of the profession of teaching. Through the use of General Semantics (5) the student begins to understand the language and perceptions of the profession of teaching by actual participant-observer experiences in the classroom.

Following the introductory course, the student begins the professional semester in the senior year. This full semester consists of five weeks of on-campus study, followed by eight to nine weeks of student teaching. During the five weeks of on-campus work, student teachers learn specific methods in their specialization areas, as well as readings and discussions involving adolescence, personal awareness, motivation, the research base of the program and interpersonal relationship skills that promote a positive self-concept. Role playing, videotaping and other human relations approaches are used in order to give the student teachers a personal frame of reference before entering the student teaching experience.

In keeping with the program's emphasis on a holistic view of the person, physical fitness is another area of concern. Not only are emotional and intellectual development important considerations, but also physical development. Pre and post physical fitness tests (Harvard Step Test and the twelve-minute mile) are taken by everyone (including the faculty) in the program. Self-reports indicate that being physically in shape increases energy levels in the classroom.

In addition, students choose among off-campus experiences that provide opportunities to test out their learning and skill training in the field. Department staff offer three to four three-day basic encounter groups (15; 4, pp. 1–27) in which the participants personally experience a high trust climate in which positive regard, empathy and genuineness serve as the key characteristics. The groups are held in a University-owned mountain lodge (Catamount) where staff and students come to know each other as people. Throughout the total experience, a person-centered approach (16) is encouraged and modeled. Congruence becomes the watchword; that is, the faculty not only must teach genuineness, care, respect and empathy, but must live and be those variables. The faculty must themselves be rich and growing people: who trust, who care, and who are open and understanding. The use of first names, so simple an act, has a profound effect. Community builds and faculty-student distance all but disappears.

In recent years, due to the lack of available teaching positions and to a new thrust of the department, half of those seniors participating in the professional semester do not try for teaching positions. Peter Ladd, the Coordinator, meets with underclass people of the Teacher Education Program and describes the coming semester as one incredibly rich with opportunities for personal growth and experience. To leave the safety of note-taking, sitting behind texts and desks of the college classroom is an exciting, if not scary venture. Many of those students participating do not intend ever to teach. However the experience gives them an excellent opportunity to test themselves as well as their understanding of their subject matter. It should be noted that the student teaching period is meant to be an experiential learning process and not designed to emulate actual teaching in an occupational sense, but rather to provide personal-intellectual exploration.

Increasingly, during the first five weeks, tensions rise and a very real anxiety emerges. We believe this is not only natural, but healthy. We are glad that the student-teachers-becoming-persons are concerned. However, when their anxiety reaches the point where their effectiveness as a person is diminished then we provide a process for them to get control of it. Fantasy Relaxation Technique (8, pp. 199–200) is a method whereby individuals are taught how to become aware of debilitating panic and how to relax themselves. The technique, while behavioral, is person-centered, since individuals make the choice to learn how to control their anxiety and they also then have the choice of learning how to relax themselves. Seminars are held during the semester for those choosing to learn this additional skill which helps them gain more autonomy and control over their own worlds. As they learn to reduce their own anxiety, gain greater control through relaxation, they become more sure and positive about themselves.

SOME PROBLEMS ENCOUNTERED

The authors are frank in telling of the challenges and obstacles encountered in developing the program.

The first test of the person-centered approach in teacher education falls directly on the faculty. It means a total commitment to students and colleagues as people, but more than that it means the faculty must set the mood and example. Soon it became apparent just what consequences this kind of commitment generated. Occasionally we were "sniped at," misinterpreted and misunderstood. Continually we had to model the higher levels of trust of the psychologically facilitative climate. This was so often interpreted as being "buddy-buddy" with students. The experiment was seen as a challenge to university standards and academic traditions and policies. Not only were we often challenged by our colleagues and administrators, but also we were confusing to some students who were simply not used to being treated as individuals, who were not able to adjust easily to taking responsibility for their own learning and who were not used to being listened to and accepted. Instead they demanded to be told, passively listening and filling their notebooks, interacting in the conventional classroom styles of distance between students and teacher, invariably maintaining rigid roles. In addition, the school systems within which our students practiced their teaching found the person-centered approach threatening and in some cases even questioned the motives of the program.

We have found ourselves in the delicate position of wanting to foster change in a rigid system, yet at the same time having to "walk softly." Our students who choose to enter teaching rarely find themselves in a progressive and humanistic setting. By and large they obtain employment in typically traditional school systems. Consequently the St. Lawrence program has not pushed the varied methods and techniques associated with "humanistic education" and the open classroom concepts. Rather, we've stressed the power of the "facilitative psychological attitudes" which include unconditional positive regard, empathy, and genuineness in and, especially, out of the classroom. We are reminded that Aspy and Roebuck's work (2, pp. 163–71) was done in conventional schools, not in the ideal setting of free schools, private experimental schools, or experimental curricula.

In addition to these issues of faculty commitment and finding a secure niche in a conventional university, and geographic area, there are the ever present problems involved in evaluation—of the students and of the program.

General accountability to the university and both program and personal evaluation have been real issues with which the entire community has had to wrestle. We walk the fine line between the necessity of evaluation and the avoidance of a judgmental stance, the latter a very real inhibition to learning as well as to self-awareness and self-expansion. It has, for example, been difficult to move from an institutional letter grade system to a pass-no-credit method of evaluation.

Then, in order for the programs to be certified, we had to meet certain criteria set down by the New York State Department of Education. Our persistent dilemma was trying to fit a person-centered approach to the State mandated competency model. The evaluation procedures, particularly the process for assessing competencies, are unique; nevertheless, *all* of the St. Lawrence programs are fully certified by the State of New York. Thus, a phenomenological model for teacher education is certifiable under the competency format; a struggle and a victory with which we are pleased.

EVALUATION PROCEDURES:
ACHIEVING ACCOUNTABILITY

Here is a somewhat more formal account of the way in which this innovative approach to teacher education worked in a solid way to achieve state approval. In their efforts they also developed a novel, complex and complete method of evaluation of the students. Their work can well serve as a model in similar situations.

One of the most taxing and difficult problems in the St. Lawrence program has been to fit a process-flow oriented model to the linear cause-effect model demanded by the New York State Education Department's mandated Competency Based Teacher Education. The staff has seriously struggled with this dilemma for many years. The question is simply how to fit Rogers' person-centered approach of teacher education to a competency model? It can be done, however, and it is the authors' contention that David and Virginia Aspy and Flora Roebuck of the National Consortium for Humanizing Education have certainly been unsung heroes of the movement to humanize education (1, pp. 10–14; 2, pp. 163–71). Their effort has not been one of exploring the philosophical issues involved nor making the popular attacks on schools and public education. They opted for the non-popular approach of merging technology with humanism and have done this through a decade of hard research. They have taken the basic tenets of Rogers and have tested them in the classroom. For example, one of the exciting outcomes of Aspy's research was the finding that teacher empathy was the single best predictor of achievement in school. Thus, for evaluation purposes our students are given a modified pre-post instrument on listening from Gazda (6). In terms of competency, minimal levels of success are delineated and students must reach these on a paper and pencil test.

In testing accountability another competency predictor was used during the student teaching experience. Arrangements were made to analyze student teachers' classroom interactions (on cassette) through the National Consortium for Humanizing Education. Analyses using Flanders Interaction, Bloom's Cognitive Taxonomy as well as positive regard, empathy, genuineness, success promotion and student involvement scales were returned to' the student teacher as a frame of reference regarding his/her progression during the student teaching experience. By working through an outside agency such as the National Consortium for Humanizing Education, the student teachers were given an additional alternative perspective regarding their competence in the development of a unique teaching style.

An additional difficulty of merging a process approach with a competency format comes about during the everyday interactions of the student teacher in the classroom. On the one hand, a person-centered approach focuses on the self-awareness, and process of growth of the student teacher, whereas competency based education has its focus on the student teacher's ability to meet specific expectations which regulate and control the academic product put out by a student teaching program. The result of this combination at St. Lawrence has been the development of a Competency Based Workbook, where specific person-centered concepts, such as the ability to actively listen and the ability to act with positive regard, etc., are presented in journal form in order to give each student teacher a self-initiated, self-evaluative frame of reference (see Figure 1 as one example). The difference in this evaluative procedure is that the student teacher does not actively go into the classroom and attempt to complete certain competencies, but approaches the student teaching experience from a "disciplined naivete" (13), where he/she reflects on the everyday process of student teaching from three specific perspectives: 1) The Education Department at St. Lawrence has developed a number of research based, person-centered expectations, 2) Each supervising teacher is required to list in the workbook those expectations that they feel are most significant for their specific situation and 3) The students themselves develop a list of expectations which they wish to gain from the experience. With all expectations (competencies) listed in the workbook the student teacher reflects/dwells on the everyday interactions of student teaching and then records those specific interactions which fulfill the expectations of the Education Department, supervising teachers and themselves. The workbook also focuses on *where* the student teacher actually accomplished these expectations. By developing an awareness of the expectations of the total program and where these expectations are accomplished, the student begins to map out his/her unique process-of-becoming a professional teacher.

The workbook also becomes the foundation for weekly seminars held during the student teaching experience. Each student brings to the seminars those expectations which have emerged as strengths within their styles or those which have become critical problems. Through weekly theme-centered encounter groups the expectations of the entire program are re-clarified according to the unique needs of each student teacher. Such themes as discipline strategies, nervousness/panic, communication breakdowns, etc. are discussed. During the last week of the semester, student teachers are then asked to self-evaluate the expectations found in their workbooks. This is combined with the evaluations of their supervising teachers and that of

FIGURE 1 To Act-Listen Emphatically in the Classroom (Active Listening).

Resources Used in Achieving Expectations
(Briefly cite personal notes, dates, titles, etc., of seminars, classes, books, etc., used to achieve expectations or goals)

weekly seminars	classroom presentations	books
conferences with supervising teacher	discussions with students	others

effective	very effective	effective	very effective	effective	very effective
Student's Own Evaluation		Education Department Evaluation		Other Person's Evaluation (optional)	

St. Lawrence University Department of Education

the Education Department at St. Lawrence in order to give the student a final perspective on their progress.

A further attempt at self-awareness is in the use of other students involved in a person-centered approach. Full-time graduate students in the counseling and human development program at St. Lawrence have worked, in the past, with two or three student teachers during the professional semester. The graduate students are not teaching supervisors, method experts or master teachers, but rather are support people who will listen and help when student teachers request it. Hopefully, by building a good relationship, the student teachers and their graduate student create one more nourishing climate in which all can benefit.

During the last week of the teaching field experience, student teachers train their pupils to take a ten-point questionnaire. This questionnaire is a student's view of how they perceived the degree of respect, empathy and genuineness, their student teacher conveyed. For greater phenomenological accuracy, students respond to each item by designating those people in their lives who are most and least typical of the intent of the question. For example, under positive regard, they would place the initials of that person who, they believe, shows the highest level of care and regard and then the initials of the person in their lives who shows the least care and respect, followed by a check along the continuum for their student teacher. When compared, there has been a high relationship between questionnaire results and cassette tape evaluations.

At present, work continues on the development of a similar questionnaire that administrators, students and colleagues would use to evaluate recent graduates who hold teaching positions. It would result in helpful feedback so vital for accountability in the program.

A footnote to this very complete and self-respecting, student-respecting evaluation process is provided by the authors. They state that in the final oral evaluation—a dialogue between the college supervisor and the student teacher—more than one hundred definitions of teaching style have emerged. These are factual, operational definitions given by the student teacher. These definitions are vital testimony to the uniqueness of each prospective teacher who is in the process of becoming more aware of self, more capable of evaluating his or her work. It highlights the absurdity of attempting to promote a common teaching style in training programs.

A CRITICAL ELEMENT—THE
SUPERVISOR TEACHER

The authors tell of another challenge with which the program is coping.

The role of the supervising teacher is vital. In the past difficulties arose when student teachers were placed with supervisors unfamiliar with our approach. Student teachers were trapped when their on-campus experiences and learnings were in direct contradiction to the supervisory teachers' beliefs and behavior.

We have struggled over the years to build a cadre of "sponsor" teachers, often former graduates of the undergraduate teacher-training program or the graduate counseling and human development program, to work closely with the St. Lawrence Program. From this pool of personnel we select "adjunct instructors" who teach and demonstrate institutional methods in all the subject areas. In this manner we have managed to move method instruction from the college's academic departments to the field. This has been of significant value, for the credibility of methods instructors has increased. Now, student teachers are able to see a person-centered approach carried out in conventional classrooms in secondary schools. They witness first hand the theory and the skills implemented daily in the "adjunct instructor's" classes.

We find ourselves continually in process of change and moving in the direction of increased coherence. With sponsor teachers familiar with a person-centered approach, and carefully recruited adjunct methods instructors, the research, ideas and skills promoted in the on-campus experience have an impact that is resulting in greater cohesiveness.

THE REALITIES

In the final sections of their paper, the authors give a revealing and vivid picture of what it means to be involved in such a program, so contrary to the usual college-level teaching, so at odds with the educational system as a whole.

As professionals, we often wrestle with selection criteria of our students, yet at St. Lawrence, we've found selection of faculty the far more critical issue. It is very difficult to find a faculty whose interests and natural bent are centered around the student as a person. For example, it has involved almost thirteen years of searching to produce a faculty at St. Lawrence capable of carrying out a humanizing program. The success or failure of a program of this nature cannot be the responsibility of the students, but must be the responsibility of the faculty.

Thus far, the description of our program may appear clear and matter of fact. However, all is not neat and rosy. The creation and implementation of a teacher education program modeled after the person-centered approach is harrowing, draining and painful. To respect students as persons, to believe in giving power and control to individuals, to convey an unconditional respect, to stop and truly listen to another's deeper feelings and to be aware, genuine and sharing of one's own ongoing experience often are met with suspicion and incomprehension. The basic stance of simply respecting a student as a person is for many a frightening heresy, so new that it muddles and confuses. These are not the rantings and ravings from brief and superficial encounters with the system, but rather the combined experience of the authors one of whom has been trying to humanize classrooms for over twelve years. There are the times of loneliness best expressed as the end product of being misunderstood. There are the days and nights of inner questioning, doubting; are we so out of step with the world? There are the continual doubts of self and purpose. Being misunderstood is one thing; it is lonely and it hurts, yet being categorically dismissed without the chance to explain, to dialogue, to discuss the research evidence, is a bitter frustration. We have learned of the basic fear that this approach engenders in the system. We survive because we have allies. We have deep relationships with friends many of whom are colleagues and students. We have each experienced the person-centered approach and its power for growth and personal enrichment and realization. But, there is a price for the dream and we each must be willing to pay it if we are to succeed in humanizing the school.

Conclusion

We have described the methods, techniques, and the program for a person-centered teaching approach. However, we cannot describe the more fundamental and critical interpersonal climate that must exist day by day if such a program is to succeed. Here, within the climate of unconditional positive regard and respect, empathy and personal genuineness a community of people emerges, sharing the hopes, the fears, the excitement and courage to have an impact on a deadening, human wasteland. Thus, our goal at St. Lawrence is to facilitate the growth and development of human beings.

> The rare nourishing teachers, have that skill, that ability to excite and to throw sparks into the otherwise stifling classrooms. By and large, these nourishers are able to bring themselves, their genuine humanness into the classroom. There is a real concern not only for the subject matter, but also for the constant human encounters that take place over and over again in a myriad of forms. Learning is living and these rare teachers are alive in their own learning and thus in their teaching. (7, pp. 193–94)

WHAT STUDENTS LEARN

This then is the picture of the program. But how do students react? What do they get out of it? I have examined the twenty-two student reports turned in by students in one section of the program during one recent semester. There was not one truly negative response, though I am told that occasionally a student does turn in a negative evaluation.

There follow a few of these reports. Note how students have gained in self-esteem, in insight, in confidence in their career choice, in an understanding of children, in personal maturity, in ability to handle difficult situations with responsibility and courage. I will put the most negative reaction last.

> As I think back on my four years of college, I realize that though I learned a lot it didn't really help me grow as much emotionally as it did intellectually. This last semester has been the most rewarding, trying, difficult and overall most growing experience I've encountered. My goal at the beginning of this semester was to gain self-confidence and after endless years of trying, I have made considerable gains. It has been the most rewarding because I've touched so many lives in a personal sense as well as helping them grow intellectually. I've made good friends and close ties. I am honored to be a confidant and respected person to my students. Though now I reap the benefits, I must acknowledge that they did not come easily. The emotions I felt over this 14-week period were intense and often frustrating. I recommend this experience to anyone who not only is considering teach-

ing, but anyone in search of a growing, rewarding, soul-searching experience that will help you retouch yourself as well as the real world.

*   *   *

I am not very good at words of wisdom or knowing how to express myself in words, so I don't really know what to write on this card.

Student teaching, whether you choose teaching as a career or not, is a worthwhile experience. When you go into a classroom of students, you are going to learn your weaknesses and your strengths. In almost any other course of study at college, you can escape or avoid these facts. HOWEVER, in student teaching they "hit you right in the face." This is probably why this semester will have a *big* impact on my life. As I learned my strong points and weak points, they were realized and accepted by my supervisor and my education advisors; therefore, I could accept them. This allowed me to grow as a person. I could build and improve on what I learned about myself. Whether I use that knowledge in teaching or another field, what could be more valuable than knowing what you have within yourself to build on and work with?

*   *   *

The St. Lawrence University Education Program has been my greatest educational experience during my four years of college.

The program taught me how to handle the freedom to work in my own way, in a responsible, adult way.

I feel that I have grown up a lot this semester—I don't believe this growing would have occurred if I had not put this challenge upon myself.

I thank you because without you, it would not have been possible. I believe this program is special—you not only teach well, but you practice what you preach and that made all the difference in the world.

Thank you for giving the room to be myself and the room to grow!

*   *   *

Frustration, anxiety, confusion, hostility and inability were all emotions of familiarity these last nine weeks. As I write this all the events are fresh in my mind and all too vivid. Some of these days I'd like to rip from my mind like leaves from my notebook; maybe it's fortunate I can't. These nine weeks allowed me to realize my stamina and how positive my self-concept is. Through days of pressure and put-down, I continued to feel my self-worth. This is a victory for me. Throughout the days of doubt about my artistic ability and technical knowledge the thought that I had more to give, is what kept me from giving up. Without the five weeks at St. Lawrence University, I might not have known that. Now that it is over, I realize that I did touch others and leave behind some love, caring and encouragement.

Asked, "Are you glad you did it?" Others overwhelmingly answered, "Yes!" Today, I say, "No." A week, month or year from now, maybe the reply will be "most definitely." Right now, I feel scarred by stress from two of my supervising teachers, but unlike scar tissue, I will have more feeling, if not for myself, for others. The fact that so many, if not all the others said "yes" I know that my experience was much different than theirs. I do know that from my frustration came growth and for that I am thankful. I also know that I have changed in many positive respects and thank the St. Lawrence University program for much of that.

*   *   *

What does the Professional Semester mean to me? That's a hard question because it (the Professional Semester) has so many different facets to it that they are hard to explain. First of all, it was a chance to try out teaching to see if I liked it. Well, through nine weeks of excitement, exhaustion, frustration and exhilaration, I learned that I really like teaching. But I learned much, much more. The first five weeks, I learned to write a lesson plan, understand the work of men like Carl Rogers, Art Combs and other educational researchers, to be prepared for just about anything and to trust and share myself with other people. During the nine weeks of actual teaching, I learned to put into effect all the things taught to me in the first five weeks. But I also learned that I've got a lot more to learn! Through trial and error, I learned how to deal with 9th and 10th graders—how to handle my feelings when they disliked me and how to feel great when they showed how they cared. I learned to deal with other people—mostly older people. I learned to accept the aid and advice offered by teachers, supervisors and peers. I learned to use myself—my past experiences and constant feelings and ideas— as an unlimited source of strength. I developed confidence in myself which I was definitely lacking before this experience.

The feelings I have about this whole semester experience are such that I could never fully describe it in words. I would recommend the Professional Semester to anyone whether they were interested in teaching or not. I learned as much about myself and what I want to do with my life this semester as I have in the past three years here at SLU.

*   *   *

I feel that my experience student teaching had an immense impact on me. I've become more aware of my positive aspects through student teaching. Usually, I'm very critical of myself and tend to put myself down, but after this experience, I've learned to be more optimistic.

Another important change came about from teaching and that is the ability to discipline myself to sit down and work. I actually liked planning lessons.

My confidence soared from being in the classroom. It was a great feeling to know that you can get up and teach a lesson—you do know more than the students. Four years of college finally starts to pay off.

*   *   *

During the first five weeks of the semester, I was not overly enthused about the department's approach. I was getting rather tired of humanistic ideas; I wanted practical methods taught to me. It was only at Catamount, and afterwards, that I realized the value of the semester to me—the value of a group of close-knit caring people, sharing a common experience.

What did the semester mean to me? I think it increased my self growth, self-worth, and independence at a very crucial period in my life. I learned to value "my kids" at school, and to value what I could give to them. I still have a lot of growing to do in my young and ever-changing life, but I am thankful that I had this semester to learn to understand myself again. I now know better who I am.

As to my future, the Professional Semester has reinforced an idea I have long held, i.e., that I would like to work in the field of education.

From the bottom of my heart, thanks a bunch.

*   *   *

In the beginning of the program, I felt the instructors were not organized. Because of this, I feel time was wasted. I also feel that there was a lack of communication between instructors which was to the disadvantage of the students. I think there was a lot of repetition between the methods course and Educational Psychology. I do feel that I had a valuable experience student teaching. I learned a lot of my supervising teacher's philosophy. I do feel this program is good because the busy-work of preparing for student teaching is avoided.

For one professional semester to have produced reactions such as the above, with their obvious evidence of marked personal and professional development, is testimony to the effectiveness of the Program. Clearly these students have been reached in very important ways.

THE PRESENT PICTURE

Recent comments from Hugh Gunnison bring the picture of the program up to date.

The program has more than survived; it is flourishing. There were difficulties, times of misunderstanding, occasional sharp, yet fair questioning; however, in the long run the Department of Education had the foresight and courage to press for a program of this nature to continue.

While enrollment in teacher training programs throughout the country has generally fallen off, enrollment at St. Lawrence has not. In part this is due to the way the St. Lawrence program is presented. The professional semester is not seen as vocational training, but rather a logical extension of liberal arts education, a semester of valuable personal experiences in which individuals are encouraged to explore self-awareness. Students see this as a rare opportunity to spend one semester of their senior year leaving the role of college student behind. For fifteen weeks they can choose to leave the safety of their college classrooms and participate in experiences designed to encourage personal growth, awareness and interpersonal communication. The student teaching experience offers individuals an opportunity to test themselves as well as their understanding of their major academic discipline.

The attacks and challenges continue. However, a strong camaraderie exists within an expanding community and the program has become familiar beyond the rural northern area of Canton, New York. Yet the struggle is not over. The moves toward 'back to basics,' toward more impersonal kinds of learning, toward tighter trends in discipline, toward greater control and structure all offer a challenge to our Program. The deadening effect of lethargy and the stagnating aspects of complacency must be guarded against.

We still have as great a challenge to keep these hopes for learning, for people, and for education alive.

Comments

I had the privilege of visiting the teacher training program at St. Lawrence University a few years ago. I was deeply impressed.

The difficulty of enlisting faculty who were willing to share power with students, to be human and personal with students, was evident in many of the accounts that were given to me. I was nevertheless surprised that it had taken twelve struggling years to assemble such a faculty.

One outstanding experience of my visit was the first two hours of contact with the program. I had requested that I be given the opportunity to meet some of the students and teachers who were, or had been, in the program. This was set up as the very first aspect of my visit. I had had no chance to talk with faculty, to learn the specifics of the program, nor to visit any of the classes. Yet here I was, faced with a large number of students, former students now, teachers, and faculty. What was I to do?

I simply opened the session by explaining my situation, and then I said something of this sort, "I would like to learn from you what it has been like for you to be a part of this program—what it has been like personally and professionally. I hope we can be open, and speak up about the flaws and disappointments you have experienced, as well as the positive elements. I would like to hear from you what your experience in this program has meant to you—whether the meanings have been positive, negative, or indifferent."

During and after that session, I *wished* that it could have been recorded—and played back in every teacher training institution. It was an inspiring outpouring. Here were young people helping younger people to grow. They were excited by what they were doing, delighted at finding themselves respected by the faculty, obviously feeling their own strength and power and confidence. I remember one black man, who was, judging from his speech, from a ghetto background, telling of his experiences now in dealing with tough, "incorrigible" young black students. He told of the challenge it had been, how they would not believe at first that he trusted them, and the astonishing results he was now achieving. There were many accounts, similar, but not always as dramatic. The only disappointments voiced were by those who had been placed with supervising teachers who did not understand a person-centered approach and seemed to be threatened by it.

Perhaps a little of the flavor of that meeting is contained in an excerpt from a letter from one of these students received after I returned home.

> For me the graduate Counseling Program at St. Lawrence which I started in 1967 was part of a turning point in my life. Other things happened that year too—personal and social, individual and national. I became more aware of myself as a person. The climate that I experienced was person-centered, although I didn't know what it was at the time. It was something I had experienced only in bits and pieces before that time. It helped me to value

the things that had led up to this period in my life. It has affected me deeply since then.

He gives his account of the meeting.

As I and others speak, you listen and react. Your personhood is confirmed and mine is reaffirmed. I feel very lucky to have support available to me from Fritz, Gunner, you and other like-minded people in the room. I am moved that so many people have come to be with their allies for this meeting. I feel valued and prized by you and others, and especially by me. I feel it's worth taking the risk of being me.

His letter suggests the quality of that meeting. As I continued my visit, that quality was confirmed. My overall reaction is contained in a few paragraphs from a talk I gave before I left, to the whole St. Lawrence audience.

I want to tell you what a remarkable and confirming experience it has been for me to get to know the work in the development of educators which is being carried on at St. Lawrence University.

I have met with the undergraduate students in education, with the graduate students, with some of those from other fields who teach the methods courses, with student teachers, with some of their supervisors, and with administrators who are responsible for this process of preparation and development of teachers. I have observed and listened, and I am deeply thrilled and excited by what is going on.

This is the only place I know where a consistently person-centered philosophy runs through the whole sequence—from the first day the student enters a class in education to his or her functioning as a teacher outside, and then beginning to function as a supervisor or as instructor in methods for those who are still in the process of preparation.

It seems to me to be a total, unified, coherent experiment in teacher training. It is aimed toward trusting students, toward respecting them as persons and as learners. It is operating not only at an intellectual level, but as a way of being which is experienced by all those in the program. I find the morale of faculty, students, and former students exceedingly good.

But is it working? If you could have been in a meeting which I attended which included many former graduates, there could be no doubt in your mind. Confidence in themselves as professional persons, the ability to facilitate learning, the capacity for living as human beings in relationship with their students was evident in almost every statement that was made. As one of them said, "It works!" I could not help but agree.

I'm sure if I stayed longer, I would see more of the flaws, more of the mistakes being made. I've learned of a few already. But I have also seen enough to know that you have every right to be proud of the richly significant way in which St. Lawrence University is educating teachers, and equally proud of the courage and farsightedness of those who have brought this program into being. I congratulate you.

The View from Within

What was it like after the St. Lawrence program? Did it help or hinder the beginning teacher? One of the clearest statements I have encountered comes from a student, Kyle Blanchfield, who went through the program. It is heartening; it is deeply depressing. It is well worth careful study, and I am indebted to its author for making it available.

The St. Lawrence Program: One
Student's Experience

I have wanted to be a teacher for most of my life. When I came to St. Lawrence's Education Program, the idea of being an effective teacher was very vague to me. I knew that I wanted to be myself, yet I also knew from what I had been told that education programs were usually the sort of thing that we had to go through in order to become certified and not much more. This perspective of wanting to be myself with the students, was not the way several others in the program perceived it. It seemed they were constantly waiting for the instructors to tell them how they were "supposed" to teach. The amazing thing was the incredible confusion and anxiety that most of the students went through when the instructors would say things like: "How do you feel you should teach?" or, "What do you feel your style is?" I was personally relieved that someone was asking me to be myself instead of telling me how it ought to be. As the program went on, it appeared that others slowly were becoming more comfortable with the fact that they were going to have to be aware of themselves before they could ever be aware of the students in the public schools.

This slow process of getting comfortable with ourselves, the instructors and the fact that soon we were going to have to teach students, came to a climax at what St. Lawrence calls, "The Catamount Experience." Here we all went to a mountain lodge and for three days experienced a Basic Encounter Group. After, people were very positive and really felt supported. We had risked together at Catamount and had practiced the skills of active listening and effective responding, along with our own authentic feelings of positive regard and genuineness. After this was over I had the energy and the confidence to go to New York City and begin my student teaching. Fortunately, I had the instructors at St. Lawrence to thank for being there when I needed them. They helped me process a lot of what I saw in the public schools. By the time the experience had ended, I felt that I had a fairly good understanding of my personal style of teaching, plus I had gained insight into my personal self. This, more than anything, gave me confidence as well as made me very optimistic.

After graduating from St. Lawrence I realized that there was yet another degree required for permanent certification in New York State. So, I enrolled in a graduate program in Urban Education at a major East Coast university. Here is where, for the first time, my methods of teaching and of being myself were both questioned and negated. Basically for one year I became a permanent substitute in a public school. For all practical purposes I had entered the world of my new profession. At first, I was very enthusiastic, mainly because I felt that this was a great opportunity to work with many different age groups, along with being in many different teaching situations. My enthusiasm was extinguished quickly by administrators, other teachers and the faculty and students in the graduate school. They all seemed to be incredibly threatened by my rapport with the children and their ability to get their work done when in class with me. I just could not figure out why anyone would be upset with kids learning and having fun. What finally happened was that I was removed from my first school because I would not use physical discipline on the children. Of course that was not what was said, because it seemed as though a straight answer was very hard to come by in this school. After a lot of tears and a few calls to Peter Ladd at St. Lawrence, I decided to go into the next school and again try out my ideas.

At the second school I was able to find at least two allies, which helped quite a bit. Nevertheless, things again began to get miserable. At first I had a lot of teaching assignments, but as people became aware of the fact that I listened and was really involved with the students, the previous popularity I had with staff quickly diminished. I found myself doing menial tasks like xeroxing things, or hall duty, etc. The teachers, and the administration did not want me with the kids. This left me very disillusioned. I blamed myself, doubted myself and what I was about, and also rationalized my situation by saying, "maybe if I had my own classroom?" This finally led me to getting a transfer to another school where I would have my own class.

Unfortunately, having my own classroom was not the problem. Even when protected from the other teachers by my own classroom I began to start doubting. My confidence was being eroded. I was losing sight of myself and my students. The pressures were the same. The public school personnel were still living in a climate of fear and now I was losing my trust. I was very lonely and very afraid. I thought the people at St. Lawrence were not only idealistic, but also unrealistic and a bit crazy. They had set me up to be myself and now myself was getting murdered. I felt that they betrayed me. They had let me find my own style and now my style was not only being rejected by my profession, but questioned by myself. By the end of the academic year I was totally disillusioned and decided to quit teaching and go into a more realistic profession. As far as the St. Lawrence Program was concerned, I felt that the whole thing was dangerous and too idealistic.

Yet, I decided to give it one last try in an Upward Bound Program the following summer. This time my bosses were trusting, caring administrators who cared about the students and the faculty. Slowly, my self-confidence came back to me. I had allies who were both staff and students. All those ideas which seemed to reflect the way I teach and the way I am were put into action. By the end of the summer these students, who were considered the rejects of public school, were crying along with me because we would have to end the experience we were having. I had it back, all of it, and I was flying very high.

Just a note to end this. It is not that St. Lawrence's Student Teaching Program is too idealistic or that the people in it are too naive as to what the real world is all about. What it really is can be summed up in the faces of those students and teachers whom I encountered during hard times in the public schools. What I'm trying to say is that there are a lot of people afraid to be themselves. The most unrealistic thing about public schools, from my experience, is the *fear*. The most realistic thing I have experienced from being a teacher is caring and listening to the kids. If that is too idealistic for most people then I can say fortunately I went through a program which did not forget this. And, it was not easy.

Comments

This report by one who has been through the program depicts, in a startling way, the strangely revolutionary character of a person-centered approach in our schools.

It is clear that Kyle is a born teacher, and the St. Lawrence program confirmed her in a warm, human, student-centered way of being a teacher. But in the system she was unacceptable to both faculty and administrators. Her statement bears repeating. "They all seemed to be incredibly threatened by my rapport with the children and their ability to get their work done when in class with me. *I just could not figure out why anyone would be upset with kids learning and having fun.*" This was her crime—that her students *enjoyed* learning and *enjoyed* her.

She was only a substitute teacher, the lowest on the totem pole of the system. How could she possibly be a threat? Her experience set out in bold relief two convictions which run so deep in our schools that at times it seems hopeless to change them. Here they are.

1. Learning must be painful and unpleasant.
2. The teacher must, at all costs, preserve a status superior to the student.

Kyle did not openly challenge these convictions. She was simply a living contradiction of them, and as such she could not be tolerated in the system.

When will our society implement the vision of our founding fathers and put into practice the belief that all persons "are created free and equal?" When will it be considered acceptable to be a unique, warm, growing teacher, with a respect for the uniqueness and strength of each student? Clearly the time is not yet, but coherent, comprehensive programs such as that at St. Lawrence, will help to bring that time closer.

REFERENCES

1. Aspy, David N. "Empathy: Let's Get the Hell on with It." *The Counseling Psychologist* 5 (1975):10–14.
2. Aspy, David N. and Roebuck, Flora N. "From Humane Ideas to Human Technology and Back Again Many Times." *Education* 95 (1974):163–71.
3. Belanger, W. A. Personal correspondence, 1977.
4. Coulson, W. "Inside a Basic Encounter Group." *The Counseling Psychologist* 2 (1970):1–27.
5. Fox, W. "A Study of the Impact of a Course in General Semantics on the Educational/Operational Assumptions of Prospective Teachers." *ETC.: A Review of General Semantics* 31 (1974):295–305.
6. Gazda, G. M. *Human Relations Development: A Manual for Educators.* Boston: Allyn and Bacon, 1973.
7. Gunnison, Hugh. "Education: A Diatribe." *ETC.: A Review of General Semantics* 29 (1972):189–200.

8. Gunnison, Hugh. "Fantasy Relaxation Technique." *Personnel and Guidance Journal* 55 (1976):199–200.
9. Gunnison, Hugh. "Humanistic Education and Teacher Education." *ETC.: A Review of General Semantics* 33 (1976):162–70.
10. Gunnison, Hugh. "The St. Lawrence Experiment." Unpublished manuscript, Department of Education, St. Lawrence University, 1980.
11. Gunnison, Hugh and Ladd, P.D. "Teacher Education from a Person-centered Approach." *The Humanist Educator* 17 (1):23–32. Copyright © American Association for Counseling and Development. Reprinted with permission. No further reproduction authorized without permission of AACD.
12. Hall, E. T. *Beyond Culture.* New York: Doubleday, 1977.
13. Merleau-Ponty, M. *Phenomenology of Perception.* London: Routledge, Kegan Paul Ltd., 1962.
14. Renick, T. F. "Self-understanding and Self-awareness in a Counselor Education Program." *Humanist Educator* 15 (1976):91–97.
15. Rogers, Carl R. *Carl Rogers on Encounter Groups.* New York: Harper & Row, 1970.
16. Rogers, Carl R. *Carl Rogers on Personal Power.* New York: Delacorte, 1977.
17. Symons, M. Personal correspondence, 1978.

The Politics of
Education

✒

A humanistically oriented teacher often finds that she simply does not fit into a conventional school. We saw evidence of this in the personal account in the final pages of the preceding chapter. The humanistic teacher may feel herself to be an alien being in a conventional system. This is not surprising, because there are two sharply different approaches to the learning process. I would like to consider these in more detail.*

Traditional education and person-centered education may be thought of as the two poles of a continuum. I think that every educational effort, every teacher, every institution of learning could locate itself at some appropriate point on this scale. You may wish to think of yourself or the school or educational enterprise with which you are connected and consider its fitting placement on this continuum.

The Traditional Mode

I believe that the following are the major characteristics of conventional education, as we have known it for a long time in this country and as it is experienced by students and faculty.

● *The teacher is the possessor of knowledge, the student the expected recipient.* The teacher is the expert who knows the field. The student sits with poised pencil and notebook, waiting for the words of wisdom. There is a great difference in the status level between the instructor and student.

*A portion of this chapter is adapted, with permission, from *Carl Rogers on Personal Power* (New York: Delacorte Press, 1977), pp. 69–74.

● *The lecture, the textbook, or some other means of verbal intellectual instruction are the major methods of getting knowledge into the recipient. The examination measures the extent to which the student has received it. These are the central elements of this kind of education.* Why the lecture is regarded as a major means of instruction is a mystery. It made sense before books were published, but its current rationale is almost never explained. The increasing stress on the examination is also mysterious. Certainly its importance in this country has increased enormously in the last couple of decades. It has come to be regarded as the most important aspect of education, the goal toward which all else is directed.

● *The teacher is the possessor of power, the student the one who obeys.* The administrator is also the possessor of power, and both the teacher and the student are the ones who obey. Control is always exercised downward.

● *Rule by authority is the accepted policy in the classroom.* New elementary school teachers are often advised, "Make sure you get control of your students the very first day." Another common maxim, expressing the grimness of this control is "Don't smile at your kids before Christmas." The authority figure—the instructor—is very central in this education. Whether greatly admired as a fountain of knowledge or despised as a dictator, the teacher is always the center.

● *Trust is at a minimum.* Most notable is the teacher's distrust of the student. The student cannot be expected to work satisfactorily without the teacher's constant supervision. The student's distrust of the teacher is more diffuse—a lack of trust in teacher's motives, honesty, fairness, competence. There may be a real rapport between an entertaining lecturer and those who are being entertained. There may be admiration for the instructor, but mutual trust is not a noticeable ingredient.

● *The subjects (students) are best governed by being kept in an intermittent or constant state of fear.* Today there is not as much physical punishment in schools, but public criticism and ridicule and a constant fear of failure are even more potent. In my experience, this state of fear appears to increase as we go up the educational ladder because the student has more to lose. The individual in elementary school may be an object of scorn or regarded as stupid. In high school there is added to this the fear of failure to graduate, with its vocational, economic, and educational disadvantages. In college all these consequences are magnified and intensified. In graduate school sponsorship by one professor offers even greater opportunities for extreme punishment due to autocratic whim. Many graduate students have failed to receive their degrees because they have refused to conform to every wish of their major professor. Their position is often analogous to that of some slave, subject to the life-and-death power of an Oriental despot.

● *Democracy and its values are ignored and scorned in practice.* Students do not participate in choosing the goals, the curriculum, or the manner of working. These things are chosen for the students. Students have no part in the choice of teaching personnel, nor any voice in educational policy.

Likewise the teachers often have no choice in choosing their administrative officers. Often they, too, have no part in forming educational policy. All this is in striking contrast to all the teaching about the virtues of democracy, the importance of the "free world," and the like. The political practices of the school stand in the most striking contrast to what is taught. While being taught that freedom and responsibility are the glorious features of our democracy, students are experiencing themselves as powerless, as having little freedom, and as having almost no opportunity to exercise choice or carry responsibility.

● *There is no place for the whole person in the educational system, only for her intellect.* In elementary school the bursting curiosity of the normal child and the youngster's excess of physical energy are curbed and, if possible, stifled. In secondary school the one overriding interest of all the students is sex and the emotional and physical relationships between the sexes. Teachers almost totally ignore this interest and certainly do not regard it as a major area for learning. There is very little place for emotions in the secondary school. In college the situation is even more extreme—only the rational *mind* is welcomed.

The Politics of Conventional Education

In discussing the politics of this traditional mode, I use the term *politics* in its sociological sense, as in "the politics of the family," the "politics of psychotherapy," or "sexual politics." In this sense, politics has to do with control and with the making of choices. It has to do with the strategies and maneuvers by which one carries on these functions. Briefly, it is the process of gaining, using, sharing, or relinquishing power and decision making. It is also the process of the complex interactions and effects of these elements as they exist in relationships between persons, between a person and a group, or between groups.

Looked at from this perspective, the politics of traditional education is exceedingly clear. Decisions are made at the top. "Power over" is the important concept. The strategies for holding and exercising this power are (1) the rewards of grades and vocational opportunities; and (2) the use of such aversive, punitive, and fear-creating methods as failure on exams, failure to graduate, and public scorn.

It is the politics of a "jug and mug" theory of education, wherein the faculty (the jug) possess the intellectual and factual knowledge and cause the student to be the passive recipient (the mug) so that the knowledge can be poured in.

We see this concept of conventional education practiced all around us. It is not often openly defended as the *best* system. It is simply accepted as the inevitable system. Occasionally, however, it acquires a spokesperson, as in the case of Dr. Jay Michael, vice president of the University of California. Michael strongly opposed two recommendations that have been made to the legislature. One recommendation was that a small percentage of the budget be set aside for innovation in education. This suggestion was completely unacceptable to him. The other recommendation was that education should include *both* affective and cognitive learning. Of this, Michael said, "There is knowledge that exists separate and apart from how a person feels . . . and that accumulation of knowledge is *cognitive*. It can be transmitted, it can be taught and learned." To include affective learning would, he feared, reduce the importance of cognitive learning "to a level unacceptable to scholars."* Here is explicit support for the politics of the jug and mug theory. Teachers know best what is to be transmitted to the student.

The Person-centered Mode

The person-centered approach is at the opposite end of the scale. It is sharply different in its philosophy, its methods, and its politics. In our present educational culture, it cannot exist unless there is one precondition. If this precondition exists, then the other features listed may be experienced or observed at any educational level, from kindergarten through graduate school.

● *The precondition is: a leader or a person who is perceived as an authority figure in the situation is sufficiently secure within herself and in her relationship to others that she experiences an essential trust in the capacity of others to think for themselves, to learn for themselves.* She regards human beings as trustworthy organisms. If this precondition exists, then the following aspects become possible, and tend to be implemented.

● *The facilitative teacher shares with the others—students, and possibly also parents or community members—the responsibility for the learning process.* Curricular planning, the mode of administration and operation, the funding, the policy making, are all the responsibility of the particular group involved. Thus, a class may be responsible for its own curriculum, but the total group may be responsible for overall policy. In any case, responsibility is shared.

● *The facilitator provides learning resources, from within herself and her own experience, from books or materials or community experiences.* She encourages the learners to add resources of which they have knowledge, or in which they have experience. She opens doors to resources outside the experience of the group.

● *The student develops her own program of learning, alone or in cooperation with others.* Exploring one's own interests, facing this wealth of resources, the student makes the choices as to her own learning direction and carries the responsibility for the consequences of those choices.

● *A facilitative learning climate is provided.* In meetings of the class or of the school as a whole, an atmosphere of realness, of caring, and of under-

* As reported in Los Angeles *Times*, 3 December 1974.

standing listening is evident. This climate may spring initially from the person who is the perceived leader. As the learning process continues, it is more and more often provided by the learners for each other. Learning from each other becomes as important as learning from books or films or work experiences.

● It can be seen that *the focus is primarily on fostering the continuing process of learning.* The content of the learning, while significant, falls into a secondary place. Thus, a course is successfully ended not when the student has "learned all she needs to know," but when she has made significant progress in learning *how to learn* what she wants to know.

● *The discipline necessary to reach the student's goals is a self-discipline* and is recognized and accepted by the learner as being her own responsibility. Self-discipline replaces external discipline.

● *The evaluation of the extent and significance of the student's learning is made primarily by the learner,* although this self-evaluation may be influenced and enriched by caring feedback from other members of the group and from the facilitator.

● *In this growth-promoting climate, the learning tends to be deeper, proceeds at a more rapid rate, and is more pervasive in the life and behavior of the student than is learning acquired in the traditional classroom.* This comes about because the direction is self-chosen, the learning is self-initiated, and the whole person (with feelings and passions as well as intellect) is invested in the process.

The Politics of Person-centered Education

Consider the political implications of person-centered education. Who has the essential power and control? It is clear that it is the learner, or the learners as a group, including the facilitator-learner.

Who is attempting to gain control over whom? The student is in the process of gaining control over the course of her own learning and her own life. The facilitator relinquishes control over others, retaining only control over herself.

I see two strategies used in relation to power. The facilitator provides a psychological climate in which the learner is able to take responsible control. The facilitator also helps to de-emphasize static or content goals and, thus, encourages a focus on the process, on *experiencing* the way in which learning takes place.

The decision-making power is in the hands of the individual or individuals who will be affected by the decision. Depending on the issue, the choice may be up to the individual student, the students and facilitators as a group, or may include administrators, parents, members of the local government, or community members. Deciding what to learn in a particular course may be entirely in the hands of each student and the facilitator. Whether to build a new building affects a much larger group and would be so dealt with.

Each person regulates the modes of feeling, thought, behavior, and values through her own self-discipline.

It is obvious that the growing, learning person is the politically powerful force in such education. The *learner* is the center. This process of learning represents a revolutionary about-face from the politics of traditional education.

The Threat

I have slowly realized that it is in its *politics* that a person-centered approach to learning is most threatening. The teacher who considers using such an approach must face up to the fearful aspects of sharing her power and control. Who knows whether students can be trusted and whether a process can be trusted? One can only take the risk; and risk is frightening.

Person-centered education is threatening to the student. It is much easier to conform and complain than to take responsibility, make mistakes, and live with the consequences. In addition, students have been directed for so many years that they long for the continuance of the security of being told what to do. Just this week, a faculty member told me of sharing with students the responsibility for learning in a course on marriage and the family. Even in a course with such an enormous potential for significant personal development, the initial student reactions were largely ones of alarm. "How will we be graded?" "How many exams?" "How much of the text are we supposed to study?" Clearly, responsible choice is frightening, a fact we do not always recognize.

I hardly need to mention the threat to the administrator. Time and again I have observed that if one teacher in a traditional system, without talk or fanfare, institutes a person-centered process of learning in *one* classroom, that teacher becomes a threat to the whole system. The ferment of responsible freedom and shared power is recognized for what it is—a *revolutionary force*—and is suppressed if possible.

Naturally, the conventional members of the system do not *say* that they are opposed to a democratic process or to responsible freedom. The most frequent reaction to the threat is, "This idealistic notion is very commendable as a dream, but it just wouldn't and couldn't work in practice."

The Evidence

This last statement implies that person-centered education is neither practical nor effective. The statement is completely contradicted by the facts. Some evidence has been presented in previous chapters, but the overwhelming research confirmation will be found in the section, "What Are the Facts?"

The day is now past when teachers or administrators can dismiss the person-centered approach as an impossible mode of conducting education or as ineffective in promoting learning. The facts are all on the side of a person-centered approach. The superiority of this mode of education has been clearly demonstrated in many countries and in solid research studies, especially in the United States and Germany.

The Political Implications of the Evidence

The "facilitative conditions" studied make a profound change in the power relationships of the educational setting. To respect and prize the student, to understand what the student's school experience means to her, and to be real as a human being in relation to the pupil is to move the school a long way from its traditional authoritarian stance. These conditions make of the classroom a human, interactive situation, with much more emphasis upon the student as the important figure who is responsible for the evaluation of her own experience. And the research demonstrates that politics of this humane sort foster all kinds of constructive learning, both personal and intellectual. Furthermore, a lack of such a humane environment works against such learning and is associated with *less* than normal progress. Under a sharply and measurably defined humane politics, students improve in their way of perceiving themselves and in their social behavior. All this is a striking affirmation of the value of a person-centered approach in education.

CAN WE INFLUENCE A PROFESSION?

Would it be possible to move a whole profession toward a more humanistic, person-centered approach? Obviously if we were to attempt this, the strategic approach would be to provide person-centered experiences for those who were involved in the preparation of the professionals. We have seen in the preceding chapter how individual teacher-training institutions may make a difference. But there exists an interesting example of an effort to involve a whole profession, the medical field. The story is one from which we may learn.

More than ten years ago Orienne Strode-Maloney, a member of our Center, whose former husband had been a physician until his death, initiated a plan for helping physicians to be more human in their relationships. She elicited support and encouragement from the dean of Johns Hopkins University Medical School and from others, including me. A program was developed; it was aimed at medical educators, the persons most responsible for the attitudes of young physicians.

The first four-day workshop on Human Dimensions in Medical Education was held in June 1972. We had been apprehensive that high-status medical personnel would not respond to a program carried on by a nonmedical staff. Consequently, we were surprised and pleased that more than fifty chose to come, a large proportion being deans of medical schools or chairmen of departments. We found the attendees to be generally dubious that the experience would be worthwhile. For a few, the program was not very profitable, but the great majority left the workshop with many new personal and professional learnings. We also included some medical students and interns, so that the viewpoint of the physician-in-training would be represented. This proved to be a very wise move.

The staff was surprised to find that those attending this conference and the succeeding ones felt that they gained more of what they wanted from the small, often highly personal intensive groups than from the sessions on how institutions might be changed. Consequently, the small groups were made more of a central focus of the conferences.

What did the participants gain? I think it might be best to let a few of them speak for themselves through their letters and questionnaire responses.

Enjoy "teaching" more—don't feel the fantastically unreal drive to "keep up" or "get ahead" or get "one-up" as much—don't feel guilty when haven't read the latest. Relate on a much more human level to students, faculty, and personnel. (Faculty member)

In these weeks since our experience, I'm still gaining drive, understanding, warmer relations at home, an urge to know colleagues better, an ability to relate to others. . . . It works! I sense a closeness to my group members that has rarely happened before. (Medical School Dean)

It gave me a far greater awareness of students as persons. (Professor)

My experience there was the most meaningful and valuable part of my medical education to this date. The exposure to genuine, dynamic interactions between people from the medical community has sustained me throughout the process of becoming a physician. (Third-year Medical Student)

To say it in a few words, I learned a lot. Medicine and medical education desperately need what sessions like this have to offer. On the plane coming back I decided to build a requirement for training in human relations into our surgical internship and residency program as we develop it. (Chairman, Department of Surgery)

Notice that many of these responses indicate a freer communication and a greater sharing of power.

Since that beginning, the program has grown very rapidly. There have now been many of these four-day conferences with more than one thousand participants. Nearly every medical school in the United States has been represented, and members of foreign schools are beginning to attend.

A number of those attending wished they might have more extensive training in group facilitation so that they could be more effective "back home." As a consequence, a number of ten-day conferences have been held. Somewhat more cognitive material has been presented in them, although the best training for a facilitator is still the experience of learning to be more of oneself with a group.

A frequent reaction was the wish that others in one's department or medical school attend. Consequently, team attendance was encouraged. A number of medical schools have had five to fifteen educators attend. They constitute a support group for each other when they return to their school.

Most important of all have been the many requests to hold similar conferences in the medical school itself.

I would be interested in pursuing the idea of a cooperative venture between your group and perhaps four medical schools to set up a specific program aimed toward the development of the whole physician and a more humanistic approach to the teaching and practice of medicine. (Chairman, Department of Surgery)

A number of medical schools have now initiated such humanistic programs, adopting different forms suitable to the situation, but having a common goal of turning out doctors with experience and training in effective interpersonal relationships.

In one of these medical schools, a unique and pioneering program was strongly supported by the dean, who had himself attended one of the early workshops. This school recently held a four-day conference, involving intensive group experience, for all of their incoming students, the thirty faculty members who will be dealing with those students and the school staff (registrar, secretaries, librarians). The facilitators of the intensive groups were physicians from other medical schools in the region who had attended our ten-day programs. Deep levels of communication were achieved among faculty, students, and staff. Can you imagine a situation in which ninety incoming students and spouses are on a first-name basis with all of their teaching faculty, having shared as equals their hopes, dreams, anxieties, concerns, fears—interacting as *persons* in their classes, not as roles? The situation constitutes a revolution in professional education! Feedback from all levels has been enthusiastic. This same group of students and their teaching faculty will be meeting in a two-day, off-campus conference every six months throughout their medical school career. Another revolution!

This whole program for humanizing medical education has led to dramatic changes in curricular thinking in a number of schools. It is bringing about in faculty and students the very attitudes we have described as being effective in promoting a humanized process of learning. It is creating a person-centered context for turning out physicians who are both competent *and* human.

Conclusion

I ask myself why such a program is growing so rapidly in medical education, while there is no comparable program, nor so far as I know any desire for such a program, in our schools of education and teacher-training institutions. I believe there are several answers. In the first place, physicians are accustomed to changing their practice as new knowledge and new ways of treatment develop. A doctor eagerly seizes upon the newest, most effective way of dealing with an old disease and is rewarded for so doing. I believe there are very few rewards in the teacher-training field for educators who are trying out new ways. Another element is that the physician is continually exposed to feedback and is accustomed to learning from mistakes. An autopsy tells her she made a mistaken diagnosis. A patient who develops a damaging side effect from some new drug confronts her with the necessity of fresh learning. It is to her political advantage to be openminded and changing. But long-term feedback is very rare in education. An educator almost never learns of the curiosity she has killed or the persons she has damaged. Feedback is too politically threatening.

My conclusion is that we may see a person-centered approach to education developing strong roots in alternative schools, in universities-without-walls, and in specialized situations such as medical education, before it has a major impact on our larger teacher-training institutions. A rigid power structure in most of these schools of education is resistant to the political threat posed by change.

Yet the challenge and the possibility remain. Clearly, steps could be taken in teacher education, not unlike those beginning to have a real influence on physician education, with the purpose of bringing about a more human and effective learning climate in our classrooms. Do we, as educators, wish to take those steps, or will the politics of traditional education continue to stand in the way?

What Are the Facts?

Researching Person-centered Issues in Education

꽃

Why Read This Chapter?

*P*eople often avoid anything labeled research, especially if they see some tables of data and a few statistical terms. But this is one of the most important chapters in the book for anyone interested in being human in the classroom. I want to give several reasons why that is so.

The major reason is that this research provides convincing evidence—from two teams based on two continents—showing that students *learn more, attend school more often* (financially important), are more *creative,* more *capable of problem solving,* when the teacher provides the kind of human, facilitative climate that has been described in this book. If you are humanistically inclined and are in touch with skeptical administrators or boards of education, this chapter provides the facts and the support you need. It shows conclusively that a human approach is definitely superior, in a great many basic ways, to the traditional approach.

One can report that the concepts presented in the preceding chapters have been successfully used, not only in the classes and schools described, but in such unlikely spots as the teaching of human relations to military officers in the Army, Navy and Air Force, in the Orient, in Europe, in the United States. But such descriptions of the fruitful use of these concepts are often unconvincing to those at the top. This chapter provides the hard data that administrators and executives seek.

The research studies reported here are among the largest and most exhaustive ever carried out in the field of education. They are based on tape recordings of thousands and thousands of hours of classroom interaction in eight countries. These come from all levels of education, many different ethnic and national groups, a wide spread of geographical locations. They cannot be dismissed as inconclusive.

You still may be put off by the figures and tables. I would like to reassure you that you can, if you wish, read the whole chapter without looking at the tables since the meaning of each table is described separately in plain language.

You will, in addition to the major findings, come across some fascinating tidbits. What happens to school attendance when all the teachers in one school decide to increase the amount of direct eye contact they have with their students? What percentage of average classroom time is taken up by teacher talk: 20 percent? 40 percent? 60 percent? 80 percent? You will find out. What proportion of student time involves actual *thinking* behavior? More important, what percentage of teacher time is spent in *thinking* in class? Would it be 10 percent? 1 percent? Or less? You cannot come away from this chapter without ideas about altering your own way of being in the classroom.

What kind of people devote years of their lives to gathering, rating, using computers, analyzing, writing up such material? It is hard, tedious, difficult work. Are they just grubby researchers, remote from real life? I would like to let them very briefly speak for themselves.

Flora Roebuck writes of the fact that many studies in education are vulnerable to attack because of their research procedures.

> So, all those years ago, Dave Aspy and I decided that we had enough faith in the effectiveness of person-centered education to put it on the line; to subject it to the most rigorous possible tests in the toughest arena—the real world of the everyday classroom.
>
> Since then we've been too busy researching and training and speaking and looking for funds for more research and writing-up individual studies to put all the results together in one package and take a look at it. Writing this chapter has given us a chance to do that—and I am pleased with it. I think those years of effort have been well spent. The documentation that we have compiled is irrefutable. Person-centered education works—it works in the real world of schools and in the computer world of statistics.

With the Drs. Tausch, the story is even more moving.

> When I—Reinhard—came home after having served six years in the German Army in the Second World War, I more and more realized: German National Socialism and Hitlerism correlated with the upbringing of German children and the quality of interpersonal relations in schools and families. That is why Anne-Marie and I have committed ourselves to work very intensely on these research projects over the last decades in order to facilitate a change of school and family life which so often lacks humanity.
>
> We did not carry out this research work for the sake of our so-called scientific career; on the contrary, we often had to face rejection and contempt. I received my professorships in Cologne and in Hamburg *in spite of* these

investigations into bringing up children and into the person-centered approach.

So, without more ado, I welcome you to a chapter of fact-gathering, by four very idealistic human people, and the exciting conclusions which can be drawn from their untiring efforts.

Our Research and Our Findings
David Aspy and Flora Roebuck

THE BASIC QUESTION

The bottom line for many people is, "So what? What makes these class-rooms with person-centered freedom any better than others?" The National Consortium for Humanizing Education (NCHE) has conducted research into that issue for seventeen years in forty-two states and seven foreign countries. The results of these investigations reveal that there are some very positive effects from applying person-centered principles to daily prac-tice in schools.

The NCHE findings can be briefly summarized in one statement: *Students learn more and behave better when they receive high levels of understand-ing, caring, and genuineness, than when they are given low levels of them.* It pays to treat students as sensitive and aware human beings. (8)

This statement is based upon almost two decades of research and training projects in which we have focused upon interpersonal relationships in class-rooms (13). NCHE activities have included both research and training and have employed both subjective (phenomenological) and scientific proce-dures. Through a variety of approaches, we have examined relationships between Rogers' facilitative conditions (empathy, congruence, positive re-gard) and a variety of factors such as attitudes (toward self, school, others), discipline problems, physical health, attendance, I.Q. changes, and cogni-tive growth. These investigations involved all levels of schools and included elementary, secondary, and college populations. In all, we have worked with more than two thousand teachers and twenty thousand students. We would like to share our technology and our findings with you.

THE NCHE APPROACH

As we see the problem of humanizing interpersonal relationships in schools, the primary need is to use person-centered models to develop viable pro-grams that humanize the *daily* procedures of persons in schools. NCHE has pioneered that type of program for interpersonal relationships in edu-cation. It established the kind of model appropriate for humanistic inter-vention at this time. This approach involved three major steps:
1. Adoption of a theoretical model of humanistic interpersonal relationships,
2. Formulation of logistics to gather information about that theoretical model in *real* school settings, and
3. Dissemination of the obtained information to the profession.

NCHE *first* took a fairly precise position on what humanistic interpersonal relationships were; *second*, it explored that position in a range of studies; and *third*, it told professional educators what it had found.

CHOOSING A MODEL

We chose one model of humanistic interpersonal relationship for our work. It was necessary to make a choice because there are so many options for a theoretical stance.

For exactness in carrying out research, we selected as the NCHE model some aspects of interpersonal relationships that could be defined rather precisely (23). The terms of the model could be quantified and analyzed with adequate scientific accuracy, while they considered the intangible factor of interpersonal behavior, which we call *feelings* or *emotions*. The model we used is shown in Figure 12–1.

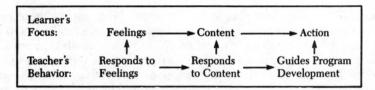

FIGURE 12–1: Model of Interpersonal Relationships in Teaching

We further defined the model by determining that the "responses to feelings" with which we were concerned were Rogers' facilitative conditions of empathy, congruence, and positive regard (43). We found ways to measure those conditions as they were expressed by teachers in a school setting. Similarly, we defined responses to content on the basis of Flanders' Interaction Analysis and Bloom's Cognitive Categories (20). Responses to action were defined as Carkhuff's technology for program development (25).

This definition of the model allowed us to move from subjective data toward precise measures. For example, when a verbal interaction was observed we could assess rather clearly whether there was (1) a response to the expressed feelings, (2) a response to the content, or (3) a planned course of action.

The question of whether the responses were *accurate* could not be answered so precisely with hard data; the measurement of accuracy rested upon the statistical reliability of observations by judges. However, the predictive validity of those observations was demonstrated in a variety of settings (17,12). Unbiased, trained raters expressed high levels of agreement (.90+) about the accuracy of responses to feelings (40). Additionally, those ratings correlated significantly with performance by students on a variety of behavioral indexes such as (1) I.Q. changes, (2) achievement test gains, (3) behavioral difficulties, (4) absences, (5) cognitive process, (6) self-concept, and (7) self-disclosure. All of these relationships were in the expected directions and at statistically significant levels; that is, it is unlikely they could have happened by chance. In addition, they were "meaningful" in the real world. In other words, the relationships we observed were large enough to be evident as real differences in the effectiveness of the persons studied as well as in the "numbers" we collected. For example, in one study comparing training results in schools with high facilitative principals versus schools led by principals who were poor facilitators, we found that teachers in a school led by a high facilitator frequently *signed* their names to data which we had asked them to give us on an *anonymous* basis. In a matching "low" school, the teachers often failed to provide any data and *never* with personal identification attached to it (14)!

LOGISTICS

We wanted to examine Rogers' facilitative conditions (empathy, congruence, and positive regard) as they impacted on everyday life in classrooms. This meant that we would need a precise record of classroom events so that those events could be investigated repeatedly from many points of view. One practical concern was that the cost of such data had to be relatively low without destroying the integrity of the data.

Through repeated investigations, an audio tape recording was found to be a valid source of information about the interpersonal behaviors in a classroom (2, 3, 4). Additionally, such recordings are inexpensive and cause a minimal intrusion into the normal classroom setting. Using audio tape recordings, NCHE members conducted a series of studies, which examined interpersonal behaviors in classrooms according to the conceptual model described above.

We found that the most difficult component of these studies was the logistics for managing the people who made the observations of the events. Difficulty was reduced considerably by bringing the audio recordings to a central location where trained observers assessed them. In this way, the observers were highly experienced technicians whose observational reliability could be assessed systematically through inter-rater and intra-rater studies (5). Both indexes exceeded $r = .90$ routinely. In one assessment of our technology, tapes that had been rated by a crew of raters in the fall of 1971 were re-rated by a different crew of raters in the spring of 1974. Inter-crew rating reliability was .914 for empathy, .898 for positive regard, and .906 for congruence (40). All of these reliabilities were significant at $p < .01$. (In other words, there was less than one chance in 100 that the results were due to chance.)

Empathy, congruence and positive regard were rated on five-point scales developed by Aspy.* The general levels of the scales were:

5.0	Adding, encouraging, exploring responses
4.0	Responses adding significantly to experience
3.0	Minimally effective responses
2.0	Hurting responses
1.0	Crippling responses

Each of the constructs (empathy, congruence, and positive regard) was rated on its own scale in which specific dimensions of the facilitative condition were designated for each level of the scale. In addition, the scales employed terminology suitable for application within educational settings.

In order to allow teachers to develop personal meaning for the research and training programs, NCHE adopted a feedback procedure so that those participating in the studies could benefit from the data obtained from their classroom teaching. The procedure was the following: (1) *RATE* the audio

---

*To differentiate the application of the constructs in educational versus counseling settings, the names but not the basic meaning of the constructs were changed. Thus, *empathy* became "understanding the meaning to the student of his experiencing" (called "Meaning" for short), *congruence* became "genuineness," and *positive regard* became "respect." For copies of the scales and details of development, see (5).

recording for Flanders' Interaction Analysis, Bloom's Taxonomy of Educational Objectives, and Aspy's Scales for Interpersonal Processes of Empathy, Congruence and Positive Regard; (2) *ANALYZE* by feeding the results into a computer which printed out a summary of the results from each scale; and (3) *SHARE* by sending the printout to the teacher. Before receiving the computer printout, each teacher was taught the general concept and procedures of each scale. Finally, each teacher had access to a consultant if she wished to discuss the results.

As the teachers received their feedback, they formulated goals they wanted to attain in their classroom teaching, and they were given systematic training in the chosen area. Some wanted to improve in question asking, others wished to respond more effectively to students' feelings, others to accept student ideas, etc. Each area was approached through a systematic training program that had clear-cut procedures and goals (18). The alternation of training and feedback helped teachers both determine their goals and assess the attainment of those goals.

During the training/feedback period, the NCHE staff compiled other outcomes of the teacher's work—achievement tests, I.Q., attendance, etc.— so that the participants could see the long-range benefits of the daily shifts in the classroom processes. At a higher level, an entire school could see the changes in its behavior in relation to its level of facilitative conditions (34). In one instance this feature was starkly evident. The school's interpersonal functioning fell to a very low level, and subsequently, there was (1) a student revolt, (2) a student rape, and (3) an attack on the principal. The levels of interpersonal functioning clearly preceded and were predictive of the dire events (14).

All of the data collection, analysis, and feedback was completed in such a way that the identity of the participants remained anonymous. This was accomplished through a code system which permitted the computerization of the results for both feedback and research. In this manner, the NCHE conducted sophisticated studies that gave computer feedback to teachers about their interpersonal functioning in the classrooms. At the same time, the computer could tell those same teachers about their students' performances on a variety of indexes they normally would not be able to follow because of time and personal constraints. Therefore, we concluded that a technology used in a humane way was both a conceptual and logistical possibility.

FACILITATIVE CONDITIONS AND
STUDENT OUTCOMES

Of course, the computer also kept tabs on all the data from teachers and students so that we could analyze it later. In one study involving 600 teachers and 10,000 students (13), the students (from kindergarten to grade twelve) of teachers who were trained to offer high levels of empathy, congruence, and positive regard were compared with control students of teachers who did *not* offer high levels of these facilitative conditions. The students of the high facilitative teachers were found to
1. Miss fewer days of school during the year;
2. Have increased scores on self-concept measures, indicating more positive self regard;

3. Make greater gains on academic achievement measures, including both math and reading scores;
4. Present fewer disciplinary problems;
5. Commit fewer acts of vandalism to school property;
6. Increase their scores on I.Q. tests (grades K-5);
7. Make gains in creativity scores from September to May; and
8. Be more spontaneous and use higher levels of thinking.

In addition, these benefits were cumulative; the more years in succession that students had a high functioning teacher, the greater the gains when compared with students of low functioning teachers. Tables 12–1 and 12–2 present some of the data from this study (13).

The finding, presented in Table 12–1, that students of high empathy teachers came to school an average of four days *more* per child than students of low empathy teachers was an important finding for us. First, it showed clearly that person-centered teaching resulted in benefits which were tangible in the "real" world of observable behaviors. But second, and perhaps even more importantly, this finding could be translated into the kind of dollars-and-cents data school administrators could appreciate—more days of attendance meant a higher average daily census and yielded more dollars from state (foundation) support formulas. As a result, more administrators were willing to listen when we asked for cooperation in research or training projects.

TABLE 12–1: Results of Analysis of Variance of Differences in Absenteeism Between Students of High and Low Functioning Teachers*

Level of Teacher Functioning	N of Teachers	Average Days Absent Per Student	N of Students	Significance level
High Empathy**	121	5.0 days per year	3410	P < .005
Low Empathy	119	9.0 days per year	3199	

*Analysis of Variance is a procedure which researchers frequently use to find out whether two or more groups of people perform differently on some test or other measure of skill or behavior. In order to decide whether the groups are alike or different, the researcher compares the pattern (distribution) of the scores made by persons in one group against the patterns for the other groups. If a group is different *enough* from the other groups and from the total or overall group, it is then said to be a significant difference.

* *Above 3.2 level on Aspy Scale of Meaning (Empathy)

The data in Table 12–2 speaks most loudly to teachers since they can see that, at every grade level, relating to students in a person-centered manner resulted in gains on the achievement indices for which they are being held accountable, including the basic skills of reading and math. For us "back to the basics" meant returning to the fundamental premise of our model: productive classrooms are those in which facilitative teachers help students grow both personally and academically.

But this process of relating to students takes time and patience. Many times, teachers complained in our training sessions, "I did what you said, but I feel as though all we did all day was have fun! We didn't work at all!" Yet, those same teachers were the ones whose students were more productive on all the indices we measured. We wanted to know what was going on in their classrooms that caused the teachers to characterize their day as "having fun and not work." We found that learning activities in the classrooms of high-facilitative teachers were characterized by more frequent occurrence of certain specific student behaviors than were activities in classrooms of low-facilitation teachers (6, pp. 370–76; 9, pp. 3–10; 35).

TABLE 12–2: Mean Differences in Adjusted Gain* Between Students of Trained (Facilitative) Teachers and Untrained Teachers

Grade Level	Reading Achievement	Math Achievement	English Achievement
1-3	+ 10.88***	Not Tested	Not tested
4-6	+ 3.66**	+ 15.44***	+ 18.66***
7-9	+ 2.96**	+ 4.10**	+ 11.75***
10-12	+ 1.56*	+ 1.94*	+ 0.96 NS

*p < .05   + In favor of experimental (training) group
**p < .01   − In favor of control (no training) group
***p < .001

NS = Not significant

*Covariates were I.Q. and pre-test standing.

In the classrooms of teachers who were more empathic, more congruent, and more respectful of their students, there was:

1. More student talk
2. More student problem solving
3. More verbal initiation
4. More verbal response to teacher
5. More asking of questions
6. More involvement in learning
7. More eye contact with teacher
8. More physical movement
9. Higher levels of cognition
10. Greater creativity

We had anticipated (or, at least, hoped) that the students of teachers who had been trained to offer higher levels of interpersonal skills (the Experimental Group) would make greater gains in self-concept than the control students. But we were *horrified* to find that part of the statistical significance of the difference in gains was due to the fact that, in many cases, the control students (whose teachers did *not* receive the training) had suffered a *decrease* in their self-concept scores! (See Table 12–3.) They were more negative about their physical appearance, their interpersonal adequacy, their sense of autonomy. Certainly, teaching a person to like himself *less* is not a process that we felt should be going on in schools (13).

In another study, we investigated interpersonal conditions and their relationship to cognitive processes (11, pp. 365–68). We assessed both student and teacher behavior according to Bloom's Taxonomy of Cognitive Objectives, which defines six categories of mental processes. Such a large percentage of behavior occurred in the first category (memory) that it was difficult to find behaviors that could be called thinking or problem solving. The typical classroom in our samples employed the lowest order of cognitive behavior (memory) almost exclusively.

Classes were assigned to Group I if we found no incidence of student cognitive functioning above Level One of Bloom's Taxonomy and to Group

TABLE 12–3: Results of Comparisons of Adjusted* Treatment Means From *How I see Myself* Test Scores

HISM Factor	Grades 3-6			Grades 7-12		
	Experimental Means	Control Means	Sig. p<	Experimental Means	Control Means	Sig. p<
Teacher-School	2.56	1.61	.05	1.52	0.53	NS
Physical Appearance	1.45	−0.96	.01	1.81	0.01	.05
Interpersonal Adequacy	2.87	2.20	.05	1.99	−0.28	.01
Autonomy	0.96	−1.89	.01	2.19	0.89	.01
Academic Adequacy	1.25	0.02	.05	0.86	0.30	.05
Total School	8.61	1.08	.001	6.85	0.92	.001

*Covariates were I.Q. and pre-test standing
NS = Not significant at p ≤ .05

TABLE 12–4: Relationship Between Teacher Levels of Interpersonal Functioning and Student Levels of Cognitive Functioning

Interpersonal Variable	Group I†	Group II†	Total Teachers		Biserial Coefficient
	Means	Means	Means	Standard Deviation	$r$bis.
Empathy	2.56	2.83	2.69	.53	.322
Congruence	2.57	2.81	2.68	.57	.262
Positive Regard	2.58	3.35	2.96	.59	.821*

*Significant at p < .001

†Groups differentiated according to levels of cognitive functioning (on Bloom's Taxonomy) attained by students. Group I attained *only* Level 1. Group II had at least occasional occurrence of Levels 2–6.

II if we found students functioning at least occasionally on a level higher than memory. Then the levels of the teacher's facilitative functioning were assessed. It was clear that teachers were more person-centered in the classrooms where students were thinking. (See Table 12–4.)

The results were surprising to most teachers who thought they were eliciting high orders of cognitive behaviors from their students. They were even more disturbed by discovering that they themselves rarely used higher order cognitive behavior in the classroom. That is, they neither modeled nor requested thinking from their students. In one sample of 692 hours of secondary school teaching provided by ninety teachers, the total time devoted to thinking behaviors by *all teachers combined* was one hour and three minutes (17).

Without stretching the data too far it seems logical to infer from the foregoing that teachers do not show a great deal of *intellectual* respect for their students. This conclusion seems warranted by the fact that they rarely ask them to solve problems in class. Of course, it may be that most teachers do not know how to elicit problem-solving behavior from students, and, thus, cannot do so.

It seemed to us that if teachers did not respect their students, negative feelings might be reciprocated, so we took a look at the relationship of facilitative levels and disruptive behavior in the classroom. We assessed eighty-eight classes in grades two through six for levels of teacher empathy and respect and the frequency with which the teacher gave praise, accepted student ideas, and asked for thinking from students. We also collected the number of disruptive behavior incidents that occurred in each classroom for a month. Then we tried to "predict" from the teacher measures which classes had had the most disruptive behavior. As you can see in Table 12–5, from 16 to 45 percent of the variance of disruptive behavior can be predicted if you know the teacher's levels of person-centered conditions (33). That is, *more* disruptive behavior occurred in classes whose teachers were *low* in empathy, respect, praising, accepting student ideas, and asking for thinking.

This area of investigation expanded into indexes such as discipline, attendance, and attitudes. Thus, as the results of the studies accumulated, it was possible to conclude that, *in general, positive human relations are related to positive human behaviors.*

Since many of our studies cut across all socio-economic levels and two or three racial groups, the question arose as to whether the observed benefits were produced by high scores of middle- and upper-class students masking

TABLE 12–5: Prediction of Disruptive Behavior

Variable	Mean	Standard Deviation	MCR^2 With Teachers' Levels of Interpersonal Skills[1]
PHYSICAL AGGRESSION			
Against Teacher	0.4	1.31	(.08)
Against Pupil	2.4	2.85	.21*
Against Object	0.5	1.02	.22*
VERBAL AGGRESSION			
Against Teacher	2.6	4.45	.16*
Against Pupil	3.9	4.79	.22*
Against Object	0.4	0.81	.21*
PASSIVE RESISTANCE	1.2	1.96	.37*
ANNOYING PERSONAL BEHAVIOR			
Intended	1.9	2.89	.33*
Unintentional	1.2	2.26	.45*
TOTAL DISRUPTIVE BEHAVIOR	14.7	13.52	.33*

( ) = Not Significant at $p < .05$
* = Significant at $p < .05$
MCR^2 = Multiple Correlation Coefficient Squared
[1]Interpersonal skills used as predictors of disruptive behavior were: Empathy, Congruence, Respect for Student, Student Success Promotion, and Student involvement

little or no gain by children from less verbal and less achievement-oriented levels of society. Accordingly, we examined separately data for all students in grades two through six who were scoring significantly below their age-expectancy norms on academic achievement measures, regardless of the reason for such under-achievement (41). The study involved 296 students from seventy-five classrooms. (See Tables 12–6 and 12–7.) Findings were that "educationally handicapped" students of teachers offering high levels of empathy, congruence, and positive regard

1. Missed fewer days of school during the year;
2. Maintained or increased their scores on self-concept measures (while students of teachers offering low levels of empathy, congruence and positive regard had decreases on self-concept measures);
3. Maintained or increased their scores in I.Q. tests as opposed to decreases for students of low level teachers;
4. Made greater gains on academic achievement measures.

The level of person-to-person conditions the teacher offers to under-achieving students more frequently produced significant main effects on school attendance, gain in reading and math achievement, and change in I.Q. scores and self-concept than any of the following variables: I.Q. levels, race/sex groups, and socio-economic status. In other words, *for students identified as having learning difficulties, the teacher's level of interpersonal facilitation was the single most important contributor to the amount of gain on all outcome measures* (41).

Furthermore, interaction effects with race, sex, and socio-economic status supported the hypothesis that teachers operating at low levels of empathy, congruence and positive regard were also responding to students on the basis of stereotypes, whereas teachers operating at high levels responded *differentially* (responded to each student in terms of the student's needs and goals). From the student's viewpoint, this means that when she has a facilitative teacher she is *not* responded to as "That lazy, fat sloppy kid," but as "Janey" who has "lots of creative and achievement potentials but needs some help in activating them."

One other smaller study of the Consortium (NCHE) is of interest here because it sheds some light on how well students will choose when allowed self-direction. Martha Gallion, a teacher in the Garland Independent School District, completed a course offered by Texas Woman's University that used the NCHE training program as its content. With the permission of her principal, she decided to put her new skills to work by offering the chance to design their own reading program to the students in her "educationally handicapped" third grade classroom. Every student in the classroom was reading one or more years below grade level.

At first, the students found it difficult to believe that they really could design their own program. When they did begin to make suggestions, many of them were negative ones: "We don't want to read out loud in circles every day;" "We don't want to do workbooks every day;" "No wall-chart of what we haven't finished." But they also came up with constructive suggestions: "Could we have a quiet time every day where everybody just reads, including you, teacher?" "Can we just read for you to hear—not everybody else?" "Can we read something else more than the reading book?"

The reading program, as finally designed by the students, included: (1) one half-hour of silent reading every day, with the teacher reading her own

TABLE 12–6: Results of Analysis of Co-Variance† for Treatment Effects on Reading Achievement, Math Achievement, I.Q. Score, and Self-Concept of Educationally Handicapped Students

GRADE LEVEL	READING*			MATH*			I.Q. SCORE*			SELF-CONCEPT‡		
	Mean Change		Sig. Level	Mean Change		Sig. Level	Mean Change		Sig. Level	Mean Change		Sig. Level
	Hi	Lo		Hi	Lo		Hi	Lo		Hi	Lo	
02	+0.9	+0.5	.02	—	—	—	+5.3	−2.3	.008	—	—	—
03	+1.5	+0.7	.03	+1.3	+0.8	.04	+5.7	−0.6	.05	—	−1.2	.04
04	+1.4	+0.7	.04	+0.7	+0.2	.002	+3.1	−1.7	.009	+2.5	+0.5	.04
05	+0.8	+0.5	NS	+1.1	+0.6	.04	+0.9	−5.6	.03	+4.2	+0.5	.02
06	+1.9	+1.2	.05	+1.5	+0.9	.04	+3.2	+0.5	.007	+2.5	+0.4	.05

† = Covariate was pre-test standing on criterion variable

Sig. Level = Level of significance of f-test

Hi = students of teachers functioning above 3.0 on scales of empathy, congruence and positive regard

Lo = students of teachers functioning below 3.0 on scales of empathy, congruence and positive regard

* = Change in grade-level equivalents

= Change in I.Q. points

‡ = Change in raw score points

+ = gain

− = loss

— = no test at this grade for this outcome measure

TABLE 12–7: Results of Analysis of Variance for Treatment Effects on Absenteeism of Educationally Handicapped Students

Grade Level	Absenteeism Mean* for Year		Difference Lo-Hi	F-Test Level of Significance
	High Group	*Lo Group*		
02	7.9	11.8	3.9	.04
03	8.0	9.6	1.6	.05
04	6.0	9.3	3.3	.04
05	6.3	7.2	0.9	.05
06	6.9	8.2	1.3	.03

*Mean days absent per student

Hi = Students of teachers functioning above 3.0 on scales of empathy, congruence, and positive regard

Lo = Students of teachers functioning below 3.0 on scales of empathy, congruence, and positive regard

materials, (b) reading aloud to the teacher twice a week, (c) doing skills materials during two half-periods a week, (d) reading in the basal reader once a week, (e) reading orally with a partner once weekly, (f) one half-hour a week in which they could do anything related to learning to read that they liked (read aloud to a friend, play a learning game, read to the teacher, read silently, visit the library, or any other activity they could justify as being related to reading).

Martha added two other elements to the total classroom program, although they were not considered part of the reading program designed by the students. Each day, one half-hour was set aside in the morning in which students could tell the whole class anything important about themselves that they wished their classmates to know. A second, shorter, period was set aside in the afternoon in which students could come individually to Martha to talk with her about anything they wanted her to know, including anything that was bothering them about school, or themselves, or exciting things they wanted to share just with her.

At the end of the year, not one of these "educationally handicapped" children had made less than eleven months progress in reading; some had made as much as *three years'* growth. An analysis of variance was conducted to compare their gains with the gains of students in the three other third-grade classrooms in the same school. The resulting f was 4.475; $p < .01$. (Thus there is only a 1% probability that the superior gains are due to chance.)

To sum it all up, the research evidence clearly indicates that when students' feelings are responded to, when they are regarded as worthwhile human beings, capable of self-direction, and when their teacher relates to them in a person-to-person manner, good things happen. To the Consortium researchers, it seems that children who are in person-centered classrooms learn some important things about themselves, which make it possible for them to grow more healthily and achieve more effectively. Those "extra" self-learnings seem to be as follows:

1. My feelings are acceptable.
2. It's all right to be me. . . . I'm unique and valued.

3. My feelings are a good way to decide what's good and what's bad for me.
4. Everyone has feelings, and everyone has the right to express their own feelings.
5. Doing things that are important and exciting *to me* is worthwhile.
6. My experience can guide my learnings, and my learnings can help me interpret my experience.

In short, students learn that they *can* learn, and in so doing they are free to become productive and involved—more fully functioning in every way.

THE INTERPERSONAL SKILLS OF TEACHERS

In several studies in which NCHE assessed the levels of facilitative conditions which teachers offer to students, we found that teachers who provided high levels of empathy were also characterized by a cluster of other behaviors (16, pp. 216–22; 37, 39). That is, they also tended to provide:
1. More response to student feeling.
2. More use of student ideas in ongoing instructional interactions.
3. More discussion with students (dialogue).
4. More praise of students.
5. More congruent teacher talk (less ritualistic).
6. More tailoring of contents to the individual student's frame of reference. (Explanations tend to be created to fit the immediate needs of the learners.)
7. More smiling with students.

Furthermore, their classroom activities tended to reflect similar general characteristics:
1. The learning goals are derived from cooperative planning between teacher and students.
2. The classroom is individualized for and by the present class to meet its needs. There are more projects and displays created by students. The room looks "lived-in."
3. More freedom from time limits. There are fewer deadlines and more flexible sequences of order.
4. More emphasis upon productivity and creativity than upon evaluation. It's more important to carry out a meaningful project than to critique performance. Therefore, there is less emphasis upon grades and tests.

These behaviors are clearly contained within the broader boundaries of those described by Rogers as being person-centered. Unfortunately, and despite a rather general misconception that most teachers have well-developed interpersonal skills, these behaviors do not occur frequently in the average classroom. In fact, the broad-based data of the NCHE indicates that most teachers (principals and supervisors, too) generally operate at a *low* level of interpersonal skills (14). (See Table 12–8.) They need very basic training in procedures for responding to other people.

To illustrate the need for basic skills, one of our studies found that some teachers cannot maintain eye contact with another person for more than a fleeting moment. Furthermore, some students *never* receive *favorable* eye contact from a teacher and receive negative eye contact only when they are being disruptive. As a result of these findings (15), we made eye-to-eye contact one school's humanizing goal for an academic year; attendance in-

TABLE 12–8: Teacher Means by Geographic Groups of Naturally Occurring (Before Training) Levels of Interpersonal Functioning

Location	N	Mean
Florida	400	2.3
Kansas	120	2.0
Kentucky	36	2.3
Louisiana	60	2.1
Massachusetts	20	2.2
North Carolina	40	2.1
Texas	600	2.2
Virginia	100	2.3

creased significantly (p<.01). This kind of basic skill seems to be the proper starting point of interpersonal training programs for some educators.

In general, our findings about the distribution of facilitative conditions can be summarized in seven points:

1. The mean level of empathy, congruence, and positive regard among teachers was about the same as that of the general population.*
2. The average level of interpersonal skills for teachers who had not been trained to offer facilitative conditions was below the minimally effective threshold of 3.0 on the process scales for empathy, congruence, and positive regard. (14)
3. The mean level of interpersonal skills among principals and counselors untrained in the humanistic education technology was below 3.0 on the process scales. (10, pp. 163–71)
4. The mean level of interpersonal skills among professors of teacher education who had not received interpersonal-skill training was below the minimally facilitative (3.0) threshold. (15)
5. The distribution of naturally occurring (untrained) levels of interpersonal skills was not related to sex, race, years of experience in educational settings, or geographical location. (36, pp. 9–14; 38, pp. 86–92)
6. The mean level of interpersonal skills among teachers in the United States was not significantly different from that in seven foreign countries. (10, pp. 163–71)
7. There was a deterioration across the year from September to May in the levels of facilitative conditions offered students by their teachers. (17)

INCREASING THE INTERPERSONAL SKILLS OF TEACHERS

The early work by the NCHE indicated that most classroom teachers were *not* concerned deeply about maintaining facilitative interpersonal behaviors in their classroom as *an end in itself*. On the other hand, *they were interested* in those things that affect their students' immediate schooling behaviors—learning, discipline, and attendance. Thus, we wanted to close the gap between researchers and practitioners by depicting the relationship between facilitative interpersonal behaviors and outcomes the teachers valued.

*For mean level of teacher functioning, see (13). For levels of general public, see (24).

The human relations specialist tends to view interpersonal behavior as pre-eminent and substantive content as secondary; the classroom teacher, particularly at the high-school level, views substantive content as primary and human relations as secondary. Our studies revealed that for enhancing learning outcomes the teacher was the most important interpersonal factor in the classroom; and it was essential to present interpersonal behavior training as an adjunct to effective instruction. Thus, we introduced our training by explaining that our past work indicated that certain types of teacher behaviors were related to increased student learning. We also tied our interpersonal model to an appropriate learning model with which teachers could identify (23). This extended model is shown in Figure 12–2.

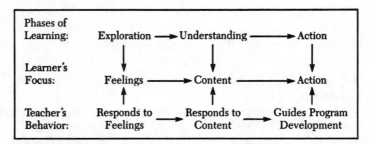

FIGURE 12–2: Expanded Model of Learning and Interpersonal Relationships

In order to introduce the idea of interpersonal events, we employed Flanders' Interaction Analysis because it was couched in "teacher's language" and seemed to communicate to teachers that their behavior has some relationship to student behaviors. At a broad level, the teacher discovered the amount of classroom time occupied by teacher talk and, conversely, that proportion used for talk by students. This simple component of interpersonal relationships was a significant learning for most classroom teachers, who found that about 80 percent of their classroom time was teacher talk, 10 percent student talk (all of them), and 10 percent silence or confusion. Many teachers were surprised at this finding and began to seek ways to decrease *their* talk while *increasing* that of their students.

Incidentally, NCHE has recently completed a study of teaching in colleges of education in ten universities throughout the nation. In most of the college classrooms, student talk was the largest component of the verbal interaction; but it was *not* spontaneous, conversational talk. It was students giving reports—mini-lectures—on some assigned topic. It was not dialogue or real verbal interaction. It seems that professors in colleges of education have decided that students should talk more in class, but their skill repertoire is limited to delegating the responsibility for conducting a monologue to someone else. Apparently, teacher educators do not know how to engage students in conversational dialogue. Thus, human relations in most classrooms tend to be formal and rigid, because we do not have functional behaviors to relax them. At least, the evidence suggests that our teaching mentors do not use such behaviors in *their* classrooms.

We described the use of feedback from tape-recordings while discussing our technology earlier in this article. Our overall finding is that teachers can be trained to use higher levels of intepersonal facilitative conditions. In a three-year study of the effects of training educational personnel to offer higher levels of empathy, congruence, and positive regard to their students, NCHE had the following results (17):

1. Teachers, principals, and counselors were successfully trained to function above the minimally effective threshold (3.0 on the scales for empathy, congruence, and positive regard) through training programs employing a didactic/experiential model.
2. There was no systematic differential response to this training by subgroups of teachers differentiated according to characteristics of race, sex, years of teaching experience, or geographical location. In other words, anybody *could learn* to be more facilitative.
3. In order to reach the 3.0 level of facilitative functioning, in general, secondary teachers required training programs of longer duration or greater intensity than did elementary teachers.
4. The teachers learned more effectively in programs that (a) combined training in interpersonal processes with training in applying those skills to learning interactions, (b) provided periodic feedback of the teachers' level of functioning in the classroom, and (c) were conducted by instructors who were themselves functioning above the 3.0 level of empathy, congruence, and positive regard.
5. When principals and school-system administrators supported the training program by providing incentives for teacher involvement in the training, then (a) the teachers participated more regularly, (b) more teachers participated, (c) the teachers made greater gains in skills, and (d) the gains in levels of empathy, congruence, and positive regard were more frequently put into practice in the classroom.
6. The trained levels of interpersonal skills produced growth in students just as the naturally occurring, high levels of these facilitative conditions do.
7. When principals were trained to use higher levels of interpersonal and interactional skills with their faculties, the teachers (a) used higher levels of skills with their students, (b) reported that their working environment and instructional tasks were more attractive, and (c) had decreased turnover rates and absence rates.
8. The teachers' level of empathy was the single most frequently recurring predictor of other teacher and student behavior in the classroom as well as of outcome behaviors in terms of student growth on self-concept, achievement measures, attendance, and less disruptive behavior.

We used the same model for training as for research—a model that placed the facilitative conditions within a context of the phases of learning. In working within this model, the NCHE developed training procedures to enhance teacher levels of functioning in interpersonal skills. It is important to underscore the term *skill* in interpersonal relationships because it assumes significance in the model we employed. By this we mean that interpersonal skills were defined somewhat narrowly; and, as such, they were steps forward in the process delineating the critical variables of interpersonal relationships. Specifically, we defined a *skill* as *a replicable act on call to the person*. (We can do it when we want.) The objective of interpersonal skills programs becomes that of training for the skills that theory suggests and research supports as being significantly related to effective interpersonal functioning.

In its teacher training programs, the NCHE increased its effectiveness when it used well-defined interpersonal skills and systematic training programs. It seemed that teachers learned more effectively when they understood the skills and could evaluate whether or not they were acquiring them. The fear of interpersonal training seemed to yield to a systematic approach in which each interpersonal skill became as tangible as all other human behaviors. In short, the teacher training programs worked.

INTERPERSONAL SKILLS AND
PHYSICAL FITNESS

Several investigations of the physical fitness dimension supported a relationship of that factor and the interpersonal skills dimension. Findings from these studies (8, 14, 22, 42) included the following:

1. In case studies of school administrators, 93 percent of the high-functioning principals were involved in some regular physical exercise program; 60 percent of these person-centered principals (aged forty-five and older) were able to run two miles in less than fifteen minutes.
2. In general, teacher responsiveness toward students declines within each week from Monday morning to Friday afternoon and recovers on the following Monday.
3. When only the data from the high-physical-fitness group is examined, the pattern is different (from that described in 2)—the highest peak of responsiveness is reached on Friday afternoon at the time the students most need it.
4. Physical fitness was a significant predictor of gain in both immediate skills learning and subsequent performance in the classrooms of teachers who participated in in-service training workshops designed to increase constructive responsiveness to students.
5. Teachers' hearts beat approximately twelve times more per minute when teaching than when engaged in physically equivalent non-teaching activity. That is, there is some real physical wear and tear in the teaching process.
6. When teachers are responding to students, they have significantly ($p<.02$) faster pulse rates than when they are initiating structure.
7. The finding for number 6, above, does not hold true for physically fit teachers.
8. The teacher's level of physical fitness was significantly ($p<.001$) correlated with the frequency with which he made eye contact with students and the number of times he smiled while teaching.
9. Physical fitness was a better predictor of practicum performance of student teachers and student nurses than grade point average.
10. Comparisons of student teachers from a college located in flat terrain with one located in mountainous terrain indicated: (1) no significant differences between the two groups in demographic characteristics such as age, sex, socioeconomic status, and race; and (2) a difference in physical fitness with students from mountainous terrain being significantly ($p<.01$) more fit, as measured on a twelve-minute walk/run test.
11. Student teachers with higher levels of physical fitness accepted their students' ideas more often and criticized their students less often than did student teachers with lower levels of physical fitness ($R^2 = 0.483$; $p<.002$).
12. The single best predictor of the counselor's helpfulness (as rated by the client) was listening stress levels; the more effective counselors listened dynamically (heartbeat rate elevated ten to fifteen beats per minute while the client was talking).

We concluded that fatigue, poor nutrition, and lack of physical exercise are deterrents to positive interpersonal relationships. The data from subsequent work suggests strongly that physical fitness is necessary for sustaining constructive interpersonal relationships across long periods of time. It seems that all teachers who *understand* constructive human relationships can be humane for a *short* period of time, but their levels of physical fitness determine the *durability* of their interpersonal facilitation.

One point that must be made clear is that physical fitness is not the only factor in constructive interpersonal behavior. That is, a person may be quite fit physically and be inept interpersonally. *Physical fitness seems to be a necessary, but not a sufficient, condition for sustaining high levels of interpersonal functioning.* Also, we *cannot* say that all of those teachers who provide good interpersonal facilitation are physically fit. It seems that we *can* say that our levels of physical fitness determine the length of time we can employ our highest interpersonal skills. Of course, if our skills are very limited, then high levels of physical fitness would not enhance them.

These findings about physical fitness and interpersonal functioning are so compatible with common sense as to be obvious and barely worth mentioning except for the fact that our investigations indicate that, as a group, teachers are unfit physically. Additionally, many school practices do not encourage physical fitness for either students or teachers. For instance, few schools provide exercise facilities for teachers, and lunch periods are often very short and associated with stressful conditions of noise, responsibility for student behavior, isolation from adult peers, and so on. In the light of the data relating physical fitness and interpersonal functioning, there is little wonder that teachers often provide low levels of interpersonal facilitation.

If we were to summarize the bits and pieces of our work, it would be something like this: Physical fitness seems to be the foundation out of which interpersonal skills can develop, and they, in turn, lay the basis for intellectual growth. This is not a new set of formulations. It is a reaffirmation of some things we have undersupported for a long time in our schools.

NCHE STUDIES IN NONSCHOOL SETTINGS

Recently, the interest of the consortium researchers has turned to investigating the effects of Rogers' facilitative conditions in settings other than schools. Major findings from these studies include:
1. When parents of special education (resource room) children are trained in Interpersonal Skills, the students perceive their home environments as more understanding and express less anxiety about parent-teacher conferences. (28)
2. When parents of primary-grade children are trained in both interpersonal (humanistic interaction) skills and communication skills in the language arts areas, the students (a) talk more about their school experiences with their parents, (b) express more enthusiasm for language arts activities, (c) read more books at home, and (d) more frequently choose reading-related activities and games during free times at school. (26)
3. When teenage pregnant girls are taught about contraception and family planning by high affect teachers, they learn more information and become more confident of their ability to exercise control over what happens to them than do girls who are taught by low affect teachers. (15)

4. Teenagers with gonorrhea who have come to a clinic for diagnosis and treatment and have been given their epidemiologic interview and taught about the disease and its consequences by interviewers who have been trained to offer high levels of interpersonal skills, return for their test-of-cure about twice as frequently as those whose interviewer had not received the interpersonal skills training. (33)

5. When physicians offer high levels of empathy while taking a patient history, their histories are more complete and the information received is more directly relevant to the subsequent diagnosis (as judged by a panel of independent physicians) than were histories taken without offering empathic statements to the patients. (19, pp. 1–14)

IMPEDIMENTS

When one views the evidence supporting humanistic interpersonal relationships, it usually leads to questions of why they do not receive more emphasis in our schools. The answers are nearly as varied as are our thousands of school systems. Fortunately, however, common threads occur in many situations. A few of these are the following:

1. There is a tendency for researchers/educators to dichotomize "interpersonal skills" and "on-the-job success." This spirit is depicted by the phrase, "It's nice to be nice, but you gotta teach them something." It seems that most of us have not yet integrated our responsive interpersonal dimension with our assertiveness dimension. The effect of this polarization is that we find teachers choosing between being tender or tough. Those who select tenderness often find that they also choose nonpromotion; those who opt for toughness discover that isolation and loneliness come with it.

2. There is a tendency for schools to operate in terms of immediacy rather than of long-range needs. This tendency is enhanced when resources are limited in time of economic problems. In this context, interpersonal relations receive emphasis in proportion to the crisis levels in a given school; we are often limited to crisis intervention and remedial functions for our entries to the scene of operations. Thus the growth and prevention dimensions of interpersonal skills tend to be neglected in many school settings.

3. Interpersonal skills training programs often focus upon horizontal and downward relationships. This focus helps educators relate more effectively to colleagues and students, but not to administrators, parents, board members, and so on. The outcome is that teachers tend to retreat from "others" and form mutually reinforcing support groups. Although the latter are necessary, they are incomplete because some of the important interfaces are untouched.

4. As alluded to earlier, human relations specialists tend to be somewhat overzealous for interpersonal relationships and neglectful of the school's substantive responsibility. This happens when the human relations specialist fails to employ his own skills for entering the teacher's frame of reference. In those instances, we find a kind of struggle between teachers and the interpersonal programs.

5. Interpersonal skills programs frequently are not based on individual readiness levels and fail to bring success to many of the trainees. Teachers and principals and supervisors do not enjoy failure (or the lack of success) any more than their students do. (1; 7, pp. 57–60)

A BRIEF SUMMARY OF OUR JOURNEY

This concludes our presentation of our years of research. We have presented the model from which we drew our hypotheses; the logistics by which we accumulated a massive amount of data; the measurement of the facilitative attitudinal conditions in teachers and administrators; the effects of these teacher attitudes and behaviors on students—their achievement, the quality of their thinking, their morale; the degree to which teachers possess these attitudes and skills; the effective means we discovered for increasing these skills; the relationship of physical fitness to these attitudes, especially their lasting quality; some studies showing how these attitudes and skills affect parents and teenagers in non-school situations; and finally some of the obstacles to the more widespread use of training in interpersonal skills.

Now we turn to studies made in another country which tested our findings in a very different cultural setting.

Corroboration from Germany

When Reinhard and Anne-Marie Tausch learned of the Aspy-Roebuck studies that have been presented in this chapter, they were challenged. Would the same results be found in German schools?

For a decade, they pursued these questions, replicating in their own way the Aspy-Roebuck studies. Working with their students, many doctoral dissertations and a host of masters' theses were completed bearing on these questions. These have been published in a variety of German journals.

FINDINGS REGARDING TEACHER-STUDENT INTERACTION

The Drs. Tausch wrote a summary of these researches, which shows the imagination and ingenuity with which they pursued not only the major thrust of the Aspy-Roebuck studies, but probed many other fascinating interactions, beyond those of teacher and student. It is unfortunate that lack of space prevents us from presenting their full report. Instead we will let them summarize their findings and suggest some of the implications.

> In all of the school studies, empathic understanding, genuineness, warm respect, and nondirective activities proved to significantly facilitate the quality of the pupils' intellectual contributions during the lesson, their spontaneity, their independence and initiative, their positive feelings during the lesson, and their positive perception of the teacher. Teachers who were rated high on all four dimensions felt more content with themselves and their lessons. Furthermore, all the studies indicated that low ratings on understanding, genuineness, respect, and nondirective facilitation and high ratings on directive leading accompanied lower levels of pupil intellectual performance and significantly negative emotional experiences.
>
> If we want to diminish stress, aversion, and impairment of physical and emotional health in schools and at the same time facilitate the development of personality and the quality of intellectual performance, then we will need a different kind of teacher than we seem to produce at present. Teachers

are needed who can create in their classes an atmosphere in which there is empathic understanding, pupils receive warmth and respect, genuineness is encouraged, and the teacher can be facilitative in nondirective ways. (47)

THE ENCOUNTER GROUP AS A MEANS
OF HELPING TEACHERS

In one very important study,

twenty-six teachers from different types of schools took part in person-centered encounter groups for two-and-a-half days along with psychotherapy clients. There were at least two teachers in each encounter group. Teachers waiting to participate in an encounter group experience served as controls. Results of the study showed that 73% of the encounter-teachers had long-lasting changes in their personalities. Their self-concepts and their personal relationships improved; they decreased their negative self-communication, and they had fewer emotional problems. The encounter-teachers also changed their teaching behavior after having been in the group. Their school problems decreased (discipline problems, lack of time); they felt they had a better understanding of their pupils' emotions; and they considered their students' feelings more frequently during lessons. They improved their relations with their colleagues. Their pupils became more trusting of the teacher and enjoyed more self-determination. And finally, 96% of the encounter-teachers thought that such person-centered encounter groups were important and helpful for their work at school. (48)

OTHER FINDINGS

In one study child-centered counseling was provided for maladjusted and disadvantaged kindergarten and primary school children. The results were very positive (46). A similar study of many difficult and anxious students in intermediate school showed that those who received counseling became, in teachers' judgments, more psychologically stable and improved (32). The researchers even trained older pupils to be group facilitators of younger 5th and 6th graders, with very good results (49). In each of these studies there were adequate control groups.

Other studies involved the effectiveness of two-and-a-half day encounter groups with neurotic adults: results very positive (21). They also studied individual therapy of a person-centered sort (45, 44).

Their general conclusions deserve to be quoted in full.

If teachers, parents, psychotherapists, members of groups, and people in general, could to a significant extent be genuine, empathic, and understanding, provide each other warm respect, and interact in nondirective ways, the consequences would be substantial. Such behavior would facilitate constructive development of personality, lead to enhanced psychological health, and promote intellectual development. If these qualities were found in teachers, parents, psychotherapists, and group leaders, then the lives of children and adult members of groups of all kinds would be more humane and full of growth.

Unfortunately, such qualities seem relatively rare in professional, helping persons at present. Our evidence indicates that only about 10% of teachers approach their classes in a person-centered way, for example (29, 30, 31). If person-centered encounter groups could be made available to teachers, teachers-in-training, therapists and leaders of groups, then it is reasonable to assume that this would greatly influence their effectiveness in facilitating change in others. (47)

Brief Comments

It is most unusual for research in the social sciences to be replicated. Here a large-scale study was repeated, using slightly different methods, in another culture. The fact that the findings are, in all essential respects, in agreement, is a remarkable validation of the outcomes. The results in each country reinforce the results in the other country, thus, increasing the trustworthiness of the basic findings.

In one respect the two studies differ. In the effort to improve the facilitative attitudes of the teachers, Aspy, Roebuck, and colleagues used a training approach based on skills. The Tausch researchers enrolled teachers in brief but intensive encounter groups.

There has been much criticism of training in interpersonal relations that is based on narrowly defined *skills*. This kind of emphasis frequently leads only to a change in the *form* of the person's response. It does not necessarily lead to the *experiencing* of a different *attitude*. Personally, I have many reservations about this kind of training. Experience in an encounter group, on the other hand, frequently changes the person's *attitudes*, which then may be expressed in a number of spontaneous and diverse forms. My preference is for this type of approach.

It is of interest to me that positive results in the improvement of facilitative attitudes were achieved in both studies. Hence, we cannot say from these reports that one approach is better than the other.

There is no doubt that the skills type of training is more readily adaptable to large numbers, and I am aware that learning a skill *can* lead to a real change in attitude. Nevertheless in helping teachers develop in a totally humanistic way, an encounter group or a teacher-training program such as that at St. Lawrence University, is, in my judgment, preferable to a narrower training in the *skills* of interpersonal relationship.

Aside from this cautionary statement, which in no way detracts from the primary findings, I regard these two studies as landmarks in the field of education.

Some Final Questions—and Answers

Let me bring this chapter to a close by posing a number of questions to teachers, to supervisors, to administrators, and to those involved in the training of teachers.

Within the educational domain for which you have responsibility, would you find it desirable if:

1. Students learned reading, math and other subjects at a more accelerated rate?
2. Student absenteeism was reduced, thus increasing outside financial aid?
3. Pupils had more self-confidence, valued themselves more, were more able to know and express their own feelings?
4. Discipline problems and disruptive behavior in the classroom were diminished?
5. Vandalism by students decreased?
6. Many pupils made a gain in I.Q.?
7. Students developed the higher thinking processes—problem-solving and decision-making abilities?
8. Students gave evidence of more creativity?
9. Students were more spontaneous and initiated more activity, more conversation?
10. Students were more eager learners, asking more questions, making more contributions, enjoying learning?
11. Students were not mere memorizers?
12. Students became more self-directing, able to choose their own areas of study, and responsibly carry through their own plans?
13. Students liked their teachers?
14. Students developed more ability to work together cooperatively?

To the extent that your answer to these questions is "yes," the studies reported in this chapter show how these results may come about. Every one of these outcomes is significantly more likely in classrooms where the teachers rate high on the facilitative conditions: where they are themselves as genuine persons in class; where they respect the uniqueness of each student; where they let students know that their feelings and the meaning that the school experience has for them is understood.

This statement is accurate whether we are speaking of white children, black, or Mexican Americans; of German children, of Israeli children. It is accurate whether we are speaking of young children in elementary schools or adolescents in secondary schools or young people in technical schools. It holds for educationally disadvantaged children and for the gifted. Present knowledge indicates that it applies to all of education.

But where are such teachers to come from? It is clear that teachers with these qualities and attitudes would vastly improve our educational system. But their numbers are relatively small.

Here, too, the studies give an encouraging answer. When teachers are supplied—in a confidential and nonjudgmental way—with the facts about their own attitudes and behaviors in the classroom, they are much more willing to undertake cognitive and experiential training focused on just these qualities. And this training is effective in raising the qualitative level of teacher-student interaction so that teachers become more facilitative. This is especially true when their instructors are persons who themselves rate high on these qualities.

Principals and administrators can also learn from such intensive training, which includes both intellect and heart, and the very best classroom and student outcomes occurred when the principal and the teachers exhibited high levels of the facilitative qualities. In these schools there was less teacher turnover and absenteeism, and high morale. The whole school became a place for *learners*.

All of these positive outcomes are more likely when teachers and administrators are physically fit, a condition that is also capable of improvement.

I will not attempt to summarize the many secondary findings of these researches. I want to simply stress the main point.

We know—as this chapter clearly demonstrates—how a school—*any* school—may become a situation in which there are eager learners, thinking creatively, rapidly and responsibly; where teachers enjoy their work and their students; where morale is high and both students and teachers *want* to come to school. We know this from elaborate research. We know it because it has been demonstrated. Schools have changed in these directions. These are not speculations. These are facts.

This constitutes a challenge to every teacher, every administrator, every member of a board of education, and perhaps especially to those responsible for the preparation of teachers. How will we respond to that challenge?

REFERENCES

1. Aspy, David N. "Better Self-concepts through Success." *Journal of Negro Education*, December, 1970.
2. Aspy, David N. "The Effect of the Teacher's Inferred Self-Concept upon Student Achievement." Paper presented at the annual meeting of the American Educational Research Association, February 1968, Los Angeles.
3. Aspy, David N. "The Effects of Teacher-Offered Conditions of Empathy, Positive Regard, and Congruence upon Student Achievement." *Florida Journal of Educational Research* 11 (1969): 39–48.
4. Aspy, David N. "The Relationship of the Trainer's Level of Interpersonal Functioning and Change in Teacher Behavior." *Educational Leadership Research Supplement* 28 (1971).
5. Aspy, David N. *Toward a Technology for Humanizing Education.* Champaign, Illinois: Research Press Company, 1972.
6. Aspy, David N., Black B., and Roebuck, Flora N. "The Relationship of Teacher-Offered Conditions of Respect to Behaviors Described by Flanders' Interaction Analysis." *Journal of Negro Education* 61(1972): 370–76.
7. Aspy, David N. and Hutson, B. A. "Promotion of Student Success." *Journal of Educational Research* 66 (October, 1972): 57–60.
8. Aspy, David N. and Roebuck, Flora N. "Client Centered Therapy in the Educational Process." Invited Paper for the *Proceedings of the European Conference on Client Centered Therapy.* Wurtzburg, Germany: University of Wurtzburg Press, 1975.
9. Aspy, David N. and Roebuck, Flora N. "A Discussion of the Relationship Between Selected Student Behavior and the Teacher's Use of Interchangeable Responses." *Humanist Education*, September, 1975, pp. 3–10.
10. Aspy, David N. and Roebuck, Flora N. "From Humane Ideas to Humane Technology and Back Again Many Times." *Education* 92 (Winter, 1974): 163–71.
11. Aspy, David N. and Roebuck, Flora N. "An Investigation of the Relationship Between Student Levels of Cognitive Functioning and the Teacher's Classroom Behavior." *Journal of Educational Research* 65 (1973): 365–68.

12. Aspy, David N. and Roebuck, Flora N. "An Investigation of the Relationship Between Trainers' Levels of Interpersonal Functioning and Changes in Their Trainees Classroom Behavior." *Journal of Negro Education,* 1975.

13. Aspy, David N. and Roebuck, Flora N. *Kids Don't Learn from People They Don't Like.* Amherst, Massachusetts: Human Resource Development Press, 1977.

14. Aspy, David N. and Roebuck, Flora N. *A Lever Long Enough.* Dallas, Texas: The National Consortium for Humanizing Education, 1976.

15. Aspy, David N. and Roebuck, Flora N. "The National Consortium for Humanizing Education: An Update of Research Results." Presentation to the annual meeting of the American Educational Research Association, San Francisco, California, April 12, 1979.

16. Aspy, David N. and Roebuck, Flora N. "The Relationship of Teacher-Offered Conditions of Meaning to Behaviors Described by Flanders' Interaction Analysis." *Education* 95 (Spring, 1975): 216–22.

17. Aspy, David N. and Roebuck, Flora N. *Research Summary: Effects of Training in Interpersonal Skills.* Interim Report No. 4 for NIMH Grant Number 5 PO I MH 19871. Monroe, Louisiana: Northeast Louisiana University, October, 1974. Abstracted in *Resources in Education,* October, 1975. (ERIC Document # ED 106733).

18. Aspy, David N.; Roebuck, Flora N.; Willson, M. A.; and Adams, O. B. *Interpersonal Skills Training for Teachers.* Interim Report No. 2 for NIMH Grant Number 5 PO I MH 19871. Monroe, Louisiana: Northeast Louisiana University, August, 1974.

19. Blalock, and Aspy, David N. "The Effect of Interpersonal Skills upon the Amount of Information Obtained in a Medical Interview." *Research Reports, Carkhuff Institute of Human Technology* 3 (1980): 1–14.

20. Bloom, B. S., ed.; Englehart, M.D.; Furst, E. J.; Hill, W. H.; and Krathwohl, D. R. *A Taxonomy of Educational Objectives; Handbook I, the Cognitive Domain.* New York: Longmans, Green, 1956.

21. Bruh, M., Schwab, R. J., und Tausch, R. Die Auswirkungen intensiver personenzentrieter Gesprächsgrupper bei Klienten und seelischer Beeinträchtigungen. Zeitschrift für Klinische Psychologie, 1980.

22. Buhler, J. H. and Aspy, David N. *Physical Health for Educators: A Book of Readings.* Denton, Texas: North Texas State University Press, 1975.

23. Carkhuff, R. R. *The Development of Human Resources.* New York: Holt, Rinehart and Winston, Inc., 1971. (The model was drawn from the Human Resource Development paradigms proposed by Carkhuff.)

24. Carkhuff, R. R. *Helping and Human Relations: A Primer for Lay and Professional Helpers. Vol I Selection and Training. Vol II Practice and Research.* New York: Holt, Rinehart and Winston, 1969.

25. Carkhuff, R. R. *How to Help Yourself: The Art of Program Development.* Amherst, Massachusetts: Human Resource Development Press, 1974.

26. Committee on Communication Skills, Primary Level. *Parental Involvement Administrator's Manual.* Baton Rouge, Louisiana: Louisiana Office of the Southwest Educational Development Laboratory, 1973.

27. Flanders, N. A. *Teacher Influence on Pupil Attitudes and Achievement.* U.S. Department of Health, Education and Welfare, Cooperative Research Monograph No. 12, Washington, D.C.: Government Printing Office, 1965.

28. Hettrick, E. *Training Parents in Facilitative Communication Skills.* Unpublished dissertation, Psychology Department, Texas Woman's University, 1976.

29. Hoder, J., Tausch, R., und Weber, A. Förderliche Dimensionen des Lehrerverhaltens und ihr Zusammenhang mit der Qualität der Unterrichtsbeitrage der Schuler. Im Manuskript, 1976.

30. Joost, H. Förderliche Dimensionen des Lehrerverhaltens in Zusammenhang mit emotionalen und kognitiven Prozessen bei Schuler, Psychol. in Erz. u. Unterricht, 25, S. 69–94 (1978).
31. Klyne, P. Dimensionen des Lehrerverhaltens in ihrem Zusammenhang mit Vorgangen der Schuler, Im Manuskript, 1976.
32. Pize-Kettner, U.; Ahrbeck, B.; Scheibel, B.; und Tausch, A. Personenzentrierte Gruppen-und Einzelgespräche mit psychisch beeinträchtigen Hauptschulern aus 5.6 Klassen. Zeitschrift für Klinische Psychologie, 1978, Band 7, Heft I, S. 28–40.
33. Roebuck, Flora, N. "Cognitive and Affective Goals of Education: Towards a Clarification Plan." Presentation at Annual Meeting of the Association for Supervision and Curriculum Development, Atlanta, Ga., March, 1980.
34. Roebuck, Flora N. "Delivering HRD Skills in the Public Schools." Abstracted in *Resources in Education*, February 1975. (ERIC Document # ED 096579).
35. Roebuck, Flora N. "Humanistic Education from a Human Resources Development Viewpoint." In *Humanistic Education: Visions and Realities*, Phi Delta Kappa Symposium on Education Research, Berkeley, California: McCutchan, 1977.
36. Roebuck, Flora N. "Human Thoughts and Humane Procedures—Effective Behavior." *Peabody Journal of Education*, October, 1975, pp. 9–14.
37. Roebuck, Flora N. "Polynomial Representation of Teacher Behavior." Address presented at AERA National Convention, Washington, D.C., March 31, 1975. Abstracted in *Resources in Education*, October, 1975. (ERIC Document # ED 106718).
38. Roebuck, Flora N. and Aspy, David N. "Grade-Level Contributions to the Variance of Flanders' Interaction Categories." *The Journal of Experimental Education*, Spring, 1974, pp. 86–92.
39. Roebuck, Flora N. and Aspy, David N. *Response Surface Analysis*. Interim Report No. 3 for NIMH Grant Number 5 PO I MH 19871. Monroe, Louisiana: Northeast Louisiana University, September, 1974. Abstracted in *Resources in Education*, October, 1975 (ERIC Document # ED 106732).
40. Roebuck, Flora N.; Aspy, David N.; Sadler, V.; and Willson, M. A. *Maintaining Reliability*. Interim Report No. 1 for NIMH Grant Number 5 PO I MH 19871. Monroe, Louisiana: Northeast Louisiana University, July, 1974. Abstracted in *Resources in Education*, October, 1975. (ERIC Document # ED 106730).
41. Roebuck, Flora N., Buhler, J. H., and Aspy, David N. *A Comparison of High and Low Levels of Humane Teaching/Learning Conditions on the Subsequent Achievement of Students Identified as Having Learning Difficulties*. Final Report: Order No. PLD-6816-76-rc, the National Institute of Mental Health, HEW, Denton, Texas: Texas Woman's University Press, 1976.
42. Roebuck, Flora N. and Buhler, J. H. "The Relationship between Physical Fitness of a Selected Sample of Student Teachers and Their Performance on the Flanders' Verbal Interaction Scale." In Buhler, J. H. and Aspy, David N., eds. *Physical Health for Educators: A Book of Readings*. Denton, Texas: North Texas State University Press, 1975.
43. Rogers, Carl R. "The Necessary and Sufficient Conditions of Therapeutic Personality Change." *Journal of Consulting Psychology* 21 (1957): 95–103.
44. Rudolph, J., Langer, I., und Tausch, R. Prüfung der psychischen Auswirkungen und Bedingungen von personenzentrierter Einzelpsychotherapie. Aus: Zeitschrift für Klinische Psychologie, 1980, 9, S. 23–33.
45. Rudolph, J. *Psychische Anderungen durch Gesprächpsychotherapie und deren Bedingungen in der Sicht der Klienten*. Doctoral dissertation, Department of Psychology, University of Hamburg, 1975.

46. Tausch, A.; Kettner, U.; Steinbach, I.; und Tonnies, S. E. Effekte kindzen-trierter Einzel- und Gruppengespräche mit unter-privileglierten Kindergarten-und Grundschulkindern, Psychol. in Erz. u. Unterricht, 20, Jg., S. 77–88 (1973).
47. Tausch, R. and Tausch, A-M. *Verifying the Facilitative Dimensions in German Schools—Families—and with German Clients.* Unpublished manuscript, 1980.
48. Tausch, A., Wittern, O., und Albus, J. Erzieher-Kind-Interaktionen in einer Vorschul-Lernsituation im Kindergarten, Psychol. in Erz. u. Unterricht, 23, Jg., S. 1 - 1 (1976).
49. Theig, G., Steinbach, I., und Tausch, A. Schuler führen hilfreiche Gespräche mit Schulern, Psychol. in Erz. u. Unterricht, 25, Jg., S. 75–81 (1978).

Some
Disappointments
in Innovation

A Pattern of Failure

It may have been evident that there was a significant omission in the many examples of the effectiveness of the person-centered approach. There was no description of a whole educational institution built around such an approach sustaining itself successfully over a period of years. This is because humanistic, innovative educational organizations have a poor record in regard to permanence. There seems to be a disappointing succession of failures in this regard. I would like to face up to that pattern of failure by giving a number of thumbnail sketches of such institutions. Then I wish to explain what seem to me to be the reasons for these failures.

The description of each such situation will be very brief, and therefore oversimplified. It cannot do full justice to the facts. For that reason I will endeavor to give references that will enable the interested reader to study each situation in greater depth.

Louisville, Kentucky

I was privileged to be an active observer of a historic period of change in an inner city school system. The Louisville schools were marked by steady deterioration and a staff in despair. In a few short years they were transformed into exciting places of learning with a staff full of hope and determination. I would like to give a few of the highlights of that story.

The Louisville school system, in 1969, was literally a "horrible example" of the depths to which an inner city can sink. The poverty of the community,

227

the level of unemployment, the despair and alienation were the backdrop. As one example, 34 percent of the students came from families with yearly incomes of $2,000 or less! In the schools, teachers were becoming policemen; pupils resented the irrelevant material they were forced to confront (even if they could not be forced to learn). Achievement in all subjects was disastrously low and each year lower. Morale among teachers and students was sinking. It was out of honest desperation that the school board realized that some drastic changes must be made. And they acted on this determination. They employed Newman Walker as superintendent.

Over a period of time I formed a close relationship with Newman Walker, the new superintendent who initiated the innovations. I found him to be an exceedingly honest, self-critical person whose strongest belief was that teachers, students, and parents are persons to be *trusted*. They are not subordinates to be ordered about nor inferiors to be manipulated nor adversaries to be defeated. This trusting attitude is one of the rarest characteristics to be found in educators.

Walker had been effective in lowering the dropout rate in another city. He brought to the Louisville situation a knowledge and competence in the fields of elementary and secondary education, group dynamics, communication, personnel selection and administration. He selected central office staff who shared his philosophy.

With this staff he took some bold steps to meet a desperate situation. During a six-month period in the spring and summer, he enrolled 1600 members of the system in week-long human relations workshops—intensive group experiences held in a residential retreat setting. Included were Walker himself, the whole board of education, principals, teachers, central office staff and clerical workers. In these "labs" people came to know each other as persons and to confront differences. They communicated informally and learned about themselves and how they were perceived by others. They were more open in expressing their feelings. The cognitive was not ignored. They learned new ways of working with students, new ways of promoting learning. I have read the reactions of many of the participants, and for most it was a highly positive experience. It proved to be a ferment which influenced everything that happened later.

That fall, in schools chosen for their first project, an enthusiastic group of principals and teachers with the assistance of young teacher interns turned the classrooms upside down. Open classrooms, team teaching, giving students much freedom of choice—all kinds of innovative things were done. The result, in many instances, was turbulent and chaotic. Kids who had been under authoritarian control for years burst out in various ways when given a taste of freedom. Criticism came from all angles.

But the turbulence was constructive. It was a "purposeful controlled chaos in the classroom" (5). It was recognized that enthusiasm and freer communication with students were not enough. So the staff rethought their purposes, regrouped to learn how to teach, without giving up this aim of creating an environment where students could choose and learn responsibly.

Gradually the project schools became a coherent educational program, operating well in all essential respects. In a relatively short period of years, the impact of this first project, and the impact of all the other projects—similar in aim, but diverse in form—was tremendous. A ghetto school system had been turned around. With the aid of large federal grants, a model had been established which could be utilized in other inner city systems. The decline in achievement scores had stopped. Staff and student morale was high.

Racial balance had been achieved in the staff, though it was impossible to achieve in the schools, because the city was predominantly black. I wrote at the time, "I believe this is the most promising broadscale venture in public education in the United States."

The whole story is extremely complex, and these general paragraphs do not even hint at the complexity. A book-length manuscript was completed, telling of all the projects undertaken, the staunch backing of the Board, the criticisms and attacks from left and right, the gradual emergence of a revolutionary, well functioning system. Unfortunately, by the time Jack Lyne (5) had completed the book, the nationwide emphasis was "back to basics," and he could not find a publisher. Other references which tell of different facets of the experiment are Dickenson et al. (2), Moorefield (6), Borton (1), Capitol Publications (4), Rogers (8).

I cannot possibly give a complete account, but perhaps a few vignettes will give more of the flavor of the boldness involved.

● Early in the situation Walker was talking to the principals about granting more autonomy in the schools. Some principals began to gloat that "it was about time" that they be given the opportunity to run their own schools. Walker said, "I don't believe you heard what I just stated. I said that I was willing to give you as much autonomy *as you are willing to give the teachers and students in your school.*" And he meant just that.

● In the fourteen schools selected for the first project, he wanted to have only teachers who *desired* to participate in an innovative system. So he terminated all appointments in those schools. Then the teachers were selected from those who wished to be a part of the new project. The others were assigned to other schools. Thus, the innovations were given a fair trial without having to meet resistance in the teaching staff.

● A teacher learned that a meeting of the John Birch Society was to be held that night to "expose" the awful things going on in the schools. She notified Walker, and he suggested that the two of them attend. They sat in the rear of the room while their program was being roundly condemned although the criticisms seemed somewhat muted because the speaker recognized Walker. During the question period, he finally said, "Well, ask the *Man*. He's here." So Walker and the teacher answered the questions openly, nondefensively, admitting they did not know the answers to some. One question (raised many times in the community) was "Is it true that in some classrooms the teacher sits in a circle with the students, *on the floor?*" (For some reason this seemed to many a *terrible* thing.) Walker and the teacher expressed their belief in equality of teachers and learners and the value of informality. But then he added, "We don't know the answers to all your questions, and if you wish to hold another meeting, I'll come with the principal and more of the teachers and you can ask them. But even more important, we need volunteers to help us. If some of you would volunteer to work with us, it would be greatly appreciated." Amazingly, four women volunteered. Two lasted throughout the year, though one insisted to the end that she did not like what was going on.

This incident illustrates the extent to which the new administration was willing to answer any questions, respond to any criticism, with complete honesty.

● Here is an observation taken from a report I wrote at the time: I was particularly pleased that the opportunity to visit a classroom of Project 8 was given me, a project designed to assist the learning of potential dropouts. This program has already been in operation for a year and now is running smoothly. When I visited one of these classes, it was very hard indeed to realize that the children in the group are composed of the most difficult, and even incorrigible, students in the system. I never would have guessed this from their behavior. The class was quiet. Small groups of students were working intently on different kinds of problems. When I was there, a teacher was showing pamphlets to a boy telling him the contents and quality of each pamphlet. The teacher was, in other words, doing his job in providing the resources for learning. Suddenly, the boy said, "I want to take that one home." I asked him later to show me the pamphlet he had chosen. It was a pamphlet on astronomy—the relation of the earth to the sun, the moon, the planets, a quite technical but well-illustrated pamphlet. Here was an instance of the responsible, personally initiated learning which the whole program leans toward. I looked at this boy and thought, "This is an incorrigible youngster?" It is obvious that he has become a learning student. I felt a certain degree of awe at the change that must have taken place in him.

● The administration worked as rapidly as possible to develop neighborhood school boards. The Board of the Roosevelt School proved to be one of the most vital. It was composed of parents, teachers, teacher-interns, and it took in the new principal, Car Foster. He had been one of the prime movers in the human relations groups and in getting the transformation underway. Now he wanted more of a front line position, and he left the central office staff to become the principal at Roosevelt. I will let him tell of the first significant action of the board.

The validity of the board as a decision-making body had to be tested. Parents had to discover that they could make decisions. The opportunity came when parents, for various reasons, wanted to establish a seventh grade at Roosevelt. (The school had only grades one through six.) A poll taken in the community by one of the parents was included in a letter to the Louisville Board of Education requesting that a seventh grade be established at Roosevelt. The letter was hand-carried to the central board of education, which later gave an affirmative answer. On the surface, this appears to be a rather simple, logical action occurring through normal operational channels, but it was more. Its importance was expressed by the dry quivering throat and sweaty palm of one of the scared parents who, for the first time in her life, had confronted power and won. Its importance was also expressed by the fact that this was the first time any of these parents had dared go into the building that housed the Louisville Board of Education.

Thoughts, doubts, fears and excitement mingled and tossed and churned some long held values and feelings. This quake was never to settle; growth had begun. (3, pp. 147–48)

This was only a first step. The board gradually acquired the courage to select teachers—and, later to evaluate them and to sever some. They slowly developed their own educational philosophy. They made a decision that the principal opposed, and they made it stick. They had to live with the consequences, which were not good. But it gave them confidence in the principal, who had respected their decision even though he was opposed.

One more incident will illustrate the growth that was involved for all concerned. In one board discussion

a teacher asked, "Why don't more of you parents come into my classroom and tell me what you like or dislike?" There was a long silence. One parent somehow found the courage to risk, saying, "I'm afraid to. I'm just a parent; who am I to tell you how to teach?"

This honest, trusting, self-disclosure was second only to what followed from the teacher.

"You're afraid to! WOW! I'm scared to death of parents. I feel so young and inexperienced, yet you trust me to educate your children. I'm afraid I might blow it—so afraid that I really get up-tight when parents come to my room."

Both teacher and parent looked at each other, mouths open, as the insight slammed them both into silence. Could this have been another learning moment? Incidents such as this, where open, honest confrontation brings people's worlds together for a moment of sharing have contributed more to our growth, individually and communally, than any single factor. (3, pp. 151–52)

The story of the many crises faced by the board and the development of poorly educated black parents, experienced teachers, young teacher-interns, and the principal into a closely knit, expressive, confrontational, caring, working unit, is an exciting one. It enables Foster and Back to write:

Can parents make educational decisions in "their" school? Can they determine school philosophy? Can they select curriculum and develop staffing patterns? Can they interview and recommend the hiring of their teachers? Can they evaluate these teachers? YES, they can! They are doing these things daily at Roosevelt Elementary School. (3, p. 145)

Several years later, I asked a teacher, Martha Redden, who had been a part of these exciting years, "What was outstanding?" She did not hesitate. "It was the sense of *autonomy*. We all felt it—the principals, the teachers, and gradually the students. And, of course, that's what Newman gave us."

"What was the most difficult aspect?" "The hardest thing of all was to learn to share the power—not to give up your own power to be in charge of yourself, but to give others that same right, to be in charge of themselves. It was hard, too, to learn to respect differences."

"How do you feel about it now?" "It was a marvelous experiment, and it *worked*. It worked because of the experiences and ideas of a few people—Newman Walker, Car Foster, you, and other 'radicals' in the field of education" (7).

THE TRAGEDY

So here was an increasingly successful innovative program in that most difficult of educational arenas, the impoverished inner city. It was working.

Then a tragic set of circumstances having nothing to do with the innovative policies in the system brought an end to the whole experiment. Court orders, the merger of two antithetical systems, personal and cultural animosities, anti-busing riots—an "unholy mess" of events—buried the growingly constructive enterprise.

Some of the key points in the "unholy mess" were that though racial balance had been achieved in the Louisville staff, the only way the *schools* could be integrated was to merge the white suburban schools with the inner city schools in one system. The court ordered this to be done.

Who would head up the new system? Walker was hated and feared by the suburbanites. Yet a compromise was worked out whereby he would be deputy superintendent in charge of the programs he had inaugurated, and the man who headed the county system would be superintendent. Before the compromise took effect, the county superintendent, perhaps foreseeing what a difficult task would be his, supervising the massive busing necessary, resigned. This left Walker in an impossible situation. He would not be permitted to be superintendent and was now a deeply divisive factor in the situation. He accepted a superintendency in another city and resigned.

All hell broke loose in regard to busing, and the larger Louisville community was now the scene of anti-busing riots, violence, hatred. The inner city program was effectively diluted and stopped, though elements, like the Roosevelt School and the Roosevelt Neighborhood School Board, continued to fight on. But for all practical purposes, the "marvelous experiment" was dismantled. Due to circumstances having nothing to do with educational philosophy or practice, the humanistic learning programs came to an end.

LOGIC—AND ILLOGIC

I wish to look at the situation first from a logical point of view. Newman Walker had achieved a nationally recognized degree of success. He and his group had effectively rescued a system from disaster, and inaugurated a self-directing, self-confident educational process in what had been a dismal situation. So when the city and county schools were merged, this highly respected man would be the logical choice for the new superintendency. Right? *Wrong*—completely wrong. In Lyne's words, both Walker and the Louisville Board that had backed him, had earned "the undying enmity of the area's white, conservative suburbanites" (5).

What were the reasons for this hostility? Some were circumstantial, some cut much deeper. It behooves us to understand them.

● Walker and his group had been highly successful in obtaining federal funds for their innovations. The county had not.

● Walker and the Louisville Board had refused to slash the education budget. I assume this meant that the county tax rate was not reduced. It touched the pocketbook of county citizens.

● Walker's group had brought large numbers of black administrators, teachers and teacher-interns into the system. The county had not.

● Walker's group had trusted principals and teachers to be as autonomous as possible. There was no such trust in the suburban communities.

● The city system had given students freedom to learn, to choose responsibly. This policy was anathema to the county. It undermined authority in the classroom.

● Walker, Foster, and their staff had empowered parents, even uneducated black parents, to participate in curriculum decisions, teacher selection and evaluation, and policy decisions in their neighborhood schools. This was an incredibly threatening thing. After the schools were merged, the new board made recurring efforts to close Roosevelt School, which had the most powerful neighborhood board. Various reasons were given, but the primary one appeared to be that here was a functioning grassroots democracy in a strictly hierarchical system. It could not be tolerated.

● The whole trend in the Louisville system had been toward a participatory democracy in which students, young interns, teachers, parents, principals, the central staff and superintendent, were all empowered to take part in decisions affecting their own learning, growth, and functioning. This was simply too much for suburban citizens to take. Their whole experience—in school, at home, in their work—had been one in which they were controlled. To trust all these people to make healthy, wise, responsible choices was a risk they could not take.

● The result? They hated and feared Walker and all that he stood for.

That, essentially, marked the end of years of dedicated effort by many persons, lay and professional, to make the Louisville schools a human environment for personal learning. It richly deserved a continuing chance, but it did not get it.

Immaculate Heart

In 1965 and 1966 I was dreaming of and eagerly looking for an opportunity to try out my ideas in a public school system. With the help of colleagues, I drafted a proposal which we sent to a number of foundations for funding—without result. I then published the proposal as an article (10), ending with the question, "Any takers?"
The spirit of the proposal is contained in one paragraph.

A way must be found to develop, within the educational system as a whole, and in each component, a climate conducive to personal growth, a climate in which innovation is not frightening, in which the creative capacities of administrators, teachers, and students are nourished and expressed rather than stifled. A way must be found in the *system* in which the focus is not upon *teaching,* but on the facilitation of self-directed *learning.* Only thus can we develop the creative individual who is open to all of his experience; aware of it and accepting it and continually in the process of changing. (10, p. 718)

THE PROJECT

The most promising "taker" of the proposal proved to be the Immaculate Heart system in Los Angeles, composed of a college, several high schools, and a score or more of elementary schools. A limited amount of funding was obtained. The experiment had the backing of the head of the nuns and the president of the College, which was noted for its innovative character. Planning sessions were held with a number of Immaculate Heart leaders, and we were ready to begin.

As I look back, I realize that we inundated the system. At least twenty members of our La Jolla staff (of the Center for Studies of the Person) took part, and we made frequent trips to Los Angeles to lead the encounter groups, which were the heart of the plan, and its first phase.

Within ninety days, we had held encounter groups—all voluntary, though some faculty felt a subtle pressure to attend—for the following:

45 administrators and faculty of the College;
36 high school administrators and faculty;
40 student leaders from the high schools;
180 teachers, principals, and administrative staff from 22 elementary schools.

These individuals met in groups of ten to fifteen, each facilitated by one of our staff. The general pattern was to meet for one full weekend, and then a second weekend approximately one month later. There were criticisms of the groups. Some facilitators were felt to be less than competent. Some individuals did not involve themselves in the second weekend, feeling that the first had been too upsetting. Some faculty, especially older College faculty, objected to the emphasis on *persons.* They felt they were a role— biology teacher, English instructor, etc.—as much as they were a person and felt that their professional roles were not sufficiently honored in the encounter groups.

In addition to the groups, large meetings were held with the College faculty, and with the students of the College, explaining the plan and answering questions.

The initial proposal had hypothesized that the groups would bring changes in administrators, teachers, and students. It was believed that following the intensive group experience the teacher, among other changes:

—will be more able to listen to students, especially to the feelings of students;

—will be able better to accept the innovative, challenging, "troublesome," creative ideas which emerge in students, rather than reacting to these threats by insisting on conformity;

—will tend to pay as much attention to his relationship with his students, as to the content material of the course;

—will be more likely to work out interpersonal frictions and problems with students, rather than dealing with such issues in a disciplinary or punitive manner;

—will develop a more equalitarian atmosphere in the classroom, conducive to spontaneity, to creative thinking, to independent and self-directed work (10, pp. 723–24).

For a great many of the participants, changes of this sort did occur. We asked for letters or statements following their experience. Here is one from an elementary school teacher.

> You asked me what happened to me . . . pure and simple someone got to me—the inside "new" me . . . I listened. And I heard, have heard and am hearing things I have never listened to before . . . and love it. Results? All I know is it's fun. I've *listened* to my students. I asked them if I had previously turned any off or not listened—the biggest *thugs* all raised their hands. Also—they are the most sensitive . . . I've had the busiest, most arousing, sapping, exciting, fun-filled, fulfilling, and happiest month since I started teaching, and it hasn't stopped yet. (12, p. 332)

A College faculty member writes:

> My classroom behavior is radically different. I have been able to confess anxiety to my classes, and consequently feel more comfortable in the classroom than I have ever felt before. I invited the girls to call me by my first name, and after a couple of weeks, they are doing so. This allows for a lot of free exchange. I am not giving grades, and am not even giving exams. They are writing their own questions—the ones that are meaningful to them in terms of the material, and then discussing them. (12, p. 333)

A high school student shows more exuberance. One of our learnings was that the less status the individual had to protect, the more he or she tended to get out of the encounter group experience.

> I should state clearly right now that the workshop was one of the most important and beautiful experiences of my (relatively short) lifetime. I find personally that I am very much changed in my attitude toward teachers, fellow students, and just plain everybody. I am far more open now (or at least I try very hard to be) than I have ever been. (11, p. 180)

The encounter groups tended to polarize the community, especially the College faculty. Those who were most strongly opposed and even hostile were those who had not been participants in any of the groups.

THE PHASES

The project can be summarized in various phases.

● The period of joint planning in which the two organizations became acquainted with each other and developed cooperative plans for carrying on the project.

• The period of very intensive planned encounter groups, many of which have been mentioned.

• The period of invitation. The La Jolla staff was invited to facilitate many groups—classes, courses, and informal groups of students. One of the most heated and long-lasting was a black-white seminar initiated by black students.

• The period of administrative risk. Because we had been strongly backed by two of the top administrative officials, we naively supposed that all the administrators would involve themselves in the program. The opposite proved to be the truth. The administrative group in the College felt quite threatened by the whole program, and most did not involve themselves in the encounter groups. However, as the program continued, the Administrative Council of the College, an influential group of eight administrators and faculty members, decided they wanted to deal with their problems. They were fearful of an encounter group but they had learned about task-oriented groups which were being conducted in industry to improve administrative functioning and decided they would like to try this. Consequently, they invited Dr. Sheldon Davis, experienced in the industrial field, and me, to facilitate the group. Our meetings cleared up many deep misunderstandings in the administrative structure, brought about changes in policies, and helped the administrative council to become a much more unified group.

• The period of rejection and criticism. Toward the end of the first year, and acquiring great strength in the second year, there was a strong feeling on the part of the students and many faculty that the program had been an intrusion and that they did not wish further contact with the "La Jolla Group." This was a curious phenomenon since there seemed no tendency to reject the gains that had been made nor to reject the idea of the intensive group experience as being an effective tool. I believe I am being objective in saying that it was somewhat of an adolescent phenomenon where people took the attitude, "The La Jolla Group did things quite imperfectly. We can do them much better ourselves." Although it was a little hard on the program staff to be on the receiving end of these feelings, we could not deny their exceedingly healthy import. The whole system was saying, "We want to move ahead but we want to move ahead in our own fashion. You get out of our way."

• The period of assimilation and acceptance of their own purposes. Since the project staff was no longer on the campus, criticism gradually died down and in its place came an increasing number of innovations. I think that all of these have been in the direction of involving greater student participation, greater student initiative, more self-responsibility, self-discipline, and deeper cooperation between faculty and students. Such changes went on in the teaching of languages, philosophy, teacher education, music, theatre arts, an interdisciplinary seminar involving scientists—almost the whole range of the college curriculum.

• A responsible acceptance by the College of the intensive group experience as a part of their ongoing program. Judith Glass came to the College as a new faculty member at the very time the project started, "wondering what it would be like to work with nuns." I will let her tell of a very significant program which developed, heavily influenced by the project.

Immaculate Heart College succeeded in actualizing many of the values of humanistic education. It was a nurturing and challenging place in which to be a student and a faculty member. One of its programs, the Teacher Preparation Program (TPP), illustrates the ways in which humanistic values were translated into programs.

My own involvement began when, during the first encounter weekend, I became friends with Bonnie Flynn McWhinney, who was responsible for teacher education. Through her, I became involved with both the educational change project and with a student-faculty-administration steering committee which was responsible for designing a new Teacher Preparation Program. This was clearly an act of faith for me and for the college, since I had had no prior experience with elementary education. It also illustrates what IHC offered me as a faculty member: an opportunity to grow beyond the confines of my Ph.D., colleagues who trusted me to learn new things all the time and who valued my ideas, a chance to work creatively with people I liked, and students to whom I could respond in a full and human way.

The result of our efforts was one of the most significant teacher preparation programs not only in California, but in the United States. We started from the premise that there were many right ways of being a teacher, and that a teacher preparation program should provide students with opportunities to observe and participate in many different modes of teaching so they could then choose modes consonant with their strengths.

Included in the requirements of the program were:
1. Reflective Learning: students had to develop over the course of their years in the program a statement about their philosophy of education, including its roots in a concept of human nature and the relationship of that concept to teaching and learning;
2. Cognitive Skills: theories about the teaching of reading, math, social studies, and science were formulated;
3. Experiences with art and music;
4. Teaching Experiences: in many different classrooms, open and closed, trying out different methods, and choosing the ways in which they could effectively teach.

The design of the entire program was oriented toward successful outcomes, whether or not the student chose teaching. Because students were in the classroom every semester, not only when they reached the stage of student teaching, they had many opportunities to assess whether or not teaching was the right choice. They had a review committee of faculty members and others whose guidance they valued with whom to discuss their experiences, and if teaching was not for them, they could choose to leave the program without stigma before they invested four years. Because of this process, the students who graduated with a credential were sure of their career choice, were self-directed, and became some of the most creative teachers in the school district. (9, pp. 75–76)

THE CLOSING OF IMMACULATE HEART

Shortly after our heaviest involvement with the system, the Immaculate Heart Community suffered a heavy blow. The sisters had insisted on formulating their own rules for themselves. The Cardinal was equally insistent that they follow his much more rigid set of rules. The dispute was finally carried to the Vatican, and the decision went against the Order. They refused to submit, and with much stress became a lay Order outside the governance of the Church. The Cardinal then dismissed all the sisters teaching in the parochial schools of Los Angeles. Thus, the schools lost a splendid group of teachers, and they, in turn, lost their jobs.

The College and its high school continued in their innovative ways, but financial contributions, necessary to support the work, became more and more difficult to obtain. After a number of crises, the College could no longer meet its obligations, and closed in August, 1980.

I will let Judith Glass speak for me in posing the final questions.

Why did this college which was so responsive to the needs of its students and faculty, which helped people to learn and grow in a humane, concerned way, which was a truly healthy place, why did this college fail while other schools thrive, even though they are factories and treat people like ciphers? Were we so out of step with our society, so subversive, that people with money were not interested in giving it to us? Or did we not look in the right places? The college could have continued to serve the community for the cost of one jumbo jet, but we were not able to persuade society that IHC was more valuable. (9, p. 76)*

Union Graduate School

"UGS," as it is familiarly known, has been in existence for more than a decade. Two of the important founding spirits were Dr. Goodwin Watson, formerly of Teachers College, Columbia, and Dr. Roy Fairfield, a Harvard Ph.D., writer, and teacher. It was begun as an innovative program at the graduate level offering Master's and Doctor's degrees in several areas including education.

THE PROGRAM

UGS was developed to provide independent study programs for those who were able and willing to assume a major responsibility for their own education, with skillful facilitative help from the core faculty and the adjunct professors. It was unique in the degree to which students shared in governance of the school. There were students on the national policy board. Students participated heavily in the selection of their own doctoral committees, which included student members. Peer evaluation was an important concept throughout.

Two of the more unusual features will indicate the extent of the responsible freedom given to the student. The learner nominated and essentially chose the six-person committee which would guide and facilitate his/her work, culminating in the fulfillment and conclusion of the "learning contract." The student was the chairperson of his/her own committee. There were to

*Reprinted from J. Glass and J. Glass, "Humanistic Education: A Tale of Two Professors," *Journal of Humanistic Psychology*, Vol. 21, No. 2, © 1981 by The Association for Humanistic Psychology, with permission of Sage Publications, Inc.

be, as members of that committee, two peers, two adjunct faculty, and a core faculty. The core professor had considerable power if things were going badly, but in many instances simply served as a member.

The learning contract included many types of learning, but one of its features was a Project Demonstrating Excellence—the PDE. Although somewhat similar to a thesis or a dissertation, it was part of the *total* program of learning for the student. When all aspects of the contract, including the PDE, were finished and acceptable to the six committee members, there was a final step. This was the "terminar," a presentation of one's work and a celebration. It was not an agonizing "final oral," but a joyous entry into mature involvement in the work and life of the "real" world.

The students have been a diverse group, from every portion of the United States and many foreign countries. The quality of their work has been such that the school was for a time fully accredited by national organizations. Perhaps something of the spirit of the undertaking can be conveyed by a brief description of the key aspects of the venture, taken from Fairfield (14).

● Application is encouraged by those who cannot get the advanced training they require in more conventional programs.

● Admission depends upon high intelligence and the demonstrated capacity for self-direction and disciplined effort toward self-chosen objectives.

● Students are encouraged to use the world as their classroom, developing workable plans, implementing them by drawing upon resources both within and outside academic institutions, and fitting means to need; each program is a tailor-made one, with students participating with faculty in selection of advisors, evolving a learning contract jointly with a committee comprised of a minimum of two adjunct professors (specialists in their fields), two UGS peers, and a UGS core faculty member.

● Each student's program consists of a study component ("What do you want to learn?"), an experimental component (an internship or practicum, broadly defined), and a Project Demonstrating Excellence (PDE).

● Since a student either passes or drops out, there are no credits, grades, or points; a cumulative record, consisting of log materials, papers, anything he or she and the committee deem relevant, becomes the basis of evaluation.

● A Project Demonstrating Excellence or PDE (we eschew the terms *thesis* and *dissertation*) may acquire any number of forms and is limited only to the imagination and daring of the student and his committee. He may publish a book or a number of scholarly articles, design and implement a project of significant social change, create poetry, painting, sculpture, musical composition, dances, films, or other art forms that win recognition (14, pp. 17–18).

UGS has turned out high quality products, and high quality persons. Its development, its "agonies and ecstasies," are vividly described by Roy Fairfield in a book which brims over with humor, wit, and wisdom—*Person-Centered Graduate Education.*

THE DECLINE

For all its brilliant record, UGS began to alter its humanistic approach and to retreat from its person-centered goals. These changes coincided with the retirement (and later death) of Goodwin Watson, and the decreased in-

volvement, and eventual resignation of Fairfield. Without going into complicated details, the persons chosen to head the institution dropped much of
the student participation, dismissed faculty members, made it a much more
conventional hierarchical organization. There was much active protest from
the students and former students, and many battles were won, during a
traumatic period of upheaval. A top administrator was literally forced out by
the protesting group. The school lost its accreditation. It had to file for
bankruptcy.

During the difficult period of reorganizing the school, much of its innovative nature was lost. Students no longer participate in policy decisions;
there are many more rules and regulations, in the interest of "quality control;"
there are more administrators in proportion to the number of students; there
is hierarchical management.

In the possibly biased view of Fairfield, the school has moved, as is the
tendency of institutions, "from charisma and creativity to bureaucracy and
routinization" (13).

Yet, in the opinion of many, the school continues to provide a good
alternative to the conventional university. There is no doubt, however, that
many of its more humanistic procedures, and even its goals, have changed in
the direction of conventionality. Its leading administrator has spoken publicly
of his opposition to student involvement in university administration. The
initial vision and spirit are gone.

Johnston College

The beginnings, the life, the eventual death of Johnston College are
described in a moving, witty, sad, joyous series of five articles (15, 16, 17,
18, 19). I shall not attempt to do more than mention a few of the major
aspects.

Johnston College was made possible by James Johnston, the founding
donor, and the University of Redlands, which sponsored this new experimental venture. The life span was approximately a decade, 1969–79.

POLICIES AND PROBLEMS

A group of educational pioneers planned the policies of the college. It
was to have no grades, no departments, personal growth labs as an important
continuing feature, decision by consensus, the individual learning contract
as one of its major means of encouraging independent study. The larger aim
was to create a living-learning environment, in which both experiential and
cognitive learning could flourish.

The college believed that it had been given full autonomy by the University of Redlands. The president of the university and his trustees had a
different concept—that autonomy of the college existed only at their discre-
tion and within certain ambiguous guidelines. Particularly they were determined to control the Johnston lifestyle. Governance of the dormitories, and
rules for dormitory living, became a focus of this struggle between the college
and the university.

The students tended to fall into two categories: students who were attracted by the possibilities of self-directed learning and students who were rebels against any and all authority. One participant describes the "positive center" of Johnston as being "a set of balances: freedom balanced against responsibilities; group authority versus respect for individual 'rights;' cognitive education versus affective learning; 'establishment' thought versus peripheral thinking" (19, p. 19).

From the accounts one gets the impression of enormous ferment—serious work, rowdy and comic behavior of students and faculty at times, passionate confrontations, power struggles—a whole gamut of lively but often unpredictable events.

To mention only one of its unusual features, the college tried to avoid hurtful power struggles by developing the DTF—the Disappearing Task Force. Rather than setting up permanent administrative units or committees, groups were organized to carry out a specific function. At its conclusion, the group dissolved.

Within eighteen months, the first chancellor was fired in the dispute over autonomy. It was not until 1979 that the college was "absorbed" by the University of Redlands, finishing its existence as an experimental college.

Something of the quality of its life is contained in the conclusion of an article by Dr. Williams, one of the older faculty members, who served one year as acting chancellor, and seven years as dean.

> In spite of the relatively short duration of Johnston College, what I hope emerges from the totality of these comments is a picture of one of the most memorable, intense, tortured, yet beautiful moments in the lives of most of us. Most of us still brightly remember the faces (and even names) of those who went through all that with us. Those were times that taught how magnificent the human spirit can be. And we were welded together, as a group, in a way that surpasses comparisons to anything else I've ever experienced. (19, p. 21)

The trustees and the university president reached their limit of tolerance fairly early in the game. The unconventional behavior of the students—including their insistence on a coed dorm—the battles over the extent to which the college had the power to govern itself, the close relationship between faculty and students—often an alliance against the university—proved to be more than the university administration could take. And so a very promising experiment, its strength wasted battling for lost causes, was gradually brought to an end.

Kresge College

The University of California at Santa Cruz opened in 1965, in a wooded campus above Monterey Bay. It was initiated on the "cluster college" model, starting a new college each year. The hope was that relatively small colleges, each with a unique character, would provide a community spirit, within the resources of a larger university.

When Kresge College was being planned, to open in 1971, the university chose a young biologist with excellent scientific credentials to be its founding chancellor. He endeavored to explain his strong interest in a humanistic approach to education, and the administration was skeptical. It is doubtful whether they grasped the depth of his commitment to those views and the extent to which he would go in implementing them. He had been a member of the faculty group with which I had worked for three years (on a monthly basis) at the California Institute of Technology. His views had been supported and enlarged by John Weir at Caltech and by other humanistic psychologists.

He rather quickly gathered a core group of five faculty members who essentially shared his philosophy. This made it possible for him to start Kresge as a genuinely experimental educational venture. Such an experiment had never been understood, accepted, or sponsored by the campus administration.

Thus, the experiment was never intended by the university. Nor was its innovative program chosen by the students. Many of the students enrolled in Kresge simply because they had not been accepted by the other more traditional colleges of UCSC. Michael Kahn points out in a thoughtful analysis (20, p. 63) that the initiation of an experimental college was, from the university point of view, an accident.

Perhaps the most outstanding characteristic of the Kresge experiment was its intensity for both faculty and students. For example a student in the core course would attend, each week, the following:
—a three hour lecture, with the whole class;
—a small seminar group of co-residents, with their faculty advisor, discussing the lecture, and the book on which it was based;
—a T-group (sensitivity training group) facilitated by an outside consultant. In this group the faculty advisor was just another member.

Each of these sessions was long, demanding preparation and concentration, with opportunity for the highly intellectual and the deeply personal. All the groups were optional. The purpose of the T-group was to help the student relate to others in a living-learning environment, and to find purpose and meaning in his/her life. As is evident, a very close relationship with faculty members was built into the program.

After two years, only those aspects of the program that were acceptable to the majority of the students were continued throughout the college.

Those students and faculty who chose to participate fully in the original plan drew off into a "Corner of the College" (20, p. 66). This group of four faculty and forty-eight students became a very close-knit group. They started the year with a week-long orientation retreat. They had the living-learning experiment they had dreamed of. "For two years this mini-experiment flourished and, in the opinion of most of its participants, fulfilled the promise of the original Kresge ideas. At least one of the faculty members found it the most completely satisfying academic experience of a long career. Almost without exception, students reported it as rich and life-changing" (20, pp. 66–67).

THE DISSOLUTION

As Kahn sees it, this "corner group" came to an end because new faculty could not be recruited. The commitment required was very heavy in time and personal energy. Junior faculty could not make this commitment because of the "publish or perish" dictum and because their careers might be hurt if they were linked with a program around which controversy was swirling. The only senior faculty interested in the experiment were already involved.

Then came dropping enrollment and budget cuts. A new chancellor was given the mandate to reorganize the campus and to get rid of the counter-culture image. It was reorganized in conventional ways, built on strong campus-wide departments. Primary emphasis was on these departments, not on colleges. The faculty members of all the colleges were redistributed, and the Kresge faculty was scattered throughout the campus.

One of the major issues which had most offended the campus administration was the endeavor to bring the emotions, the body, as well as the mind, into the college. The administration, while believing in the emotional, physical, and erotic aspects of life, was convinced that these elements should be sharply divided from the intellectual. Only reason and the intellectual had a place in the university. The failure to recruit faculty was the practical reason for the end of the experiment. This profound philosophical disagreement was the substantive reason for its death.

The curriculum was now placed firmly in the hands of the chancellor and the deans. There would be no further experiments either by accident or design.

The Experimental College at San Francisco State

Tumultuous and exciting, though short-lived, the mushrooming adventure in learning which took place at what was then San Francisco State College, deserves our attention. It is vividly described by two of its active leaders (21).

It was born in the context of the "radical 60s," and it was a most creative and far-out adventure. It was entirely student-initiated. One student gathered together a group who were interested in discussing education. Out of the discussion arose an alternative program in education, challenging the conventional one. They enlisted faculty help. Soon there were 22 courses available. By the summer of 1966, even more courses were presented, and the "Experimental College" was formed. In an astonishingly short time, there were 70 courses involving 1400 students.

One of its unusual features was that any student could organize a course. Ian Grand, a student, first became involved by organizing a course to study the way in which certain ecstasy religions used the body to affect altered states of consciousness. He became more and more active in the experiment and was eventually named the coordinator of the new venture. He says, "The learnings, the cross-fertilization of ideas, the contact in this milieu was incredible. The process itself, finding oneself forming a direction of study along the lines of one's interests, was exhilarating" (21, p. 81).

The course labels ranged from "Culture and the City" and "Contemporary Soviet Social Thought" to "Grass, Acid and Zen" and "Exploring New Forms of Sexual Relationship." Even the registration process was strange and involving. It was held in a student lounge.

> All the course organizers would set up at various tables and they would have signs and costumes and music playing. The idea was that people should be able to talk with their course planners about what they were trying to cover in the course and how they were going to teach it. People would go from table to table seeing what was offered and talking to each other. What resulted was an incredible marketplace of ideas and forms of learning, all dealing with innovative educational content and process, swirls of activity. These registrations were attended by thousands of people. You could take these courses, organize new courses, and get credit for doing it. We had discovered that there were mechanisms within the structure of the school that nobody had ever used that would enable students to apply alternate course credits toward their degree requirements and enable faculty to be involved. (21, p. 82)

It was a college within a college, full of infectious excitement. It aroused national and media interest, which made it possible to bring in leading young thinkers. Soon the EC was not only involved in a most unusual learning process. It was challenging the conventional educational process in the whole school.

One of its features was to make full use of the community as a learning environment. Students taught in the community, studied it, took part in it, in such ways as setting up a "Trades-Skills Community Center."

The aim of the leaders of the EC was clear. They were aiming toward

> creating the environment whereby students come to identify, *be fired with,* a path of learning that they can then follow in such a fashion that they form out of that a body of knowledge and a body of experience. (21, p. 93)

THE ENDING

There were always meetings, always crises, but the college flourished. In 1968 there was, however, a movement in the board of trustees to disband the EC or to bring it under conventional control. In an important board meeting the Experimental College was defended not only by the president of San Francisco State, but by a representative of the U.S. Office of Education, who had been much impressed by the learning that was going on. The motion to disband the EC was tabled—for the time being.

Then came the much-publicized student strike at San Francisco State, the impounding of student funds, the locking of the doors of the office of the Experimental College. It was all over by the spring of 1969.

I will let Ian Grand tell of the process and the product that was the goal of the EC. It had been the hope that students would come through their education *with their passion intact and enhanced*. Rather than the image of dispassionate learning and dispassionate discourse, there would be an image of impassioned concern. They would be able to think passionately and well. They would be capable of being passionately involved in whatever direction they followed, including work that requires protracted discipline. They would value and learn from experience as well as abstractions. And they would be able to think through, feel through, and critique problems and situations in society and in the mind, to form for themselves images, ideas, connections, and directions.

The role of the teacher in this model is to fire the imagination; to give it room; to begin with the interests of the student and to broaden them, to bring to bear his or her own commitment, concern, and knowledge; to encourage both the rigors of discipline and a sense of the great achievements of the past. The drive of the students would be to create anew, to explore, and to find their own place in humankind's development.

An education along these lines would enable people to make important contributions to whatever milieu they found themselves in, whether academic, industrial or governmental—important contributions to the culture as a whole. (21, p. 95)

Reasons for Impermanence

The various organizations I have described—humanistic, innovative, person-centered—have failed to survive. How can we account for this pattern of short-lived success? I can see several reasons.

THEY POSE A THREAT

When an organization is truly democratic, when persons are trusted and empowered to act freely and responsibly, this poses an enormous threat to conventional institutions. Our culture does not as yet believe in democracy. Almost without exception the "establishment"—and the people—believe in a pyramidal form of organization, with a leader at the top, who controls his or her subordinates, who in turn control those further down the line. When some form of organization, other than authoritarian, flourishes and succeeds, it challenges a way of being that is deeply rooted in our society.

This is most obvious in the case of the Experimental College at San Francisco State. The program was initiated, planned, and conducted by students. It was a grass roots, democratically oriented program. It was regarded as successful in promoting important learnings—not only by the student learners, but by the president of the university, and by the U.S. Office of Education. In other words, those who should know endorsed it as a successful educational venture. Yet the board of trustees of the university was determined to dismantle the program. The only possible reason is that they felt threatened by a successful program which they did not and could not control.

In Louisville, the inner city area and the Louisville School Board were proud of their innovative system and its surprising achievements. But the middle and upper class suburban areas with whom they were forced to merge, by a court order, took a different view. They were frightened by the innovation, the openness, the boldness, the degree of freedom in the city schools. This was certainly a major factor in their determination to rid the school systems of the man who was primarily responsible for the innovations. The city system put its primary emphasis on freeing students to be responsible learners. The county system put authority and discipline and order as their top priorities. They wanted control.

At Immaculate Heart, the system was able to encourage innovation, not simply tolerate it. There was dissension over these new and more human procedures, but they grew and were nurtured. But the outside support of Immaculate Heart, necessary if it was to survive, came largely from wealthy contributors. General economic conditions may have accounted for some of the shrinkage in gifts, but there was surely another factor. It must indeed have been disturbing to the contributors to have such striking evidence of a definitely democratic Catholic organization—making its own rules, in defiance of authority, encouraging students to be self-directed learners, encouraging self-discipline rather than discipline by an external authority. Support dwindled.

In Johnston College the issues became very muddled, but there was only one extremely sharp difference between the university and the college. Who was to control the lifestyle of the students? Was it to be primarily the students themselves, with help and facilitation from the faculty and staff of the college, or was it to be the board of trustees? To the trustees it was clear that the students were too young, too immature to be self-governing. The college believed otherwise. The trustees were motivated by the understandable fear that "wild" decisions would be made, that irresponsible behavior would predominate. And in the final analysis they believed they must control.

So I see, as one of the major factors in the shortened lives of these organizations, the fears of the "establishment"—fear of self-directing individuals and enterprises, fear of any entity deeply rooted in a democratic way of being.

THE LACK OF A POOL

Thus far, there are only a few institutions which trust the individual, or believe in the capacity of a group to be self-governing. Consequently when the founding leaders leave or retire, where is the group to look for leadership? There are a number of people who believe in a person-centered philosophy. A smaller number tries actually to *live* in that way. Of these a still smaller group have any experience in utilizing this way of being in the leadership or administration of an enterprise. Hence the pool of individuals from which to choose is very limited indeed.

This appears to be very clear in the case of Union Graduate School. When the original leaders disappeared from the scene, individuals were chosen who gave lip service to a humanistic approach, but they were lacking in skill and experience in implementing this approach in an administrative process. Perhaps to a lesser degree, this may have been true at Johnston College. It is not easy to find educators who believe in empowering the individuals in their group, and who understand how that belief might be put into practice.

CREEPING BUREAUCRACY

Fairfield (14, Chap. 5) has an excellent chapter pointing out the tendency of every organization to develop routinized, bureaucratic ways of operation. He says:

> Anybody who has been involved in developing an institution—public school, private hiking club, business, church, or whatever—knows that it is easy to apply some kind of rational system to persuade others to conform to recommended viewpoints, codes, or rules. Hence, it seems probable that any institution advocating a liberal, radical, or freedom-seeking end is virtually bound to reinvent autocratic reasons for *not* acting in accordance with its own goals. (14, p. 100)

Anything can become an imposed rule, even freedom. There is more than a modicum of truth in the old cartoon of the child in a "progressive" school saying plaintively, "Do I *have* to do what I want to do?" In the structureless freedom of an encounter group, participants frequently discover norms to which they are expected to conform. So the accumulation of customary procedures all too easily slides into becoming the codification of rules for *required* procedures.

Another element involved in bureaucracy is the tendency to act as if, because an organization has been formed, it should be continued. Temporary committees become permanent. We say that the organization tends to perpetuate itself. It would be more accurate to say that the persons in the organization find themselves striving to maintain the status quo, rather than seeking to achieve their original goals. Examples could be found, I'm sure, in each of the organizations described to illustrate this trend.

This is why, to me, two of the most interesting bits I have come across in reviewing these enterprises are the "learning blob" of UGS, and the "Disappearing Task Force" of Johnston College. They represent positive action to try to halt the drift toward bureaucracy.

The "learning blob" was formed to pursue learning about some specific problem, issue or area. It was composed of faculty, students, outside experts, resource people. They worked cooperatively to achieve their goals. When, by their work and interaction, they had learned what they set out to learn, the "blob" dissolved.

The "DTF" usually had a practical goal involving the solution of some administrative problem. It would be composed of those whose interests were involved. Once the problem was solved—or proven insoluble—the task force "disappeared." These two ways of working, both in the educational and administrative areas, appear to be highly useful models for slowing the development of dehumanizing and rule-bound procedures. It ensures the continuation of a human approach. One of Fairfield's most challenging sentences is this. "The learning blob which self-destructs . . . may be the most stable element assuring UGS continuity" (22, p. vi).

THE LACK OF EXPERIENCE

For a group to empower itself, as did the student-formed College at San Francisco State, is a rare experience in our culture. For members of a group to discover that they are being empowered, as in the Louisville situation, is equally rare. So it is apparent that most of us have little or no experience in being a part of a self-directing group process. The only patterns of behavior with which we are familiar are hierarchical and authoritarian, so we tend to fall back on those. We lack the practical know-how.

Another challenging difficulty is that there can never be a codifiable pattern for the operation of a person-centered institution. By empowering the members of the group, we guarantee that each situation will be unique, and must be dealt with by the group in its own special way. I first recognized this at the University of Chicago. In the eyes of the university I was the responsible person in charge of the Counseling Center. I handled that responsibility by empowering all the staff, myself included, to operate the organization. I have written about that period.

> I learned many strange things from the experience at the Counseling Center. It was quite dismaying to me at first that we never seemed to be able to find the *right* way of operating the Center. First all decisions were made by consensus. That was too burdensome. We delegated decision-making to a small group. That proved slow. We chose a coordinator, and agreed to abide by his/her decisions, though like a prime minister he/she could be given a vote of no confidence. Only gradually did I realize that there is no right way. The life and vitality and growth of the Center was closely bound up with its lack of rigidity, with its continually surprising capacity to change its collective mind, and to utilize a new mode of operation.
>
> I found that when power was distributed, it was no big thing to be the coordinator or chairman of the budget committee or whatever. Consequently administrative tasks were very often sought by the newest members of the staff, because it was an avenue of becoming acquainted with the workings of the operation. An intern might chair a group making up next year's budget. The newest staff member might head a planning group, or a group to pass on membership or promotions. Senior members of the group were freed to spend more time on research and therapy, knowing that if the various administrative task groups failed accurately to represent the sentiment of the members, their decisions would be rejected by the staff as a whole.
>
> I found the enormous importance of personal feelings in administrative matters. Often the staff would spend *hours* (or so it seemed) in arguing some trivial issue, until a perceptive member would see and state the feelings underlying the issue—a personal animosity, a feeling of insecurity, a competition between two would-be leaders, or just the resentment of someone who had never really been heard. Once the *feelings* were out in the open, the issue which had seemed so important became a nothing. On the other hand when the staff was in open communication with one another, heavy issues such as the allocation of the budget for the following year, the election of a coordinator, the adoption of an important policy might take only minutes to decide. (23, pp. 94–95)

Perhaps that account gives some feeling for the strangeness inherent in a person-centered organization. Few of us have had experience in working in the fluid ways that seem fitting in such a task.

THE LURE OF "POWER OVER"

There is one final element which may help to account for the relatively short life of most institutions which aim to respect the dignity, worth, and capacity of the individual. It can best be illuminated by examining a significant case history from the business world.

> I know a man who has, for 15 years, been a consultant for a very large industrial firm. The business of this firm is diversified, but for the most part its units of manufacture are small and widely used.
>
> This man has, by his way of being, by his training approach, and through cognitive methods, brought into being in this organization a person-centered way of management—not with the whole organization, of course, but with a sizable number of middle and upper management personnel.
>
> So highly has he been regarded, and so effective the managers who had trained with him, that a number of years ago he was permitted to set up an "experiment." Three factories were set aside as experimental manufacturing plants, where the consultant had trained, and continued to work with, management and nonmanagement personnel. Three other plants were designated as control units. It should be stressed that this is a very modern industrial giant, with generally good labor relations, a high level of efficiency compared with other firms manufacturing the same types of items, and of course a rigorous cost-accounting system. Hence both the control and experimental plants started the experiment as "well run" systems.
>
> During the past nine years the people in the experimental plants have become more and more deeply involved with a person-centered philosophy. Employees tend to be trusted by those in charge, rather than having their work closely supervised, inspected, and scrutinized. Likewise, employees tend to trust each other. The degree of mutual regard among the employees is unusually high, as is their respect for each other's capabilities. The emphasis of the consultant and of the plant personnel has been upon building up good interpersonal relations, vertical and horizontal two-way communication, and a dispersion of responsibility, choice, and decision-making.
>
> Now the results are clearly apparent. In the experimental plants the average cost of a particular unit is about 22¢. In the control plants the average cost of the same item is 70¢! In the experimental plants there are now three to five managers. In the control units of comparable size there are seventeen to twenty-three managers! In the experimental units workers and supervisors come sauntering in from the parking lots in earnest conversation, generally about their work. In the control plants they come in quickly, mostly singly, to punch the time clock. (23, pp. 101–2)

Here is a remarkable success story. Surely the conclusion should be that these person-centered ways are now being fostered throughout the corporation. But that is *not* the way it has turned out.

Recently I talked with this consultant. He told me that while the experimental plants continue to do extremely well, and he feels pride in the work he has done with them, he regards his work with the corporation as a failure. The top management, though appreciative of the increased profits and good morale of the experimental plants, has not moved to follow this model in their other plants, even though it appears evident that overall profits would be increased. "Why not?" I inquired. His answer was most thought-provoking. "When managers from other plants look closely at what we are doing, they gradually realize how much of their power they would have to give away, have to share with their employees. And they are not willing to give up that power." When I stated that it appeared that power over people was even more important than profits—which are supposed to be the all-important goal in industry—he agreed.*

The same may be true, at least at the present time, in education. Administrators of educational institutions may place a higher value on power over people than on the enhancement of learning. Lip service is given to the latter, but the real priority is to hold onto, or gain, power over people.

This is not, I believe, a genetic characteristic, but it is highly characteristic of our culture. Along with it goes a mistrust of the person, which has deep roots in religious conceptions of man as essentially evil. Until and unless the human organism is perceived as trustworthy, those in power see it as their obligation to control. It is in these deep-seated philosophical areas that change must come about, before we can have lasting organizations based on a person-centered approach.

CONCLUDING COMMENT

It is to be hoped that we all can learn from the disappointments in these various accounts. It should be noted that every one of them was successful in promoting significant learning—some of them impressively so. But through internal flaws or external pressures and opposition they have failed to continue.

What we need to learn, it seems, are ways of gaining acceptance for a humanistic person-centered venture in a culture more devoted to rule by authority. Since ours is a pluralistic society, a humanistic option should be given the opportunity to survive. In today's world that opportunity is hard to come by.

One of the outstanding learnings from the material in this chapter is that the empowering of persons, the encouragement of self-direction, and the enhancement of learning by the whole person—with feelings as well as thoughts—constitute a profoundly revolutionary approach to education in this society.

REFERENCES

Louisville, Kentucky

1. Borton, T. "Reform Without Politics in Louisville." *Saturday Review,* 5 January 1972.

---

*An interesting footnote to this story is that as managers in the three experimental plants are offered promotions which would move them out of the experimental factories, many decline, and seek higher-level positions in organizations where there is understanding of their human way of facilitating production.

2. Dickenson, W.; Foster, Car; Walker, Newman; and Yeager, F. "A Humanistic Program for Change in a Large City School System. *Journal of Humanistic Psychology, 10 #2*, Fall 1970.
3. Foster, Car and Back, J. "A Neighborhood School Board: Its Infancy, Its Crises, Its Growth." *Education, 95* (Winter 1974): 145–162.
4. "Louisville Finds Dramatic Gains in First Grade Reading." *Report on Education of the Disadvantaged*, 2 January 1974, Washington, DC: Capitol Publications.
5. Lyne, C. Jr. *Long Ride to Where? Dreams, Decay, and City/Suburban Busing for Desegregation in Louisville.* Unpublished book manuscript, 1978.
6. Moorefield, S. "How Louisville Put It All Together." *American Education*, December 1971.
7. Redden, M. Personal communication, May 1981.
8. Rogers, Carl R. *Humanistic Innovation in Education.* 50 minute film (two reels) discussing and showing pictures of the Louisville Experiment, 1974. Washington, DC: American Personnel & Guidance Association.

Immaculate Heart

9. Glass, J. and Glass, J. "Humanistic Education: A Tale of Two Professors." *Journal of Humanistic Psychology, 21* (Spring 1981): 71–77.
10. Rogers, Carl R. "A Plan for Self-directed Change in an Educational System." *Educational Leadership, 24* (May 1967): 717–31.
11. Rogers, Carl R. "The Project at Immaculate Heart: An Experiment in Self-Directed Change." *Education, 95* (Winter 1974): 172–96.
12. Rogers, Carl R. "Self-directed Educational Change in Action." Epilogue in *Freedom to Learn*, Columbus, Ohio: Charles E. Merrill Publishing Co., 1969, pp. 327–42.

Union Graduate School

13. Fairfield, R. P. Personal correspondence, 1982.
14. Fairfield, R. P. *Person-Centered Graduate Education.* Buffalo, NY: Prometheus Books, 1977.

Johnston College

15. Blume, F. "The Role of Personal Growth Groups at Johnston College." *Journal of Humanistic Psychology, 21* (Spring 1981): 47–61.
16. Greening, T. "The First Days of Johnston College." *Journal of Humanistic Psychology, 21* (Spring 1981): 3–15.
17. Thompson, L. "A View from the Trenches." *Journal of Humanistic Psychology, 21* (Spring 1981): 23–40.
18. Watt, J. "Johnston College: A Retrospective." *Journal of Humanistic Psychology, 21* (Spring 1981): 41–45.
19. Williams, E. "A Confirmation and Critique." *Journal of Humanistic Psychology, 21* (Spring 1981): 17–21.

Kresge College

20. Kahn, Michael. "The Kresge Experiment." *Journal of Humanistic Psychology, 21* (Spring 1981): 63–69.

The Experimental College at San Francisco State

21. Grand, Ian J. and Bebout, J. "Passionate Discourse: The Experimental College at San Francisco State." *Journal of Humanistic Psychology, 21* (Spring 1981): 79–95.

Reasons for Impermanence

22. Fairfield, R. P. *Person-Centered Graduate Education*. Buffalo, NY: Prometheus Books, 1977.
23. Rogers, Carl R. *Carl Rogers on Personal Power*. New York: Delacorte Press, 1977.

The Philosophical
and Value
Ramifications

A Modern Approach to
the Valuing Process

*T*he work of the teacher and educator, like that of the therapist, is inextricably involved in the problem of values. The school has always been seen as one of the means by which the culture transmits its values from one generation to the next. But now this process is in upheaval with many of our young people declaring themselves "dropouts" from the confused and hypocritical value system that they see operating in the world. How are educators—how are citizens—to orient themselves in relation to this complex and perplexing issue?

While on vacation in Jamaica, many years ago, watching the abundant sea life through my snorkel, and the equally fascinating development of three of our grandchildren, I attempted an essay on this problem based largely on my experience in psychotherapy.* When I had finished, I felt quite dissatisfied with it, but it has, for me, stood the test of time, and I now feel good about its venturesome quality. I feel in regard to it, as with a small number of other papers, that I was writing more than I consciously "knew," and that it took my intellect some time to catch up with what I had written. I have also found that it has had significant meaning for many other people.

I did not at that time foresee the tremendous shift in values that would so markedly change our culture, yet in a profound way, I believe I did see something of the process by which that change would come about.

*A condensed version of this chapter was first published as "Toward a Modern Approach to Values," *Journal of Abnormal and Social Psychology* 68 (1964): 160–67. Copyright © 1964 by the American Psychological Association. Adapted by permission of the publisher and author.

255

Recently the social researcher, Daniel Yankelovich, studying a great mass of data from national polls, tried to picture something of that shift. "Americans show unmistakably that the search for new meanings is an outpouring of popular sentiment and experimentation . . ." involving perhaps 80 percent of all adults. "It is as if tens of millions of people had decided simultaneously to conduct risky experiments in living, using the only materials at hand—their own lives" (6).

A picture of the way in which this shift in values has come about, and some of the outcomes that have come to be culturally accepted, will be found in this chapter, the body of which was written several years ago. I will let it speak for itself.

There is a great deal of concern today with the problem of values. Youth, in almost every country, is deeply uncertain of its value orientation; the values associated with various religions have lost much of their influence; sophisticated individuals in every culture seem unsure and troubled as to the goals they hold in esteem. One does not have to look far to find the reasons. The world culture, in all its aspects, seems increasingly scientific and relativistic, and the rigid, absolute views on values that come to us from the past appear anachronistic. Even more important, perhaps, is the fact that the modern individual is assailed from every angle by divergent and contradictory value claims. It is no longer possible, as it was in the not too distant historical past, to settle comfortably into the value system of one's forebears or one's community or one's church and live out one's life without ever examining the nature and the assumptions of that system.

In this situation it is not surprising that value orientations from the past appear to be in a state of disintegration or collapse. Men question whether there are, or can be, any universal values. It is often felt that we may have lost, in our modern world, all possibility of any general or cross-cultural basis for values. One natural result of this uncertainty and confusion is that there is an increasing concern about, interest in, and searching for, a sound or meaningful value approach which can hold its own in today's world.

I share this general concern. I have also experienced the more specific value issues which arise in my own field, psychotherapy. The client's feelings and convictions about values frequently change during therapy. How can she or we know whether they have changed in a sound direction? Or does she simply, as some claim, take over the value system of her therapist? Is psychotherapy simply a device whereby the unacknowledged and unexamined values of the therapist are unknowingly transmitted to an unsuspecting client? Or should this transmission of values be the therapist's openly held purpose? Should he become the modern priest, upholding and imparting a value system suitable for today? And what would such a value system be? There has been much discussion of such issues, ranging from thoughtful and empirically based presentations to more polemic statements. As is so often true, the general problem faced by the culture is painfully and specifically evident in the cultural microcosm which is called the therapeutic relationship.

I should like to attempt a modest approach to this whole problem. I have observed changes in the approach to values as the individual grows from infancy to adulthood. I observe further changes when, if she is fortunate, she continues to grow toward true psychological maturity. Many of these observations grow out of my experience as a therapist, where I have had the rare opportunity of seeing the ways in which individuals move toward a richer life. From these observations I believe I see some directional threads emerging that might offer a new concept of the valuing process, more tenable in the modern world. I have made a beginning by presenting some of these ideas partially in previous writings (4, 5); I would like now to voice them more clearly and more fully.

I would stress that my vantage point for making these observations is not that of the scholar or philosopher: I am speaking from my experience of the functioning human being, as I have lived with him or her in the intimate experience of therapy, and in other situations of growth, change, and development.

Some Definitions

Before I present some of these observations, perhaps I should try to clarify what I mean by values. There are many definitions that have been used, but I have found helpful some distinctions made by Charles Morris (3). He points out that *value* is a term we employ in different ways. We use it to refer to the tendency of any living beings to show preference, in their actions, for one kind of object or objective rather than another. This preferential behavior he calls "operative values." It need not involve any cognitive or conceptual thinking. It is simply the value choice that is indicated behaviorally when the organism selects one object, rejects another. When the earthworm, placed in a simple Y maze, chooses the smooth arm of the Y, instead of the path that is paved with sandpaper, he is indicating an operative value.

A second use of the term might be called "conceived values." This is the preference of the individual for a symbolized object. Usually in such a choice there is anticipation or foresight of the outcome of behavior directed toward such a symbolized object. A preference for "Honesty is the best policy" is such a conceived value.

A final use of the term might be called "objective values." People use the word in this way when they wish to speak of what is objectively preferable, whether or not it is in fact sensed or conceived of as desirable. What I have to say involves this last definition scarcely at all. I will be concerned with operative values and conceptualized values.

The Infant's Way of Valuing

Let me first speak about the infant. The living human being has, at the outset, a clear approach to values. She prefers some things and experiences, and rejects others. We can infer from studying her behavior that she prefers those experiences which maintain, enhance, or actualize her organism, and rejects those which do not serve this end. Watch her for a bit:

> Hunger is negatively valued. Her expression of this often comes through loud and clear.
>
> Food is positively valued. But when she is satisfied, food is negatively valued, and the same milk she responded to so eagerly is now spit out, or the breast

which seemed so satisfying is now rejected as she turns her head away from the nipple with an amusing facial expression of disgust and revulsion.

She values security and the holding and caressing which seem to communicate security.

She values new experience for its own sake, and we observe this in her obvious pleasure in discovering her toes, in her searching movements, and in her endless curiosity.

She shows a clear negative valuing of pain, bitter tastes, and sudden loud sounds.

All of this is commonplace, but let us look at these facts in terms of what they tell us about the infant's approach to values. It is first of all a flexible, changing, valuing *process*, not a fixed system. She likes food and dislikes the same food. She values security and rest, and rejects it for new experience. What is going on seems best described as an organismic valuing process, in which each element, each moment of what she is experiencing is somehow weighed, and selected or rejected, depending on whether, at that moment, it tends to actualize the organism or not. This complicated weighing of experience is clearly an organismic, not a conscious or symbolic function. These are operative, not conceived values. But this process can nonetheless deal with complex value problems. I would remind you of the experiment in which young infants had spread in front of them a score or more of dishes of natural (that is, unflavored) foods. Over a period of time they clearly tended to value the foods which enhanced their own survival, growth, and development. If for a time a child gorged herself on starches, this would soon be balanced by a protein "binge." If at times she chose a diet deficient in some vitamin, she would later seek out foods rich in this very vitamin. She was utilizing wisdom of the body in her value choices, or perhaps more accurately, the physiological wisdom of her body guided her behavioral movements, resulting in what we might think of as objectively sound value choices.

Another aspect of the infant's approach to value is that the source or locus of the evaluating process is clearly within herself. Unlike many of us, she *knows* what she likes and dislikes, and the origin of these value choices lies strictly within herself. She is the center of the valuing process, the evidence for her choices being supplied by her own senses. She is not at this point influenced by what her parents think she should prefer, or by what the church says, or by the opinion of the latest "expert" in the field, or by the persuasive talents of an advertising firm. It is from within her own experiencing that her organism is saying in non-verbal terms—"This is good for me," "That is bad for me," "I like this," "I strongly dislike that." She would laugh at our concern over values, if she could understand it. How could anyone fail to know what she liked and disliked, what was good for her and what was not?

The Change in the Valuing Process

What happens to this highly efficient, soundly based valuing process? By what sequence of events do we exchange it for the more rigid, uncertain, inefficient approach to values that characterizes most of us as adults? Let me try to state briefly one of the major ways in which I think this happens.

The infant needs love, wants it, tends to behave in ways which will bring a repetition of this wanted experience. But this brings complications. A boy pulls baby sister's hair and finds it satisfying to hear her wails and protests. He then hears that he is "a naughty, bad boy," and this may be reinforced by a slap on the hand. He is cut off from affection. As this experience is repeated, and many, many others like it, he gradually learns that what "feels good" is often "bad" in the eyes of others. Then the next step occurs, in which he comes to take the same attitude toward himself that these others have taken. Now, as he pulls his sister's hair, he solemnly intones, "Bad, bad boy." He is introjecting the value judgment of another, taking it in as his own. To that degree he loses touch with his own organismic valuing process. He has deserted the wisdom of his organism, giving up the locus of evaluation, and is trying to behave in terms of values set by another, in order to hold love.

Or take another example at an older level. A boy senses, though perhaps not consciously, that he is more loved and prized by his parents when he thinks of being a doctor than when he thinks of being an artist. Gradually he introjects the values attached to being a doctor. He comes to want, above all, to be a doctor. Then in college he is baffled by the fact that he repeatedly fails in chemistry, which is absolutely necessary to becoming a physician, in spite of the fact that the guidance counselor assures him he has the ability to pass the course. Only in counseling interviews does he begin to realize how completely he has lost touch with his organismic reactions, how out of touch he is with his own valuing process.

Let me give another instance from a class of mine, a group of prospective teachers. I asked them at the beginning of the course, "Please list for me the two or three values that you would most wish to pass on to the children with whom you will work." They turned in many value goals, but I was surprised by some of the items. Several listed such things as "to speak correctly," "to use good English, not to use words like ain't." Others mentioned neatness: "to do things according to instructions"; one expained her hope that "When I tell them to write their names in the upper right-hand corner with the date under it, I want them to do it *that way,* not in some other form."

I confess I was somewhat appalled that for some of these young women the most important value to be passed on to pupils were to avoid bad grammar or meticulously to follow teacher's instructions. I felt baffled. Certainly these behaviors had not been *experienced* as the most satisfying and meaningful elements in their own lives. The listing of such values could only be accounted for by the fact that these behaviors had gained approval—and thus had been introjected as deeply important.

Perhaps these several illustrations will indicate that in an attempt to gain or hold love, approval, esteem, the individual relinquishes the locus of evaluation that was hers in infancy and places it in others. She learns to have a basic *distrust* for her own experiencing as a guide to her behavior. She learns from others a large number of conceived values and adopts them as her own, even though they may be widely discrepant from what she is experiencing.

Because these concepts are not based on her own valuing, they tend to be fixed and rigid, rather than fluid and changing.

SOME INTROJECTED PATTERNS

It is in this fashion, I believe, that most of us accumulate the introjected value patterns by which we live. In this fantastically complex culture of today, the patterns we introject as desirable or undesirable come from a variety of sources and are often highly contradictory in their meanings. Let me list a few of the introjections which are commonly held.

• Sexual desires and behaviors are mostly bad. The sources of this construct are many—parents, church, teachers.

• Disobedience is bad. Here parents and teachers combine with the military to emphasize this concept. To obey is good. To obey without question is even better.

• Making money is the highest good. The sources of this conceived value are too numerous to mention.

• Learning an accumulation of scholarly facts is highly desirable.

• Browsing and aimless exploratory reading for fun is undesirable. The source of these last two concepts is apt to be the school, the educational system.

• Abstract art is good. Here the people we regard as sophisticated are the originators of the value.

• Communism is utterly bad. Here the government is a major source.

• To love thy neighbor is the highest good. This concept comes from the church, perhaps from the parents.

• Cooperation and teamwork are preferable to acting alone. Here companions are an important source.

• Cheating is clever and desirable. The peer group again is the origin.

• Coca-Cola, chewing gum, electric refrigerators, color TV, and automobiles are utterly desirable. This conception comes not only from advertisements, but is reinforced by people all over the world. From Jamaica to Japan, from Copenhagen to Kowloon, the "Coca-Cola culture" has come to be regarded as the acme of desirability.

This is a small and diversified sample of the myriads of conceived values that individuals often introject and hold as their own without ever having considered their inner organismic reactions to these patterns and objects.

COMMON CHARACTERISTICS OF
ADULT VALUING

I believe it will be clear from the foregoing that the usual adult—I feel I am speaking for most of us—has an approach to values that has these characteristics:

• The majority of her values are introjected from other individuals or groups significant to her but are regarded by her as her own.

• The source or locus of evaluation on most matters lies outside of self.

• The criterion by which values are set is the degree to which they will cause her to be loved or accepted.

• These conceived preferences are either not related at all, or not clearly related, to her own process of experiencing.

• Often there is a wide and unrecognized discrepancy between the evidence supplied by her own experience, and these conceived values.

• Because these conceptions are not open to testing in experience, she must hold them in a rigid and unchanging fashion. The alternative would be a collapse of her values. Hence her values are "right"—like the law of the Medes and the Persians, which changeth not.

• Because they are untestable, there is no ready way of solving contradictions. If she has taken in from the community the conception that money is the *summum bonum* and from the church the conception that love of one's neighbor is the highest value, she has no way of discovering which has more value for *her*. Hence a common aspect of modern life is living with absolutely contradictory values. We calmly discuss the possibility of dropping a hydrogen bomb on a country we regard as our enemy, but then find tears in our eyes when we see headlines about the suffering of one small child.

• Because she has relinquished the locus of evaluation to others, and has lost touch with her own valuing process, she feels profoundly insecure and easily threatened in her values. If some of these conceptions were destroyed, what would take their place? This threatening possibility makes her hold her value conceptions more rigidly or more confusedly, or both.

The Fundamental Discrepancy

I believe that this picture of the individual, with values mostly introjected, held as fixed concepts, rarely examined or tested, is the picture of most of us. By taking over the conceptions of others as our own, we lose contact with the potential wisdom of our own functioning and lose confidence in ourselves. Since these value constructs are often sharply at variance with what is going on in our own experiencing, we have in a very basic way divorced ourselves from ourselves, and this accounts for much of modern strain and insecurity. This fundamental discrepancy between the individual's concepts and what she is actually experiencing, between the intellectual structure of her values and the valuing process going on unrecognized within—this is a part of the fundamental estrangement of the modern person from his or her self. This is a major problem for the therapist.

RESTORING CONTACT WITH
EXPERIENCE

Some individuals are fortunate in going beyond the picture I have just given, developing further in the direction of psychological maturity. We see this happen in psychotherapy where we endeavor to provide a climate favorable to the growth of the person. We also see it happen in life, whenever life provides a therapeutic climate for the individual. Let me concentrate on this further maturing of a value approach as I have seen it in therapy.

In the first place let me say somewhat parenthetically that the therapeutic relationship is *not* devoid of values. Quite the contrary. When it is most effective, it seems to me, it is marked by one primary value: namely, that this person, this client, has worth. She as a person is valued in her separateness and uniqueness. It is when she senses and realizes that she is prized as a person that she can slowly begin to value the different aspects of herself. Most importantly, she can begin, with much difficulty at first, to sense and to feel what is going on within her, what she is feeling, what she is experiencing, how she is reacting. She uses her experiencing as a direct referent to which she can turn in forming accurate conceptualizations and as a guide to her behavior. Gendlin (1, 2) has elaborated the way in which this occurs. As her experiencing becomes more and more open to her, as she is able to live more freely in the process of her feelings, then significant changes begin to occur in her approach to values. It begins to assume many of the characteristics it had in infancy.

INTROJECTED VALUES IN RELATION TO
EXPERIENCING

Perhaps I can indicate this by reviewing a few of the brief examples of introjected values that I have given, and suggesting what happens to them as the individual comes closer to what is going on within him or her.

- The individual in therapy looks back and realizes, "But I *enjoyed* pulling my sister's hair—and that doesn't make me a bad person."
- The student failing chemistry realizes, as she gets close to her own experiencing: "I *don't* value being a doctor, even though my parents do; I don't like chemistry; I don't like taking steps toward being a doctor; and I am not a failure for having these feelings."
- The adult recognizes that sexual desires and behavior may be richly satisfying and permanently enriching in their consequences, or shallow and temporary and less than satisfying. She goes by her own experiencing, which does not always coincide with the social norms.
- She considers art from a new value approach. She says, "This picture moves me deeply, means a great deal to me. It also happens to be an abstraction, but that is not the basis for my valuing it."
- She recognizes freely that this communist book or person has attitudes and goals which she shares as well as ideas and values which she does not share.
- She realizes that at times she experiences cooperation as meaningful and valuable to her, and at other times she wishes to be alone and act alone.

Valuing in the Mature Person

The valuing process that seems to develop in this more mature person is in some ways very much like that in the infant, and in some ways quite different. It is fluid, flexible, based on this particular moment, and the degree to which this moment is experienced as enhancing and actualizing. Values are not held rigidly, but are continually changing. The painting that last year seemed meaningful now appears uninteresting; the way of working with individuals that was formerly experienced as good now seems inadequate; the belief that then seemed true is now experienced as only partly true, or perhaps false.

Another characteristic of the way this person values experience is that it is highly differentiated, or as the semanticists would say, extensional. As the members of my class of prospective teachers learned, general principles are not as useful as sensitively discriminating reactions. One says, "With this little boy, I just felt I should be very firm, and he seemed to welcome that, and I felt good that I had been. But I'm not that way at all with the other children most of the time." She was relying on her experiencing of the relationship with each child to guide her behavior. I have already indicated, in going through the examples, how much more differentiated are the individual's reactions to what were previously rather solid, monolithic, introjected values.

In another way the mature individual's approach is like that of the infant. The locus of evaluation is again established firmly within the person. It is her own experience that provides the value information or feedback. This does not mean that she is not open to all the evidence she can obtain from other sources. But it means that this is taken for what it is—outside evidence—and is not as significant as her own reactions. Thus she may be told by a friend that a new book is very disappointing. She reads two unfavorable reviews of the book. Thus her tentative hypothesis is that she will not value the book. Yet if she reads the book her valuing will be based upon the reactions it stirs in her, not on what she has been told by others.

There is also involved in this valuing process a letting oneself down into the immediacy of what one is experiencing, endeavoring to sense and to clarify all its complex meanings. I think of a client who, toward the close of therapy, when puzzled about an issue, would put his head in his hands and say, "Now what *is* it that I'm feeling? I want to get next to it. I want to learn what it is." Then he would wait, quietly and patiently, trying to listen to himself, until he could discern the exact flavor of the feelings he was experiencing. He, like others, was trying to get close to himself.

In getting close to what is going on within himself, the process is much more complex than it is in the infant. In the mature person it has much more scope and sweep, for there is involved in the present moment of experiencing the memory traces of all the relevant learnings from the past. This moment has not only its immediate sensory impact, but it has meaning growing out of similar experiences in the past. It has both the new and the old in it. So when I experience a painting or a person, my experiencing contains within it the learnings I have accumulated from past meetings with paintings or persons, as well as the new impact of this particular encounter. Likewise the moment of experiencing contains, for the mature adult, hypotheses about consequences. "I feel now that I would enjoy a third drink, but past learnings indicate that I may regret it in the morning." "It is not pleasant to express forthrightly my negative feelings to this person, but past experience indicates that in a continuing relationship it will be helpful in the long run." Past and future are both in this moment and enter into the valuing.

I find that in the person I am speaking of (and here again we see a similarity to the infant) the criterion of the valuing process is the degree to which the object of the experience actualizes the individual. "Does it make her a richer, more complete, more fully developed person?" This may sound as though it were a selfish or unsocial criterion, but it does not prove to be so, since deep and helpful relationships with others are experienced as actualizing.

Like the infant, too, the psychologically mature adult trusts and uses the wisdom of her organism, with the difference that she is able to do so knowingly. She realizes that if she can trust all of herself, her feelings and intuitions may be wiser than her mind, that as a total person she can be more sensitive and accurate than her thoughts alone. Hence she is not afraid to say, "I feel that this experience (or this thing, or this direction) is good. Later I will probably know *why* I feel it is good." She trusts the totality of herself.

It should be evident from what I have been saying that this valuing process in the mature individual is not an easy or simple thing. The process is complex, the choices often very perplexing and difficult, and there is no guarantee that the choice that is made will in fact prove to be self-actualizing. But because whatever evidence exists is available to the individual, and because she is open to her experiencing, errors are correctable. If this chosen course of action is not self-enhancing this will be sensed and she can make an adjustment or revision. She thrives on a maximum feedback interchange and thus, like the gyroscopic compass on a ship, can continually correct the course toward the true goal of self-fulfillment.

Some Propositions Regarding the
Valuing Process

Let me sharpen the meaning of what I have been saying by stating two propositions that contain the essential elements of this viewpoint. While it may not be possible to devise empirical tests of each proposition in its entirety, yet each is to some degree capable of being tested through the methods of science. I would also state that though the following propositions are stated firmly in order to give them clarity, I am actually advancing them as decidedly tentative hypotheses.

I. *There is an organismic base for an organized valuing process within the human individual.*

It is hypothesized that this base is something the human being shares with the rest of the animate world. It is part of the functioning life process of any healthy organism. It is the capacity for receiving feedback information that enables the organism continually to adjust its behavior and reactions so as to achieve the maximum possible self-enhancement.

II. *This valuing process in the human being is effective in achieving self-enhancement to the degree that the individual is open to the experiencing that is going on within.*

I have tried to give two examples of individuals who are close to their own experiencing: the tiny infant who has not yet learned to deny in her awareness the processes going on within; and the psychologically mature person who has relearned the advantages of this open state.

There is a corollary to this second proposition that might be put in the following terms. One way of assisting the individual to move toward openness to experience is through a relationship in which she is prized as a separate person, in which the experiencing going on within is empathically understood and valued, and in which she is given the freedom to experience her own feelings and those of others without being threatened in doing so.

This corollary obviously grows out of therapeutic experience. It is a brief statement of the essential qualities in any growth-promoting relationship. There are empirical studies that give support to such a statement.

Propositions Regarding the Outcomes of the Valuing Process

I come now to the nub of any theory of values or valuing. What are its consequences? I should like to move into this new ground by stating bluntly two propositions as to the qualities of behavior which emerge from this valuing process. I shall then give some of the evidence from my own experience as a therapist in support of these propositions.

III. *In persons who are moving toward greater openness to their experiencing, there is an organismic commonality of value directions.*

IV. *These common value directions are of such kinds as to enhance the development of the individual, of others in the community, and to contribute to the survival and evolution of his species.*

It has been a striking fact of my experience that in therapy, where individuals are valued, where there is greater freedom to feel and to be, certain value directions seem to emerge. These are not chaotic directions but instead have a surprising commonality. This commonality is not dependent on the personality of the therapist, for I have seen these trends emerge in the clients of therapists sharply different in personality. This commonality does not seem to be due to the influences of any one culture, for I have found evidence of these directions in cultures as divergent as those of the United States, Holland, France, and Japan. I like to think that this commonality of value directions is due to the fact that we all belong to the same species—that just as a human infant tends, individually, to select a diet similar to that selected by other human infants, so a client in therapy tends, individually, to choose value directions similar to those chosen by other clients. As a species there may be certain elements of experience which tend to make for inner development and which would be chosen by all individuals if they were genuinely free to choose.

Let me indicate a few of these value directions, as I see them in my clients as they move in the direction of personal growth and maturity.

● They tend to move away from façades. Pretense, defensiveness, putting up a front tend to be negatively valued.

● They tend to move away from "oughts." The compelling feeling of "I ought to do or be thus and so" is negatively valued. The client moves away from being what he "ought to be," no matter who has set that imperative.

● They tend to move away from meeting the expectations of others. Pleasing others, as a goal in itself, is negatively valued.

● Being real is positively valued. The client tends to move toward being herself, being her real feelings, being what she is. This seems to be a very deep preference.

● Self-direction is positively valued. The client discovers an increasing pride and confidence in making her own choices, guiding her own life.

● One's self, one's own feelings come to be positively valued. From a point where she looks upon herself with contempt and despair, the client comes to value herself and her reactions as being of worth.

● Being a process is positively valued. From desiring some fixed goal, clients come to prefer the excitement of being a process of potentialities being born.

● Perhaps more than all else, the client comes to value an openness to all of her inner and outer experiences. To be open to and sensitive to her own *inner* reactions and feelings, the reactions and feelings of others, and the realities of the objective world—this is a direction which she clearly prefers. This openness becomes the client's most valued resource.

● Sensitivity to others and acceptance of others is positively valued. The client comes to appreciate others for what they are, just as she has come to appreciate herself for what she is.

● Finally, deep relationships are positively valued. To achieve a close, intimate, real, fully communicative relationship with another person seems to meet a deep need in every individual, and is very highly valued.

These then are some of the preferred directions that I have observed in individuals moving toward personal maturity. Though I am sure that the list I have given is inadequate and perhaps to some degree inaccurate, it holds for me exciting possibilities. Let me try to explain why.

I find it significant that when individuals are prized as persons, the values they select do not run the full gamut of possibilities. I do not find, in such a climate of freedom, that one person comes to value fraud and murder and thievery, while another values a life of self-sacrifice, and another values only money. Instead there seems to be a deep and underlying thread of commonality. I dare to believe that when the human being is inwardly free to choose whatever she deeply values, she tends to value those objects, experiences and goals which contribute to her own survival, growth, and development, and to the survival and development of others. I hypothesize that it is characteristic of the human organism to prefer such actualizing and socialized goals when she is exposed to a growth-promoting climate.

A corollary of what I have been saying is that in *any* culture, given a climate of respect and freedom in which she is valued as a person, the mature individual would tend to choose and prefer these same value directions. This is a highly significant hypothesis which could be tested. It means that though the individual of whom I am speaking would not have a consistent or even a stable system of conceived values, the valuing process within her would lead to emerging value directions which would be constant across cultures and across time.

Another implication I see is that individuals who exhibit the fluid valuing process I have tried to describe, whose value directions are generally those I have listed, would be highly effective in the ongoing process of human evolution. If the human species is to survive at all on this globe, the human being must become more readily adaptive to new problems and situations, must be able to select that which is valuable for development and survival out of new and complex situations, must be accurate in the appreciation of reality if she is to make such selections. The psychologically mature person as I have described her has, I believe, the qualities that would cause her to value those experiences that would facilitate the survival and enhancement of the human race. She would be a worthy participant and guide in the process of human evolution.

Finally, it appears that we have returned to the issue of the universality of values, but by a different route. Instead of universal values "out there," or a universal value system imposed by some group—philosophers, rulers, or priests—we have the possibility of universal human value directions emerging from the experiencing of the human organism. Evidence from therapy indicates that both personal and social values emerge as natural, and experienced, when the individual is close to her own organismic valuing process. The tentative conclusion is that though modern humans no longer trust religion or science or philosophy or any system of beliefs to *give* them their values, they can find an organismic valuing base deep within themselves, which, if they can learn to be in touch with it, will prove to be an organized, adaptive, and social approach to the perplexing value issues which face all of us.

Summary

I have tried to present some observations, growing out of experience in psychotherapy, that are relevant to humankind's search for some satisfying basis for an approach to values.

I have described the human infant as she enters directly into an evaluating transaction with her world, appreciating or rejecting her experiences as they have meaning for her own actualization, utilizing all the wisdom of her tiny but complex organism.

I have said that we seem to lose this capacity for direct evaluation, and come to behave in those ways and to act in terms of those values that will bring us social approval, affection, esteem. To buy love we relinquish the valuing process. Because the center of our lives now lies in others, we are fearful and insecure, and must cling rigidly to the values we have introjected.

But if life or therapy gives us favorable conditions for continuing our psychological growth, we move on in something of a spiral, developing an approach to values that partakes of the infant's directness and fluidity but goes far beyond in its richness. In our transactions with experience we are again the locus or source of valuing, we prefer those experiences that in the long run are enhancing, we utilize all the richness of our cognitive learning and functioning, but at the same time we trust the wisdom of our organism.

I have pointed out that these observations lead to certain basic statements. Humans have within themselves an organismic basis for valuing. To the extent that we can be freely in touch with this valuing process in ourselves, we will behave in ways that are self-enhancing. We even know some of the conditions that enable us to be in touch with our own experiencing process.

In therapy, such openness to experience leads to emerging value directions that appear to be common across individuals and perhaps even across cultures. Stated in older terms, individuals who are thus in touch with their experiencing come to value such directions as sincerity, independence, self-direction, self-knowledge, social responsivity, social responsibility, and loving interpersonal relationships.

I have concluded that a new kind of emergent universality of value directions becomes possible when individuals move in the direction of psychological maturity, or more accurately, move in the direction of becoming open to their experiencing. Such a value base appears to make for the enhancement of self and others, and to promote a positive evolutionary process.

REFERENCES

1. Gendlin, E. T. *Experiencing and the Creation of Meaning*. New York: The Free Press of Glencoe, Division of the Macmillan Co., 1962.
2. Gendlin, E. T. *Focusing*. New York: Everest House, 1978.
3. Morris, Charles W. *Varieties of Human Value*. Chicago: University of Chicago Press, 1956.
4. Rogers, Carl R. *Client-centered Therapy*. Boston: Houghton Mifflin Co., 1951.
5. Rogers, Carl R. "A Theory of Therapy, Personality and Interpersonal Relationships." In *Psychology: A Study of a Science*, edited by S. Koch, pp. 185–256. Vol. III. *Formulations of the person and the social context*. New York: McGraw-Hill, 1959, pp. 185–256.
6. Yankelovich, D. "New Rules in American Life: Searching for Self-fulfillment in a World Turned Upside Down." *Psychology Today*, 15 (1981): 39.

Freedom and
Commitment

‌꘏

Freedom to learn or choose; *self-directed* learning; these are completely untenable concepts in the minds of many behavioral scientists, who believe that man is simply the inevitable product of his conditioning. Yet these are terms that I have used freely in this book, as though they have real meaning.

I endeavored to face this discrepancy squarely in a talk I gave at the time I was honored as "Humanist of the Year" by the American Humanist Association. I do not pretend that I resolved the age-old problem of freedom and determinism, but I have, for myself, formulated a way of living with it. I hope my statement will be clarifying to those who are perplexed by differences between the mechanistic-behaviorist point of view in education and the humanistic approach to learning.

One of the deepest issues in modern life is the question as to whether the concept of personal freedom has any meaning whatsoever in our present day scientific world. The growing ability of the behavioral scientist to predict and to control behavior has brought the issue sharply to the fore. If we accept the logical positivism and strictly behavioristic emphases that are predominant in the American psychological scene, there is not even room for discussion.

But if we step outside the narrowness of the behavioral sciences, this question is not only *an* issue; it is one of the primary issues that define modern man. Friedman in his book (5, p. 251) makes his topic "the problematic of modern man—the alienation, the divided nature, the unresolved tension between personal freedom and psychological compulsion which follows on 'the death of God.' " The issues of personal freedom and personal commitment have become very sharp indeed in a world in which the individual feels the division between her awareness and those elements of dynamic functioning of which she is unaware. If she is to wrest any meaning from the universe, which for all she knows may be indifferent, she must arrive at some stance that she can hold in regard to these timeless uncertainties.

So, writing as both a behaviorial scientist and as one profoundly concerned with the human, the personal, the phenomenological and the intangible, I should like to contribute what I can to this continuing dialogue regarding the meaning of and the possibility of freedom.

Man Is Unfree

Let me explain, first of all, that to most psychologists and workers in the behavioral sciences, the title of this chapter would seem very strange indeed. In the minds of most behavioral scientists, man is not free, nor can he as a free man commit himself to some purpose, since he is controlled by factors outside of himself. Therefore, neither freedom nor commitment is even a possible concept to modern behavioral science as it is usually understood.

To show that I am not exaggerating, let me quote a statement from Dr. B. F. Skinner of Harvard, who is one of the most consistent advocates of a strictly behavioristic psychology. He says,

> The hypothesis that man is not free is essential to the application of scientific method to the study of human behavior. The free inner man who is held responsible for his behavior is only a prescientific substitute for the kinds of causes which are discovered in the course of scientific analysis. All these alternative causes lie *outside* the individual. (12, p. 477)

This view is shared by many psychologists and others who feel, as does Dr. Skinner, that all the effective causes of behavior lie outside of the individual and that it is only through the external stimulus that behavior takes place. The scientific description of behavior avoids anything that partakes in any way of freedom. For example, Dr. Skinner (11, pp. 90–91) describes an experiment in which a pigeon was conditioned to turn in a clockwise direction. The behavior of the pigeon was "shaped up" by rewarding any movement that approximated a clockwise turn until, increasingly, the bird was turning round and round in a steady movement. This is what is known as operant conditioning. Students who had watched the demonstration were asked to write an account of what they had seen. Their responses included the following ideas: that the pigeon was conditioned to *expect* reinforcement for the right kind of behavior; that the pigeon *hoped* that something would bring the food back again; that the pigeon *observed* that a certain behavior seemed to produce a particular result; that the pigeon *felt* that food would be given it because of its action; that the bird came to *associate* his action with the click of the food dispenser. Skinner ridicules these statements because they all go beyond the observed behavior in using such words as *expect, hope, observe, feel,* and *associate.* The whole explanation from his point of view is that the bird was reinforced when it emitted a given kind of behavior;

the pigeon walked around until the food container again appeared; a certain behavior produced a given result; food was given to the pigeon when it acted in a given way; and the click of the food dispenser was related in time to the bird's action. These statements describe the pigeon's behavior from a scientific point of view.

Skinner goes on to point out that the students were undoubtedly reporting what they would have expected, felt, and hoped under similar circumstances. But he then makes the case that there is no more reality to such ideas in the human being than there is in the pigeon, that it is only because such words have been reinforced by the verbal community in which the individual has developed, that such terms are used. He discusses the fact that the verbal community that conditioned them to use such terms saw no more of their behavior than they had seen of the pigeon's. In other words the internal events, if they indeed exist, have no scientific significance.

As to the methods used for changing the behavior of the pigeon, many people besides Dr. Skinner feel that through such positive reinforcement human behavior as well as animal behavior can be "shaped up" and controlled. In his book, *Walden Two*, Skinner says,

> Now that we know how positive reinforcement works and how negative doesn't, we can be more deliberate and hence more successful in our cultural design. We can achieve a sort of control under which the controlled, though they are following a code much more scrupulously than was ever the case under the old system, nevertheless *feel free*. They are doing what they want to do, not what they are forced to do. That's the source of the tremendous power of positive reinforcement—there is no restraint and no revolt. By a careful cultural design we control not the final behavior but the *inclination* to behave—the motives, the desires, the wishes. The curious thing is that in that case *the question of freedom never arises*. (13, p. 218)

Another psychological experiment, done by Dr. Richard Crutchfield at Berkeley (3), again illustrates a way in which behavior may be controlled, in which it appears the individual is unfree. In this experiment five subjects at a time are seated side by side, each in an individual booth screened from one another. Each booth has a panel with various switches and lights. The subject can use the switches to signal his judgments on items that are projected on the wall in front of the group. The lights are signal lights that indicate what judgments the other four members are giving to the items. The subjects are told that they will be given identifying letters *A, B, C, D,* and *E* and are instructed to respond one at a time in that order. However, when they enter the cubicles, each discovers that he is letter *E*. They are not permitted to talk during the session.

Actually the lights in each booth are controlled by the experimenter and do not express the judgments of the other four members. Thus, on those critical items where the experimenter wishes to impose group pressure, he can make it appear that all four members, *A* through *D*, agree on an answer that is clearly at variance with the correct answer. In this way each subject is confronted with a conflict between her own judgment and what she believes to be the consensus of the group. Thus, for example, the question may be,

"Which of these two irregular figures is larger, X or Y?" The individual sees clearly that X is larger than Y, yet one after another the lights flash on indicating that all of the other four members regard Y as being the larger figure. Now it is her turn to decide. How will she respond? Which switch will she press? Crutchfield has shown that given the right conditions almost everyone will desert the evidence of her senses or her own honest opinion and conform to the seeming consensus of the group. For example, some high level mathematicians yielded to the false group consensus on some fairly easy arithmetic problems, giving wrong answers that they would never have given under normal circumstances.

Here again there would seem to be evidence that the behavior of the individual is shaped by the outside stimulus, in this case a social stimulus, and that there is no such thing as freedom in choosing one's behavior. It helps to explain how Skinner in his book, *Walden Two,* can have his hero say:

> "Well, what do you say to the design of personalities? Would that interest you? The control of temperaments? Give me the specifications and I'll give you the man! What do you say to the control of motivation, building the interests which will make men most productive and most successful? Does that seem to you fantastic? Yet some of the techniques are available and more can be worked out experimentally. Think of the possibilities. . . . Let us control the lives of our children and see what we can make of them." (13, p. 243)

An experience I had some time ago in a university on the West Coast further illustrates the "unfreedom" of man. Some psychologists were studying the ways in which individual patterns of behavior in a group can be changed. Four male subjects are seated around a table. Each has in front of him a shielded light bulb invisible to the others. They are given a topic on which to talk. Notice is taken of the individual who seems least dominant in the group, who never takes a leadership role. Then for the second part of the experiment, this individual is given a paper in which he is told that the discussion is being listened to and observed by experts, and that when these experts think he is contributing usefully to the group process, his light will blink. He will have to judge for himself what he is doing that is helpful. The other, more dominant, three are given similar sheets of instructions, except that each is told that his light will blink when he is *not* contributing helpfully. They are then given another question to discuss with the instruction that by the end of the half hour they are to try to arrive at conclusions in regard to this problem. Now, every time that the "shrinking violet" speaks, his light blinks. And whenever the others speak their lights also blink, but with the opposite meaning, that they are *not* contributing. After half an hour of such conditioning, the shy member is nearly always the perceived leader of the group. Furthermore, this pattern seems to carry over through an additional half hour in which no use is made of lights. The story is told of three mature scientists and one young graduate student who were put through this procedure. In the first session, the young student took almost no part. In the session with the blinking lights, he became so dominant that at the end when the group was asked for a summary of what had gone on, the older men turned to him and said, "Why don't you summarize it? You're the one best able to do that."

Here again it seems as though behavior is extremely manipulable and that there is no such thing as freedom. The members of the group are behaving like puppets on a string at the whim of the experimenters.

One more example of the degree of control which scientists have been able to achieve involves an experiment with rats. Years ago, Dr. James Olds (7) found that he could implant tiny electrodes in the septal area of the brain of laboratory rats. When one of these animals presses a bar in his cage, it causes a minute current to pass through these electrodes. When the electrode has penetrated just the right area of brain tissue, this appears to be such a rewarding experience that the animal goes into an orgy of bar pressing, often until he is exhausted. However, the subjective nature of the experience seems to be so satisfying that the animal prefers it to any other activity. Even after exhaustion, with a brief rest and a small bit of food and water, the rat returns to its orgy of pleasure. In one experiment, rats went on in this fashion for twenty-four hours a day for three weeks straight. Curiously enough, there seemed to be no physical or mental damage to the rats then or later. One can only speculate what this procedure might bring forth if applied fully to human beings.

There are not only experiments of this sort with animals, but there are beginning to be situations in which such electronic stimulation of the brain is utilized for a number of medical purposes in humans. Obviously there cannot be the experimentation with human beings that there has been with animals. Yet already we know that these tiny electronic currents passing through minute portions of the brain elicit feelings of happiness, rage or terror, and even depress feelings of extreme pain.

I think it is clear from all of this that man is a machine—a complex machine, to be sure, but one that is increasingly subject to scientific control. Whether behavior will be managed through operant conditioning as in *Walden Two* or whether we will be "shaped up" by the unplanned forms of conditioning implied in social pressure, or whether we will be controlled by electrodes in the brain, it seems quite clear that science is making out of man an object and that the purpose of such science is not only understanding and prediction but *control*. Thus, it would seem to be quite clear that there could be no concept so foreign to the facts as that man is free. Man is a machine, man is unfree, man cannot commit himself in any meaningful sense; he is simply controlled by planned or unplanned forces outside of himself.

Man Is Free

I am impressed by the scientific advances illustrated in the examples I have given. I regard them as a great tribute to the ingenuity, insight, and persistence of the individuals making the investigations. They have added enormously to our knowledge. Yet for me they leave something very important unsaid. Let me try to illustrate this, first from my experience in therapy.

I think of a young man classed as schizophrenic with whom I had been working for a long time in a state hospital. He was a very inarticulate man, and during one hour, he made a few remarks about individuals who had recently left the hospital; then he remained silent for almost forty minutes. When he got up to go, he mumbled almost under his breath, "If some of *them* can do it, maybe I can too." That was all—not a dramatic statement, not uttered with force and vigor, yet a statement of choice by this young man to work toward his own improvement and eventual release from the hospital. It is not too surprising that about eight months after that statement he was out of the hospital. I believe this experience of responsible choice is one of the deepest aspects of psychotherapy and one of the elements that most solidly underlies personality change.

I think of another young person, this time a young woman graduate student, who was deeply disturbed and on the borderline of a psychotic break. Yet after a number of interviews in which she talked very critically about all of the people who had failed to give her what she needed, she finally concluded: "Well, with that sort of a foundation, it's really up to *me*. I mean it seems to be really apparent to me that I can't depend on someone else to *give* me an education." And then she added very softly: "I'll really have to get it myself." She goes on to explore this experience of important and responsible choice. She finds it a frightening experience, and yet one that gives her a feeling of strength. A force seems to surge up within her that is big and strong, and yet she also feels very much alone and sort of cut off from support. She adds, "I am going to begin to do more things that I know I should do." And she did.

I could add many other examples. One young fellow talking about the way in which his whole life had been distorted and spoiled by his parents finally comes to the conclusion that, "Maybe now that I *see* that, it's up to *me*."

Let me spell out a trifle more fully the way such choosings occur in therapy. An immature, highly religious sixteen-year-old high school girl, brought up in a very strict family, had rather obviously been patterning herself upon a masculine ideal of work and scholarly achievements that was almost certainly beyond her abilities. The previous year she had had a "nervous breakdown," which overwhelmed her. Some months after her break, she came to me for help. To take just one theme of the many that she pursued through the interviews, I will focus on her views about being a woman, as quite fully reported in my notes. During the early interviews, she made it clear that she disliked children, that she did not wish marriage, that she wished she were a man or could act like a man. These feelings were accepted.

Later on she says, "I admire masculine qualities so much that I wish I could be a man. Maybe somebody ought to set me straight and show me that I could be a fine young woman." This more ambivalent attitude was again accepted as being her own.

Two interviews later she talks about her dislike for small children but adds thoughtfully, "Maybe my dislike has been more or less forced. Maybe I just thought I'd be that way."

In a later interview she talks rather freely of her fear of childbirth, her fear that marriage would interfere with a career, saying that she is still mixed up on all these issues, showing very definite ambivalence.

In one of the closing interviews, she says, "You know I've thought about that femininity thing again and I'm going to see if I can put it into words. I'm a woman. I'm going to accept it, not as fate, not in a spirit of submission, but as meant for the best. I can probably do a lot more good by being myself and developing my own talent rather than trying to do something different. I'm going to accept it as a challenge. I feel that I've almost lost that feeling that I wanted to be masculine. I just want to be myself. Maybe before I get through I'll really be glad I'm feminine."

Here again we see a slowly growing experience of personal choice which appeared to be basic to all of the change in personality and behavior that occurred. She chose, freely, to perceive herself in a different way, and out of that different perception there flowed many changes in attitude and behavior.

Or perhaps I could somehow communicate best the significance of free and responsible choice by quoting one sentence from a confused, bitter, psychotic individual who had been in a state hospital for three admissions, the last admission having lasted two and one-half years at the time I began working with him. I think the changes that gradually took place were based on and epitomized by one sentence in one of his interviews when he was feeling particularly confused. He said, "I don't know *what* I'm gonna do; but *I'm* gonna do it." For me, that speaks volumes.

The film *David and Lisa,* made a number of years ago, illustrates exactly what I have been discussing. David, the adolescent schizophrenic, goes into a panic if he is touched by anyone. He feels that "touching kills," and he is deathly afraid of it and afraid of the closeness in human relationships which touching implies. Yet toward the close of the film he makes a bold and positive choice of the kind I have been describing. He has been trying to be of help to Lisa, the girl who is out of touch with reality. He tries to help at first in an intellectually contemptuous way, then increasingly in a warmer and more personal way. Finally, in a highly dramatic moment, he says to her, "Lisa, take my hand." He *chooses,* with obvious conflict and fear, to leave behind the safety of his untouchableness, and to venture into the world of real human relationships where he is literally and figuratively in *touch* with another. You are an unusual person if the film does not grow a bit misty at this point.

Perhaps a behaviorist could try to account for the reaching out of his hand by saying that it was the result of intermittent reinforcement of partial movements. I find such an explanation both inaccurate and inadequate. It is the *meaning* of the *decision* that is essential to understanding the act.

What I am trying to suggest in all of this is that I would be at a loss to explain the positive change that can occur in psychotherapy if I had to omit the importance of the sense of free and responsible choice on the part of my clients. I believe that this experience of freedom to choose is one of the deepest elements underlying change.

The Meaning of Freedom

Considering the scientific advantages that I have mentioned, how can we even speak of freedom? In what sense is a client free? In what sense are any of us free? What possible definition of freedom can there be in the modern world? Let me attempt such a definition.

In the first place, the freedom that I am talking about is essentially an inner thing, something that exists in the living person quite aside from any of the outward choices of alternatives that we so often think of as constituting freedom. I am speaking of the kind of freedom that Viktor Frankl vividly describes in his experience of the concentration camp, when everything—possessions, status, identity—was taken from the prisoners. But even months and years in such an environment showed only "that everything can be taken from a man but one thing: the last of the human freedoms—to choose one's own attitude in any given set of circumstances, to choose one's own way" (4). It is this inner, subjective, existential freedom that I have observed. It is the realization that "I can live myself, here and now, by my own choice." It is the quality of courage which enables a person to step into the uncertainty of the unknown as she chooses herself. It is the discovery of meaning from within oneself, meaning that comes from listening sensitively and openly to the complexities of what one is experiencing. It is the burden of being responsible for the self one chooses to be. It is the recognition of a person that she is an emerging process, not a static end product. The individual who is thus deeply and courageously thinking her own thoughts, becoming her own uniqueness, responsibly choosing herself, may be fortunate in having hundreds of objective outer alternatives from which to choose, or she may be unfortunate in having none. But her freedom exists regardless. So we are first of all speaking of something that exists within the individual, something phenomenological rather than external, but nonetheless to be prized.

The second point in defining this experience of freedom is that it exists not as a contradiction of the picture of the psychological universe as a sequence of cause and effect, but as a complement to such a universe. Freedom rightly understood is a fulfillment by the person of the ordered sequence of her life. The free person moves out voluntarily, freely, responsibly, to play her significant part in a world whose determined events move through her and through her spontaneous choice and will.

I see this freedom of which I am speaking, then, as existing in a different *dimension* than the determined sequence of cause and effect. I regard it as a freedom that exists in the subjective person, a freedom which she courageously uses to live her potentialities. The fact that this type of freedom seems completely irreconcilable with the behaviorist's picture of man is something which I will discuss a bit later.

FREEDOM MAKES A DIFFERENCE

Curiously enough, there is scientific evidence of the importance of this sense of freedom. For example, in the study done by Crutchfield (3) which I mentioned earlier, I stated that under especially extreme circumstances, nearly everyone yielded in some degree to group pressure. Yet there were sharp individual differences, and these are found to be definitely correlated with personality characteristics. For example, the individuals who tended to yield, agree, conform, the ones who could be controlled, gave general evidence of incapacity to cope effectively with stress, while the nonconformists did not tend to panic when placed under pressure of conflicting forces.

The conformist also tended to have pronounced feelings of personal inferiority and inadequacy, while the person who did not yield to pressure had a sense of competence and personal adequacy. She was more self-contained and autonomous in her thinking. She was also a better judge of the attitudes of other people.

Most important of all for our purposes is the fact that those who yielded, the conformists, tended to show a lack of openness and freedom in emotional processes. They were emotionally restricted, lacking in spontaneity, tending to repress their own impulses. The nonconformists, those who made their own choices, were, on the other hand, much more open, free and spontaneous. They were expressive and natural, free from pretense and unaffected. Where the conformist tended to lack insight into her own motives and behavior, the independent person had a good understanding of herself.

What is the meaning of this aspect of Crutchfield's study? It seems to imply that the person who is free within herself, who is open to her experience, who has a sense of her own freedom and responsible choice, is not nearly so likely to be controlled by her environment as is the person who lacks these qualities.

Another story of research in this field, one with which I was closely connected, had a very decided impact on me in the years following the experience. A competent student doing his graduate work under my supervision many years ago chose to study the factors that would predict the behavior of adolescent male delinquents. He made careful objective ratings of the psychological environment in the family, the educational experiences, the neighborhood and cultural influences, the social experiences, the health history, and the hereditary background of each delinquent. These external factors were rated as to their favorableness for normal development on a continuum from elements destructive of the child's welfare and inimical to healthy development to elements highly conducive to healthy development. Almost as an afterthought, a rating was also made of the degree of self-understanding, since it was felt that although this was not one of the primary determining factors, it might play some part in predicting future behavior. This was essentially a rating of the degree to which the individual was open and realistic regarding himself and his situation, a judgment as to whether he was emotionally acceptant of the facts in himself and his environment.

These ratings on seventy-five delinquents were compared with ratings of their behavior and adjustment two to three years after the initial study. It was expected that the ratings on family environment and social experience with peers would be the best predictors of later behavior. To our amazement the degree of self-understanding was much the best predictor, correlating .84 with later behavior, while quality of social experience correlated .55 and family environment .36. We were simply not prepared to believe these findings and laid the study on the shelf until it could be replicated. Later it was replicated on a new group of seventy-six cases, and all the essential findings were confirmed, although not quite so strikingly. Furthermore, the findings stood up even in detailed analysis. When we examined only the delinquents who came from the most unfavorable homes and who remained in those homes, it was still true that their future behavior was best predicted, not by the unfavorable conditioning they were receiving in their home environment, but by the degree of realistic understanding of themselves and their environment that they possessed (10).

The significance of this study was only slowly driven home to me. I began to see the significance of inner autonomy. The individual who sees himself and his situation clearly and who freely takes responsibility for that self and for that situation is a very different person from the one who is simply in the grip of outside circumstances. This difference shows up clearly in important aspects of his behavior.

The Emergence of Commitment

I have spoken thus far primarily about freedom. What about commitment? Certainly the disease of our age is lack of purpose, lack of meaning, lack of commitment on the part of individuals. Is there anything that I can say in regard to this?

It is clear to me that in therapy, as indicated in the examples that I have given, commitment to purpose and to meaning in life is one of the significant elements of change. It is only when the person decides, "I am someone; I am someone worth being; I am commited to being myself," that change becomes possible.

At a very interesting symposium at Rice University, Dr. Sigmund Koch sketched the revolution that is taking place in science, literature, and the arts, in which a sense of commitment is again becoming evident after a long period in which that emphasis has been absent.

Part of what he meant by that may be illustrated by talking about Dr. Michael Polanyi, the philosopher of science, formerly a physicist, who has presented his notions about what science basically is. In his book, *Personal Knowledge*, Polanyi makes it clear that even scientific knowledge is personal knowledge, committed knowledge. We cannot rest comfortably on the belief that scientific knowledge is impersonal and "out there," that it has nothing to do with the individual who has discovered it. Instead every aspect of science is pervaded by disciplined personal commitment, and Polanyi makes the case very persuasively that the whole attempt to divorce science from the person is a completely unrealistic one. I think I am stating his belief correctly when I say that in his judgment logical positivism and all the current structure of science cannot save us from the fact that all knowing is uncertain, involves risk, and is grasped and comprehended only through the deep, personal commitment of a disciplined search.

Perhaps a brief quotation will give something of the flavor of his thinking. Speaking of great scientists, he says:

> So we see that both Kepler and Einstein approached nature with intellectual passions and with beliefs inherent in these passions, which led them to their triumphs and misguided them to their errors. These passions and beliefs were theirs, personally, even though they held them in the convic-

tion that they were valid, universally. I believe that they were competent
to follow these impulses, even though they risked being misled by them.
And again, what I accept of their work today, I accept personally, guided by
passions and beliefs similar to theirs, holding in my turn that my impulses
are valid, universally, even though I must admit the possibility that they
may be mistaken. (8)

Thus, we see that a modern philosopher of science believes that deep
personal commitment is the only possible basis on which science can firmly
stand. This is a far cry indeed from the logical positivism of forty years ago,
which placed knowledge far out in impersonal space.

Let me say a bit more about what I mean by commitment in the psychological sense. I think it is easy to give this word a much too shallow meaning,
indicating that the individual has, simply by conscious choice, committed
himself to one course of action or another. I think the meaning goes far deeper
than that. Commitment is a total organismic direction involving not only the
conscious mind but the whole direction of the organism as well.

In my judgment, commitment is something that one *discovers* within
oneself. It is a trust of one's total reaction rather than of one's mind only. It
has much to do with creativity. Einstein's explanation of how he moved
toward his formulation of relativity without any clear knowledge of his goal is
an excellent example of what I mean by the sense of commitment based on a
total organismic reaction. He says:

> During all those years there was a feeling of direction, of going straight
> toward something concrete. It is, of course, very hard to express that feeling
> in words but it was decidedly the case and clearly to be distinguished from
> later considerations about the rational form of the solution. (14, pp. 183–
> 84)

Thus, commitment is more than a decision. It is the functioning of an
individual who is searching for the directions that are emerging within himself. Kierkegaard has said, "The truth exists only in the process of becoming,
in the process of appropriation" (6, p. 72). It is this individual creation of a
tentative personal truth through action that is the essence of commitment.

Persons are most successful in such a commitment when they are functioning as integrated, whole, unified individuals. The more that they are
functioning in this total manner the more confidence they have in the directions that they unconsciously choose. They feel a trust in their experiencing,
of which, even if they are fortunate, they have only partial glimpses in their
awareness.

Thought of in the sense in which I am describing it, it is clear that
commitment is an achievement. It is the kind of purposeful and meaningful
direction that is only gradually achieved by individuals who have come increasingly to live closely in relationship with their own experiencing—a relationship in which their unconscious tendencies are as much respected as
are their conscious choices. This is the kind of commitment toward which I
believe individuals can move. It is an important aspect of living in a fully
functioning way.

The Irreconcilable Contradiction

I trust it will be very clear that I have given two sharply divergent and irreconcilably contradictory points of view. On the one hand, modern psychological science, and many other forces in modern life as well, hold the view that the person is unfree, that she is controlled, that words such as *purpose, choice, commitment* have no significant meaning, that the individual is nothing but an object that we can more fully understand and more fully control. Enormous strides have been and are being made in implementing this perspective. It would seem heretical indeed to question this view.

Yet, as Polanyi has pointed out in another of his writings (9), the dogmas of science can be in error. He says:

> In the days when an idea could be silenced by showing that it was contrary to religion, theology was the greatest single source of fallacies. Today, when any human thought can be discredited by branding it as unscientific, the power previously exercised by theology has passed over to science; hence science has become in its turn the greatest single source of error.

So I am emboldened to say that over against this view of man as unfree, as an object, is the evidence from therapy, from subjective living, and from objective research as well, that personal freedom and responsibility have a crucial significance, that one cannot live a complete life without such personal freedom and responsibility, and that self-understanding and responsible choice make a sharp and measurable difference in the behavior of the individual. In this context, commitment does have meaning. Commitment is the emerging and changing total direction of the individual, based on a close and acceptant relationship between the person and all of the trends of his or her life, conscious and unconscious. Unless, as individuals and as a society, we can make constructive use of this capacity for freedom and commitment, humans are, it seems to me, set on a collision course with fate.

What is the answer to the contradiction I have described? For myself, I am content to think of it as a deep and lasting paradox. While paradoxes are often frustrating, they can still be very fruitful. In physics, there is the paradox that light is a form of wave motion, and at the same time it can be shown to exist in quanta, the contradiction between the wave theory and the corpuscular theory of light. This paradox has been irreconcilable, and yet on the basis of it, physics has made important advances.

Friedman, the philosopher, believes that much the same point of view is necesssary when we face the philosophical issue of meaning. He says: "Today, meaning can be found, if at all, only through the attitude of the man who is willing to *live* with the absurd, to remain open to the mystery which he can never hope to pin down" (5, p. 468).

I share this conviction that we must live openly with mystery, with the absurd. Let me put the whole theme of my discussion in the form of a contradiction.

A part of modern living is to face the paradox that, viewed from one perspective, man is a complex machine. We are every day moving toward a more precise understanding and a more precise control of this objective mechanism that we call *man*. On the other hand, in another significant dimension of his existence, man is subjectively free; his personal choice and responsibility account for the shape of his life; he is in fact the architect of himself. A truly crucial part of his existence is the discovery of his own meaningful commitment to life with all of his being.

If in response to this you say, "But these views *cannot* both be true," my answer is, "This is a deep paradox with which we must learn to live."

AN UPDATE

Since those words were written, scientists have moved a long way in recognizing the deficiencies of a mechanistic world view and the inadequacy of the linear cause-effect science on which behaviorism rests. The universe is far more mysterious than it seemed, and we find prominent physicists likening this view of the cosmos to that of Oriental mystics.

As to the issues I have discussed in this chapter, I will give some quotations from Fritjof Capra, a theoretical physicist, though the same ideas have been expressed by other scientists and philosophers of science.

First the modern world view, including the disappearance of a narrow cause-effect science, as seen by Capra. "The universe is thus experienced as a dynamic, inseparable whole which always includes the observer in an essential way. In this experience the traditional concepts of space and time, of isolated objects, and of cause and effect lose their meaning. Such an experience, however, is very similar to that of the Eastern mystics" (1, p. 81).

Then an extensive quotation bears directly on the question of choice. "A living organism is a self-organizing system, which means that its order in structure and function is not imposed by the environment, but is established by the system itself. . . ." Living systems interact with the environment continually, "but this interaction does not determine their organization. . . .

"The relative autonomy of self-organizing systems sheds new light on the age-old philosophical question of free will. From the systems point of view, both determinism and freedom are relative concepts. To the extent that a system is autonomous from its environment it is free; to the extent that it depends on it through continuous interaction its activity will be shaped by environmental influences. The relative autonomy of organisms usually increases with their complexity, and it reaches its culmination in human beings.

"This relative concept of free will seems to be consistent with the view of mystical traditions that exhort their followers to transcend the notion of an isolated self and become aware that we are inseparable parts of the cosmos in which we are embedded. The goal of these traditions is to shed all ego sensations completely and, in mystical experience, merge with the totality of the cosmos. Once such a state is reached, the question of free will seems to lose its meaning. If I *am* the universe, there can be no 'outside' influences and all my actions will be spontaneous and free" (2, 269–270).

I look back to my statement earlier in this chapter, that "The free person moves out voluntarily, freely, responsibly, to play her significant part in a world whose determined events move through her and through her spontaneous choice and will." For me these words acquire an added meaning and a new richness in the light of Capra's statement. It is a confirming thing to find that views based primarily on experience in psychotherapy are paralleled by the thinking of theoretical physicists, based on experimentation and mathematics. The paradoxical quality of our freedom is still there, but it is a paradox with its roots in the nature of the universe.

REFERENCES

1. Capra, Fritjof. *The Tao of Physics*. Boulder, Colorado: Shambala Press, 1975.
2. Capra, Fritjof. *The Turning Point*. New York: Simon & Schuster, 1982.
3. Crutchfield, Richard S. "Conformity and Character." *American Psychologist, 10* (1955): 191–198.
4. Frankl, V. E. *From Death Camp to Existentialism*. Boston: Beacon Press, 1959.
5. Friedman, M. *The Problematic Rebel*. New York: Random House, 1963.
6. Kierkegaard, S. *Concluding Unscientific Postscript*. Edited by Walter Lowre. Princeton: Princeton University Press, 1941.
7. Olds, James. "A Physiological Study of Reward." In *Studies in Motivation,* edited by D. C. McClelland. New York: Appleton-Century Crofts, 1955.
8. Polanyi, M. *Personal Knowledge*. Chicago: University of Chicago Press, 1958.
9. Polanyi, M. "Scientific Outlook: Its Sickness and Cure." *Science, 125* (1957): 480–84.
10. Rogers, C. R., Kell, B. L., and McNeil, Helen. "The Role of Self-Understanding in the Prediction of Behavior." *Journal of Consulting Psychology, 12* (1948): 174–86.
11. Skinner, B. F. "Behaviorism at Fifty." In *Behaviorism and Phenomenology: Contrasting Bases for Modern Psychology,* edited by T. W. Wann. Chicago: University of Chicago Press, 1964.
12. Skinner, B. F. *Science and Human Behavior*. New York: Macmillan, 1953.
13. Skinner, B. F. *Walden Two*. New York: Macmillan, 1948.
14. Wertheimer, M. *Productive Thinking*. New York: Harper, 1945.

The Goal: The Fully
Functioning Person

W hat are we striving for? Why is it that we desire the *best* (however we define that term) in family life, in the school, in the university, in the community? It is, I believe, because we hope to develop the *best* of human beings. But rarely do we give explicit thought to the exact meaning of this goal. What sort of human being do we wish to grow?

A number of years ago, writing as a psychotherapist, I tried to state my personal answer to this question (2). I make no apology for the fact that this chapter is cast in the framework of therapy. To my mind the *best* of education would produce a person very similar to the one produced by the *best* of therapy. Indeed, it may be of help to teachers and educators to think of this issue in a setting outside the school. It may make it easier for them to see, in sharper focus, those points where they agree with the picture I paint and those points where they disagree.

I suspect that each one of us, from time to time, speculates on the general characteristics of the optimal person. If education were as completely successful as we could wish it to be in promoting personal growth and development, what sort of person would emerge? Or, speaking from the field in which I have had the most experience, suppose psychotherapy were completed in optimal fashion, what sort of person would have developed? What is the hypothetical end-point, the ultimate, of psychological growth and development? I wish to discuss this question from the point of view of therapy, but I believe the tentative answers that I formulate would be equally applicable to education or to the family or to any other situation that has as its aim the constructive development of persons. I am really raising the issue, what is the goal? What is the optimal person?

I have often asked myself this question and have felt an increasing dissatisfaction with the kind of answers that are current. They seem too slippery, too relativistic, to have much value in a developing science of personality. They often contain, too, I believe, a concealed bias which makes them unsatisfactory. I think of the commonly held notion that the person who has completed therapy or is fully mature will be adjusted to society. But what society? Any society, no matter what its characteristics? I cannot accept this. I think of the concept, implicit in much psychological writing, that *successful therapy* means that a person will have moved from a diagnostic category considered pathological to one considered normal. But the evidence is accumulating that there is so little agreement on diagnostic categories as to make them practically meaningless as scientific concepts. And even if a person becomes *normal,* is that a suitable outcome of therapy? Furthermore, the experience of recent years has made me wonder whether the term *psychopathology* may not be simply a convenient basket for all those aspects of personality that diagnosticians as a group are most afraid of in themselves. For these and other reasons, change in diagnosis is not a description of therapeutic outcome that is satisfying to me. If I turn to another type of concept, I find that the person whose psychological growth is optimal is said to have achieved a positive mental health. But who defines *mental health?* I suspect that the Menninger Clinic and the Center for Studies of the Person would define it rather differently. I am sure that the Soviet state would have still another definition.

Pushed about by questions such as these, I find myself speculating about the characteristics of the person who comes out of therapy, if therapy is maximally successful. I should like to share with you some of these tentative personal speculations. What I wish to do is to formulate a theoretical concept of the optimal end-point of therapy, or, indeed, of education. I would hope that I could state it in terms which would be free from some of the criticisms I have mentioned, terms that might eventually be given operational definition and objective test.

The Background From Which the Problem Is Approached

I shall have to make it clear at the outset that I am speaking from a background of client-centered or person-centered therapy. Quite possibly all successful psychotherapy has a similar personality outcome, but I am less sure of that than formerly and hence wish to narrow my field of consideration. So I shall assume that this hypothetical person whom I describe has had an intensive and extensive experience in client-centered therapy, and that the therapy has been as completely successful as is theoretically possible. This would mean that the therapist has been able to enter into an intensely personal and subjective relationship with this client—relating not as a scientist to an object of study, not as a physician expecting to diagnose and cure, but as a person to a person. It would mean that the therapist feels this client to be a person of unconditional self-worth; of value no matter what his condition, his behavior, or his feelings. It means that the therapist is able to let himself go in understanding this client; that no inner barriers keep him from sensing what it feels like to be the client at each moment of the relationship; and that he can convey something of his empathic understanding to the client. It means that the therapist has been comfortable in entering this relationship fully, without knowing cognitively where it will lead, satisfied with providing a climate which will free the client to become himself.

For the client, this optimal therapy has meant an exploration of increasingly strange and unknown and dangerous feelings in himself; the exploration proving possible only because he is gradually realizing that he is accepted unconditionally. Thus he becomes acquainted with elements of his experience which have in the past been denied to awareness as too threatening, too damaging to the structure of the self. He finds himself experiencing these feelings fully, completely, in the relationship, so that for the moment he *is* his fear, or his anger, or his tenderness, or his strength. And as he lives these widely varied feelings, in all their degrees of intensity, he discovers that he has experienced himself, that he *is* all these feelings. He finds his behavior changing in constructive fashion in accordance with his newly experienced self. He approaches the realization that he no longer needs to fear what experience may hold, but can welcome it freely as a part of his changing and developing self.

This is a thumbnail sketch of what client-centered therapy might be at its optimum. I give it here simply as an introduction to my main concern: What personality characteristics would develop in the client as a result of this kind of experience?

The Characteristics of the Person after Therapy

What then is the end-point of optimal psychotherapy, of maximal psychological growth? I shall try to answer this question for myself, basing my thinking upon the knowledge we have gained from clinical experience and research, but pushing this to the limit in order better to see the kind of person who would emerge if therapy were most effective. As I have puzzled over the answer, the description seems to me quite unitary, but for clarity of presentation I shall break it down into three facets.

1. *This person would be open to his experience.*

This is a phrase that has come to have increasingly definite meaning for me. It is the polar opposite of defensiveness. *Defensiveness* we have described in the past as being the organism's response to experiences that are perceived or anticipated as incongruent with the structure of the self. In order to maintain the self-structure, such experiences are given a distorted symbolization in awareness, that reduces the incongruity. Thus, the individual defends himself against any threat of alteration in the concept of self.

In the person who is open to his experience, however, every stimulus, whether originating within the organism or in the environment, would be freely relayed through the nervous system without being distorted by a defensive mechanism. There would be no need of the mechanism of "subception" whereby the organism is forewarned of any experience threatening to the self. On the contrary, whether the stimulus was the impact of a configuration of form, color, or sound in the environment on the sensory nerves, or a memory trace from the past, or a visceral sensation of fear or pleasure or disgust, the person would be "living it," would have it completely available to awareness.

Perhaps I can give this concept a more vivid meaning if I illustrate it from a recorded interview. A young professional man reports in the forty-eighth interview the way in which he has become more open to some of his bodily sensations, as well as other feelings.

> *Client:* "It doesn't seem to me that it would be possible for anybody to relate all the changes that I feel. But I certainly have felt recently that I have more respect for, more objectivity toward my physical makeup. I mean I don't expect too much of myself. This is how it works out: It feels to me that in the past I used to fight a certain tiredness that I felt after supper. Well now I feel pretty sure that I really am *tired*—that I am not making myself tired—that I am just physiologically lower. It seemed that I was just constantly criticizing my tiredness."
>
> *Therapist:* "So you can let yourself *be* tired, instead of feeling along with it a kind of criticism of it."
>
> *Client:* "Yes, that I *shouldn't* be tired or something. And it seems in a way to be pretty profound that I can just not fight this tiredness, and along with it goes a real feeling of *I've* got to slow down, too, so that being tired isn't such an awful thing. I think I can also kind of pick up a thread here of why I should be that way in the way my father is and the way he looks at some of these things. For instance, say that I was sick, and I would report this, and it would seem that overtly he would want to do something about it but he would also communicate, 'Oh, my gosh, more trouble.' You know, something like that."
>
> *Therapist:* "As though there were something quite annoying, really, about being physically ill."
>
> *Client:* "Yeah, I am sure that my father has the same disrespect for his own physiology that I have had. Now last summer I twisted my back, I wrenched it, I heard it snap and everything. There was real pain there all the time at first, real sharp. And I had the doctor look at it and he said it wasn't serious, it should heal by itself as long as I didn't bend too much. Well this was months ago—and I have been noticing recently that—hell, this is a real pain and it's still there—and it's not my fault, I mean it's—"
>
> *Therapist:* "It doesn't prove something bad about you—"
>
> *Client:* "No—and one of the reasons I seem to get more tired than I should maybe is because of this constant strain and so on. I have already made an appointment with one of the doctors at the hospital that he would look at it

and take an X-ray or something. In a way I guess you could say that I am just more accurately sensitive—or objectively sensitive to this kind of thing. I can say with certainty that this has also spread to what I eat and how much I eat. And this is really a profound change, as I say. And of course my relationship with my wife and the two children is—well you just wouldn't recognize it if you could see me inside—as you have—I mean—there just doesn't seem to be anything more wonderful than really and genuinely—really *feeling* love for your own child and at the same time *receiving* it. I don't know how to put this. We have such an increased respect—both of us—for Judy and we've noticed just—as we participated in this—we have noticed such a tremendous change in her—it seems to be a pretty deep kind of thing."

Therapist: "It seems to me you are saying that you can listen more accurately to yourself. If your body says it's tired, you listen to it and believe it, instead of criticizing it; if it's in pain you can listen to that; if the feeling is really loving your wife or child, you can *feel* that, and it seems to show up in the differences in them too."

Here, in a relatively minor but symbolically important excerpt, can be seen much of what I have been trying to say about openness to experience. Formerly he could not freely feel pain or illness, because being ill meant being unacceptable. Neither could he feel tenderness and love for his child because such feelings meant being weak, and he had to maintain his façade of being strong. But now he can be genuinely open to the experience of his organism—he can be tired when he is tired, he can feel pain when his organism is in pain, he can freely experience the love he feels for his daughter, and he can also feel and express annoyance toward her, as he went on to say in the next portion of the interview. He can fully live the experiences of his total organism, rather than shutting them out of awareness.

I have used this concept of availability to awareness to try to make clear what I mean by openness to experience. This might be misunderstood. I do not mean that this individual would be self-consciously aware of all that was going on within himself, like the centipede who became aware of all of his legs. On the contrary, he would be free to live a feeling subjectively, as well as be aware of it. He might experience love, or pain, or fear, living in this attitude subjectively. Or he might abstract himself from this subjectivity and realize in awareness, "I am in pain," "I am afraid," "I do love." The crucial point is that there would be no barriers, no inhibitions, which would prevent the full experiencing of whatever was organismically present, and availability to awareness is a good measure of this absence of barriers.

2. *This person would live in an existential fashion.*

I believe it would be evident that for the person who was fully open to his experience, completely without defensiveness, each moment would be new. The complex configuration of inner and outer stimuli which exists in this moment has never existed before in just this fashion. Consequently our hypothetical person would realize that "What I will be in the next moment, and what I will do, grows out of that moment, and cannot be predicted in advance either by me or by others." Not infrequently we find clients expressing this sort of feeling. Thus, one, at the end of therapy, says in rather puzzled fashion, "I haven't finished the job of integrating and reorganizing myself, but that's only confusing, not discouraging, now that I realize this is a continuing process. . . . It is exciting, sometimes upsetting, but deeply encouraging to feel yourself in action and apparently knowing where you are going even though you don't always consciously know where that is."

One way of expressing the fluidity that would be present in such existential living is to say that the self and personality would emerge *from* experience rather than experience being translated or twisted to fit a preconceived self-structure. It means that one becomes a participant in and an observer of the ongoing process of organismic experience, rather than being in control of it. I have tried to describe how this type of living seems to me.

> This whole train of experiencing, and the meaning that I have thus far discovered in it, seem to have launched me on a process which is both fascinating and at times a little frightening. It seems to mean letting my experience carry me on, in a direction which appears to be forward, toward goals that I can but dimly define, as I try to understand at least the current meaning of that experience. The sensation is that of floating with a complex stream of experience, with the fascinating possibility of trying to comprehend its everchanging complexity.

Such living in the moment, then, means an absence of rigidity, of tight organization, of the imposition of structure on experience. It means instead a maximum of adaptability, a discovery of structure *in* experience, a flowing, changing organization of self and personality.

The personality and the self would be continually in flux, the only stable elements being the physiological capacities and limitations of the organism, the continuing or recurrent organismic needs for survival, enhancement, food, affection, sex, and the like. The most stable personality traits would be openness to experience, and the flexible resolution of the existing needs in the existing environment.

3. *This person would find his organism a trustworthy means of arriving at the most satisfying behavior in each existential situation.*

He would do what "felt right" in this immediate moment and he would find this in general to be a competent and trustworthy guide to his behavior.

If this seems strange, let me explain the reasoning behind it. Since he would be open to his experience he would have access to all of the available data in the situation on which to base his behavior; the social demands, his own complex and possibly conflicting needs; his memories of similar situations, his perception of the uniqueness of this situation, etc., etc. The dynamic aspects of each situation would be very complex indeed. But he could permit his total organism, his consciousness participating, to consider each stimulus, need, and demand, its relative intensity and importance, and out of this complex weighing and balancing, discover that course of action that would come closest to satisfying all his needs in the situation. An analogy that might come close to a description would be to compare this person to a giant electronic computing machine. Since he is open to his experience, all of the data from his sense impressions, from his memory, from previous learning, from his visceral and internal states, is fed into the machine. The machine takes all of these multitudinous pulls and forces which were fed in as data and quickly computes the course of action that would be the most economical avenue of need satisfaction in this existential situation. This is the behavior of our hypothetical person.

The defects which in most of us make this process untrustworthy are the inclusion of nonexistential material or the absence of data. It is when memories and previous learnings are fed into the computation as if they were *this* reality, and not memories and learnings, that erroneous behavioral answers arise. Or when certain threatening experiences are inhibited from awareness, and hence are withheld from the computation or fed into it in distorted form, this too produces error. But our hypothetical person would find his organism thoroughly trustworthy because all the available data would be used, and it would be present in accurate rather than distorted form. Hence, his behavior would come as close as possible to satisfying all his needs—for enhancement, for affiliation with others, and the like.

In this weighing, balancing, and computation, the organism would not by any means be infallible. It would always give the best possible answer for the available data, but sometimes data would be missing. Because of the element of openness to experience however, any errors, any following of behavior which was not satisfying would be quickly corrected. The computations, as it were, would always be in process of being corrected because they would be continually checked in behavior.

Perhaps you will not like my analogy of an electronic computing machine. Let me put it in more human terms. The client I previously quoted found himself expressing annoyance to his daughter when he "felt like it," as well as affection. Yet he found himself doing it in a way which not only released tension in himself, but which freed this small girl to voice her annoyances. He describes the differences between communicating his angry annoyance or imposing it on her. He continues, "Because it just doesn't feel like I'm imposing my feelings on her, and it seems to me I must show it on my face. Maybe she sees it as 'Yes, Daddy is angry, but I don't have to cower.' Because she never does *cower*. This in itself is a topic for a novel, it just feels that good." In this instance, being open to his experience, he selects, with astonishing intuitive skill, a subtly guided course of behavior which meets his need for the release of his angry tension, but also satisfies his need to be a good father, and his need to find satisfaction in his daughter's healthy development. Yet he achieves all this by simply doing the thing that feels right to him.

On quite another level, it seems to be this same kind of complex organismic selection that determines the behavior of the creative person. He finds himself moving in a certain direction long before he can give any completely conscious and rational basis for it. During this period, whether he is moving toward a new type of artistic expression, a new literary style, a new theory in the field of science, a new approach in his classroom, he is simply trusting his total organismic reaction. He feels an assurance that he is on his way, even though he could not describe the end-point of that journey. This is the type of behavior that is, I believe, also characteristic of the person who has gained greatly from therapy, or of the person whose educational experience has enabled him to learn how to learn.

The Fully Functioning Person

I should like to pull together these three threads into one more unified descriptive strand. It appears that the person who emerges from a theoretically optimal experience of personal growth, whether through client-centered therapy or some other experience of learning and development, is then a fully functioning person. He is able to live fully in and with each and all of his feelings and reactions. He is making use of all his organic equipment to sense, as accurately as possible, the existential situation within and without. He is using all of the data his nervous system can thus supply, using it in awareness, but recognizing that his total organism may be, and often is, wiser than his awareness. He is able to permit his total organism to function in all its complexity in selecting, from the multitude of possibilities, that behavior which in this moment of time will be most generally and genuinely satisfying. He is able to trust his organism in this functioning, not because it is infallible, but because he can be fully open to the consequences of each of his actions and correct them if they prove to be less than satisfying.

He is able to experience all of his feelings, and is afraid of none of his feelings; he is his own sifter of evidence, but is open to evidence from all sources; he is completely engaged in the process of being and becoming himself, and thus discovers that he is soundly and realistically social; he lives completely in this moment, but learns that this is the soundest living for all times. He is a fully functioning organism, and because of the awareness of himself which flows freely in and through his experiences, he is a fully functioning person.

SOME IMPLICATIONS OF THIS
DESCRIPTION

This, then, is my tentative definition of the hypothetical end-point of therapy, my description of the ultimate picture which our actual clients approach but never fully reach, the picture of the person who is continually learning how to learn. I have come to like this description, both because I believe it is rooted in and is true of my clinical and educational experience, and also because I believe it has significant clinical, scientific, and philosophical implications. I should like to present some of these ramifications and implications as I see them.

A. APPROPRIATE TO CLINICAL EXPERIENCE

In the first place it appears to contain a basis for the phenomena of clinical experience in successful therapy. We have noted the fact that the client develops a locus of evaluation within himself; this is consistent with the concept of the trustworthiness of the organism. We have commented on the client's satisfaction at being and becoming himself, a satisfaction associated with functioning fully. We find that clients tolerate a much wider range and variety of feelings, including feelings that were formerly anxiety-producing; and that these feelings are usefully integrated into their more flexibly organized personalities. In short, the concepts I have stated appear to be sufficiently broad to contain the positive outcomes of therapy as we know it.

B. LEADS TOWARD OPERATIONAL HYPOTHESES

While the formulation as given is admittedly speculative, it leads, I believe, in the direction of hypotheses which may be stated in rigorous and operational terms. Such hypotheses would be culture free or universal, I trust, rather than being different for each culture.

It is obvious that the concepts given are not easily tested or measured, but with our growing research sophistication in this area, their measurability is not an unreasonable hope.

C. EXPLAINS A PARADOX OF PERSONAL GROWTH

We have found, in some of our research studies in psychotherapy, some perplexing differences in the analyses of before-and-after personality tests, by different outside experts. In clients whose personal gain in therapy is amply supported by other evidence, we have found contradictions among the experts in the interpretation of their personality tests. Briefly, psychologists who are oriented strictly toward personality *diagnosis,* who are comparing the individual with general norms, tend to be concerned over what they see as a lack of personality defenses, or a degree of disorganization, at the conclusion of therapy. They may be concerned that the person is "falling apart." The psychologist who is therapeutically oriented tends to see the same evidence as indicative of fluidity, openness to experience, an existential rather than a rigid personality organization.

To me it seems possible that the "looseness," the openness, of the person who is undergoing marked personal growth may be seen, in terms of population norms, as deviating from those norms, as "not normal." But these same qualities may indicate that all personal growth is marked by a certain degree of disorganization followed by reorganization. The pain of new understandings, of acceptance of new facets of oneself, the feeling of uncertainty, vacillation, and even turmoil within oneself, are all an integral part of the pleasure and satisfaction of being more of oneself, more fully oneself, more fully functioning. This to me is a meaningful explanation of what would otherwise be a puzzling paradox.

D. CREATIVITY AS AN OUTCOME

One of the elements that pleases me in the theoretical formulation I have given is that this is a creative person. This person at the hypothetical endpoint of therapy could well be one of Maslow's "self-actualizing people." With his sensitive openness to the world, his trust of his own ability to form new relationships with his environment, he would be the type of person from whom creative products and creative living emerge. He would not necessarily be "adjusted" to his culture, and he would almost certainly not be a conformist. But at any time and in any culture he would live constructively, in as much harmony with his culture as a balanced satisfaction of needs demanded. In some cultural situations he might in some ways be very unhappy, but he would continue to be himself, and to behave in such a way as to provide the maximum possible satisfaction of his deepest needs.

Such a person would, I believe, be recognized by the student of evolution as the type most likely to adapt and survive under changing environmental conditions. He would be able creatively to make sound adjustments to new as well as old conditions. He would be a fit vanguard of human evolution.

E. BUILDS ON TRUSTWORTHINESS OF HUMAN NATURE

It will have been evident that one implication of the view I have been presenting is that the basic nature of the human being, when functioning freely, is constructive and trustworthy. For me this is an inescapable conclusion from more than forty years of experience in psychotherapy. When we are able to free the individual from defensiveness, so that he is open to a wide range of his own needs, as well as the wide range of environmental and social demands, his reactions may be trusted to be positive, forward-moving, constructive. We do not need to ask who will socialize him, for one of his own deepest needs is for affiliation with and communication with others. When he is fully himself, he cannot help but be realistically socialized. We do not need to ask who will control his aggressive impulses, for when he is open to all of his impulses, his need to be liked by others and his tendency to give affection are as strong as his impulses to strike out or to seize for himself. He will be aggressive in situations in which aggression is realistically appropriate, but there will be no runaway need for aggression. His total behavior, in these and other areas, when he is open to all his experience, is balanced and realistic, behavior which is appropriate to the survival and enhancement of a highly social animal.

I have little sympathy with the rather prevalent concept that persons are basically irrational, and thus their impulses, if not controlled, would lead to destruction of others and self. Our behavior is exquisitely rational, moving with subtle and ordered complexity toward the goals the organism is endeavoring to achieve. The tragedy for most of us is that our defenses keep us from being aware of this rationality, so that consciously we are moving in one direction, while organismically we are moving in another. But in our hypothetical person there would be no such barriers, and he would be a participant in the rationality of his organism. The only control of impulses that would exist or that would prove necessary, is the natural and internal balancing of one need against another, and the discovery of behaviors which follow the avenue most closely approximating the satisfaction of all needs. The experience of extreme satisfaction of one need (for aggression, or sex, etc.) in such a way as to do violence to the satisfaction of other needs (for companionship, tender relationship, etc.)—an experience very common in the defensively organized person—would simply be unknown in our hypothetical individual. He would participate in the vastly complex self-regulatory activities of his organism—the psychological as well as physiological thermostatic controls—in such a fashion as to live harmoniously, with himself and with others.

F. BEHAVIOR DEPENDABLE BUT NOT PREDICTABLE

There are certain implications of this view of the optimum human being that have to do with predictability, which I find fascinating to contemplate. It should be clear from the theoretical picture I have sketched that the particular configuration of inner and outer stimuli in which the person lives at this moment has never existed in precisely this fashion before; and also that his behavior is a realistic reaction to an accurate apprehension of all this internalized evidence. It should, therefore, be clear that this person will seem to himself to be dependable but not specifically predictable. If he is entering a new situation with an authority figure, for example, he cannot predict what his behavior will be. It is contingent upon the behavior of this authority figure, and his own immediate internal reactions, desires, etc. He can feel confident that he will behave appropriately, but he has no knowledge in advance of what he will do. I find this point of view often expressed by clients, and I believe it is profoundly important.

But what I have been saying about the client himself would be equally true of the scientist studying his behavior. The scientist would find this person's behavior lawful and would find it possible to postdict it, but could not forecast or predict the specific behavior of this individual. The reasons are these. If the behavior of our hypothetical person is determined by the accurate sensing of all of the complex evidence that exists in this moment of time, and by that evidence only, then the data necessary for prediction is clear. It would be necessary to have instruments available to measure every one of the multitudinous stimuli of the input, and a mechanical computer of great size to calculate the most economical vector of reaction. While this computation is going on, our hypothetical person has already made this complex summation and appraisal within his own organism and has acted. Science, if it can eventually collect all this data with sufficient accuracy, should theoretically be able to analyze it and come to the same conclusion and thus postdict his behavior. It is doubtful that it could ever collect and analyze the data instantaneously, and this would be necessary if it were to predict the behavior before it occurred.

It may clarify this if I point out that it is the maladjusted person whose behavior can be specifically predicted, and some loss of predictability should be evident in every increase in openness to experience and existential living. In the maladjusted person, behavior is predictable precisely because it is rigidly patterned. If such a person has learned a pattern of hostile reaction to authority, and if this "badness of authority" is a part of his conception of himself-in-relation-to-authority, and if because of this he denies or distorts any experience which should supply contradictory evidence, *then* his behavior is specifically predictable. It can be said with assurance that when he enters a new situation with an authority figure, he will be hostile to him. But the more that therapy, or any growth-promoting relationship, increases the openness to experience of this individual, the less predictable his behavior will be. This receives some crude confirmation from the Michigan study (1) attempting to predict success in clinical psychology. The predictions for the men who were in therapy during the period of investigation were definitely less accurate than for the group as a whole.

What I am saying here has a bearing on the common statement that the long range purpose of psychology as a science is "the prediction and control of human behavior" a phrase which for me has had disturbing philosophical implications. I am suggesting that as the individual approaches this optimum of complete functioning his behavior, though always lawful and determined, becomes more difficult to predict; and though always dependable and appropriate, more difficult to control. This would mean that the science of psychology, at its highest levels, would perhaps be more of a science of understanding than a science of prediction, an analysis of the lawfulness of that which has occurred, rather than primarily a control of what is about to occur.

In general this line of thought is confirmed by our clients, who feel confident that what they will do in a situation will be appropriate and comprehensible and sound, but who cannot predict in advance how they will behave. It is also confirmed by our experience as therapists, where we form a relationship in which we can be sure the person will discover himself, become himself, learn to function more freely, but where we cannot forecast the specific content of the next statement, of the next phase of therapy, or of the behavioral solution the client will find to a given problem. The general direction is dependable, and we can rest assured it will be appropriate; but its specific content is unpredictable.

G. RELATES FREEDOM AND DETERMINISM

I should like to give one final philosophical implication which has meaning for me. For some time I have been perplexed over the living paradox that exists in psychotherapy between freedom and determinism, as I have indicated in the preceding chapter. I would like to add one more thought on that topic. In the therapeutic relationship some of the most compelling subjective experiences are those in which the client feels within himself the power of naked choice. He is *free*—to become himself or to hide behind a façade; to move forward or to retrogress; to behave in ways that are destructive of self and others, or in ways that are enhancing; quite literally free to live or die, in both the physiological and psychological meaning of those terms. Yet as we enter this field of psychotherapy with objective research methods, we are, like any other scientist, committed to a complete determinism. From this point of view every thought, feeling, and action of the client is determined by what precedes it. The dilemma I am trying to describe is no different from that found in other fields—it is simply brought to sharper focus. I tried to bring this out in a paper written some time ago contrasting these two views. In the field of psychotherapy,

> Here is the maximizing of all that is subjective, inward, personal; here a
> relationship is lived, not examined, and a person, not an object, emerges,
> a person who feels, chooses, believes, acts, not as an automaton, but as a

person. And here too is the ultimate in science—the objective exploration of the most subjective aspects of life; the reduction to hypotheses, and eventually to theorems, of all that has been regarded as most personal, most completely inward, most thoroughly a private world. (3)

In terms of the definition I have given of the fully functioning person, the relationship between freedom and determinism can, I believe, be seen in a fresh perspective. We could say that in the optimum of therapy the person rightfully experiences the most complete and absolute freedom. He wills or chooses to follow the course of action which is the most economical vector in relation to all the internal and external stimuli, because it is that behavior which will be most deeply satisfying. But this is the same course of action which from another vantage point may be said to be determined by all the factors in the existential situation. Let us contrast this with the picture of the person who is defensively organized. He wills or chooses to follow a given course of action, but finds that he *cannot* behave in the fashion that he chooses. He is determined by the factors in the existential situation, but these factors include his defensiveness, his denial or distortion of some of the relevant data. Hence it is certain that his behavior will be less than fully satisfying. His behavior is determined, but he is not free to make an effective choice. The fully functioning person, on the other hand, not only experiences, but utilizes, the most absolute freedom when he spontaneously, freely, and voluntarily chooses and wills that which is absolutely determined.

I am quite aware that this is not a new idea to the philosopher, but it has been refreshing to come upon it from a totally unexpected angle, in analyzing a concept in personality theory. For me it provides the rationale for the subjective reality of absolute freedom of choice, which is so profoundly important in therapy, and at the same time the rationale for the complete determinism which is the foundation stone of present day science. With this framework I can enter subjectively the experience of naked choice that the client is experiencing; I can also as a scientist, study his behavior as being absolutely determined.

Conclusion

Here then is my theoretical model of the person who emerges from therapy or from the best of education, the individual who has experienced optimal psychological growth—a person functioning freely in all the fullness of his organismic potentialities; a person who is dependable in being realistic, self-enhancing, socialized, and appropriate in his behavior; a creative person, whose specific formings of behavior are not easily predictable; a person who is ever-changing, ever developing, always discovering himself and the newness in himself in each succeeding moment of time.

Let me stress, however, that what I have described is a person who does not exist. He is the theoretical goal, the end-point of personal growth. We see persons moving *in this direction* from the best of experiences in education, from the best of experiences in therapy, from the best of family and group relationships. But what we observe is the imperfect person moving *toward* this goal. What I have described is my version of the goal in its "pure" form.

I have written this chapter partly to clarify my own ideas. What sort of persons tend to come from my classes, from my groups, from my therapy? But much more important, I have written it to try to force educators to think much more deeply about their *own* goals. The assumption has been prevalent for so long that we all know what constitutes an "educated man," that the fact that this comfortable definition is now *completely irrelevant* to modern society is almost never faced. So this chapter constitutes a challenge to educators at all levels. If my concept of the fully functioning person is abhorrent to you as the goal of education, then give *your* definition of the person who should emerge from modern day education, and publish it for all to see. We need many such definitions so that there can be a really significant *modern* dialogue as to what constitutes our optimum, our ideal citizen of *today*. I hope this chapter makes a small contribution toward that dialogue.

REFERENCES

1. Kelley, E. L. and Fiske, Donald W. *The Prediction of Performance in Clinical Psychology.* Ann Arbor: University of Michigan Press, 1951.
2. Rogers, Carl R. "The Concept of the Fully Functioning Person." *Psychotherapy: Theory, Research, and Practice,* 1 (1963): 17–26.
3. Rogers, Carl R. "Persons or Science: A Philosophical Question." *American Psychologist,* 10 (1955): 267–78.

Do We Dare?

Some Reflections

As I look back over what I have written in this book, I fall into a somewhat dreamy, reflective state. I hope you can enter this inner world of mine and enrich it with your own memories, experiences, and thoughts.

The Miracle of Childhood

I get flashes, pictures of the young children I have known and observed, children before they have been exposed to school. Some of these are memories of my children and grandchildren when they were young. Some are recent glimpses of my three great-grandchildren. But there are children of friends, children I have observed on the streets, in homes, and in supermarkets with their parents. There are the youngsters I have seen in China and Japan, in Brazil, in Austria, and in England—children all over the world.

I see a small boy pounding nail after nail into a large wooden box until it is studded with the metal heads. I see a little girl insisting stubbornly that she will wear only the dress *she* has chosen, not the one selected by her mother. I see a child in a supermarket, trying to feel every can, box, bunch of vegetables, stopped only temporarily by a mother's slap on his hands. There is a small girl trying to imitate the big words she had just heard. There is a boy turning over rocks and boards, looking for the harmless snakes he loves to collect. I see a group of children playing with clay, laughing at the forms they create. I see youngsters learning to thwart parental rules, manipulate parental behavior. I hear a small boy asking over and over, "What letter is *that?* And what letter is *that?*" I see the homeless "street children" of Brazil, unloved and unwanted, roaming the streets, stealing, searching for bread in the trash cans, deceiving and manipulating adults, struggling to survive. I see children on the beach, building sand castles, carrying buckets of water to and fro. I see children counting out pennies for a candy bar. I see and hear a small boy kicking an empty can along a city street. I hear the ever-repeated questions, "Why?" "How?" *"Why* does water run downhill?" *"How* does the baby get inside the mother?" *"Why* is he talking so loud?" *"How* do you make it go?"

The activities are ceaseless, the curiosity endless. Young children are eager to find out, wanting to do, to shape, to create. They are soaking up information through eyes, ears, nose, mouth, fingers. They are moving, restless, spontaneous, determined. They are assimilating knowledge, perceiving patterns, acquiring a language, improving skills.

They are learning, learning, learning—probably at a rate they will never again equal.

And then their "education" begins. Off they go to school. What will they find? The possibilities are almost endless, but I will sketch two of the extremes, recognizing that there are many schools whose methods, attitudes, procedures, would fall between these two extremes.

One Pathway to Education

A small boy enters school, his first day. He is eager to go, because it is a step toward being grown up. He knows that big boys go to school. On the other hand, he is frightened. It is a strange new situation, full of fearsome possibilities. He has heard stories about school—about punishments, about exciting times, about report cards, about teachers, friendly and unfriendly. It is a scary uncertainty.

He is directed to his room. His teacher is businesslike. Here is his desk and chair, one in a straight row of desks and chairs. Here are his books, and pencils. The teacher greets the group with a smile but it seems forced. Then come the rules. He cannot leave his seat, even to go to the toilet, without first raising his hand and receiving permission. He is not to whisper or talk to his neighbors. He is to speak only when called upon. No one is to make unnecessary noise.

He thinks of yesterday. He was continually on the move, making as much noise as he pleased, shouting to his friends. School is so very different.

Then classes begin—the reading book, letters and words on the board. The teacher talks. One child is called upon and is praised for a correct response. He is called on. He makes a mistake. "Wrong! Who can give Johnny the right answer?" Hands go up, and he is soon corrected. He feels stupid. He leans over to tell his neighbor how he happened to make the mistake. He is reprimanded for talking. The teacher comes and stands by his seat to make clear that she is watching him, that he must abide by the rules.

Recess is fun—much shouting, running, some games—all too short.

Then the ordeal begins again. His body squirms, his mind wanders. Finally lunch. Not until they are all lined up in a perfectly straight row are they permitted to walk, silently, to the lunch room.

His educational career has commenced. He has already learned a great deal, though he could not put it into words.

He has learned that:
- there is no place for his restless physical energy in the school room;
- one conforms or takes the unpleasant consequences;
- submission to rules is very important;
- making a mistake is very bad;
- the punishment for a mistake is humiliation;
- spontaneous interest does not belong in school;
- teacher and disciplinarian are synonymous;
- school is, on the whole, an unpleasant experience.

At the end of the day, he asks his parents, "How long do I have to go?" Gradually, he will learn that he has been sentenced to a very long term.

As the days, months, years roll by he learns other things. He learns that:
- most textbooks are boring;
- it is not safe to differ with a teacher;
- there are many ways to get by without studying;
- it is okay to cheat;
- daydreams and fantasy can make the day pass more quickly;
- to study hard and get good grades is behavior scorned by one's peers;
- most of the learning relevant to his life takes place outside of school;
- original ideas have no place in school;
- exams and grades are the most important aspects of education;
- most teachers are, in class, impersonal and boring.

Small wonder that he looks forward to vacations as being the time when one really lives. Graduation becomes desirable as a release from boredom, constriction, and coercion.

So this is one pathway, one type of school experience. I believe it is a pathway experienced by millions of children and young people. Have I painted it in too gloomy terms? Here is a statement from a letter written by a professor of education in a university. She has taught for many years, been involved in the training of teachers, has kept in close touch with the schools in her large city. After describing some experiences in which students show how frightened they are by the possibility of learning in an academic setting, she bursts out with some strong feelings. "It seems to me schools not only murder feelings, they also destroy the power of thought and the capacity for learning anything outside of authority-stipulated, to-be-memorized isolated details—if that can be called learning! People are turned into appendages for assembly-line machinery. My heart is pounding as I write this. The poisonousness of the school has never been so glaringly apparent to me before. I have thought the notion of 'deschooling society' a hare-brained one, believing we must transform the school from within. But I wonder now—is it humanly possible? And here I feel like crying, out of sheer frustration and a sense of helplessness, and anger."

I believe this passionate statement expresses the feelings of many as we observe some of the tragic realities: ghetto schools that are literally nothing but prisons, with students held against their will, learning only hatred for everything that passes under the label of education; school administrators who are but political connivers, with no concept of what learning can mean; teachers who are bored and burned out, hanging on only to obtain their pensions. It is not a pretty picture.

A Second Way to Learning

We have seen in the preceding chapters that there is another path, another way. Let me sketch that picture very briefly.

A small girl goes to school for the first time. The atmosphere is friendly and informal. Part of her fear and anxiety disappear as the teacher greets her warmly and introduces her to some of the other children.

When it is time for school to begin, they sit in a circle with the teacher. She asks the children to tell of one thing they are interested in, one thing they like to do. The teacher's interest in each youngster is evident, and the little girl relaxes even more. This may be fun.

There are all kinds of interesting things in the room—books, maps, pictures, building blocks, crayons and paper, some toys—and soon the children are investigating their environment. Our small girl looks at a picture book of children in another country.

When the teacher calls them together again, she asks the girl if she could tell a little story. Our youngster starts to tell about going shopping with her mother. The teacher prints part of the story on the board and points out the words and letters. And so the day has begun.

What has this small girl learned? She has learned that:

- her curiosity is welcomed and prized;
- the teacher is friendly and caring;
- she can learn new things, both on her own and with the teacher's help;
- there is room for spontaneity here;
- she can contribute to the group learning;
- she is valued as a person.

We don't need to follow her school career further because it has all been described in earlier chapters. But in this humanistically oriented school, we will find various elements as she continues through the years.

- She will have a part in choosing what she wishes and needs to learn.
- She will learn reading and mathematics more rapidly than her friends in other schools.
- She will find an outlet for her creativity.
- She will become more expressive of both feelings and thoughts.
- She will develop a confidence in, and a liking for herself.
- She will discover that learning is fun.
- She will look forward to going to school.
- She will like and respect her teachers and be liked and respected in turn.

● She will find a place in school for all of her many and expanding interests.

● She will develop a knowledge of resources, ways of finding out what she wants to know.

● She will read about, think about, and discuss the crucial social issues of her time.

● She will find some things very difficult to learn, requiring effort, concentration and self-discipline.

● She finds such learning very rewarding.

● She learns to attack tasks cooperatively, working with others to achieve a goal.

● She is on the way to becoming an educated person, one who is learning how to learn.

What We Know

We have already discovered, as we have journeyed through this book, the elements that make this second school possible.

We know, with some precision, the attitudes, the ways of being, which create a learning climate.

We have found that prospective teachers can be helped to develop in these ways, as facilitators of learning.

It is also possible to help teachers on the job develop such attitudes and ways, in relatively short intensive experiences.

We have found that these facilitative ways are learned most rapidly in schools where the administrator maintains a facilitative environment for the teachers.

The hard-headed facts show that more learning, more problem-solving, more creativity, is found in classrooms which have such a climate.

We have seen teachers, from elementary classrooms to graduate school seminars, finding ingenious ways to help students to learn and choose and grow.

We have watched students develop in responsibility, in self-discipline, in ability to work.

We know, in short, that it is possible for any teacher to move in the direction of becoming more real, more sensitively understanding, more caring in relation to his or her students. We have learned that it is possible, in such a climate, for students to become reliably self-directing; to choose, and bear the responsibility of the consequences of their choice; to learn more than in the traditional classroom; and to do so with enthusiasm.

So the logical conclusion from this is that every school would wish to become more of a center for freedom to learn, more of a place where human qualities in teacher and student would be prized.

Such is not the case. Great sections of our educational system seem wedded to a traditional mode of education, and incredibly resistant to change. Other institutions in our culture—industry, government, marriage, the family—have all changed greatly in recent decades to meet modern conditions. Schools, by and large, have shown much less change. Why is this?

No Feedback

I believe the main reason for this monolithic opposition to any change can be summed up in two words—"No autopsies!" What I mean by this cryptic phrase is that the school has an almost complete lack of evidence as to the eventual effect of its work. Medicine, too, is resistant to change, but the doctor has his autopsies—objective evidence that his diagnosis, his medication, his surgery may have been mistaken, may have harmed or killed his patient. He is forced to recognize that he has made mistakes. He has an incentive to change and improve. Industry can look at the number of products sold, the profits made or lost. It, too, has a reason for reflecting on its processes and trying to improve them. Education has no such feedback system. To be sure it has its final examinations, but these are judged only by the self-protective inner criteria of the system. It is not known what relationship they have to later success, failure, enrichment of life. They are like the final inspection of the automobile as it leaves the assembly line. All the bolts are tight, the motor runs, the car can be operated. But this may have little relation to the final verdict, which must come from consumer reports. What education needs, desperately, is feedback from its consumers.

For three years I was consultant to the California Institute of Technology, one of the most prestigious institutions for the education of top level scientists. While I was consulting with an interested group of faculty, we discussed the incredible competition for grades, even in the freshman year. (A 3.73 grade was considered definitely better, by the students, than a 3.72!! Anyone who knows the grading process knows how absurd this is.) As we discussed the matter, the majority of the group concluded that a Pass-Fail system, especially in the freshman year, would permit students to concentrate on learning what they were interested in rather than scheming how to raise their grade by one percent. Some of the group were dubious, and when the faculty as a whole was sounded out, it was evident that a majority opposed any change in their grading system because (they said) that would imply a lowering of their very high standards. Yet, a short time later, they adopted the Pass-Fail system. Why? Because a careful analysis had been made of the students who were dropping out of Caltech. They found that some of those who left simply did not have the ability to pass the courses. But they also found, to their dismay, that the dropouts included a disproportionate number of their brightest, best, most creative students. Clearly, these students did not like the cut-throat competition nor the "Mickey Mouse" of numerical grades carried to two decimal points. If their institution was to retain its highly respected place, the faculty realized they must stop this leakage of their best students. They must create a place where curious, searching, bright students could find a satisfying environment. As one step in this, they changed the grading system. An "autopsy" had shown them that they were making a serious mistake and so they acted to correct it. This is the kind of process that is so rare in schools.

Obtaining Information from the Consumer

It would not be difficult for the schools to obtain consumer feedback, and I believe that study of this information would lead to markedly improved qualities of teaching and administration. The process would not need to be elaborate. Student reactions could be obtained at the end of the elementary, secondary, and college experience, and again three to five years later. A great deal could be learned from a simple, anonymous questionnaire. The items might include such queries as the following:

• Describe two or more ways in which this school experience has met your needs.

• Name two or more ways in which the school has failed to meet your needs.

• List briefly some of the experiences—courses, teachers, students, projects, events—from which you have learned the most.

• What experiences, classes, procedures have you felt were irrelevant or a waste of time?

• To what degree do you find that this school experience has prepared you for the next step in your life? Excellently ___ Well ___ Moderately ___ Poorly ___ Very Poorly ___ Explain your response.

• Are there any changes you believe would make this school a better place for learning?

These are suggested items only. A school could develop its own instrument. A questionnaire could also be devised for parents. In addition to the questionnaires, an outside interviewer should be employed to ask these same questions of a representative sample of the students and their parents. These interviews would have more depth and would help to uncover areas of satisfaction or dissatisfaction that had not been anticipated. This same person might then be asked, as an objective outsider, to tabulate and summarize all the findings from the questionnaires and the interviews, naming names, courses, and administrators where the frequency of mention justified it. This summary could then be distributed to *all* the faculty and administrators and used as data for planning the work of the next year.

I am well aware that such self-analysis would often contain material very painful to contemplate, as well as very rewarding information. I imagine many schools would be frightened at the thought of inaugurating such a process. Yet a refusal would mean that we do not wish to know whether our students are learning in our school, nor what they are learning. Certainly responsible educators would wish to take the risks involved.

The advantages would be enormous. We invest huge amounts of effort and money in the teachers, the textbooks, the equipment, and furnishing of our schools. This would begin to let us know the extent to which this learning environment and its curricular content is being received and integrated into the life of the student. It would also bring the students alive because they would realize that they had some opportunity to participate in shaping the educational process. The cost would be very small in relation to the valuable information obtained.

It is obvious that the student reactions should not be the sole criterion in evaluating the school and its teachers, administrators and curriculum. Nevertheless, it would be a vast improvement over the present situation where we have no idea whether the high school years, for example, have promoted significant and useful learning in an individual student, or whether they have stifled it.

Other Reasons

The absence of feedback is not the only reason for the resistance to change by our educational system. I will mention briefly two more.

THE NEED FOR CONFORMISTS

Does our society, oriented as it is toward industrial, technological and military goals, need vast numbers of conformists to make it operate success-fully? I think you would find few people who would openly argue that this is our need. Yet I believe that at an unconscious or unverbalized level, there is this desire for the products of our schools to be obedient, good followers, willing to be led. Those who are independent, who think for themselves tend to "rock the boat." It is easier to manage an industry or an army with men and women who have learned to conform to the rules.

Actually this is, in our present critical situation, a most short-sighted view. Our industrial production is slowly passing into the hands of less devel-oped countries. Our technology is overreaching itself and is the cause of enormous pollution and waste. Our military, in its attempt to defend, is threatening us all with annihilation. In this situation we are in dire need of critical, independent thinking, creative problem-solving, if we are to remain a viable culture. We need precisely the kind of learners who develop in a person-centered school.

A RELUCTANCE TO SHARE POWER

Another element that makes it difficult for many educators to change is the reluctance of those in power to share that power with the group for which they are responsible. Administrators pull away from sharing power with teachers; teachers are fearful of sharing power with their students. It seems too risky. It is easier to stay with the conventional authority structure—the hierarchical order—which is so prevalent in our society.

At a deeper level this means that we are fearful of adopting a genuinely democratic philosophy. The belief that in the long run the best decisions are made by the people is a concept we rarely utilize in practice. The fact that our country was founded on the belief that those who are affected by a decision have a right to participate in making the decision, is all too easily forgotten. We do not recognize that a slogan of that time, "No taxation without representation," conveys a meaning which is relevant to every institution in our country. In our schools today it could be crudely translated into such slogans as: "No curriculum without student participation;" "No educational policies without representation of those affected by the policies."

What is represented in this book is the conviction that a democratic way, based on a fundamental trust in persons, is applicable and effective in education.

What this means—as exemplified by the many educators who have presented their experiences in these pages—is that the educator takes the risk of empowering the student to take an active participatory part in his or her own educational process. It is putting a democratic philosophy into action in the classroom. And there is ample evidence that in our society, especially at this time, this is a frightening thing to do.

The Final Issue

Here then is the challenge of this book. What do we, the people, want from our schools? What do we hope for, in the students who emerge? What sort of young citizens do we need and want in our society?

We have shown that very diverse individuals, working at various educational levels, with different intellectual interests, can bring into being a learning environment in which there is responsible freedom. These facilitators of learning create a humane climate in which, being themselves real persons, they also respect the personhood of the student. In this climate there is understanding, caring, stimulation. And we have seen students respond with an avid interest in learning, with a growing confidence in self, with independence, with creative energy.

We have made available the evidence, gleaned from far-reaching research, which shows that more effective learning takes place in such classrooms than in the traditional class. It is also clear that a host of other desirable outcomes—more regular attendance, better morale, less vandalism—follow when the teacher personifies a facilitative approach.

We have endeavored to make it clear that the philosophy underlying such a person-centered approach is one that is consistent with the values, the goals, the ideals that have historically been the spirit of our democracy.

We have set forth openly the risks, the difficulties of adopting such an approach and the obstacles society places in its way. To be fully human, to trust in persons, to grant freedom with responsibility—these are not easy to achieve. The way we have presented is a challenge. It involves change in our thinking, in our way of being, in our relationships with our students. It involves a difficult commitment to a democratic ideal.

It all boils down to the question we must ask, both individually and collectively: Do we dare?

Index